Informal Institutions and Rural Development in China

China's successful transition from a centrally planned economy to a socialist market economy, with rapid growth in rural areas since the early 1980s, is a consequence of the impact of both formal and informal institutions. Hitherto, most work undertaken on this issue has focused on formal institutions. This book shows the great importance of informal institutions on the economic and social development of rural China. It examines the relationship between informal institutions and rural development in China since the end of the 1970s, focusing in particular on three major informal institutions: village trust and rotating savings and credit associations (ROSCAs), *guanxi* community, and 'integrating village with company' (IVWC) governance. It argues that informal institutions, traditions and customs are all critical factors for facilitating modernization and social and economic development, enabling the integration of trust, reciprocity, responsibility and obligation into economic and social exchange processes, and considerably lowering risks and transactions costs. It does this by analysing case studies that illustrate how informal institutions function and support development in rural China.

Biliang Hu is Professor of Economics at the Graduate School of the Chinese Academy of Social Sciences and Senior Research Fellow of the Academy's Rural Development Institute. He received his Doctorate of Economics from the School of Economics and Management, Witten/Herdecke University in Germany. His main academic interests are in institutional analysis in relation to village governance and rural development.

Praise for *Informal Institutions and Rural Development in China*

Dr Biliang Hu's book provides valuable insights into how rural development at the village level actually worked in China when market distortions were gradually removed from the late 1970s. His in-depth empirical work helps us understand better how traditional governance structures in rural China, spontaneous cultural adaptations and the rise of informal local institutions such as village credit associations, reinforced the positive effects of the removal of policy distortions and the other elements of economic liberalization. His work is an important contribution both to our understanding of the Chinese reform process and to the relationship between institutions and rural development in general.

Dwight H. Perkins, Harvard University

Biliang Hu's remarkable insights into grass-roots rural development are based on exhaustive village-level empirical research in different parts of China. A highly original and scholarly effort to track, over many years, the positive influence of cultural factors such as village trust, *'guanxi'* networks and informal local institutions such as rotating credit associations on rural modernization since the start of China's market reforms in the late 1970s. Hu describes how in one of his villages, the spontaneous integration of traditional village governance structures and modern corporate management structures powerfully stimulated local development. The example is no doubt representative of numerous such cases in many parts of China. This book is at once an important contribution to our understanding of how rural development actually works in China and to the theory of institutional economics.

Pieter Bottelier, Johns Hopkins University

A long time study of China's rural development, Dr Biliang Hu's new book combines new theories from economics and solid empirical evidence to re-examine China's path of rural development success. Beyond the familiar role of formal policies pushed by the central government, Dr Hu argues that informal institutions were equally instrumental in helping the rural economy grow and transform. This is a book that should be read by those interested in China and those interested in development more generally.

Scott Rozelle, Stanford University

Routledge Studies on the Chinese Economy

Series Editor
Peter Nolan, University of Cambridge

Founding Series Editors
Peter Nolan, University of Cambridge and
Dong Fureng, Beijing University

The aim of this series is to publish original, high-quality, research-level work by both new and established scholars in the West and the East, on all aspects of the Chinese economy, including studies of business and economic history.

Informal Institutions and Rural Development in China

Biliang Hu

Routledge
Taylor & Francis Group

LONDON AND NEW YORK

First published 2007
by Routledge
2 Park Square, Milton Park, Abingdon, Oxon OX14 4RN

Simultaneously published in the USA and Canada
by Routledge
711 Third Ave, New York, NY 10017

*Routledge is an imprint of the Taylor & Francis Group, an informa
business*

Transferred to Digital Printing 2008

© 2007 Biliang Hu

First issued in paperback 2013

Typeset in Times New Roman by
HWA Text and Data Management, Tunbridge Wells

British Library Cataloguing in Publication Data
A catalogue record for this book is available from the British Library

Library of Congress Cataloging-in-Publication Data
Hu, Biliang.
    Informal institutions and rural development in China / Biliang Hu.
        p. cm. – (Routledge studies on the Chinese economy ; 27)
    Includes bibliographical references and index.
    1. Rural development – China – Case studies.   2. Community
organization – China – Case studies.   3. Informal sector (Economics)
– China – Case studies. I. Title.
HN740.Z9C6387217 2007
307.1´412095109045–dc22   2006038902

ISBN13: 978-0-415-42177-5 (hbk)
ISBN13: 978-0-415-54285-2 (pbk)

In memory of my father

Contents

x   *Contents*

Illustrations

Figures

Plates

Tables

Foreword

Carsten Herrmann-Pillath

When I started the study of China, still as a high school student in the 1970s, I was amazed about the zeal and vigour with which the Communist Party criticized Chinese traditional culture and its Confucian roots. Over decades, the Chinese communist movement had fought against the remnants of feudal society in China. Today, the Chinese government with the same Chinese Communist Party as the vanguard of change is supporting the establishment of a large number of Confucius Institutes in many countries which are intended to spread Chinese language and the knowledge about Chinese civilization across the globe. At the same time, the occasional visitor to China wonders whether it is precisely today that Chinese tradition is withering away under the pressures of globalization, international business and consumerism. However, those who travel more extensively in the country will rapidly notice the plurality of Chinese worlds, in particular across the rural–urban divide. This is also true for most other countries in the world but a remarkable fact in China remains that the dynamism of China's economic growth is partly rooted in the rural sector, with phenomena such as the rise of township and village enterprises in the 1980s, the large-scale migration to the export bases at the coast, or the creation of an entrepreneurial class at the grass-roots level of Chinese society.

So the question becomes an important one: how is Chinese traditional culture related to economic change and growth? This was the central concern in a collaborative research project that the writer of these lines launched together with the late Chen Jiyuan in the early 1990s, part of a larger project on China's modernization which brought together young, mostly Chinese researchers from different disciplines and which was headed by myself and the late Helmut Martin. Biliang Hu was assigned by Chen Jiyuan to be the team leader on the Chinese side. Our target was definitively immodest. We ventured to take up the lost tradition of village studies in China that had reached its zenith with the works of Fei Xiaotong in the 1930s. This we related to a special claim, namely to apply modern concepts of institutional economics on the field data that the Chinese team would collect. Finally, we also picked up the threads in the comparative studies published by Philip Huang in the 1980s and which highlighted the north/south dichotomy in Chinese social and economic history. From this, a comparative research design was created that puts data from five Chinese villages into a theoretical, historical and comparative context. The sites included three interior provinces with a northward orientation, and two coastal provinces. These regions stay in very different relations with the global economy, with the 'fifth tiger' Guangdong being the export engine of China. The interior sites included both developed and less developed regions. All the villages have some industrial production, though on different levels of modernization, hence manifesting the transition from traditional handicraft to modern manufacturing. This book gives an extensive account of the historical background of the regions which reveals that the idea of a unified and monolithic Chinese culture is highly misleading. In fact, there are divergent local traditions which are also reflected in different strands of thought in China's intellectual history, even with reference to the highly dogmatic Neoconfucian school.

The main result of the Volkswagen Foundation project was a book series with village studies and general comparative and theoretical contributions, a total of eight volumes in Chinese language. The series received highest domestic acclaim and was awarded the National Book Award in 1997. However, for personal reasons we could not transfer our work into the international realm. So we were happy when, in 2002, Stig Thøgersen made the book series the object of an exclusive review article in one of the leading international journals in Chinese social sciences, *Modern China* (Thøgersen 2002). Meanwhile, after the completion of this work, Professor Hu decided to continue with the field studies, partly in the context of smaller projects in the area of rural finance. He regularly visited the five villages to collect additional information, to conduct interviews and to follow their rapid social change. The results of this decade-long work are presented in this book. Given this huge effort, the study is unique. There are very few contributions that are also based on long-term studies of a number of single villages and which compare their development through time and across places.

The central research question of the book is: which role do informal institutions play in the process of rural development? Hu's concept of 'informal institutions' is mainly based on the Northian concept, which was being received in China in the early 1990s, when the original design of the fieldwork was drafted. I had the opportunity to present seminars on German institutional economics to the Chinese Academy of Social Sciences, with leading young scholars attending such as Fan Gang, Sheng Hong or Zuo Dapei. Just a few years ago, North's book on '*Institutions, Institutional Change and Economic Performance*' (North 1990) had been published, and I proposed this as a framework to analyse Chinese economic reforms in general and rural development in particular. This was put into practice in the analysis of the field data of the Volkswagen Foundation project.

Biliang Hu adds to this perspective in putting the concept in the broader context of modernization theory, as rural development is modernization in essence. Thus, his work is not confined to economics but adopts an interdisciplinary view. In particular, Biliang Hu wants to inquire into the question whether the transition to a modern market economy means that anonymous market relations with a governance structure of formal institutions are the predominant form of social organization emerging from modernization. This is North's hypothesis, in particular, and seems to be a major consensus of many economists. Biliang Hu wants to demonstrate that this is a biased belief. He tries to prove that informal and formal institutions continue to interact during modernization. The important conclusion is that modern market economies will always manifest a diversity of institutional forms and that modernization will not converge towards a single 'best practice' of institutional design.

In order to arrive at this result, Biliang Hu develops an analytical framework which follows earlier contributions by Daniel Little (1989) and others in arguing that to understand the interaction between culture and economy in modernization, social sciences need to develop a tool case of intermediary concepts between the macro- and the micro-level. He bases this idea on a survey of the main economic contributions to foundational institutional analysis, in particular North and Aoki, which he puts against the background of the history of ideas in economics (Veblen, Commons, Hayek *et al.*). With regard to informal institutions in particular, he points out the importance of recent contributions to three different research topics, namely trust, social capital and culture, which all seem to be related to informal institutions in different ways. For example, informal institutions cause trust to emerge, provide the behavioural foundation for social capital and display certain patterns which are perceived as 'cultural' by the observers.

Biliang Hu posits that informal institutions are an intermediary concept. His central idea is depicted in Figure 2.8. On the micro-level, he locates the individual descriptions of phenomena which the observer meets in the field studies. These are concrete institutional arrangements such as ROSCAs in a particular village. General social phenomena such as certain cultural features or social capital are assigned to the macro-level. For example, observers might agree that a special behavioural attitude towards 'relations' (*guanxi*) is a cultural phenomenon in China. However, this is a broad and abstract description which cannot be related directly to the micro-level because the specific structures of incentives and constraints are missing that actually cause the general pattern to emerge in many different places and at many different times in China. The single cases, in turn, do not easily lend themselves toward generalization. Informal institutions grasp precisely the structure of constraints and incentives that can be generalized across a number of places and times.

Biliang Hu argues that there are three kinds of informal institutions that are particularly salient in his field studies: 'village trust', '*guanxi* community' and 'integrating village with company' (IVWC). He assigns these to different theoretical concepts in the social sciences:

- 'village trust' is referred to Burt's concept of 'closed networks' as a foundation for social capital, because trust is emerging from structures of mutual surveillance, hence enabling the villagers to build complex networks of ROSCAs,
- '*guanxi* community' is related to Landa's interpretation of *guanxi* and Burt's idea of open networks based on structural holes, which actually extend

guanxi relations through entrepreneurial brokerage beyond the limits of direct acquaintance,
• the IVWC model is referred to established theories of governance, with the special twist in asking how traditional social relations are merged with modern corporate structures linked to the emergence of the modern stock market in China.

Biliang Hu argues that these theoretical concepts manifest a close relation with indigenous ideas about social relations, in particular in the area of ethics and of '*guanxi*' learning. Both had been synthesized in the traditional rules of the lineage and the clan system, which are peculiar mixes of formal and informal institutions. The Confucian doctrine is interpreted as an historical mirror of informal institutions that persist until today, as in the case of village communities and the network of status relations in them. In particular, the historical perspective allows the joining of both the ideas of '*guanxi*' and 'community' in the sense of scholars like Weber. '*Guanxi*' are normally seen as open networks of reciprocal relations: Biliang Hu emphasizes that they are based on feelings of community which, in the Western literature since Max Weber, is typically opposed to the idea of 'openness' ('Gemeinschaft' versus 'Gesellschaft'). Hu proposes that in the Chinese case this juxtaposition has become obsolete because a major aspect of Chinese culture is the capability to create communities through open network interaction. Apart from his field studies, Hu attempts at proving this point by summarizing major 'native' theories of '*guanxi*' by scholars with Chinese origin, such as Fei Xiaotong.

Biliang Hu's reports of the fieldwork are organized around theoretical concepts. His first major topic is the analysis of ROSCAs on the basis of the concept of village trust. Rotating savings and credit associations are an institutional phenomenon which can be found in many developing countries and which are especially vigorous in China, in spite of the legal suppression of informal finance. Hu gives an extensive account of the historical development and the current situation in Xiangdong village, even supported by participant research, as Hu also joined a ROSCA. His explanation of the high efficiency and the thickness of ROSCA structures relies on the idea that in Xiangdong village a high level of trust has emerged which results from an interaction between a manifold of causal determinants (history, incentives, social beliefs, etc.). Hu's second main interest is in migration and social mobility. Biliang Hu demonstrates how the migration of rural workers is organized through network relations. He focuses his study on Tunwa village, a poor place where pressure to leave is high. He collects a wealth of information on individual mobility and distinguishes between short- and long-range migration, with the typical former case being mobility induced by marriage relations. The third topic is entrepreneurship. An outstanding feature of Chinese development is rural industrialization which is fuelled by individual entrepreneurship. Biliang Hu gives an account of the general trends and collects different cases from his fieldwork on which he presents detailed descriptions to show how entrepreneurs mobilize network connections to launch their business even within an environment which does not support their activities by reliable formal institutions. The fourth and final topic is the 'integrating village with company' model. Biliang Hu reports the spectacular, though not unique, case of a company finally growing over a village, with a continuity of dualist social structures between tradition and modernity. The indigenous term for this process is *yichang daicun,* which translates as IVWC. Hu shows how the mere financial scale of a very successful TVE finally dwarfs the local public sector, and how the increasing employment in the factories leads towards a merger between social structure and corporate organization. The important point, of course, remains that this development is embedded into the continuity of the political system, with the special and autonomous role of the CPC. This leads to tensions between the corporate hierarchy, the related economic status and the political status of cadres who do not yet belong to the company, which is superimposed by kinship relations in the actual governance structure. Furthermore, the development of the village economy is deeply rooted in indigenous handicraft traditions.

From his observations of these case studies, Biliang Hu concludes that certain informal institutions enhance economic performance, which feeds back to their resilience, such that economic modernization goes hand in hand with a merger of social tradition and modernization. He strongly opposes the view that 'modernization' results in a stylized 'Western' model of formal and anonymous institutions. I think that this is the major theoretical result of this book, namely to be itself an example of how modern concepts (in this case, the concepts of economics) can be indigenized. That is, I recommend reading this book with two different lenses. One is to follow its analysis of rural development and social change and to critically receive its claims. The other is to take the book itself as an example of the Chinese process of modernization and to study the way how a Chinese intellectual struggles with the analytical concepts stemming from the West in order to understand the complexities of his society. Even if in some respects readers did not support all the claims made in the book, its value would remain very high in the second sense.

To conclude this foreword, I wish to mention the fact that I always regarded Biliang Hu as an exemplary case of personal careers in Chinese transition. I found it amazing to observe how Chinese dynamism on the macro-level can be related to an astounding degree of flexibility and creativity on the level of single individuals. Biliang Hu's interest in rural development resulted from the fact that he is himself from a rural origin. The Chinese educational system (in this respect certainly related to its civilizational roots) allowed him to arrive at the heights of the Chinese academia in his early thirties. Afterwards, he adopted a caleidic lifestyle, with being a World Bank economist for several years, serving as senior economist at an international investment bank, and even co-founding a software company that introduced the concept of offshore outsourcing software business into China. During all these activities, he constantly switched between the worlds of advising global clients on international trips, doing fieldwork as a participant observer in a rural ROSCA in China, and working on his PhD thesis under my supervision. In our common history, we became friends, and he even became godfather of one of my children who always goes crazy when receiving the many gifts of 'Uncle Hu' from China. This way of life is virtually impossible to imagine in Germany, with its fixed institutional structures and organizational constraints. I think that this high degree of flexibility and entrepreneurial alertness is the main explanation of the Chinese miracle. Biliang Hu himself shows in this book, how this might be related to traditional Chinese culture.

I am happy and grateful that Routledge, the series editors and its reviewers recognized the value of this book which is based on the author's PhD thesis. Biliang Hu announced he is refocusing on academic work in the future. I am looking forward to some exciting results.

Witten, July 2006

Carsten Herrmann-Pillath is Professor of Economics in the Faculty of Economics and Management and Chair of Evolutionary and Institutional Economics in Witten/Herdecke University, Germany, and Academic Director of Sino-German School of Governance.

Foreword

Tony Saich

The core focus of the domestic policies of General-Secretary Hu Jintao and Premier Wen Jiabao since taking office in 2002–03 has been to ameliorate the conditions of those who have not benefited so well from the economic reforms to date. This marked a clear recognition that market forces alone could not help all citizens in China and that the application of market-based polices might even produce new losers, such as the laid-off workers from state-owned enterprises. The new leadership has moved to provide minimum guarantees for livelihood in the cities, and now even in some rural areas, to improve the integration of rural migrants into urban public services, to abolish illegal fees and levies on farmers and also the agricultural tax, to make primary education universally available without regard to cost, and to get to grips with the problem of access to medical care. For rural China, these policy measures have been bundled together under the slogan of 'building a new socialist countryside'. This policy approach launched in 2006 takes village development as its core with the provision of decent public goods and services as the key. The new leadership has stressed the idea of service-oriented government (*fuwuxing zhengfu*). This belated recognition stems not only from the Chinese Communist Party's commitment to social equity but also from the realization that continued economic growth depends on a healthy and well educated population and the spread of purchasing power into the countryside.

This new policy has involved a change in signals sent to local leaders (growth alone is not enough but it is also necessary to think about the quality of that growth) as well as a significant redistribution of financial resources. However, there are limits on the extent to which the leadership will be able to reorient policy toward a pro-poor growth strategy. Not only are there financial limits but also there are political constraints that will make a substantial shift of resources away from the wealthy coastal areas to the hinterland and from China's new rich to those who have not fared so well. China remains one of the very few countries that makes net financial transfers from its poorest regions to its wealthiest and from its poorest segments of the population to the richest.

While the new central initiatives are welcome, they are insufficient. Top-down approaches to development can only be successful up to a point. They can provide more resources and a sustainable macro-economic environment that will allow local development to flourish. The central government needs to push forward the kind of growth that will increase material resources without worsening social circumstances for those at risk. This requires developing polices that deliver non-zero forms of growth that will not penalize those groups who already comprise the most economically vulnerable and that socially form the base of society. National solutions can rarely solve adequately local problems and, in some instances, may actually make them worse.

What Professor Hu's work reminds us of is just how innovative rural China has been during the reform period and that this innovation has often happened in spite of central policy. In fact, one could argue that without the innovation of local rural policy against the express wishes of the central state apparatus, China's reforms would have floundered and almost certainly failed. First, it was the households of rural China that began to abandon the collective once they had the opportunity and radically reorganized agricultural production leading to a rise in farmers' incomes and the production of better and more varied foodstuffs for the cities. This formed the platform for successful reforms in the early 1980s. Second, the spontaneous development of township and village enterprises (TVEs) absorbed some 130 million labourers at its peak thus allowing for a diversified rural economy and higher incomes. This was totally unexpected by the central leadership and even senior leader Deng Xiaoping remarked that the TVEs seemed to appear out of nowhere in a development that had not been anticipated at all by the nation's leaders. Yet, over the long-term the farmers did not benefit sufficiently from these innovations. From the mid-1980s, the focus of central policy switched to urban development and making the coastal areas prosperous through a policy of exploitation of the countryside and export-led growth. It was very successful but the new leadership is now struggling to deal with the negative consequences of that strategy.

Much development experience shows us that the local level offers the best possibilities for improving the social lot of the farmers. The localities are the most likely to respond to small-scale initiatives that when compounded may have national significance. As Hu's research shows it is at the local level, in this case the village, where innovation is most likely to be spontaneous, requiring minimal, if any, support from the state agencies. The initial post-Mao period showed us how resilient the idea of markets is and once they sprung back into life they set in train the whole reform program. Once the locality starts on this path of innovation and development the more attractive it becomes for local investment in small-scale enterprise development.

Professor Hu also shows the resilience of local culture and traditions and how cultural repertoires and practices are supremely adaptable to changing circumstances. While the Chinese Communist Party congratulates itself for the success of the reforms, Hu's research reveals a much more complex picture in which the importance of informal institutions in local development is vital. He draws on the work of institutional economists to elucidate these developments as well as the notions of trust and social capital that have become popular in development literature. His detailed case studies reveal an intricate mosaic that forms the ground of contemporary rural China. Importantly, he helps us overcome any lingering stereotypes of a monolithic process of development in China. Grafted onto the formal institutions of rural China, are a myriad of informal ones that suggest that there may be many institutional designs that will lead to development. We see divergence rather than convergence.

His decade-long study of five rural villages provides us with a fascinating picture of the role of tradition and how it engages with modernity to produce an array of informal institutions that are conducive to development. The villages are well-chosen to embrace the diversity of rural China, ranging from the affluent south and east to the impoverished northwest. He develops the idea of village trust to analyse the development of rotating savings and credit associations in the village of Xiangdong in the relatively affluent province of Zhejiang. Taking the mantra of participatory development seriously, he even became a member of one of the associations. Second, he builds on the much used notion of *guanxi* (connections or networks) to develop the idea of a *guanxi* community. In this approach social ties are more important than genetic relations. This forms the core for his understanding of how migration has been operating in, for example, Tunwa village, Shanxi Province, and the development of TVEs in Yantian, Guangdong Province.

Last he reviews the interesting development of Fuxing village (originally called Duanjia) in Hubei Province. Here the Fuxing Company has effectively taken over the organization and management of the village in what Hu calls *yichang daichun*, which he translates as 'integrating the village with the company', or literally relying on the company to lead the village. This is one of a number of examples where a powerful company has come to dominate the economic, social and eventually political life of a village community. In Fuxing, the company dominates all aspects of village life with even the party secretary of the village branch assigned by the company rather than being elected by party members. The company makes the final decisions on questions of land use rights thus usurping the rights of the village committee. In return, the company will help with the social welfare of the formal village members and improve the salary and benefits of the local officials. This is a fascinating development with far-reaching consequences for local governance in rural China. While the company prospers, many members of the village, but not all, will also thrive but what happens if the company begins to falter or even fail? Who will take the responsibility for the village community? These are not easy questions to answer but they will have major consequences for social stability and ensuring social harmony.

Professor Hu's book should be read not only by those interested in development in China but also by those who are interested in rural development and the relationship between formal and informal institutions more generally. There are very few works available on China that have engaged in such extensive research and that have been able to combine formal theory and empirical observation so effectively.

Tony Saich is Daewoo Professor of International Affairs, Kennedy School of Government, Harvard University, Director of the Asia Center, Harvard University and a Chang Jiang Scholar at the School of Public Policy and Management, Tsinghua University.

Foreword

Hiranya D. Dias

'Sleeping giant awakens'. Giants never sleep although from time to time they might rest. They are as much periods of rest as they are periods of reflection. Unlike giants who hurl themselves headlong at all and sundry thinking that their strength could overcome all opposition and find out to their chagrin that it is not so, real giants recognize the value of reflection, that is, giants who have gained wisdom through the course of time. China is such a wise giant as this book by Biliang Hu amply demonstrates.

The China that we see now through the eyes of media, mostly Western, is a country that is hurtling at a break-neck rate of economic growth. It must have been almost a decade and a half ago that such a programme described the transformation of Shanghai and said that more than 50 per cent of the giant cranes used for building skyscrapers in the world were at that time in Shanghai! This was a startling piece of information, startling because it was not given in the context of what China is, truly a giant, if not the only giant, in this world. If we recognize that it is this same China that built the Great Wall more than 2,000 years ago to protect itself from destructive forces, built the Three Gorges dam to protect its people from the floods of Yangtze River that have wrought havoc on people's lives and property year after year for centuries and to harness its waters for beneficial purposes and put men into space, then what goes on in China today should not surprise us.

This book gives us a new insight into the transformation that is taking place in China, especially in rural China. What we hear about rural China from the media is a tale of woe, focusing on income and quality of life inequalities without mentioning, of course, that such inequalities can be seen only because development (by whatever definition) is taking place. Income inequality is not something special in China. It is found even in the rich countries of the world but they do not receive the publicity in the media that China has received.

Widening income inequality is a phenomenon that has been observed by Nobel Laureate Simon Kuznets (see Kuznets 1955). It takes place as agricultural economies industrialize. R. G. Williamson (1965) showed that regional income disparities widen during the early phase of economic development. Although these views have been contested there is enough evidence to indicate that this tendency exists where economic development takes place within the framework of a market economy.

Although Kuznets and Williamson had posited that market forces would reverse this tendency once development reached a certain level, others like Gunnar Myrdal hypothesized cumulative causation would continue to widen regional disparities unless there is deliberate state intervention to reverse these tendencies. Concern about income disparities led to the slogan 'growth with equity' but this was easier said than done in the context of limited resources in developing countries, not only financial resources but also other resources. Every country must strike the balance between growth and equity appropriate to its conditions.

This was the conventional wisdom but Biliang Hu has shown in this book that rural China has found unconventional ways of achieving more equitable growth through the role that informal institutions can play in development. Limitation of financial resources has long been recognized as a serious constraint to rural development. This has been true of rural China also. Multilateral organizations as well as national governments have attempted to overcome this problem with various rural credit programmes for the past four decades and set up formal institutions to implement them. Most of these failed and governments have had to write off large amounts of irrecoverable loans. Based on the ground-breaking action research conducted by the Bangladesh Academy of Rural Development in Comilla, Grameen Bank pioneered the highly successful community based micro-credit system about the time that China was embarking on its rural reform and opening up policies. NGOs in many developing countries adopted the Grameen Bank model and adapted it to conditions in the areas where they worked. Unlike the endogenous informal institutions Biliang Hu has researched in rural China, the institutional arrangements set up by these NGOs were introduced exogenously and are formal although, like in China, they make use of local cultural and social characteristics.

Unlike the informal institutions that have emerged or re-emerged in rural China which are deeply rooted in the cultural and social traditions and values of China the exogenous nature of the institutions governmental and non-governmental organizations have set up in developing countries has raised serious questions about their sustainability. Also whereas the informal institutions that have been researched by Biliang Hu are the outcome of the ingenuity of the Chinese people which has also generated endogenous entrepreneurship in rural China, the exogenous institutions that have been introduced to rural areas in other developing countries have failed to generate entrepreneurship in spite of the efforts to promote enterprise development.

Another problem that rural people in most developing countries experience is the difficulty of marketing their products and, in some cases, obtaining required inputs. They have looked unsuccessfully to governmental organizations to overcome these problems but the enterprises in rural China have overcome these problems through the informal institutions of *guanxi* and *guanxi* community. These institutions have also been very successful in mobilizing financial and other resources from Hong Kong and overseas Chinese communities.

The informal institutions in rural China have also reduced income disparities by increasing rural incomes through generating more employment, including employment outside of the villages, increasing productivity and improving infrastructure. Both as a result of higher incomes and the commitment to social responsibility of successful enterprises, quality of life has been improved for rural people. This shows us that improvement of rural incomes and living conditions can take place simultaneously with economic growth in the rapidly industrializing metropolitan regions. This takes place through rural industrialization and rural urbanization which Biliang Hu presents as the modernization of rural society and economy. The important achievement of modernization in China is that it is the Chinese version of modernization and not merely borrowing Westernization.

This book should be read by all in the developing countries who are interested in rural development. The Chinese experience it analyses is presented in a very interesting and thought provoking manner. If I may refer to it as the 'Chinese model' (in fact China is implementing several models simultaneously), it provides alternative ways of thinking about development. Rural development need not wait until the urban industrial sector reaches a certain level of development as hypothesized by W. Arthur Lewis (1954) in his two-sector model. It is also not necessary to wait for the government to intervene as informal institutions can play a very effective role in rural development.

However, it does not provide lessons that could be applied easily or directly to promote rural development in other developing countries but it does raise the question, 'How can we apply the lessons from this Chinese experience to promote rural development in our countries?' in our minds. We have seen that rural communities in China have generated indigenous strategies in the absence of governmental organizations to support them which has been a blessing in disguise. An important lesson is that too much governmental intervention, even intervention by NGOs, discourages indigenous development. What is most important is to create conditions conducive for rural communities to generate indigenous strategies for their development and to support their initiatives.

If the readers of this book understand this message, Biliang Hu would have made a significant contribution to thinking anew about development generally and rural development particularly.

Hiranya D. Dias, Professor of Rural Development Planning, Asian Institute of Technology (AIT), Bangkok, Thailand until his retirement in 1994. He is now a member of the Board of Directors of Gemidiriya Foundation, Sri Lanka, which is a World Bank supported foundation to undertake a new approach to rural poverty alleviation.

Preface

What has been happening in China in the past 30 years is remarkable by anything that we have witnessed in development in the past few centuries. The process of modernization had taken many decades in the developed countries of the West. The 'Asian tigers' managed to collapse that process into a few decades in the latter half of the twentieth century but no one had envisaged that such a large country like China, the most populous in the world, could transform itself at the truly phenomenal rate at which it has been doing so since 1978.

China's successful transition from a centrally planned economy to a socialist market economy with rapid growth in rural areas since the early 1980s is the consequence of positive impacts of both formal and informal institutional development.

The author had the good fortune to play a key role in a research project that has studied this amazing phenomenon at the grass-roots level since 1991. The fieldwork and in-depth studies, both qualitative and quantitative, undertaken during the 10–12 years from 1991 have found expression in many forms but this is the most comprehensive piece of writing to come out of it. This work was done as a thesis submitted in partial fulfillment of the requirements for the degree of Doctor of Economics in the Faculty of Economics and Management at the University of Witten/Herdecke in Germany.

To date, most of the research undertaken focuses on formal institutions while neglecting the great importance of informal institutions in China's economic and social development. Therefore, the focus of this study is to examine the relationship between informal institutions and rural development in China since the end of the 1970s. Based on the findings in selected survey villages, it covers three major informal institutions in the context of the specific Chinese economic, social and cultural background: village trust and ROSCAs (rotating savings and credit associations), *guanxi* community and IVWC (integrating village with company) governance.

This research has enabled the author to present a hitherto largely unseen but immensely significant aspect of the transformation and modernization of China through rural industrialization and rural urbanization and the historical, social, cultural traditions of China's long and varied civilization.

Acknowledgements

Since the beginning of this research a decade ago, I have received constant support and help from a great number of people. First of all, I am very grateful to Prof. Dr. Carsten Herrmann-Pillath, who inspired my interest in this research area in the early 1990s. Under his guidance, I published two books on the impact of institutional changes on rural development in selected Chinese villages, constituting the preparatory work underpinning this research. Following this, I extended my field of study to include rural finance, rural entrepreneurship, rural markets and rural governance. This, again, was based on the most valuable advice of Prof. Herrmann-Pillath, without whose professional academic guidance and advice it would have been impossible to obtain the research findings presented in this volume.

It is a great honour to have endorsements from Prof. Dwight H. Perkins, Prof. Pieter Bottelier and Prof. Scott Rozelle, alongside those of my academic advisors and friends, Prof. Carsten Herrmann-Pillath, Prof. Hiranya D. Dias and Prof. Tony Saich, all of whom have an in-depth knowledge of China. Prof. Perkins' publications on the Chinese economy and agricultural and rural development have been especially influential in Chinese academic research and decision-making in these areas since the early 1980s. I acknowledge gratefully the generous support and valuable ideas about Chinese social science research and development strategies I gained from them.

I am indebted to Prof. Dr. Zhang Xiaoshan and Prof. Dr. Birger P. Priddat, who gave kind encouragement during the course of the research and provided valuable comments, which have been helpful in improving the results of this research. I also wish to express my gratitude to the late Prof. Chen Jiyuan who entrusted me fully with responsibility for the Chinese side of the joint German–Chinese research project in the early 1990s. The current research, built on experience acquired then, was the natural extension of that project.

People from both the Chinese and German sides offered excellent support during my research. In particular, Dr. Sigrun Caspary, Dr. Ursula Hans, Ms. Andrea Anger-Sankowsky, Dr. Zhu Qiuxia, Mr. Feng Xingyuan, Dr. Li Jing, Mr. Wang Xiaoyi, Mr. Zhang Jun, Mr. Zhang Yuanhong, Mr. Li Renqing, Dr. Liu Qiang, Ms. Li Hui, Ms. Liu Yansheng and Dr. Liu Pingqing were all helpful in various ways relating to my field surveys and the writing of the book.

I am also very thankful to friends who accompanied me throughout this period. Prof. Pieter Bottelier, Prof. Hiranya D. Dias, Dr. Ebel Wickramanayake, Dr. Ramgopal Agarwala, Dr. Erh-Cheng Hwa, Mr. Manu Bhaskaran and Prof. Flemming Christiansen have given constant encouragement and advice, and Mr. Rainer Heufers, Dr. Annette Kleinbrod, Dr. Andrzej Kwiecinski, Mr. Georg Blume, Mr. Patrick Lohlein, Dr. Tian Xiaowen, Mr. Li Kai, Mr. Wang Yan, Mr. Hu Shunyan, Mr. Ma Zengxiang, Mr. Cheng Zhengyan, Ms. Luo Guangqin, Ms. Zhang Lansong, Ms. Sun Limei, Ms. Yu Xia, Ms Yu Ying and Ms. Qin Hongyu all provided energetic support and help in my research. Their friendship was very important to me in completing this challenging research.

I am also greatly obliged to all the villagers in the survey villages in which I worked. Some of those who stand out most are Mr. Tan Gongyan, Mr. Deng Yaohui, Mr. Deng Zerong, Mr. Deng Manchang, Mr. Deng Xushu, Mr. Deng Gantian, Mr. Tan Yeliang, Mr. Zhang Zhengqun, Mr. Xiang Fanghuai, Ms. Wang Fenyu, Mr. Chen Xugen, Mr. Sun Suogui, Mr. Sun Guorong, Mr. Yang Wenzhu, Mr. Chen Wenkai, Mr. Zhao Furong, Mr. Lü Huaizhong, Mr. Yu Xueli, Mr. Yu Yimin and Mr. Li Zhengjie. During the course of my field trips, they provided a wealth of information and insight. I benefited greatly from the numerous discussions held with them throughout my research.

I also wish to express my gratitude to Prof. Hiranya D. Dias and writer and poet Erika Dias who jointly polished the English in the final version of my work. Their meticulous reading and detailed editing directly refined the research result and made this book more readable. Mr. Owen Brown and Ms. Michelle Ollett's kind help in reviewing and checking an earlier version of the work is also highly appreciated.

I am also thankful to Mr. Peter Sowden and Mr. Tom Bates at Routledge, for their very useful and careful instruction in relation to various detailed publication arrangements throughout the whole publication preparation process over the past 20 months.

Finally, the direct support of my family – that is my wife Lü Weihong, our son Hu Di, my mother Guo Lawa, and all my brothers and sisters – has been of the highest value. They persuaded me at all times to continue and not to stop halfway on the 'Long March' of this important research, since they understood very well what I was writing about.

Biliang Hu
Beijing, China

Abbreviations

ABC	Agricultural Bank of China
ADBC	Agricultural Development Bank of China
BOC	Bank of China
BTVE	Bureau of Township and Village Enterprises
CASS	Chinese Academy of Social Sciences
CBE	commune-and-brigade-run-enterprise
CCB	China Construction Bank
CCBs	city commercial banks
CDB	China Development Bank
CEB	China Everbright Bank
CHB	China Huaxia Bank
CITIC	China Industrial Trust and Investment Corporation
CMB	China Merchant Bank
CPC	Communist Party of China
Exim-Bank	Export & Import Bank of China
FDI	foreign direct investment
FRSRLO	Family Responsibility System with Remuneration Linked to Output
FSTSC	Fuxing Science & Technology Shareholding Co. Ltd.
GDB	Guangdong Development Bank
GDP	gross domestic product
GHS	German History School
GPV	gross production value
ICBC	Industrial and Commercial Bank of China
IPO	initial public offering
IVWC	integrating village with company
MOA	Ministry of Agriculture
MOF	Ministry of Finance
NBS	National Bureau of Statistics (of China)
NIE	New Institutional Economics
OIE	Old Institutional Economics
PBOC	People's Bank of China
PRC	People's Republic of China

RCBs	rural commercial banks
RCC	rural credit cooperative
RCF	Rural Credit Foundation
RMB	renminbi, Chinese currency
ROSCA	rotating savings and credit association
SDB	Shenzhen Development Bank Co. Ltd.
SPDB	Shanghai Pudong Development Bank
TVE	township and village enterprise
UCBs	urban cooperative banks
UCCs	Uuban credit cooperatives
WISC	Wuhan Iron & Steel Corporation

1 Introduction

Background to the research

Although, in many countries, modernization has now reached quite a high level, the majority of the world's population still lives in quite poor rural areas. World Bank (2003: 83) figures show that, of a total world population of 6.4 billion people, more than 3 billion still live in rural areas. The world's 1.2 billion extremely poor people, living on less than US$1 a day, reside in rural areas and most of the people in the world living on less than US$2 a day also live in rural areas. Therefore strategies to promote further rural development, especially to help impoverished residents of rural areas break out of poverty, have become an urgent global task.

From the mid to late nineteenth century, China, the world's most populous country, descended into political corruption and economic recession because of its large population as well as many other complicated factors. Until the 1940s little fundamental change occurred in China's economic and social development. After 1949, when the Communist Party of China (CPC) came to power, a series of quite radical ideas and political and administrative changes were introduced into Chinese society in a short period of time.

From 1949 to 1978, taking vast rural areas as the basis for reform, the CPC compulsorily imposed institutional changes to re-distribute farm land by re-organizing farmers through agriculture collectivization movements (from 'Farmers' Mutual Help Groups in Production' to 'Agricultural Co-operatives' and to 'People's Communes') and other strategies. These institutional changes achieved some positive results during the initial stages of their implementation, for example, from 1949 to 1957. However, in the following 20 years (1958–78), radical institutional changes brought China to the verge of economic, social, political and cultural collapse. The rural situation also faced a serious crisis at the time.

In 1976, the death of Mao Zedong, the former Chairman of CPC Central Committee, and the resulting political restructuring at the central government level provided a period of reflection for the Chinese people. In late 1978, the reform and opening up policy advocated by Deng Xiaoping was formally implemented and thus China entered a historic period of development. Within 25 years (1979–2004), China was transformed from a completely closed society into one that had entered the international community in most respects and moved from a planned system to a market economy; a modernization process that had begun to accelerate, and people's living standards had begun to improve significantly.

The same is also true in rural areas. The 25 years since China began implementing the reform and opening up policy, compared with that of the previous 30 years (1949–78), demonstrated fundamental changes in the following areas:

- transformation from a planned to a market economy in terms of agricultural management;
- rural industry became a major part of the rural economy and rural industrialization has clearly shown to be a strong trend of development;
- rapid growth of small towns in rural areas and development of metropolitan regions have accelerated the rural urbanization process; and
- democratic processes have emerged at grass-roots levels.

Radical changes in rural China

From plan to market

Before 1979, the main features of China's planned agricultural economy were as follows.

First, all major agricultural production inputs such as land, farm machines, rural credit, pesticides, chemical fertilizers, etc. were controlled and dominated by collective organizations. Farmers had no direct access to any of these means of production. China's agricultural management system at the time was the same as the former Soviet Union model with high levels of control from government and collective organizations.

Second, after 1958 all rural inhabitants were formally organized into the People's Commune system, with production teams forming the basis of the highly concentrated collectivized agricultural economy. Thus, government controlled the rural population through People's Communes, which combined both economic and government administrative functions. Rural inhabitants were not permitted to move to urban areas.[1]

Finally, adapting to a highly concentrated agricultural development model, markets for factors of production in rural areas closed and non-agricultural activities in rural areas were also prohibited by the central government. As a direct result, both agricultural production and the living standards of the rural population were quite low; for example, in 1978 total grain production was only 300 million tons, a mere 0.38 tons per rural inhabitant, or 0.31 tons per capita for the total national population; the annual per capita net income of rural inhabitants was only RMB 134 yuan, which was equivalent to US$89 at the official exchange rate of 1.5:1 at that time (Guojia Tongjiju 1979); 250 million people in rural areas were starving before rural reforms. Thus, the reforms led by Deng Xiaoping and launched in 1979 began in the agricultural sector with a focus in three areas:

1   Farm land was re-distributed from collective organizations to households. Thus rural inhabitants gained the right to farm land using the household as

the basic unit for agricultural production and consumption. This institutional change was basically completed in 1983 and 97.1 per cent of the rural population was assigned[2] a certain amount of farm land from collective organizations by the end of that year (97.9 per cent in 1984)[3] (Guojia Tongjiju 1984, 1985).

2   The People's Commune system was abolished in 1983 and 1984[4] as the re-distribution of farm land to individual family households in rural areas removed the need for this kind of organization. Correspondingly, local government in rural areas was re-organized with township governments established in 1983 and 1984 to carry out administrative work between the state and rural residents.

3   Rural markets (mainly markets for products and factors of production) were gradually re-opened from 1979. The declaration by the central government in early 2004 that various grain products were completely open to free trade, plus the public announcement made by many provinces of the removal of policies discriminating against rural–urban migrants clearly indicate that the target of transforming China's agricultural sector from a planned to a market economy had been basically achieved.[5]

Rural industrialization

From an historic point of view, China's rural economy was, for a long period of time, a kind of subsistence economy based on a combination of small farming and cottage industries, i.e., the special economic form of 'Agriculture and Handicraft Complement Each Other'. Until the 1950s, before the 'Great Leap Forward' was launched by the CPC Central Committee, the development of cottage industries in rural areas was inadequate. In 1958, when political movements such as 'Mass Steel-Making', 'Great Leap Forward', 'People's Communization' and 'Industrialization of the People's Communes' were combined together, the development of 'Five Small Industries' (small-scale iron and steel making, small-scale coal mining, small-scale chemical fertilizer production, small-scale cement production, and machinery production) in rural areas accelerated.

By June 1959, in less than one year, the number of enterprises run by People's Communes reached 700,000 nationwide and the gross production value (GPV) of China's rural manufacturing sector accounted for 10 per cent of national industrial GPV (Yu and Huang 1991: 37). However, the development of manufacturing in rural areas stimulated by these political movements was not sustainable. The majority of rural enterprises had to be shut down during the 'Three Difficult Years' of 1960, 1961 and 1962. Fortunately, these rural enterprises have recovered since the early 1980s due to Deng's policies of reform and opening up the economy.

The latest data shows the total production of China's town and village enterprises (TVEs) in terms of value-added output, a gauge that is roughly equivalent to GDP based on China's current system of national accounts, reached RMB 3.6 trillion yuan in 2003. That total accounted for 31 per cent of the national aggregate GDP and 61 per cent of the total value-added production of the entire rural economy, including both farm and non-farm production in rural areas in the same period. Production in terms of value-added from the rural manufacturing sector alone totalled RMB 2.6 trillion yuan, which accounted for 48 per cent of the total production of the country's overall manufacturing industry in 2003. In recent years TVEs have also become important engines in supporting Chinese exports; for example, TVEs made up 40 per cent of the total exports of the country in 2003.[6] In some sectors, the share is even higher, e.g., about 60 per cent of food and building materials, 50 per cent of textiles, garments and domestic appliances of the country's total exports in the same year were from TVEs. The number of workers in TVEs reached 135 million, accounting for 27 per cent of China's rural workforce or 18 per cent of the nation's total workforce (Nongyebu Xiangzhenqiyeju [Bureau of Township and Village Enterprises of the Ministry of Agriculture] 2004). Despite historic traditions, and after more than 40 years of turbulent reform, rural industrialization in China has a very strong impetus for further development.

Rural urbanization

With the rapid growth of TVEs for over 20 years, the process of urbanization in rural China has also accelerated, as shown by:

1   The number of designated towns (those officially approved by central government to be regarded as urban areas) in rural areas increased significantly and the urban population expanded rapidly. The latest official statistics show there were about 20,000 designated towns in 2003 (up from 19,811 in 2002), with a total of 110 million residents. In 1978, there were only about 2,000 towns with 10 million residents.
2   More and more rural inhabitants are moving to cities and towns. In 2003, there were 100 million rural–urban migrants, and increasingly they have become permanent urban residents after the Chinese government recently relaxed controls on people's mobility between rural and urban areas. No doubt this will also be one of the important driving forces boosting China's further 'rurbanization' (rural urbanization) in the future.
3   Development of metropolitan regions and regional integration between rural areas and local urban centres has also supported the acceleration of China's urbanization. Through the development of metropolitan regions, many villages have been incorporated into nearby cities and towns. For example, all the villages and towns in the Zhujiang River (Pearl River) Delta Area comprising twelve major cities constitute one urban system in terms of human settlement as well as economic activities. It is also true in the Changjiang River (Yangtze River) Delta Area which comprises 15 major cities. At present, the total population of these two deltas is about 100 million. It is estimated that the rural population of these two delta areas is 50 per cent, which suggests that these metropolitan regions have actually incorporated 50 million former rural residents into the urban systems of the two regions. On that basis, no less than 100 million rural residents have been

drawn into the metropolitan regions of Beijing-Tianjin-Tangshan (in Hebei province), Shenyang-Dalian in Liaoning province, Jinan-Qingdao-Yantai in Shandong province, and Fuzhou-Quanzhou-Xiamen in Fujian province. This implies that China's real urbanization rate is higher than the current official figure; however, because of the lack of rational statistical techniques, this factor has yet to be included in calculations of China's real urbanization to date.

Furthermore, about 2,000 county seats (county towns) and about 20,000 township centres also, to a certain extent, play a role in pushing forward China's urbanization. Putting all of these factors together easily suggests that a total of 350–400 million rural inhabitants have been steadily incorporated into urban systems; this accounts for nearly 50 per cent of the total rural population and 30 per cent of the national total population. Obviously, rural urbanization, by whatever route, has become the primary factor driving China's urbanization, rather than natural population growth in urban areas or the re-classification of urban areas, which were previously the two major drivers of China's urbanization process before the 1980s.[7]

Democratic processes rising from the grass roots

Democratization is a new phenomenon which has emerged recently in the process of rural development at the village level. The major manifestation of this phenomenon is the formal implementation[8] of the Law on the Organization of Villagers' Committees (LOVC) of the People's Republic of China which has villagers' self-governing organization[9] as its key point. All villages in mainland China have now implemented the villagers' self-governing system. Under this system, the villagers' committee, being a self-governing organization with independent status under law, has the power to make decisions relating to all the internal affairs of a village.

In practice, most villagers have shown a great political passion to participate in the direct election of members of the villagers' committees. Nationally, on average, fewer than 10 per cent of villagers have given up their voting rights. The villagers' self-governing system demonstrates that a democratic system can be gradually established in China drawing from village practice and then moving upward through the various levels of government administration. From this point of view, the villagers' self-governing system is extremely important and its historic significance is obvious.

In summary, comparing current agricultural and rural development in China with the first 30 years after the CPC took political centre stage, great success has been achieved in terms of improvement in people's livelihoods, rural organization, rural democracy, rural industrialization and rural urbanization. As a result, many positive changes have taken place and continue to take place. The next question to pose then is what are the major factors currently driving such changes in rural China?

Of course, the government's reform and opening up policy, i.e., formal institutional changes, have played a crucial role. However, the major argument of my research is that over the past 25 years informal institutions or cultural traditions[10] have also played a significant role in supporting all the changes mentioned already for rural development in China. In other words, this research looks at the issue of how people organize their economic activities when formal institutions are absent or are not clearly defined.

Particularly, four specific arguments relating to rural development need to be tested:

1   Because of the lack of financial support from formal financial institutions, farmers have themselves to organize credit to provide financing for rural development. As one of the informal institutions, rotating savings and credit associations (ROSCAs) work in some rural areas.
2   Since rural–urban migration became a direct driving force in pushing forward Chinese urbanization after the government relaxed control of rural people's mobility, the argument presented in our research is that rural inhabitants organized their mobility through informal institutions, for example *guanxi*, rather than through formal government regulations and organizations.
3   We already know the important contribution of TVEs to both national and rural development in China in the post-reform era; what concerns this research more is how Chinese farmers have been able to build such a large economic sector outside the government planned system in a very limited time. Again, the argument refers to the performance of *guanxi* regulation as a kind of informal institution in rural China.
4   Under an incomplete market system with weak government support for rural development during the transition period, local entrepreneurs found roles to play in accelerating rural development at grass-roots level, based on local community rules.

The major purpose of this research is to try to test these arguments through a joint German–Chinese research project.[11] Compared with many other similar research projects, this project places much emphasis on fieldwork in selected rural villages over a period of more than ten years. One of the direct reasons for doing such detailed fieldwork[12] instead of following some of the available theories, is to avoid dropping into what Philip Huang called 'the traps' in modern Chinese research, i.e., to avoid 'uncritical use' or 'ideological use' of theories, 'Western-centralism' and 'culturalism' (Philip Huang 1998). Philip Huang himself provides a good example for the research in a similar area (Huang 1990).

Background to the study

In 1991, the *European Project on China's Modernization: Contemporary Patterns of Culture and Economic Change* research project, funded by Volkswagen Foundation and directed by Carsten Herrmann-Pillath and Helmut Martin was formally initiated. The author took part throughout this research project as a key member of one of the groups focusing on rural development issues.[13]

As the first phase of the research, the team spent some time (from mid-1991 to mid-1993) discussing the questions posed by China's modernization[14] as it related to rural development. Both the Chinese and German scholars agreed to examine in the initial stage of research the development of TVEs and rural–urban migration issues. These two issues were considered to be important subjects of the research. As the research progressed, key members of the research team recognized that the village economy and culture were the key to understanding China's rural life and changes. This perception was based on the research tradition in the international academic community on village studies[15] and also on the special importance of the revival of this research tradition in Chinese studies by, for example, Fei Xiaotong's village study in the 1930s (Fei Hsiao-tung 1939), Yang's research in the 1940s (Yang 1945), etc.[16] Therefore, we finally decided to focus our research by selecting major issues related to villages. All specific research questions were put into the general framework of that agreed position. We then created a complete research programme for the investigation and designed a detailed survey handbook which formed the basis of our research.

In the second phase of the project, after repeated discussions and pilot investigations, we selected five sample villages from five provinces,[17] from both the north and the south of the country. One of the main reasons for our making the final selection of five villages based on geographic location was the experience of the research of Philip Huang (1985, 1990) and others (Nee 1992; Lin 1995), which showed that Chinese cultural features, as well as social and economic development, appear to be quite different between the north and the south of the country. Therefore we selected the sample villages from both regions so as to avoid any bias in the findings from our research. Complete and detailed fieldwork was carried out in each of the five sample villages over two and half years from May 1993 to December 1995. From this first-hand information, an eight-volume series of publications edited by Chen Jiyuan and Carsten Herrmann-Pillath was prepared under the title of *Village Economy and Culture in Contemporary China* (Chen and He 1996). The reason for describing this phase of the project is that the method of analysis in this phase was basically a very general review. In this phase, time series were important variables since the overall social, economic, political and cultural changes in the five selected sample villages were traced over almost 100 years. Based on this kind of survey, we obtained some general findings (Chen and He 1996).

However, based on the research from 1991 to 1997, if we focus our research only on the general overall level, we could hardly say that we understood the real position as regards modernization in rural areas. Therefore, specific research on specialized topics was carried out as a supplement that would carry an even more important meaning. Thus, after completing the research of *European Project on China's Modernization*, from 1998 the research team switched their focus to specialized issues. This can be regarded as the third phase of the research.

Specialized research was conducted on rural finance in the five selected villages[18] during 1998–2000. As a result, *Rural Finance and Development* (He

[Heufers] and Hu 2000) was published. Further research was conducted on rural marketing and the linkage between local centres and nearby villages,[19] during 2000–2 and, based on this, *Small Town and Regional Integration* was published (Zhang and Hu 2002). Obviously, further research of this kind which focuses on different aspects of rural development and modernization should be conducted in the future.[20]

As an important part of the research, special attention was paid from the very beginning to the relationship between institutional change and development and modernization in rural China, particularly the role of informal institutions for rural development and modernization at village level. The fieldwork in all five selected sample villages took place during the past ten years. In the initial studies of the villages of Wangjian in Shaanxi Province and Duanjia in Hubei Province (Duanjia village had changed its name to Fuxing village on 24 December 1996), more attention was paid to formal institutions and their changes.[21] From 1996, the focus of the research changed from formal institutions to informal ones. This book is largely the result of that research.

2 Village trust, *guanxi* community and IVWC governance

An interdisciplinary approach to informal institutional analysis in rural China

Major arguments

Increasingly, economists as well as other social scientists have realized that the orthodox neoclassical paradigm cannot explain people's real world correctly since neoclassical theories[1] of exchange pay no attention to the role of non-market (non-price) institutions such as trust, networks, social capital, indigenous governance, etc., under the situation of positive transaction costs (Granovetter 1985; Etzioni 1988; Hodgson 1988; Casson 1991; Herrmann-Pillath 1994; Landa 1997; Nooteboom 2002; etc.). Thus, they created new approaches to either fill the gap between reality and conventional economics, or sought to correct this shortcoming. A consensus emerging from their research is that institutions matter for economic performance and social development, and that human societies depend on two sets of institutions (market institutions and non-market institutions[2]) rather than just one type of institutions (market institutions).

On the other hand, many scholars explicitly emphasize different types of institutions by linking them closely to specific contexts of different societies or different economies with different economic development levels, different cultural, social, political and historical backgrounds and so on (provided these are not mutually exclusive). For example, under conditions of various environmental uncertainties, where the legal framework is underdeveloped, some scholars regard informal social norms and related informal institutions as being of importance. Otherwise, informal institutions do not matter at all. Therefore, developed capitalist economies can be dependent on contract law alone, while informal social norms and informal institutions need only be introduced in developing economies. Schlicht (1998: 22) even found that some prevalent ideas in relation to this point are deceptive:

> Some traditional economies may be entirely governed by custom, but in modern economies the forces of competition will erode all kinds of customary arrangements. It is held that the 'economic sphere' will eventually be coordinated by competition alone. Modernization will supplant customary arrangements by market processes.

Or, as some have concluded:

> the often-encountered view that customary arrangements are remnants of the past, to be eroded by modernization and competition.
>
> (Schlicht 1998: 207)

Based on these two arguments, my research tries to focus on institutional analysis, particularly informal institutional analysis by linking some of the theories with empirical case studies from rural China. Three informal institutions will be surveyed in this research: (1) village trust in relation to rotating savings and credit associations (ROSCAs) (Chapter 5); (2) *guanxi* community and people's mobility, and town and village enterprise (TVE) development (Chapters 6 and 7); and (3) the local governance of 'integrating village with company' (IVWC – *yichang daicun*) (Chapter 8). Through theoretical and empirical research on these three informal institutions, my research attempts to reach two major targets:

1   Showing that social structures are always governed by both formal and informal institutions simultaneously, regardless of the specific context of economic and legal development of the social organizations. The present work is one of very few empirical studies which attempts to show clearly such a close relationship between formal and informal institutions along with the evolution of social structures. This is very consistent with Mill's argument of 'the two determining agencies' of custom and competition in the market economies (Mill [1848] 1909: 242).

2   Building up some intermediate-level theories to bridge the gap between macro- and micro-institutional analysis, such as village trust and *guanxi* community, by integrating theories and concepts from anthropology, sociology, law and cultural studies such as trust, social exchange, indigenous culture, networks, social capital, customs, reciprocity, social norms and so on. These new theories play an important role in facilitating the analysis of informal institutions based on my experience of village surveys.

The literature on institutional analysis in the social sciences, particularly focusing on informal institutions, will first be reviewed in more detail. From this literature review, we will learn how scholars from differing fields explain institutions in order to gain a better understanding of how both formal and informal institutions always influence social and economic development. This will generally respond to the first argument presented at the beginning of this discussion.

In the third section of this chapter, the most important contribution of this research to institutional analysis, particularly to the study of informal institutions (i.e., the major new theoretical frameworks and concepts such as village trust, *guanxi* community and IVWC governance structure) will be highlighted. It is hoped that these contributions to the building of new theoretical frameworks and concepts will be useful in bridging macro- and micro-analysis, in bridging economic research and research from other social sciences, as well as in bridging theory and practice in the area of institutional analysis by taking case studies from rural China as an example.

Institutions in the social sciences: a general review

As was pointed out in the previous discussion, in the conventional world of economics, when people talk about trading or exchange, this usually refers to real-time trading or real-time exchange, i.e., trading or exchange with immediate payment or immediate receipt of an equivalent value. However, as trading patterns change in order to reduce transaction costs, delivery of property or merchandise and the payment process have become separated from each other. Delivery of goods becomes reliant on future payment rather than immediate payment. This directly raises the issue of credit. Broadly speaking, it is an issue of trust (Nooteboom 2002). The simple but crucial question raised by this issue is how to assure future payment. Perhaps it is better to ask whether the two sides of the transaction (or economic agents) can trust each other (Gambetta 1988). [3] Clearly, it is difficult to determine an answer based on conventional economics alone. [4]

Apart from selling and buying goods based on trust (credit), social capital and networks are two further issues that also rely very heavily on implied trust within their analysis (Herrmann-Pillath 2000a). Without trust between members within a community or within certain types of networks, it is also very difficult to address the issues of resource sharing, income distribution and social welfare arrangements based on the principles of conventional economics. From this point of view, North contends that no market can exist without trust (North 1990). Actually, without trust in any society, there would not only be no market, but there would also be no entrepreneurs and no firms. This simply implies that trust is an extremely important factor for economic analysis.

Therefore the literature on this will be reviewed from two perspectives: first, a general introduction to the basic concepts of formal and informal institutions and their functions as they relate to economic performance and social development; second, extending these basic ideas to a more important and deeper discussion of the link between informal institutions and trust, social capital, networks and culture. Hence the general conceptual analytical framework of this research derived from the macro level becomes clear.

Institutions: formal and informal

According to North (1990: 3–5), institutions are the 'rules of the game of a society' or 'the humanly-devised constraints that shape human interaction'. Therefore, all organizations such as political bodies, economic bodies, educational bodies and social bodies are not institutions[5] because they are the players, not the 'rules of the game'.

Also based on North (1990: 3, 47), institutions are composed of formal rules, informal constraints and the characteristics that enforce both. Formal institutions include constitutions, statute law, common law, property rights, contracts and regulations; conventions, norms of behaviour and self-imposed codes of conduct are informal constraints. Based on his research, North (1990: 36) believes that formal institutions (formal laws and property rights) rather than informal institutions are the foundation of capitalism and Western world development.

Although North's ideas about institutions, formal rules and informal constraints are quite clear, some research by other scholars in this area such as Schultz (1968), Nelson (1994), Hurwicz (1993), Schotter[6] (1981), Sugden (1986), Greif[7] (1989, 1994) and Bowles[8] (2001) are also very valuable and their findings significant.

Schultz (1968) made contributions to institutional research from the perspective of institutions and people's economic value. He grouped institutions into four types: institutions for reducing transaction costs (such as monetary and futures markets); institutions for managing the risks of factors allocated to production among owners (such as contracts, revenue-sharing systems, cooperatives, companies and insurance); institutions for providing the linkage between functional organization and personal income flow (property, experiences), and institutions for establishing the framework for producing and distributing public facilities and services (such as roads, airports, schools, etc.). He thinks that, as investment in human capital increases, people's economic value will be higher. The old institutions concerning the ownership of materials will lag behind real economic development. Therefore, in order to adapt to the increased economic value of people, institutional changes are inevitable.

Nelson believes that institutions are the special participants in the game. The major participants include industrial associations, technological societies, universities, courts, government departments, and judicial organs (Nelson 1994: 57). Hurwicz (1993) considers that rules must be capable of enforcement; otherwise they cannot be called institutions. Moreover, Hurwicz thinks that the design of institutions is conditioned by a series of environments, such as technology, preferences, resource endowment, etc. Game rules should be made compatible with the motives of game participants.

No doubt Aoki's research provides a good overall picture of comparative institutional analysis among economists. His own definition of institution as 'an equilibrium of a game' (compared with North's 'rules of the game') is quite a new and important concept. He regards economic process as a game process, that is economic development is a process during which individuals participating in economic activity with different motives interact and influence each other. Hence, game theory is the theoretical foundation of institutional analysis. Based on game theory, Aoki defines institution as:

> a self-sustaining system of shared beliefs about how the game is played, its substance is a compressed representation of the salient, invariant feature of an equilibrium path, perceived by almost all the agents in the domain as relevant to their own strategic choices. As such it governs the strategic interactions of the agents in a self-enforcing manner and in turn is reproduced by their actual choices in a continually changing environment.

(Aoki 2001: 26)

What is important about this research is that Aoki's idea about institutions differs from North's since his focus is very much on a self-sustaining system and the importance of interaction among players in the game, rather than the rules given from outside. From this point of view, we find that North pays more attention to the rules of the game while Aoki focuses more on the equilibrium of the game through interaction of the game players. One point coming from Aoki's research is extremely important: Aoki does not take the formal laws to be institutions if the laws are not enforced through the policy interaction of participants, including enforcers (see Aoki 2001: 13, 413 for more details).

In fact, if we compare all these concepts about institutions, especially to North's ideas (as we know that North's institutional theory is still based on the general principle of rational choice of individuals under the framework of neoclassical utility maximization), with the original institutional theories built up by the founders of the old institutional economics (OIE) like Veblen, Commons, etc., some differences are clearly evident.

For example, in Veblen's view ([1899] 1934: 190), institutions have three major characteristics: (1) they are more informal institutions biased; (2) they have very broad aspects and (3) they are evolutionary. According to him:

> The institutions are, in substance, prevalent habits of thought with respect to particular relations and particular functions of the individual and of the community [... thus] institutions must change with changing circumstances, since they are of the nature of an habitual method of responding to the stimuli which these changing circumstances afford. The development of these institutions is the development of society.[9]
>
> (Veblen [1899] 1934: 190)

This means that Veblen simply regards economic institutions as merely informal institutions, that is, a mixture of habits and customary actions (Hodgson 1988). According to Peter Burke (1992), this is actually a broad cultural concept covering customs, conventions, attitude to life and people's psychology. We will discuss this further later. From the methodology point of view, Veblen's institutions idea is rooted in an evolutionary and social historical foundation. Therefore, the concepts of habits, social interactions of the individuals within the community, human relations, etc., have significant importance in his theory of institutional economics.

In Commons' theory of institutions, 'collective action in control, liberation and expansion of individual action'[10] (Commons [1934] 1990: 648) is a simple but very important notion. Like Veblen, Commons also pays more attention in his institutional economics to informal institutions than to formal institutions. This is why 'customs' is a term often used in his writings.[11]

After systematic analysis of institutional theories from John Locke, François Quesnay and David Hume to Adam Smith, Thomas Robert Malthus and Veblen, linking historical reality, Commons drew three major conclusions in his institutional economics research: (1) 'An institution is merely collective action in control, liberation and expansion of individual action. It may be Communism, Fascism or Capitalism.' (2) The twentieth century ushered in an era of collective action. (3) 'Economic philosophy now, the world over, is the philosophy of collective action' (Commons [1934] 1990: 902). According to Commons, some collective actions such as customs do not have an organization; other collective actions, however, are carried out through organizations including families, corporations, holding companies, industrial associations, trade unions, banks, groups of associated undertakings and the state. Collective action that emerges from operating rules of either customs or institutions and organizations results in the induction of individual action (Commons [1934] 1990). At the very beginning of his institutional economics, Commons said that the theory of institutional economics he was going to discuss was a theory of the role of collective action inducing individual action and about man's relationship with man (in relation to engineering economics, this is defined as man's relationship with nature) (Commons [1934] 1990). In this man-to-man relationship, he wanted mainly to define the business rules about rights, obligations, freedom and exposure of ownership.

From the point of view of the history of economic thought, the major ideas from the American OIE school – such as those previously mentioned of Veblen and Commons (to take just two of the representatives of that school, although C. E. Ayres (1961) and Mitchell are also very important old institutional economists) – are strongly linked or even rooted in the German History School (GHS) of the mid-nineteenth century. Because the historical approach of the GHS was more Darwinian, the school regarded each society as constituting its own rules based on its history. Thus the GHS rejected general and abstract assumptions such as human rationality and maximization in favour of the economic analysis proposed at about the same time by British classical economists. Ideas from the GHS, especially those of Wilhem Roscher about the importance of non-economic factors (such as customs, property, legislation, justice, history, ethics, politics, etc.) in economic development and Gustav Schmoller's ideas about social laws, influenced American OIE to a certain extent. Both Veblen and Commons recognized this clearly in their works (Veblen 1901; Commons [1934] 1990).

In the nineteenth century, even in philosophical research, institutions referred more to conventions and customs. The research of Charles Sanders Peirce is an example. He gave increased attention to the influence of conventions (individuals' repeated acts) and customs (social compulsion), regarding them as the foundation of all sciences. However, he also pointed out that rules that came into being as a result of conventions and customs were not laws of nature but laws of collective action.

Some scholars look at institutions by linking them to social order. For example, according to Hayek, generally speaking institutions often refer to the cosmos of the spontaneous order such as customs, practices or cultural beliefs or the *nomos* of the spontaneous order such as norms, self-enforcement contracts and ethics (Hayek 1973). This means, as Hayek understands it, that the institutions that people most often refer to are informal, rather than formal, institutions.

Kasper and Streit also focus on institutions mainly from the perspectives of social order and public policy (Kasper and Streit 1998). Since they regard the major function of institutions is to safeguard and improve a stable social order, facilitate human interactions and ban unpredictable and opportunistic behaviour, thus in their theory, sanctions or punitive measures are especially important to the enforcement of any institutions: 'institutions without sanctions are useless, and only if sanctions apply will institutions make the actions of individuals more predictable' (Kasper and Streit 1998: 28). Based on their classification of two groups of institution, internal institutions[12] ('as rules that evolve within a group in the light of experience', which they also called 'soft institutions' (ibid: 100)) and external institutions[13] ('as rules that are designed externally and imposed on society from above by political action' (ibid: 100)), the nature of sanctions also differ in terms of their origins.[14] According to these definitions, the major element of internal institutions is informal institutions[15] and the resulting sanctions are mainly socially-based, rather than mechanism-based.

Summing up, most earlier authors emphasize informal institutions very much when talking about institutions, whilst modern researchers of New Institutional Economics (NIE) stress formal institutions more. The ideas and the concepts I will follow is to argue that formal institutions and informal institutions are always closely linked together and that they function simultaneously in any society. However, the focus of this research, relating to field survey material, is more on informal institutions. This framework will be discussed in more detail in a later part of this chapter.

Institutions and economic and social developments

Since the 1990s institutional economics has become one of the central focuses of economic research. Therefore the importance of institutions to economic performance has received much attention from economists. Moreover, this is due to the interdisciplinary nature of institutional analysis, especially informal institutional analysis, in different areas such as sociology, anthropology, political science, history, law, culture, etc. Research on whether 'institutions really matter' is receiving growing attention from scholars worldwide, particularly when studying the current hot topics of transitional economics and politics in China, Russia, and Eastern and Central Europe. Therefore we plan to first briefly assess, at a general level, the impact of institutions on economic performance and then turn the focus of the discussion to informal institutions.

Do institutions matter?

After the long discussion tracing the definition of formal and informal institutions in the previous section, the ideas from the literature on what are the major functions of institutions in the socio-economic development of a society will be highlighted. This review also links, to a certain extent, with the previous discussion. However, a distinction will be made between the two sections based on different focuses: basic concepts and definitions of institutions versus their functions and performance.

Again, North's major works on institutions, institutional change and economic performance (North 1981, 1990, 1994; North and Thomas 1973) seem to be recognized by the international economics community despite continued debate about his methodology and major findings. However, Stephan R. Epstein is one theorist who holds different views to North (Epstein 2000).

David Hume found that institutions support a country's economic growth. He believed that economic development, human progress and civilized society needed the support of three basic institutions, namely, protection of private property rights, free transfer of property rights and fulfilment of promises (Hume [1739] 1965). These, as well as legality and free conclusion of agreements constitute what he advocated as the institutional foundation of the development of the capitalist economy. Besides his 'free market theory', as characterized by 'the invisible hand', Adam Smith also stressed the notion that individuals should also be conditioned by the market and its competition mechanism.

Besides conceptual ideas, Veblen's contribution to the performance analysis of institutions is that he included traditions, ideology, customs, knowledge, inventions and skills in his economic analytical framework to form a preliminary theory of 'social intangible assets' (i.e., institutions, but mainly informal institutions), instead of analysing materials and utility as traditional economists did. This provides a new angle from which to explain social and economic development, and especially social and economic development under capitalism. Based on his conceptual definition on institutions, Commons (1934) found that although institutions are a kind of control for an individual, other individuals will benefit from this kind of control.

Parsons (1940) pointed out that institutions provided people with a framework for their economic action. The framework is not only organizational, but also defines the norms of people's action and social relationships, thus integrating the different possibilities of human action into a unified system. Olson (1982) valued highly the important role played by the effects of institutional change (and especially radical institutional change such as internal revolutions or defeats) in promoting economic growth by overcoming rigid institutions that hinder economic growth.

Aoki focuses on the key functions of institutions by linking with information economics:

> in a world of incomplete and asymmetric information, an institution 'enables' the bounded-rational agents to economize on the information processing needed for decision-making.

> (Aoki 2001: 13)

Furthermore, if we take the economic system as a whole, it is simply a system of a series of institutional arrangements. Kasper and Streit take China's experience of development in earlier times as a negative example to explain why China's excellent technology in the past never translated into an industrial revolution and they believe the major reason is because of 'the lack of certain social, political and legal preconditions – in short, institutions' (Kasper and Streit 1998: 18) in the country. In addition, the rules whereby officials could confiscate private property at will dealt a blow to the investment incentive for industrialists and entrepreneurs.

North's[16] major findings relating to the issue of institutions and economic performance can be summarized as:

1   economic performance is determined mainly by institutions,[17] or as he puts it, institutions 'are the underlying determinant of the long-run performance of economies' (North 1990: 107), and the development history of mankind shows that institutional changes are even the real cause of historical evolution;
2   to improve the efficiency of institutions and economic growth, it is necessary to establish efficient economic organizations;[18]
3   efficient property rights (ownership) are the foundation of efficient economic organizations;[19]
4   the necessary condition for an orderly society is manifested by a set of competition rules;[20]
5   the existence of transaction costs is the prerequisite for institutions to emerge and function;[21]
6   the state is eventually responsible for economic growth, decline or stagnation;[22] and
7   to have positive influence on economic development, institutions need the support of a reasonable ideological system.[23]

Hence, North said 'strong moral and ethical codes of a society are the cement of social stability which makes an economic system viable' (North 1990: 47).

One of North's research findings may surprise some scholars, including some economists and maybe also some historians, natural scientists and other specialists. That is, he regarded both the First Economic Revolution (commonly known as the Agricultural Revolution) and the Second Economic Revolution (usually called the Industrial Revolution) as natural results of institutional changes and not mainly due to technological revolution as many economists and historians believe (North 1981: 171).

The key reason for the former is, according to North, because of the transfer of common property rights in hunting to exclusive communal rights in agriculture. Along with the change of the property rights under the two different systems, the incentive structure also changes:

> when common property rights over resources exist, there is little incentive for the acquisition of superior technology and learning; in contrast, exclusive property rights which reward the owners provide a direct incentive to improve efficiency and productivity or, in more fundamental terms, to acquire more knowledge and new techniques.
>
> (North 1981: 82, 89)

Regarding the argument about the major reason for the industrial revolution, North's general idea is that a series of institutional changes had brought about the conditions for a series of technological changes related to the industrial revolution before the revolution happened and the technological evolution was merely a natural outcome of earlier institutional changes. For example, the source of the Industrial Revolution was the establishment of the patent system (Britain enacted Patent Law in 1624) (North 1981). Clearly defined intellectual property rights directly improved the incentive for invention and the use of new technology and led to the Industrial Revolution. According to my understanding of North's research, the basic historical logic goes like this: fully defining property rights (institutional innovation) → improving factor and product markets → market scale expanded → higher levels of specialization and division of labour (more links in production and changed organization of enterprises) → increased transaction costs (higher supervision and checking costs as a result of specialization) → changes in economic organizations (organizational innovation – improved supervision and quality control) → protection of inventions (intellectual property rights) → lower cost of innovation and higher returns from innovation → combination of science and technology (technological innovation) → the Industrial Revolution (Figure 2.1). This demonstrates that the Industrial Revolution succeeded because property rights were clearly defined (especially because of the appearance and protection of intellectual property rights). Therefore, North said that success in the Industrial Revolution hinged not on technology, but on the intellectual property rights behind technology (North 1981: 170).

To conduct in-depth case studies, North chose ancient Greece and Rome,[24] the Netherlands and Britain,[25] France and Spain[26] representing countries from Western Europe,[27] and the United States and Latin America[28] from the Americas. He drew the same conclusion from different countries in different eras, i.e., institutions are the most important factor in determining economic performance.

Informal institutions and economic and social developments

Nevertheless, a growing number of scholars have also found the impact of informal institutions on overall socio-economic development in any society is significant.

As Peter Burke (1992: 89) once said, formal organizations have long been studied by sociologists and historians,[29] but informal organizations have been relatively neglected by historians, perhaps because they are characterized by 'communitas'. Clearly, these informal organizations have been neglected not because they are unimportant but because they are not easily described. In fact, in countries with a solid traditional and cultural foundation and in most backward developing countries the influence of informal institutions on economic and social development is of special importance.

Among contemporary economists, North is a person who stresses the importance of both formal and informal institutions since he pays much attention to culture in his institutional research. For example, he argued: (1) informal institutional change always happens incrementally (or gradually),[30] (2) informal institutions

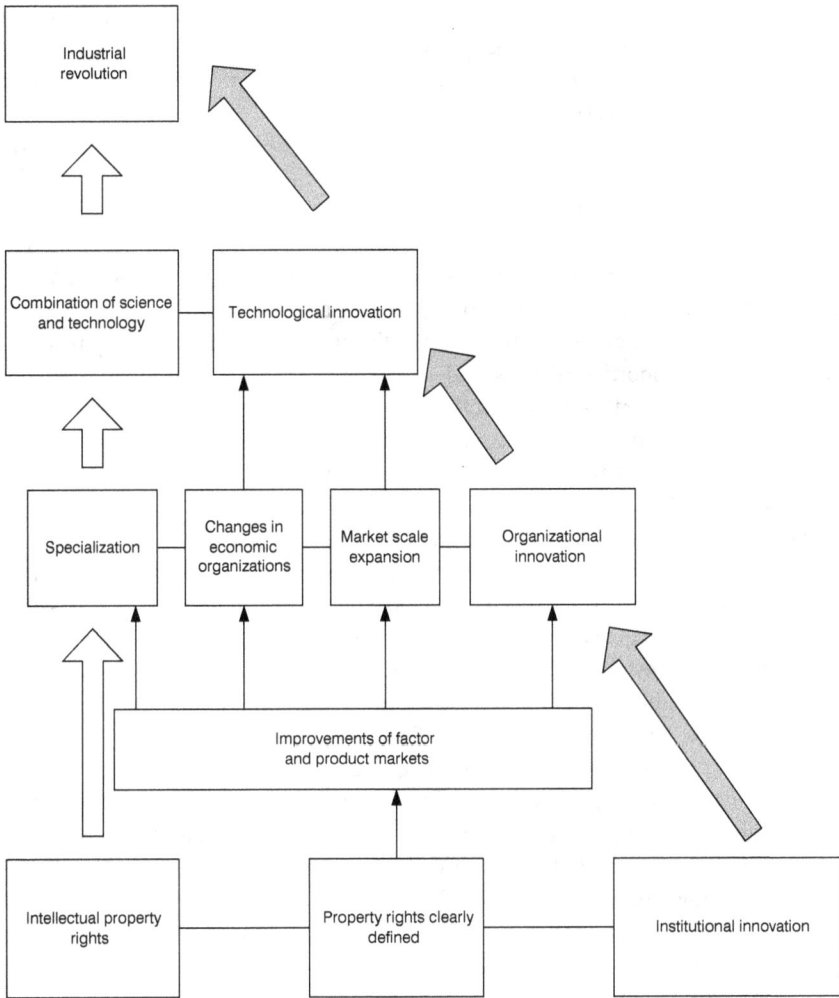

Figure 2.1 North's institutional logic on the industrial revolution (based on North 1981)

have the function of complementing formal institutions,[31] (3) informal institutions help to lower transaction costs,[32] and (4) the collapse of the manor system can be explained by institutional economics and its strong relationship to informal institutions[33] (North and Thomas 1973).

The achievements of other economists are also of note. For example, the concept of 'path dependence'[34] initially proposed by Paul David, is a very useful conceptual tool to explain the significance of informal institutions as they relate to a society's history and culture in determining the general direction of future developments of that society (David 1985, 1986). The significance of the approach is that culture and history matter (David 1988, 1992; North 1990). Platteau clarified this:

to the extent that rules and institutions are always a product of historical (social and political) processes working out their effects in a world characterized by imperfect and incomplete markets, there is no reason to expect these rules or institutions to be (even second-best) efficient.

(Platteau 1994: 787)

A further example is the concept of 'customs economy'[35] developed by John Hicks (1969) which is also important in understanding how non-market economic institutions work in feudal society. Commons ([1934] 1990: 710) also considers custom as 'the general principle' for all human actions, regardless of collective action or individual action and 'the totality of changing customs that is civilization' which is very supportive of Hicks' ideas.[36] The concept of 'conspicuous leisure and conspicuous consumption' (reflecting the reality in England, Poland and Italy in the sixteenth and seventeenth centuries) by Veblen ([1899] 1934) is also a meaningful concept for informal institutions based on explanations[37] by Pierre Bourdieu (1984) and Peter Burke (1992).

Some economists, such as Thomas Robert Malthus (1826), even firmly believed that customs were principles of decisive significance for the development of mankind and even to its survival.[38] Hodgson (1988) thought it is impossible for people to make every decision based on rational calculations in their real life under multiple constraints.[39] According to Kasper and Streit (1998), customs and conventions are able to solve problems automatically.

One of the latest contributions is from the related literature by Schlicht (1998: 6, 87, 191) who depicts custom as being *de facto* the most influential informal institution since it consists of a set of habitual, emotional and cognitive regularities. This simply means that custom is all the routines or all the conventions or even, we can say, it is the sum of cognition, emotion and action. His theory of custom shows that law is a kind of systematized custom, and common law is the general custom; firms are the islands of specialized customs emerging in the market; the whole market process is finally and totally built up based on custom since law is shaped by custom and the entitlements and obligations that have emerged from customary regulations and property rights are also rooted in custom (Schlicht 1998: 106, 151). The obvious conclusion from his research is that informal institutions based on various customary regulations will never be replaced by formal institutions and they are always fundamental for economic and social interaction in any society.

Unlike many other scholars, Thrainn Eggertsson (1990) studied the role of informal institutions from another angle. He believes that without informal constraints from self-compulsion, social customs, customary laws and value systems on the actions of individuals, all societies would be unable to effectively prevent activities that freely use resources and loot wealth. This is especially important in societies without a government and official legislators, judges, politicians and administrators (as was the case in Iceland from 930 to 1262) or in the pre-state era.

Although Burke's position on informal institutional research may be true, many scholars from disciplines other than economics have nevertheless conducted much research in this area. Most of these scholars take customs to be the major form of informal institution. However, some scholars also focused on other forms relating to informal institutions, such as the networks of power.

On the basis of some of the literature reviewed, scholars focus much of their attention on customs analysis by linking the five major aspects of (1) law, (2) social order, (3) economic and social system, (4) human behaviour and (5) human civilization.

Both François Quesnay and Edward Palmer Thompson (1991), though working in different periods, discussed customs as the foundation of various laws: for example, the natural law and rights from Quesnay's theory,[40] and the local law in Thompson's framework.[41]

Thompson's research (1991) also indicates that *Customs in Common*[42] played a very important role in maintaining the social order in Europe in the seventeenth and eighteenth centuries. Three examples particularly show the significance of customs on social functions of the time relating to the enclosure movement,[43] wife selling[44] and 'rough music' (loud noises).[45]

Generally speaking, the research of Karl Polanyi (1944) and Fernand Braudel (1981) is very closely linked to the construction of economic and social systems. According to Polanyi, the market is only one economic and social system; other systems are also available and supportive of social and economic development in societies, such as people's mutual exchange and mutual benefit system, etc.[46] Braudel mainly believes the cultural assets of capitalism consist, in part, of customs.[47]

However, John Locke[48] ([1690] 1960) and some of the psychological economists such as George Katona[49] (1951) regard customs or habits as determining human behaviour. Norbert Elias' (1976) theory[50] shows that the human civilization,[51] at least the civilization process in Western Europe, has been pushed forward by changes in various informal institutions, especially by changes of people's customs or habits as they relate to their real life.

Returning to David Hume, his ideas relating to informal rules are quite different from many others, in that he even took the role of habits as the most important factor for either individuals or societies. He simply concluded that habits decide everything, including not only the past and present but also the future (Hume [1735] 1965).

In addition, Michael Mann (1986) used his unique 'power networks' to explain the conditions for the creation and development of different civilizations. According to Mann's theory, social and historical development was mainly the outcome of the four power networks in Europe in the later period of the Middle Ages – the IEMP model – ideological, economic, military and political. The influence of the state's judicial regulation was limited – very weak, actually – consequently the norms for property rights and free exchange that were determined by local customs which played a key role in social and economic development at the time.

Informal factors such as local ideological networks are the basis for all 'power networks', according to his theory.

Informal institutions and trust

After some discussion of the basic terms of formal and informal institutions and their general impact on economic performance and social development, based on well-known literature, we now need to return to the question posed at the beginning of this chapter which is: 'How can we be assured a deal can be made if the processes of buying and selling and payment are separate from each other?' This question directly relates to the focus of discussion in this book – that is the question of informal institutions – because the most important feature of informal institutions is the way sanctions and punishment of violations under informal institutions rely totally on social sanctions or self-enforcement (Herrmann-Pillath 2000a, 2000b) and are not based on organized authorities (such as government agencies) or formal institutions (such as formal contracts and regulations). Therefore, trust becomes the most important factor in the informal institutional system since legal frameworks (formal monitoring and formal enforcement) are absent in the system. This induces us to further study of informal institutions by linking trust with both the general theories as well as empirical cases.

Nonetheless, the question raised at the beginning of this section in relation to trust is somehow an economic issue since the economic logic is quite simple and clear – trust helps to reduce transaction costs. Unfortunately, economists[52] with only some exceptions (Arrow 1971, 1974; Casson 1991; Nooteboom 2002, etc.) reject the idea that trust can be a significant factor in economics and business. Thus there is even a saying, 'there is no trust in economics' (Nooteboom in Casson and Godley 2000: 57). On the contrary, many scholars from social sciences other than economics such as anthropology, sociology, psychology and political science (Durkheim 1933; Weber 1947; Wolff 1950; Blau 1964; Elster 1979; Giddens 1984; Luhmann 1979, 1988; Zucker 1986; Shapiro 1987; Putnam 2000; Fukuyama 1995) recognized the importance of trust to either building good social relations among people and societies, or lowering transaction costs.

The function of lowering transaction costs (and maybe also enabling productive relations – Nooteboom 2002: 15) has been elaborated by many economists in their work (Arrow 1974; Powell 1990; Casson 1991, 1995; Nooteboom 1996, 2002; Dasgupta 1988; Gulati 1995). Amitai Etzioni even thought that the significance of trust is for the whole economic system, not only for reducing transaction costs, because 'without it [trust], currency will not be used, saving makes no sense … in short, it is hard to conceive a modern economy without a strong element of trust running through it' (Etzioni 1988: 7).

Moreover, according to some economists, for example, Casson (1991) and Nooteboom (2002), the fundamental issue relating to trust is that we have no choice but to trust someone and something[53] in real life for two major reasons: high uncertainty (formal institutions like contracts always leave a gap of uncertainty, we then have only the choices of 'trust or die')[54] and high monitoring costs.[55]

Taking the first point of view, trusting someone or trusting something is the only choice for us as there are no other alternatives. Even then, we cannot say that trust is totally blind because of the existence of other informal constraints and cultural factors,[56] and past experience (of certainty, honesty, reliability and confidence of others) gained from similar situations. Taking the second point of view, it is more a transaction cost issue, as has already been pointed out.

This simply means that trust is a general and universal phenomenon rather than a narrow disciplinary issue affecting only some specific cases.[57] The implication, then, is that trust is decisive in other areas, not merely economic transactions and social relations, but also in the whole economic system as well as to the whole social system. Absolutely, then, trust matters.

If trust is a general phenomenon, then all economic and social factors should relate to it to a certain extent. In other words, other social and economic actions must be embedded (Granovetter 1985) into the trust framework in certain ways, although trust itself also needs to be engineered into the processes of economic and social change. Zucker (1986) used the term 'modes of trust production' in his analysis to express these interrelations. In his framework, community, membership of family, religion, etc., are examples of characteristics, while loyalty, commitment, habituation, etc., are examples of the process (also see Nooteboom in Casson and Godley 2000).

On the basis of this theoretical background, it is planned to develop a more detailed theoretical framework in a later section of this chapter and use empirical studies of selected Chinese villages in Chapters 5, 6, 7 and 8 to determine whether the process of rural development in these communities can be explained, to a certain extent, by the trust existing in these villages.

Informal institutions, networks and social capital

Trust, however, is not an abstract concept but a characteristic closely linked to people's real life and it has been fostered and has grown in different social environments. Hence it manifests itself in different forms, for example, such as 'personal trust' and 'system trust'[58] as outlined by Niklas Luhmann (1979). In other words, different societies and communities, even different individuals, adopt different kinds of trust based on their own experience. Thus, to a certain extent, the issue of trust is linked to social networks and social capital. In particular, if we look at the issue of trust in some countries, for example China (Herrmann-Pillath 1992; Fukuyama 1995), compared with other countries, such as Sweden (Casson 1991), the situation is quite different. Trust in China is mainly based on some sub-societies such as family or clan family, the village, etc., but in Sweden, it is much more universally based and links more directly to the 'great society', to borrow a term from Hayek (1988).

From the previous discussion, we know that Luhmann (1979) proposed two kinds of trusts, i.e., system trust and personal trust. One crucial question related to that proposition is how these two kinds of trust work together in reality. One of the arguments put forward by North is that personal trust will be replaced by a system trust once society becomes well developed (North, 1990). However, Wong (in Hamilton 1991) thinks that both kinds of trust could be well integrated. Thus, we need to look closely at both networks and social capital simultaneously when we talk about trust.

While studies of both networks and social capital have drawn much attention from scholars in different disciplines, producing an abundant literature (Granovetter 1985; Coleman 1988; Burt 1992; Bourdieu 1986; Putnam 1993; Fukuyama 1995; Dasgupta and Serageldin 1999), I have determined from Herrmann-Pillath's research (Herrmann-Pillath 2000a) that, rather than separating them from each other, networks and social capital should be integrated into one analytical framework that also links into culture and trust systems.[59]

According to Herrmann-Pillath, 'a network is a commonly perceived Gestalt, i.e., a shared mental model of externalities' within the network and culture is a sort of tacit knowledge about these externalities[60] (Herrmann-Pillath 2000a: 16). Social capital is simply just the 'memory' of networks as contained in the experiences of their members[61] and this 'memory' has been identified as 'culture' (Herrmann-Pillath 2000a: 19). Obviously, the two are very closely interrelated. Through this type of integration, the changing path between networks and social capital can be clearly traced by linking trust and culture.

The real value of this new kind of integrated analytical approach, as proposed by Herrmann-Pillath, is the theoretical outcome of the significance of 'the boundaries between different networks' (a common form is various communities) within society. Because networks, to a certain extent, can be a kind of special community, social capital can also possibly, in a broad sense, be another kind of community. Therefore, when analysing networks and social capital, what is happening within a community cannot just simply be neglected.

Returning to Wong's argument mentioned earlier, it is not at all difficult to understand his point using Herrmann-Pillath's approach, namely that networks, social capital and their interactions, system trust and personal trust can be well integrated. Taking community as the entity, in which trust and culture plus networks and social capital are structured in an orderly way, the resulting integrated system should be very efficient, particularly when uncertainty exists.

Therefore, in Chapters 5, 6 and 7 we intend to look at how networks and social capital work when integrated together in certain communities[62] at the grass-roots level in rural China.

Furthermore, if both networks and social capital are strongly linked to the community, then a related question is, 'How should we build a new basis for our new community theoretical framework in line with the changing situation of a much more intensified flow of people and information (including knowledge) in modern society, compared with the conventional community conceptual framework[63] that is based on traditional methods of communication and low mobility of economic and social resources, say, before the late twentieth century?'

Reality clearly shows the serious challenges to the conventional concept of community[64] since it only focuses on the fixed place, little movement of people and old methods of face-to-face contacts, etc. In reality there is a significantly increased movement of people (including migration) from one place to another, intensified interaction between the community and the outside world, frequent changes in people's occupations, which often changes social identity as well, the rapid development of networks and so on. These changes have been happening everywhere in the world, particularly in transitional developing countries. In these circumstances, a kind of special community and its relationship to the new theoretical framework can be constituted based on the analysis in Chapter 3 of indigenous Chinese culture and concepts of networks.

Informal institutions and culture

According to many scholars (Giddens 1984; Zucker 1986; Herrmann-Pillath 2000a; Nooteboom 2000), trust is rooted in certain shared values and emotions for certain people from certain groups. This indicates clearly that trust is indeed a kind of cultural phenomenon. Also based on the observation of some scholars (Granovetter 1985; Coleman 1988; Bourdieu 1986; Putnam 1993; Dasgupta and Serageldin 1999; Herrmann-Pillath 2000a, 2000b), the boundaries of social networks and social capital also provide, *de facto,* cultural boundaries. Thus, we cannot avoid analysing culture when discussing social networks and social capital.

From the previous discussion of institutions and informal institutions, trust, networks and social capital, it can be clearly seen that all these aspects are, in certain ways, strongly linked to cultural factors. Therefore, it would be very difficult to form a correct understanding of informal institutions and related elements, in terms of both theory and practice, without first having in mind a clearer picture of culture.

Fortunately, more and more economists realize this and have begun to apply more effort in recent years to a cultural dimension in their research on economic systems (Etzioni 1988; Dasgupta 1988; Greif 1989,[65] 1994; Herrmann-Pillath 2000b; Harrison and Huntington 2000; North 1990). However, due to the nature of complexity,[66] it is not surprising to read quite diverse ideas regarding issues in the area; that has always been the situation across other disciplines since the nineteenth century.[67] Nevertheless, we do need to clarify some of the arguments relating to this research.

The basic, yet fundamental, argument is: what is culture, i.e., how should we define culture? Of course, there is no need at this time to analyse one-by-one all the nearly 200 definitions of culture collected by Kroeber and Kluckhohn (1952). However, some of the important ones need to be repeated here, for example, the initial definition proposed by Tylor in the late nineteenth century.

According to Tylor:

> culture ... is the complex whole which includes knowledge, belief, art, law, morals, custom and any other capabilities and habits acquired by man as a member of society.

> (Tylor [1871] 1924)

His definition is not clear to many people since he defined culture as a 'complex whole' of man's properties as well as all the properties of a society (including man as one of its members). It is simply too macro and too abstract. Many similar definitions followed Tylor's initial proposition.

Another influential definition offered by Weber ([1904] 1949) is simply 'a value concept'; Parsons' well-known definition (Parsons 1951: 159) is that culture 'is intrinsically transmissible from one action system to another (by learning and by diffusion)'. In current studies, North (1990) defines culture as sanctioned behaviour or the 'rule of the game' (Epstein 2000: 173). He assumes that norms and informal institutions are rooted in cultural traditions (Herrmann-Pillath 2000b); Wimmer (1996) defines culture as the dynamic process of communicating meanings that result in the demarcation of group boundaries (also see Herrmann-Pillath 2000b). However, according to Herrmann-Pillath (2000b: 43),

> culture has to be conceived of as an emerging property, based on the relationship between the observer and the observed. Culture does not exist as a property unless there is an observer. Hence, without analyzing the observer, we cannot access culture.

This suggests there are no existing universal cultural principles; rather there has to be a link between different persons, communities and different 'things' when talking about culture. This is why Herrmann-Pillath also simply defines culture as 'difference' (Herrmann-Pillath 2000a).

Definition is important not simply in itself but because the different approaches to culture by economics or other social sciences follow the various definitions.

Tylor's definition of culture is a kind of totality approach, i.e., culture is everything; Parsons' approach is a kind of universality since he believes culture is transmissible; North's cultural approach is almost the same as his approach to institutional frameworks. This is due to his strong emphasis on institutions, especially the proposition that informal institutions are rooted in cultural traditions.

But Herrmann-Pillath's approach differs. He focuses cultural analysis on the interaction between the observer (including inside learned observer and outside scientific observer) and the observed (including culture, behaviour, institutions, etc.). According to this approach, no one alone can have a full understanding of culture. Each observer can only understand part of the culture. Therefore, communication is extremely important when people study culture and related issues.

Because of the existence of such differing kinds of cultural approaches, there also arise some varied arguments in relation to informal institutions:

1 How to simultaneously link and distinguish culture from informal institutions? Based on North's approach, they can be the same thing with no significant difference between the two. This is also true for some other scholars. To the contrary, Herrmann-Pillath's approach differentiates informal institutions

from culture, putting them on different levels. The researcher's preliminary argument or hypothesis is that they should be very closely interrelated since, on the one hand, they share some important elements such as value, beliefs, emotional foundations, etc.; and, on the other hand, in reality, the boundaries and the implications must at the same time be different from each other. One of the purposes of this book is to conduct empirical study in this regard.

2　What is the relationship between traditions and informal institutions since many scholars (such as Mead, 1937;[68] Geertz [1966] 1973;[69] Boon 1972; Hayek 1988; North 1990) focus very much on the linkage of informal institutions to traditions (or 'traditional culture', or 'culture tradition')? This also relates to another argument which is whether culture must be traditional or if it can also be modernized. My preliminary argument is that informal institutions are very closely linked to culture under certain given economic, social and political backgrounds, regardless of traditions or modernity. Although I believe that culture can be traditional if the society is tradition-based, it can also be modernized if the society is modernity-based. But even if the societies or peoples are from similar (or even the same) traditional or modernized environment, the institutions, particularly the informal institutions, in different societies or communities, will also be different. This means that the most important factor for institutional analysis is the exact targeting of a group of people and the exact cultural background in which people live.

3　Is culture universal or diversified by nature? This is a much-debated issue among anthropologists because it is directly linked to the political issue of whether indigenous cultures should be conserved. Not surprisingly, there is no final conclusion arising from the debate since it involves politics deeply. What interests economists in relation to this issue is different in that it is based on whether the same or different informal institutional structures can be expected given different cultural backgrounds. My general observation is that culture is always different among different societies and different groups of people due to historic as well as natural and social factors such as climate, traditions, psychological structure, language, customs, etc. Given these differing cultural backgrounds, both formal and informal institutional choices must also be different. Otherwise the simple transformation of institutions from one society with a certain kind of cultural background to another society with a totally different cultural background would create many problems. The different results that have been achieved using different reform strategies adopted by Eastern and Central European nations and China provide good examples in this area.

In summary, culture and related social backgrounds are very important in analysing informal institutions, whilst they are also different from each other. Therefore when we study informal institutions, first of all we have to identify very carefully the cultural and social backgrounds of the research areas. Since my research is based in rural China, the cultural, historical and social development environment is very different from that of other societies. They even differ from the urban environments in the same country. Also because the selected survey villages are in different provinces with different cultural backgrounds, it is also crucial for further analysis of the research at the village level within these provinces that the researcher compares his knowledge of these provinces at the sub-culture level to Chinese culture as a whole. To achieve this more details on the cultural background at a national as well as a provincial level will be discussed in Chapters 3 and 4 respectively.

Village trust, *guanxi* community and IVWC governance structure: their themes and theoretical frameworks

No doubt informal institutions matter in China where the transaction costs are positive and where the transaction cost structure has become very complicated during China's transition from a centralized economy and society to a market economy and decentralized society. However, most scholars only pay much attention to the country's formal institutional changes, such as government policy changes, government organization structural changes and so on; very little attention has been paid to changes in informal institutions and self-governance structures. Consequently, this present research can be regarded as one of the very few attempts made in this area.

Three major informal institutions,[70] village trust linking with ROSCAs, *guanxi* community linking with people's mobility and TVE development, and IVWC system linking with rural governance at the grass-roots level, will be discussed in this present work, based on the author's background in village study over a long period and the field survey in selected villages (see Chapter 4 for details). In fact, all of these three kinds of institutions can also be regarded, simultaneously, as three different economic organizations in rural China. A common prominent feature of these three institutions is that they are all self-enforced through their own self-governance structures rather than by the state authorities, although the specific forms of self-governance structures among these three institutions are quite different from each other. Detailed discussion of their structures and methods of operation will follow in later chapters; the purpose of the present section is to discuss general theoretical foundations and frameworks so as to establish a link between specific institutions employed by people in rural China and the literature on institutions in the social sciences. Thus we can clearly establish the contribution from my current research to the related literature.

Village trust and ROSCAs

Village trust is a new institutional concept which was developed during my research. Although it is a comprehensive concept, it is quite similar in meaning to the term 'collective trust' initially proposed by Granovetter (1985). Of course, village trust and 'collective trust' analyse different targets, have different contents and express different ideas. Village trust here refers to a kind of village-based institution under conditions when people in the village are well consolidated; thus all the villagers trust each other, they then jointly 'make things happen' such as organizing ROSCAs among the villagers. This is why the concept of 'village community' is important in explaining the existence of village trust in people's real life in the village which was the subject of the survey (Chapter 5).

Detailed analysis of this institution in relation to ROSCAs will be outlined in Chapter 5. The task of this section is to discuss the theoretical basis of village trust consistent with the related social science literature; the general theoretical framework for village trust will also be conceptualized.

The concept of village trust can be explained by several theories of institutions, economic organization and economic cooperation in the social science literature. However, the theory of 'network closure as social capital' initially proposed by Coleman (1988, 1990) and developed later by Burt (2000) is directly linked, as well as being a most important theoretical foundation.

According to Coleman, network closure creates social capital[71] since he focuses very much on the risk limitation function of social capital. Network closure affects access to information (Coleman 1990) which facilitates risk minimization in a dense network. Based on Coleman's ideas, Burt's closure argument explains why network closure becomes the source of social capital. According to his argument, everyone is connected under the closure situation (dense network) and no one can then escape the notice of others; this facilitates effective sanctions. This also facilitates trust and norms (Burt 2000); thus good behaviour follows. Greif (1989) argues that this is a situation of threat of sanction creating effective reputation. However, Granovetter (1985) adds an additional condition to the successful creation of trust from such threat of sanction which is his 'embeddedness' assumption, i.e., trust created from the threat of sanction would be more likely only between people who have mutual friends (structural embeddedness).

Clearly, village trust in relation to ROSCAs in Xiangdong village (see Chapter 5) can be explained well by network closure theory since both the village community and the ROSCAs within the village are completely closed to 'outsiders' on the one hand; on the other hand, through various signalling practices, such as building the villagers' ancestral temple, celebrating ancestor worship regularly, restructuring the village church, identifying surname and kinship status, compiling genealogies, etc., the solidarity of the 'insiders' within the village has been enhanced. This is also very much consistent with Akerlof (1970) and Spence's (1974) ideas on the functions of economics of signalling in social structures.

From the network structure point of view, ROSCAs in Xiangdong village are all typical 'network closure' models of social capital. Taking 'Xiang Zujian's ROSCA' and 'Xiang Xianliang's ROSCA' as examples, apart from one villager who is also a close colleague of Xiang Zujian, the village leader, all the rest of Xiang Zujia's ROSCA members are the herd – Xiang Zujian's closest relatives; most of members of Xiang Xianliang's ROSCA are the villagers from the same village (see Chapter 5 for further information). The network structures for the two ROSCAs show very many typical 'network closure' characteristics (Figure 2.2

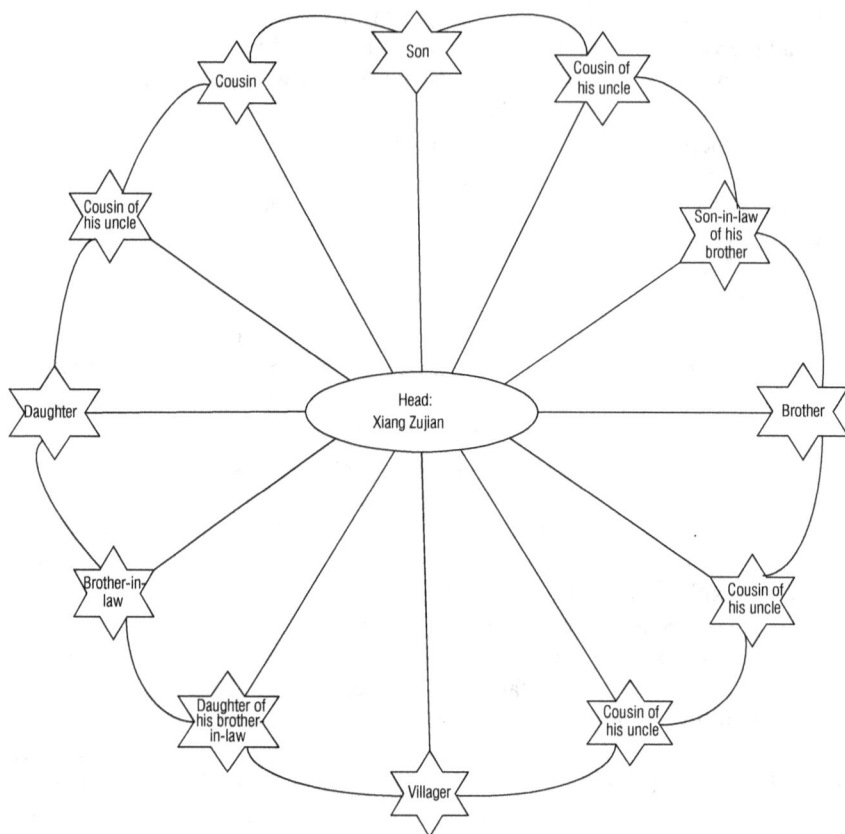

Figure 2.2 'Network Closure' structure of Xiang Zujian ROSCA

and Figure 2.3). Actually, Coleman (1988, 1990) and Biggart (2000) illustrated in their research[72] that trust advantage comes from effective risk management of the ROSCA system.

The key factor determining village trust in relation to ROSCAs within the village is closure; simply because of closure (Figure 2.2 and Figure 2.3), trustworthiness in such a small community can be reached through effective functioning of social norms and sanctions; this makes closure a special kind of social capital as Coleman (1990: 319) points out. We can also employ club theory in interpretation of the issues of village trust and ROSCAs.

The survey of Xiangdong village shows that village trust facilitates ROSCAs to establish, in practice, a kind of club-like arrangement. For instance, all the members of the ROSCAs know each other well; sanctions on the defaulters are not limited just to their credit but also to their overall economic, social and political standing, etc. (see Chapter 5). These show the ROSCA's similarity to a club. As Platteau (1994: 548–9) observes:

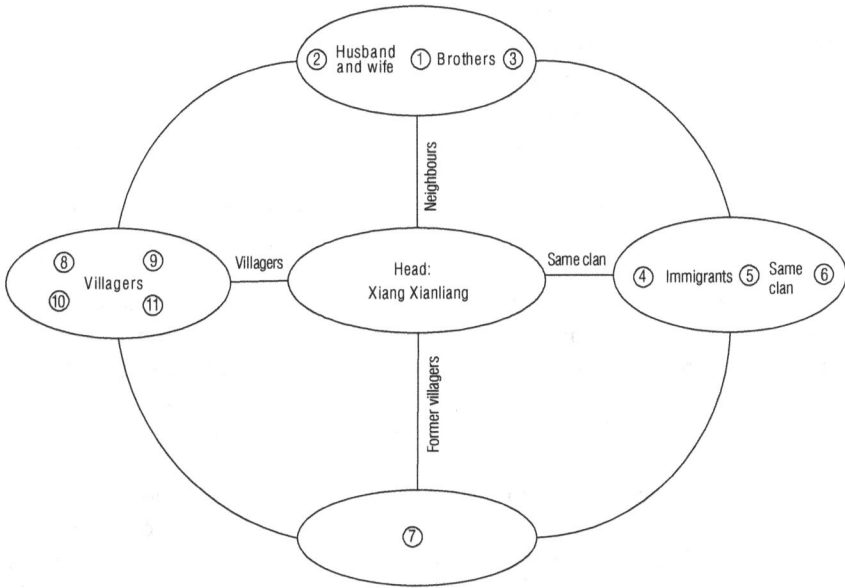

Figure 2.3 'Network Closure' structure of Xiang Xianliang ROSCA

with the dense network of small communities, like in the village community, everyone is watching everyone. Gossip about one's misconduct is circulated by word of mouth faster than any modern means of communication. In such an environment a significant cost would be incurred to a person who would violate a contract with his fellow villagers, since not only would he lose benefits from the present contract but the resulting bad reputation would deprive him of future opportunities to enter into contracts with other villagers as well.

Landa's observation (1997: 125) about the importance of the sense of shared values and norms, i.e., the sense of belonging to a certain 'moral community', to the solidarity of club membership also suggested a link between village trust and club theory. In such an environment, conformity is also important (Schlicht 1998: 14); for example, ROSCAs members in Xiangdong village tend to adapt their behaviour to the others of the group, because that behaviour is good; consequently we see positive results coming from having these kinds of arrangement in the village.

In Xiangdong village, the same group of people took part in a ROSCA for many years (see Chapter 5 for a detailed analysis). Therefore, village trust grows naturally from the repetition of interactions with the same people. Landa's argument is that it will bring reciprocity into the exchange process; once trade is repeated with the same man, the trade partners become blood brothers in some of the primitive societies (Landa 1997: 102). The most important factor for a repeated game[73] to work in a society is not determined by its primitive nature but its closure condition. This is simply because 'reputation cannot arise in an open structure' according to Colemen (1988: S107–8).

Following Landa's point about reciprocity in the trade process, as was mentioned previously, the most important precondition in creating effective reciprocity is closure.[74] Because of network closure, the non-anonymous system is powerful to demonstrate its impact through effective sanctions among the members of the group. Also because of the network closure, free diffusion of information about members among the members becomes possible. Consequently, reciprocity effects (see also Coate and Ravallion 1993; Ligon *et al.* 2002 for more details) become one of the natural results of the social structure. We can also see clearly the impact of reciprocity on people's credit behaviour in Xiangdong's ROSCAs (Chapter 5). However, so far it has not been possible to see the effects of reciprocity under closure shown by involving parents and children as discussed by La Ferrara[75] (La Ferrara 2003).

Finally, as Schlicht (1998: 36) once said very correctly, there is 'no contradiction to rationality is involved in recognizing the significance of clarity considerations'. This means that rational calculation can also be introduced into informal institutional analysis (ROSCAs analysis for example), which is consistent with the general argument presented by the researcher that formal and informal institutions are always mixed in any social structure, regardless of the contextual differences in economic and legal development status.

Guanxi *community*

Guanxi community is a new concept proposed in this research to show how the intermediate level of social theory as well as the intermediate level of social organization work consistently in social science literature and also in people's real life by linking it with our village studies in rural China. Just like kin groups in Ghana discussed by La Ferrara (2003), *guanxi* communities also perform a number of economic and social functions in China.

One of the principle reasons we find *guanxi* community concept extremely important in Chinese research is because it builds a bridge between the traditional Confucian ideas and today's real life of the Chinese. Therefore, it is planned to extend the discussion of *guanxi* community in Chapter 3 as well as Chapters 6 and 7, but to give a brief theoretical discussion in this section.

If we borrow Landa's concept (Landa 1997: 110, 130), *guanxi* community means, generally speaking, a 'group of insider people' or called 'insiders-we' compared to 'outsiders-they'. This 'group of insider people' is not purely based on clans or circles of relatives in traditional society (who are, of course, included) but it adheres to different principles, such as codes of conduct, ethnicity, religion, territory, dialects and so on. The moral factor involved in the system is much more important than the heritage factors, such as blood relations for instance – i.e., social ties are more important than genetic relations in the *guanxi* community. As a result, *guanxi* community is mainly based on social distance (Sahlins 1972) rather than genetic distance.[76] Therefore, as people's social connections change all the time, so the boundary of the *guanxi* community also changes simultaneously. This simply means that *guanxi* community is an open social structure (system).

From Figure 2.4, we find that Ego is the centre of his/her *guanxi* community. Along with the change of time frames, Ego's social distance has been extending wider and wider (the ties of blood for us are usually very limited[77]); then the boundary of Ego's *guanxi* community moves gradually to a sphere outside his surrounding. This is a typical way of *guanxi* community extension in its development process.

Since *guanxi* community is an open social structure, as we discussed above, then its structure can be theoretically explained by structural hole argument[78] proposed by Burt (1992, 2000).

According to Burt's structural hole argument, structural holes[79] as social capital generate opportunities to add value with brokerage across the holes by bridging structural holes (Burt 2000). According to Burt's argument, those who want to gain the opportunities from structural hole have to be well aware of the importance of three factors involved in the bridging process: the first is the early and better access to broad information between people in different groups; the second is to get control power on some of the common items (they can be programs, projects and other matters of common interest for people from different social groups) in order to bring people together out of their own holes; and third, willingness to learn and learning faster than others. Clearly, people with entrepreneurial spirit (network entrepreneurs) are most likely to gain from the brokering process. This is

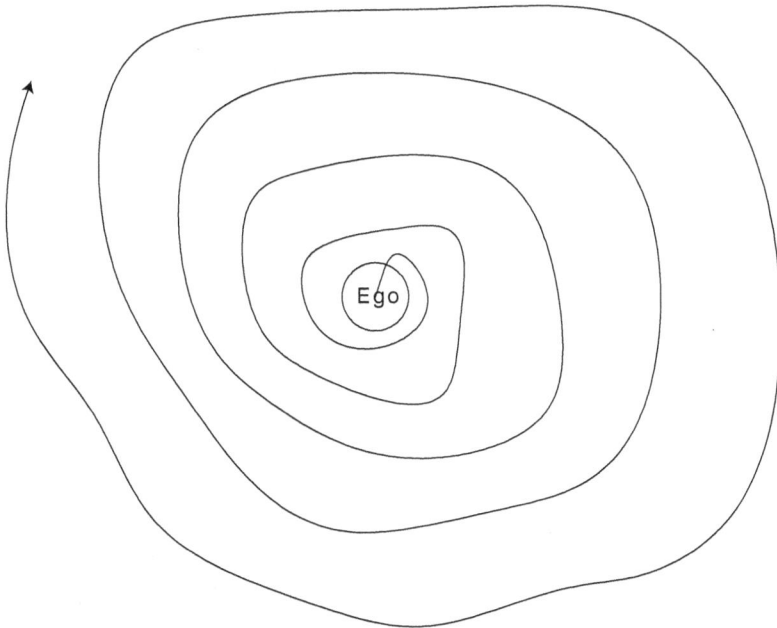

Figure 2.4 Expansion of *guanxi* community

why structural hole analysis always links with entrepreneurship or entrepreneurial networks.

However, according to Burt's observation, entrepreneurship is inherently an exercise in the social capital of structural holes on the one hand and on the other, the topic remains virtually untouched by theory and empirical research (Burt 2000). As an example, some field surveys on how entrepreneurs in rural China make advanced use of comparative advantages, coming from structural holes between rural and urban areas during the country's transitional period, have been conducted over the past few years by the present author; the detailed analysis will be presented in Chapters 6 and 7. However, two of the cases presented briefly below will be useful for us to better understand the empirical work from a theoretical framework of social capital of structural holes discussed in this section.

Figures 2.5 and 2.6 illustrate two entrepreneurs from Tunwa village who took the lead in moving to the local city from their rural origins; however, they kept frequent linkages with their native village while they developed some new networks in the city. After they had established factories in the city, they started to employ labour from their native village and their businesses have developed well in the past 20 years.

Two key theoretical issues are involved in these two cases: one is that the two entrepreneurs employed the hole strategy since they built bridges between their

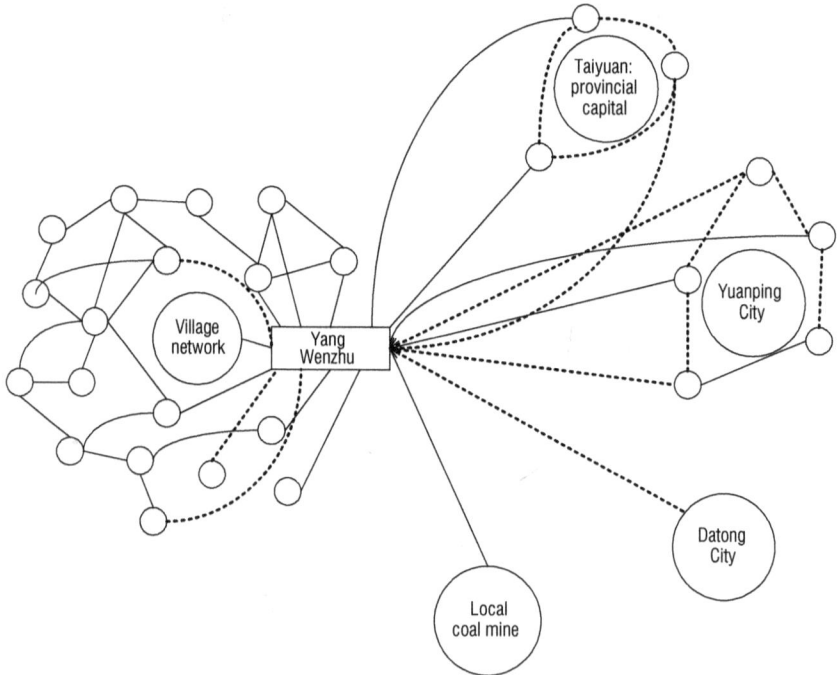

Figure 2.5 Structural holes and entrepreneurial networks (broker networks) for Yang Wenzhu

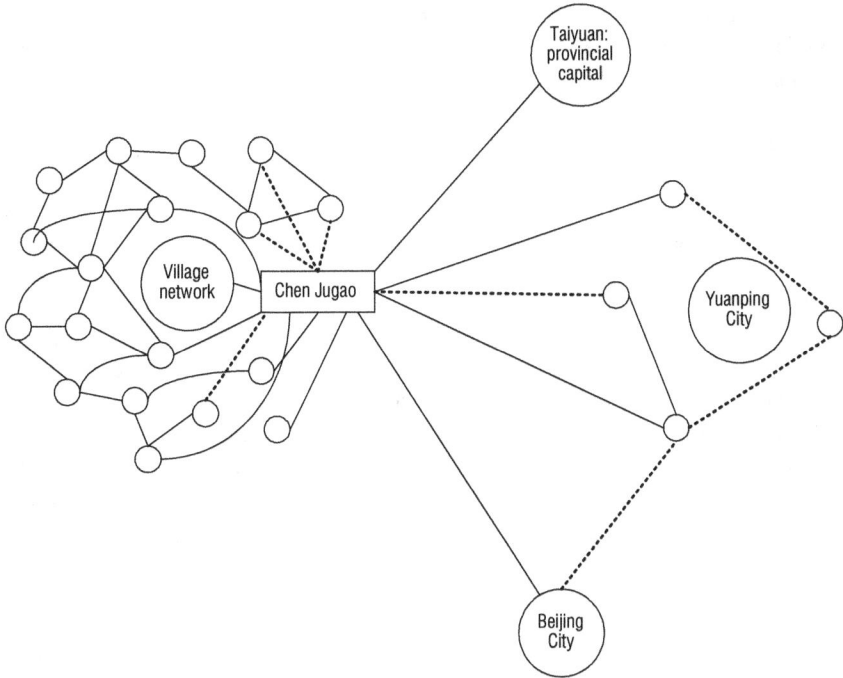

Figure 2.6 Structural holes and entrepreneurial networks (broker networks) for Chen Jugao

native village and the city where they currently live mainly by employing labour from their village of origin to work in their factories in the city; the other is that their gains from hiring labour from their native rural village is much more than their costs, since rural labour is much cheaper than urban labour because of the segmentation of labour market in China.

IVWC governance structure

'Integrating village with company' (IVWC) is a new governance structure in rural China that is jointly designed and practised by a village (Fuxing village) and a company (Fuxing Company). The IVWC governance structure is discussed in more detail in Chapter 8. The general idea is that a company run by an entrepreneur was gradually integrated with the village after the company's initial public offering (IPO) on the Chinese domestic A share market (Shenzhen Stock Exchange) (see the story in detail in Chapter 8). After the listing, some investors of the company challenged the entrepreneur about whether a modern listed company should be involved in local social provision and be involved in social issues of the villagers in the area. This inspired the case study of linking governance and firm theories.

The major argument raised by some investors in the company was that a listed public company should concentrate only on internal management issues in order to improve the company's performance and should not extend the boundaries of the company to include the local community, especially if it is a traditional village. This argument links theories of the firm and theories of governance. Therefore, the major theoretical bases of IVWC system will be explained briefly in this section as a general discussion, and the whole story and more detailed analysis will be presented in Chapter 8.

Two major interrelated theories can be used to explain IVWC system: firm theory and governance theory.

With regard to the theory of the firm, Schlicht (1998: 209) summarized two separate issues that come to mind at once: one concerns the existence of the firm, i.e., in what sense may firms be conceived of as institutions that exert some influence on the individuals composing them, rather than merely reflecting their interest? The other concerns the modes of internal control (the internal structure of the firm). If we simplify Schlicht's summary of firm theory, they are issues of the nature of the firm and its internal control modes.

The notable work on the nature of 'the firm as a nexus of contracts' (that is to say the firm as a bundle of long-term contracts), suggests that the firm is focused more on competition among individuals, as argued by Coase (1937). This is a very influential approach in this respect, since Coase looks at the firm as a kind of specialized market in order to lower transaction costs, therefore the nature of the firm according to Coase, is the *de facto* market, but it is a kind of special market where the owner of the firm and the employees sign long-term contracts (life-long or even contracts covering generations in some extreme cases). However, we should not forget that Coase (1937) also stressed very much the special function of the firm that was expected to lead to an integration of routines and customs at various levels of the firm. From Coase's idea of integration of routines and customs as well as the perception idea, some scholars proposed new approaches with 'firms as islands of custom' (each firm forms an island of custom in the ocean of market); firms were even considered as social entities with features similar to families, churches, government agencies and other associations (Putterman 1988; Schlicht 1998).

The other important issue of firm theory is about the internal control modes of the firm, as we mentioned. Initially presented by Coase (1937) and later developed by Williamson (1985), there are three modes of control in the context of the firm (that is to say, three modes of coordination of economic activities within a firm), namely, exchange[80] (market), command[81] and custom[82] (corporate culture) (see also Schlicht 1998). Two important developments in relation to control modes need to be especially mentioned here; these are (1) these three coordination modes are not mutually exclusive but are complementary – many firms combine the three mechanisms together in practice making the cultural and market factors work together in a firm; (2) these three modes of coordination have been gradually extended from a single firm organization to the community and society management. In Schlicht's words, 'all three control modes – exchange, command and custom[83] – work in various combinations, both at firm level and society level' (Schlicht 1998: 243).

An issue related to control is why the owner of a firm looks for control power. The literature in this area is mainly from Williamson (1985) and Alchian (1984) relating to their contribution of the specificity theory. According to this theory, certain inputs are 'specific' for their utilization in the firm's economic activities which brings more value added than from other uses of these inputs. As a result, the firm's performance would be enhanced by the appropriate utilization of such firm-specific resources. Thus, the owners of inputs which are 'specific' to the firm have strong incentive to gain the control power of the firm. These firm-specific resources can be material capital such as machines, equipment and so on; they can also be human capital such as good artisans, skilled technicians with special tacit knowledge ('implicit' knowledge[84]) or a good team with a strong spirit of cooperation and so forth.

After this general literature review on the theory of the firm, we refer back to the real institutional choice of IVWC as previously mentioned. Based on the theoretical discussion above, we should not be surprised that the Fuxing entrepreneur created the IVWC system because of the following three major reasons:

1   The entrepreneur attempts to establish a family-like arrangement to influence the employees' perception of working for the company, as though they were working for their own family businesses since their employer has taken more and more social responsibilities for their village development and not just for his company (most of the employees working for the Fuxing Company are from Fuxing village). This comprises the cultural and social factors, and the firm becomes a more and more influential social entity in the region.

2   The Fuxing entrepreneur has extended his control beyond his company to the surrounding community through a mixed form of coordination. As a first step the entrepreneur has controlled Fuxing village. He told the research team that he plans gradually to integrate more surrounding villages. One of the results of his extension of control power is that he gains socially and politically (see more details in Chapter 8). The mixture of three control modes has already become a common phenomenon and we can see how the Fuxing entrepreneur and his company gained comparative advantages from a balanced coordination of different control modes.

3   The reason why the Fuxing entrepreneur seeks to control not only the company but also the village is directly linked to the specificity theory, because the company's principal work is production of steel wire, based on the historic development over a long period of the traditional iron industry (such as iron forging, nail making, iron smelting, etc.) in the village (a history stretching over 600 years, see Chapter 8). Most of the workers from Fuxing village have long experience of iron- and steel-related business with certain in-built knowledge in this industry; they have become a specific resource for company development.

We mentioned in the beginning of this section that IVWC is a kind of special governance structure; this links directly with governance theory (Williamson 1975, 1979, 1985, 1996 and 1999). Generally speaking, IVWC is, in fact, a hybrid form of institution, which denotes the long-term contractual relationship between the Fuxing Company and Fuxing village according to Williamson's theory. But, if we compare the theories and IVWC institutional practice, we need also to realize that the Fuxing entrepreneur goes beyond the theoretical framework: (1) the Fuxing entrepreneur has created a kind of new institution with continuity features, as Commons emphasized (Commons 1932, 1950) but the institution the Fuxing entrepreneur has set up is not only an economic organization but also a social and cultural organization. This means that the Fuxing entrepreneur has gone beyond the economic exchange relationship of Common's 'continuity' concept; (2) clearly, as we noted, the IVWC governance structure goes beyond Coase's firm as an alternative method of coordinating production (Coase 1937); and (3) it conforms to Arrow's vertical integration of intra-firm transfers (Arrow 1969) as well as (4) Williamson's efficient economic governance structure (or the economic institutions of relational contracting) (Williamson 1985) since they all focus on efficient economic organization. The IVWC structure denotes a kind of long-term contractual relationship between a company and a village in all economic, social, political and cultural aspects.

Based on long-term observation, Fuxing entrepreneur's selection of the IVWC governance structure can be explained well by the 'adaptation' concept which, as both Hayek and Barnard agreed, is the central problem of economic organization (Hayek 1945; Barnard 1938). However, the Fuxing entrepreneur extends the adaptation from economic to socio-economic and cultural fields and into the local society by taking people in the area not only as economic actors but also as social and cultural actors of the society. Therefore, the reason for people of Fuxing, especially for Fuxing entrepreneurs, to make this adaptation is to adjust not only to changes in the market but also to changes in the 'institutional environment' on the one hand, and changes in the 'endogenous preferences' on the other hand, in accordance with Williamson's idea of governance structure (Williamson 1993). This simply means that IVWC is the natural result of institutional reform carried out by the Fuxing entrepreneur in a given macro-institutional environment and micro-indigenous cultural environment (see Chapter 3) in order to improve economic efficiency through reducing transaction costs as well as establishing 'good order and workable arrangements' [85] in the local society. Figure 2.7 illustrates the link between Williamson's governance theory and the Fuxing entrepreneur's IVWC governance structure.

We need now to formulate a composite framework from the key logical linkages presented in all of the preceding theoretical discussion in relation to the survey in the selected villages that will guide the detailed analysis in different specific areas in the following chapters (Figure 2.8).

Figure 2.7 shows what I am attempting to achieve in this research in addition to theory; I am trying to set up a comprehensive analytical structure where all the factors at different levels (macro level, meso level and micro level) are functioning

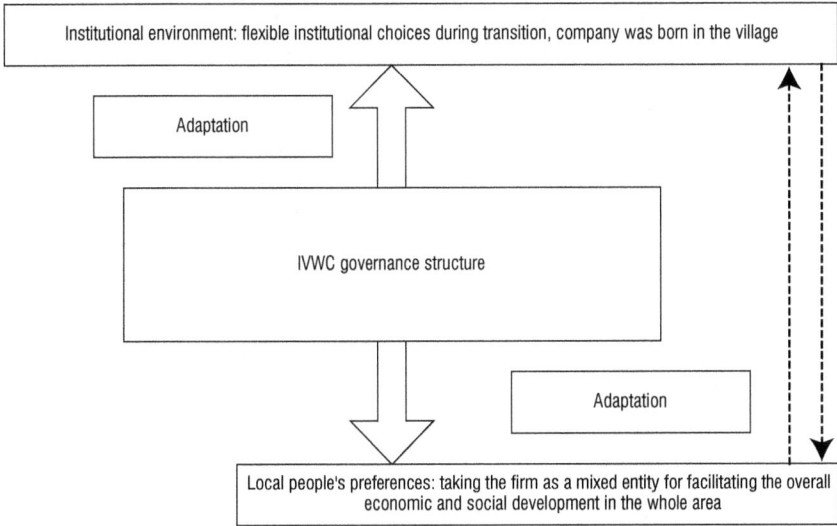

Figure 2.7 Emergence of IVWC from adaptation between macro environment and micro preferences (based on Williamson 1993)

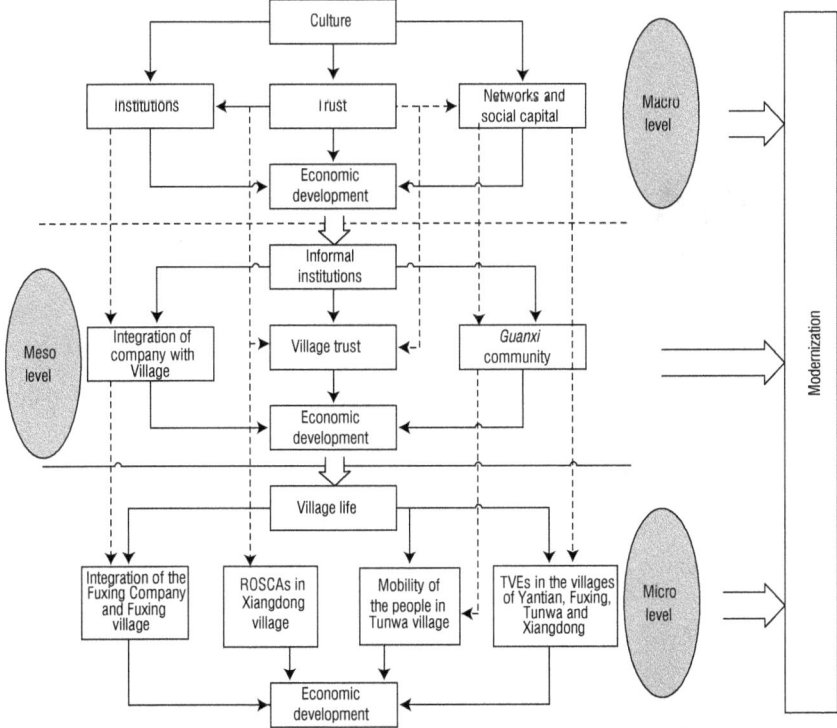

Figure 2.8 The overall analytical framework of the research

simultaneously since this reflects the true situation in the real world. From this structure, we also discover how powerful the intermediate concepts are to social science research since they form a link between the macro level and the micro level in terms of both theoretical linkages and people's interactional relations. This is also one of the other contributions to social science literature on social sciences, especially in the area of institutional studies, that I am trying to make.

3 Indigenous conceptions of networks

Before we turn to the field survey, there are still two key questions that need to be answered clearly: one is what is the bridge between general theories of institutions, trust, social capital, social norms, firm coordination, governance, culture, etc., and Chinese ideas on these concepts? The other is what is the bridge between Chinese conceptual ideas in these areas and people's real actions and practices in their related economic and social spheres? In this chapter, therefore, the focus of the discussion will be on these two 'bridges'.

Generally speaking, the first 'bridge' is what we usually call the Chinese indigenous culture and its core is the Confucian code of ethics; the second 'bridge' is what has been briefly discussed in Chapter 2 which is the new concept that has been developed in this research, namely *guanxi* community. Through the former 'bridge', we will understand better both general theories and Chinese people's behaviour; through the second 'bridge', how the theoretical gap between understanding Confucian ethics in concept and people's network in practice can be filled.

Landa's study on the institution of network exchange shows the extreme importance of identifying the status of the trading partners; virtue, rituals, customary practices and various informal social norms or codes of behaviour are the key to the 'status rights' determination and people's cooperation in the trading process (Landa 1997: 29, 107). Her comments are very true if we look at the network situation in China. Therefore, I plan to start the discussion from Chinese rules of rites and virtue in general, and then move to the intermediate or meso level by linking with *guanxi* network theories and practice in China.

The rule of rites and the rule of virtue in China

The important role of informal institutions (rules) in the process of historical development was evident not only in Europe, as mentioned previously, but also in other countries and regions of the world. This was particularly true in China, a civilization with a long history. Informal institutions played a notable role throughout China's recorded history of 5,000 years excluding the more than 500 years that comprised the Spring and Autumn Period (770–476 BC), Warring States

Period (475–221 BC) and Qin Dynasty (221–207 BC).[1] From the Western Han Dynasty (206 BC–24 AD) to the Qing Dynasty (1644–1911), China implemented a system of integrating rites with laws with the former playing the main role, supplemented by the latter; combined morality with laws with the former playing the main role, supplemented by punishment and took the rule of man to be primary and the rule of law as secondary. At some point informal institutions were formalized so that the country was basically subject to the rule of rites or the rule of virtue. The Xia Dynasty (2070–1600 BC), Shang Dynasty (1600–1100 BC) and Western Zhou Dynasty (1100–771 BC) were all typical examples of societies that implemented the rule of rites. Obviously, morality served as the foundation for ruling China through informal ways (including informal channels and self-enforcing sanctions) for a rather long period of time.

Because of such well-developed informal institutions at different levels, strong formal institutions such as the country's administrative system and the unified examination system, and so on, jointly made the Chinese civilization. It has survived continuously for several thousand years through numerous civilizations of varying descriptions, whereas other civilizations have experienced a process of 'interruption-resumption' at various stages during their historical development. An important explanation of this difference in historical development is the large variety of informal institutions both at the national level as well as at the local level (for example, non-Confucian marriage rules in some places). This is an important difference from the West where the church penetrated deeply into local communities. In this sense, Chinese civilization is, to a great extent, an institutional civilization based on rites and virtue. It is, therefore, a civilization based on the rule of rites and the rule of virtue.

Even today China still carries on these prominent elements of its culture and tradition. A mixed strategy that closely integrates formal and informal institutions still continues. On the one hand, China is attaching more and more attention to ruling the country by law and allowing the rule of law, which is a major manifestation of formal institutions, to play an increasingly important role. On the other hand, China's government continues to stress the importance of virtue in facilitating the country's development in modern times. Again, one of the differences compared to the West in this regard is that the enforcement of virtue or morality is based on a variety of informal means, whereas in the West the church is the only organization to diffuse morality at all the levels of the society.

The CPC Central Committee pointed out in the latest version of its Constitution (passed on 14 November 2002): 'The Communist Party of China leads the people in their efforts to combine ruling the country by law and ruling the country by virtue' (CPC Central Committee 2002: 57). Jiang Zemin reiterated in his report to the Sixteenth National Congress of the CPC in November 2002 that China must make sure that:

> Ruling the country by law and ruling the country by virtue complement each other. It is necessary to establish a socialist ideological and ethical system

compatible with the socialist market economy and the socialist legal standard and consistent with the traditional virtues of the Chinese nation.

(Jiang 2002: 38)

As a country with an ancient civilization, China, even at this new stage when the modernization programme is being carried out in an all-encompassing way, still places great store on informal institutions that are mainly based on morality.

In the several thousand years of China's development, informal institutions had a very rich and complicated content. In general, informal institutions that have greatly helped to maintain social stability in China have four main aspects: (1) the patriarchal clan system; (2) the system of rule of rites; (3) moral standards and the rule of virtue and (4) people's social roles and position in the society.

The patriarchal clan system

This system originated during the Western Zhou Dynasty (1100–771 BC). To be accurate, the system was a mixture of the blood clan system based on informal institutions and formal state policy. It integrated the monarch's rule with clan rule. In terms of form and structure, it was a very typical clan system but, at the same time, it was closely combined with state politics. Under this system, the family was a small state and the state was a big family so that the family and the state were integrated with each other, taking on the same structure. As a result, 'All the territory belonged to the king, and all those within the territory of the state were his subjects.' As a matter of fact, the state only belonged to the king's family or formed the family of only the king.

According to some scholars (Ma *et al.* 1999: 15; Ma 1997: 21; Feng *et al.* 1991: 197), the basic cause of the emergence of the ancient patriarchal clan system, the related feudal system and social estate system was the need to establish a proper process for succession to the throne. Having reviewed the lessons drawn from the consequences of disorderly succession during the Shang Dynasty (1600–1100 BC), rulers of the Western Zhou Dynasty established a system whereby only the emperor's eldest son, born of his wife, was entitled to the throne. His other sons had no right of succession. This rule constituted the core of the patriarchal clan system. In addition, in order to prevent younger sons from threatening the eldest son, they were forced to separate from the royal family to establish their own clans. Hence a patriarchal clan system developed whereby the eldest son led the major clan while the other sons led minor clans that were subordinate to the major one.

Being separated from the royal family, younger sons would receive large amounts of land together with its inhabitants (politically, this is known as 'investing both territories and slaves', and patriarchally, it is referred to as 'younger sons served as clan founders'). These two processes combined to form the system of enfeoffment by which nobles established states throughout the country. In this way the feudal system was established in China.

As the practice of establishing clans and states developed, the sons of the emperor founded many states throughout the country. Following the same principle, these states further developed the practice of establishing clans and states. Consequently, many ministers were appointed and territories and slaves were further invested in senior officials.

As a result, a system of clans at different levels emerged throughout the country. These were: the great clan under the king who ruled the country by order of heaven (the head of the great clan was the king or the emperor) leading to minor clans under dukes of the royal family (the head of the major clan was the duke) leading to minor clans under ministers leading to clans under senior officials (the head of the major clan at this level was a senior official) and finally clans under the sons other than the eldest sons of senior officials.

In addition, some nobles whose surnames were different from the king became related to the Western Zhou Dynasty by marriage. In this way, the whole country belonged to one family. Great changes, therefore, took place in the state structure established by the alliances that had been formed before the Western Zhou Dynasty was founded. To a great extent, the state had been replaced by the family: it had become a unified family with clans consisting of smaller sub-clans. The great clan of the royal family was in fact the state's highest management and the leader of the royal family was the king. To a great extent, state laws and management regulations were gradually replaced by the laws of the patriarchal clan and the family.

This system was copied by families at a local level in a variety of different forms but based on similar principles. Thus, the whole country showed a general trend of dominance of informal institutions in the country's economic and social development which lasted through several historic dynasties as well as in some rural areas. We will introduce more details in relation to the survey areas in the next chapter.

The system of rule of rites

This system was a series of standards and norms regarding people's behaviour developed by ancient Chinese rulers from the sacrificial customs of tribes in ancient times (from the time of the Yellow Emperor, Yao and Shun, about 2500 BC, i.e., about 4,500 years ago). These standards were elevated to become behavioural norms to maintain public order and act as laws. The system of rule of rites constituted a social system integrated with an entire set of moral teachings formed under the basic spirit of rites. In short, the system was formed by the combined action of norms of etiquette and ethical codes. Ethical codes sought to implement customs, ethics and moral principles through education. These codes were fundamental to the system of rule of rites. Covering all aspects of public activities, norms of etiquette were incidental in the system of rule of rites (Table 3.1).

Under the system of rule of rites, feudal ethical codes were more important than legal principles and norms of etiquette were more important than laws. The law was entirely integrated with customs, habits, ethics and morality.

Table 3.1 Structure of China's ancient system of rule of rites

System composition	Target designed to support	Means of implementation	Purpose
Ethical codes	Ideology	Education	To regulate the mind
Norms of etiquette	Various institutions	Punishment	To regulate behaviour

Source: Ma 1997: 24.

Serving in place of laws, rites had their most glorious development during the Xia, Shang and Western Zhou dynasties (Ma 1997: 16) and the contents and spirit of rites were found in every field of society:

> Without rites, there would be no morality, ethics, benevolence and virtue. Without rites, no education and instruction can be provided. Without rites, no law judgements can be made. Without rites, the relationships between father and son and among brothers cannot be decided. Without rites, no teachers will be respected. Without strict rites, no army can be regulated and no law can be enforced. Without rites, no solemn sacrifices can be offered to spirits.
>
> (*The Book of Rites: Quli*)

Confucianists in the Western Han Dynasty (206 BC–24 AD) summarized the main contents of rites as 'six rites' (for social ceremonies), 'seven teachings' (for human relations), 'eight regulations' (for everyday life). There were detailed rites for the king, for officials, for sons, for men and women, for the young and old, for host and the guest, for naming one's children, for marriage, for burial, for sacrifices, for everyday life, for table manners, and for behaviour (Feng *et al.* 1991: 456). Thereafter, rites served as social ideology, the state's management system and legislative principles throughout China's feudal society and China, therefore, became known as a land of ceremony and propriety.

In relation to the concept of the rule of law, the concept of the rule of rites was devised by Confucius, the founder of the Confucian school.[2] He believed the rule of rites was a better way to rule the country than the rule of law on the grounds that rites prevent illegal acts while laws merely punished these acts. As Confucius said:

> Regulated by edicts and punishments, the people will know only how to stay out of trouble, but will not have a sense of shame. Guided by virtues and rites, they will not only have a sense of shame but also know how to correct their mistakes of their own accord.
>
> (Confucius, *The Analects: Government*)

By this he meant to replace laws (punishments) with rites and to rule the country through education.

The social estate system was the prerequisite and institutional foundation of the rule of rites. Under the social estate system, filial piety, loyalty, righteousness and chastity were very important moral principles for conducting oneself in society. So morality was very much manifest in norms of conduct. For example, according to these norms, a man should love his relatives and clan members and respect his superiors, the young should respect the old, the old should love the young, and men and women should have different responsibilities. (*The Book of Rites: Dazhuan*). All these rites were based on morality as mentioned earlier: That someone should love his father best reflects the spirit of filial piety. That someone should respect the monarch the most is about the need to be loyal to the sovereign. That the young should respect the old and the old should love the young stresses the importance of the social atmosphere based on righteousness. That men and women should have different responsibilities reflects chastity (Ma 1997: 23).

In short, based on the principles that everyone should love their relatives and clan members and respect their superiors, the young should respect the old and the old should love the young, and stressing the need of filial piety, loyalty and morality, the concepts of rule of rites were ideas for ruling the country by means of education and punishment (Ma 1997: 253). The rite-related moral principles and ethics based on these ideas were at the core of China's ancient social norms.

In fact, long before Confucius put forward the idea of the rule of rites, Western Zhou rulers had already transformed rituals at religious ceremonies[3] into feudal ethical codes and put them into practice. Thereafter, rites, which merely served religious purposes, gradually changed into social norms and a social system to become a complete set of norms of conduct. With help from compatible moral education (feudal ethical codes), the Western Zhou Dynasty established a perfect society under the rule of rites. Consequently, China had a culture based on the rule of rites about 3,000 years ago which was unique in the world at the time. Later, other countries developed cultures based on the rule of law. As a matter of fact, the rule of rites based on the norms of conduct and the feudal ethical codes helped maintain social stability in China for a very long period of time.

Given the situation more than 2,000 years ago, Guanzi pointed out that 'laws came of rites which were based on customs' (Guanzi, *Guanzi: Part Shuyan*). In addition, the codes of conduct derived from accepted norms of behaviour and based on human feelings were closely connected with religious ceremonies; so they were somewhat divine. Therefore, people felt they had no other alternative but to accept them for several thousand years.

Moral standards and the rule of virtue

While they implemented the rule of rites, Western Zhou rulers also put forward the concept of virtue. They stressed the importance of replacing laws with rites and the importance of moral principles and ethics for running the country, i.e., so-called virtuous government and benevolent government. The difference between the two is that in terms of concepts and content, rites, customs and habits were not invented by Western Zhou rulers. The concept of virtue and the whole set of ideas about virtue, however, were created by Zhougong in the Western Zhou Dynasty (Feng *et al.* 1991: 329). Confucius developed these by stating that it was only natural for humans to stress benevolence and righteousness, virtue and morality and also by putting forward the idea of the rule of virtue (*The Analects of Confucius: Government*).

According to Confucian thought, moral standards mainly consist of loyalty, filial piety, chastity and righteousness. The most important principles are benevolence and righteousness, which are based on filial piety. Therefore, the most important factor of moral standards is filial piety. According to *The Book of Filial Piety*, 'Filial piety is the foundation of ethics'. As long as there is filial piety, the country can be run well (*The Book of Filial Piety*). Therefore, Mencius believed that the country could naturally be run well provided there is love between father and son, courtesy between monarch and subject, different responsibilities between husband and wife, respect between young and old, and trust between friends (*Mencius: Duke Tengwen*). That is why it was believed for a long period of time that 'filial piety is the source of all good deeds'.

Social roles and people's social positions[4]

People's roles and their positions in society played an especially important role in establishing and maintaining social, economic and political order in China. Confucius created the concept of social positions and developed its extremely rich content (Qian 1999: 44). According to him, every member of society has his own place in that society: the monarch is the monarch, subjects are subjects, the father is the father and the son is the son. None of them is expected to do anything incompatible with his social position (Confucius, *The Analects of Confucius: Yanyuan*). It is because everyone has his own social position, he should confine himself to his own duties (Confucius, *The Analects of Confucius: Xianwen*). So if the place of everyone in society is determined, the entire public order is stable. That is to say, according to Confucius, social roles and positions are a prerequisite to establish and stabilize public order. Precisely because of this, Liang Shouming (1988: 178), a representative of China's Neo-Confucianists, said that Chinese society is a village society based on people's moral places. Accordingly, the essence of Chinese laws was fully reflected by ethics (patriarchy) without much formalism. These social ethics were believed by many people to be one of the major causes of China's failure to develop capitalism.

In order that every member of China's society had his/her social role and place accurately determined and maintained over a long period of historical development, Confucian thinkers, with Confucius as the main proponent, developed a more perfect and mature ideological system based on Zhougong's rites. The core of these rites is the Three Cardinal Guides and the Five Constant Virtues.[5]

The Three Cardinal Guides are: ruler guides subject (it is essential that a subject is unconditionally loyal to the ruler); father guides son (it is essential that the son is unconditionally respectful to his father); and husband guides wife (it is essential that the wife unconditionally preserves her chastity for her husband – in the Ming Dynasty, women were not supposed to remarry after the death of their husbands).

These three guiding principles relied on benevolence[6] (care for people and loyalty), righteousness[7] (proper acts), propriety (ethical codes and norms of conduct), wisdom (ability to tell right from wrong) and credit.[8] It should be said that the Three Cardinal Guides are a development of Confucius' doctrines that 'the monarch is the monarch, subjects are subjects, the father is the father, and the son is the son'.

The Five Constant Virtues are similar to Mencius's doctrines on benevolence, righteousness, propriety and wisdom and to Guanzi's four cardinal virtues in running a country (sense of propriety, righteousness, honesty and shame).[9] Under the system of the Three Cardinal Guides and the Five Constant Virtues, the roles and places, obligations and duties of everyone are clearly defined.

As far as women are concerned, they must also be subject to the restrictions of the three obediences: to their father before marriage, to their husband after marriage and to their son after the death of husband and the four virtues of morality, proper speech, modest manner and diligent work.

All this shows that people's social position was directly related to rites. To a great extent, rites were the tools and instruments for determining the social positions of humans. Conversely, without rites, it would be difficult to determine people's social positions. The ultimate aim of either rites or determining people's social positions was to bring about social harmony (Qian 1999: 50). It was precisely because every member of the society knew his place and knew how to handle his relationship with others that social order was established and remained very stable. This is a good explanation of the fact that although China went through various wars during its several thousand years of evolution and development, Chinese civilization and Chinese society were able to maintain both the unity of such a big country and its basic social and political stability.

In short, during the past several thousand years of development, the Chinese nation established a patriarchal clan system based on blood relationships. On the basis of this system, people's interpersonal places were defined. As well as the establishment of norms of conduct and ethical codes, a system was established that closely combined the rule of rites, the rule of virtue and the rule of law, and closely integrated formal and informal institutions. Through the comprehensive effect of this system, China successfully maintained social and political stability and achieved a smooth transition from ancient civilization to modern and contemporary civilization so that the Chinese civilization continued uninterrupted for several thousand years. This greatly facilitates our study of the effect of informal institutions on social and economic development under new historical conditions.

Guanxi *community*

In the preceding section, we focused on the general indigenous culture based mainly on some of the key contents of Confucian ethics. It is a relatively macro-level discussion about indigenous culture in China. Following this macro discussion, we now need to turn our focus to a meso-level discussion of the indigenous culture in China, namely popular culture. This discussion refers to networks and their structure which link with the field studies in later sections.

In this sense, *guanxi* community is an important concept about Chinese networks that is of value for our further research, since it builds a 'bridge' for us to better understand Chinese indigenous culture at the macro level and people's real network practice at the micro level. Therefore, further discussion in this chapter will focus on this concept and the related empirical survey will be discussed in Chapters 6 and 7.

From village community to guanxi *community*

The concept of village community is of great significance in Chinese rural studies, as much theoretical exploration and debate is often conducted centring on this concept. However, the combined effect of such factors as the full introduction and further development of the modern market economy in China and the gradual relaxation of the country's policy toward the movement of people from rural to urban areas is, to a great extent, causing the collapse of the relatively complete or not-so-complete village community structure and theory which has long been familiar. Accordingly, it is essential to establish a new theory to explain the drastically changing reality in China.

The concept of village community was first introduced from Japan to historical and village studies in China. The concept originated in Japan in the early seventeenth century when Ieyasu Tokugawa founded the Tokugawa Shogunate in Edo (present-day Tokyo) (Li 2001). The development of rice production necessitated the erection of more irrigation facilities. This helped villagers to stay at their native villages, thus giving rise to the community concept of villagers closely cooperating with each other and going through thick and thin together. As the Edo Period lasted 265 years, there was a solid foundation of village community. Kunio Odaka (quoted from Li 2001) summarized the fundamental principle and spirit of village community as follows: (1) the native village was the permanent residence of villagers and villagers permanently retained their rights and obligations as members of their villages; (2) the individual interest of villagers was subordinate to the collective interests of the village; (3) the status of villagers was determined by their normal education and annual merits; (4) public order was established in villages through cooperation among villagers; the interests of communities at lower levels (families, clans, youth leagues and federations of the aged) must come after those of communities at higher levels; (5) villagers participated as a group in the assembly and the decision-making mechanism was that the village head and other elders had the final say; and (6) all the needs of villagers, including their private daily needs, were met through all these means.

For reasons of theoretical research as well as the politics in the 1930s, some of the Japanese scholars began to introduce the concept of village community into their Chinese studies. From the perspective of research, these scholars were trying to test whether the village community model that first emerged in the Edo

Period existed in China. They intended to establish an analytical methodology that was different from formalism that was prevailing in the West and from Marxism that was playing a dominant role in China. Their methodology was known as substantivism. From the perspective of politics, some Japanese scholars wanted to prove that both Japan and China were societies based on village communities, not on Western individualism. Therefore, this common social structure shared by the two countries would constitute the foundation for building the 'Greater East Asia Co-prosperity Sphere'. As a matter of fact, Japanese scholars eventually failed to reach consensus on this issue, even leaving aside their political purposes (Hatada 1972, quoted from Li 2001). Some of these scholars argued that Chinese villages were a community that integrated the power structure, religious organizations and belief. Others did not agree, believing that Chinese villages did not have fixed demarcation lines between them, nor did they share common property. They were a very scattered society in which every family operated for its own interests as an independent unit. The power of villages was based on classes and violence, not villagers' spontaneous support.

Max Weber was a renowned German sociologist and philosopher. It is, therefore, justifiable to say that he did not have the same political feelings toward this issue as some of the Japanese scholars. He thought that Chinese villages were a community with a high degree of local autonomy and strong defence capabilities (Weber 1951).

Within his framework of the moral economy of the peasant, James C. Scott (1976) established the survival ethics of the peasant and social justice. He believed that peasants' collective interests came before their individual interests and that the core of rural development was to provide peasants with better survival guarantees and reduce their risks instead of violating their survival rules through the development of market capitalism characterized by maximized income, commercialized agriculture and the bureaucratic state.

Samuel Popkin (1979), however, did not agree with Scott. He thought that the village was a loose, open organization. It was a very scattered society in which every family looked for its own interests as an independent unit. The political power structure of villages was mainly based on classes, not really the will of villagers.

The result of the research carried out by Philip C. C. Huang (1985), mainly on the basis of the information collected by researchers of The South Manchuria Railway Company during their on-the-spot survey of 33 villages on the North China Plain, indicates that many villages in the North China Plain had a relatively high degree of self-reliance from the 1920s to the 1940s. Not only were there clear demarcation lines between residences of villagers of different villages, lines were also drawn to some extent between their production and consumption areas. In addition, the relationships between villagers and their work and residence were often interwoven with their clans. So the village was basically a closed, cohesive and closely-knit community.

Using the same information from the The South Manchuria Railway Company, Prasenjit Duara (1988) developed a new model of 'culture nexus' of power in his research on China's village structure. This model includes all kinds of hierarchical organizations such as markets, clans and religions, and networks of informal relationships like relationships of blood, and relationships between patrons and their protégés and between missionaries and followers. The model incorporates imperial power, gentry culture and country folk societies into one and the same framework. It also connects such abstract concepts as power and rule with the unique cultural system in Chinese society. Obviously, Duara's concept of culture nexus puts greater emphasis on the constantly changing organizations and interpersonal relationships that exist between a village and the outside world. The culture nexus all the more demonstrates its openness as it includes such organizations as trans-village religious organizations and joint self-defence organizations of villages.

As an important representative of Western formalism, G. William Skinner (1964–5) formulated the concept of local market community on the basis of his on-the-spot investigations in Chengdu. He pointed out that although the centre of the activities of Chinese small farmers was the village it did, however, include the whole area covered by the local fair. So the foundation of China's rural social structure was not the village but the approximately 50 square km area which was affected by the fair and had 18 villages and 1,500 rural households. Later, these views were developed by Theda Skocpol (1979) into the concept of pure market community.

In short, there may be many other interpretations and theories of how large numbers of small farmers, scattered randomly, are gathered together so that order in China's rural areas and in the country as a whole is stabilized and maintained. As the general introduction to this research, it is enough for us to begin with village community. What the above-mentioned researchers said is all excellent; nevertheless, we must point out that as China is huge, has many ethnic groups with their own unique histories, culture and customs, and lacks developed transportation, the research results obtained by the researchers can hardly be summarized as a theory or model suitable for the entire country. For example, various signs show that market-oriented industry and commerce reached a rather high degree of development in China's coastal areas in the Ming and Qing dynasties whereas it was quite another situation in the country's southwestern and northern parts in the same period. By the Marxist definition, it is probable that an area in China had one or three social forms before the founding of the People's Republic in 1949.

More importantly, the reform and opening up policy introduced in China in 1978 and the country's accession to the World Trade Organization in 2001 have directly caused market, commercial and international rules to have an impact on the country's traditional rural system. To a great extent, this has also given rise to changes in the existing social structure in rural China. According to the results of the survey of five villages in five provinces that the author conducted over the period of a decade, villagers' awareness of village community increased, rather than decreased in some villages, in spite of economic development and the enhanced strength of their villages. These villages include Yantian in Guangdong

Province and Xiangdong in Zhejiang Province. Nevertheless, they have undergone substantial changes in their characteristics as communities since 1949. Although the villages have basically retained the characteristics of being closely-knit and cohesive, they are not closed. On the contrary, they are very open.

Of course, more things in present-day China show that the concept of village community is gradually becoming less and less convincing from geographic, social and cultural perspectives. On the contrary, China's reality more often conforms to Prasenjit Duara's theory of culture nexus.

On the basis of my decade-long case study of villages, I have formulated the concept of *guanxi* community, a concept of informal organization that is different from the above-mentioned concepts of village community and culture nexus and has more local characteristics. In addition, some relevant analyses will be made based on my information about the mobility of rural people into urban areas and the development of TVEs, so as to provide new explanations of the social organization and order in present-day rural China. In this part, the focus is the relevant concepts; the related case studies will be discussed in more detail in Chapters 6 and 7.

Community, **guanxi,** *and* **guanxi** *community*

Community

According to the *Contemporary Chinese Dictionary*, the Chinese term *gongtong* (common) means 'belonging to, or shared by all'; and the term *gongtongti* (community) means 'a group of people living together as a social unit and having interests, work, etc., in common' (Zhongguo Shehui Kexueyuan, Yuyan Yanjiusuo [Institute of Linguistics of the Chinese Academy of Social Sciences – CASS] 1987: 389).

In *Webster's Third New International Dictionary of the English Language Unabridged* (G. & C. Merriam Company 1976)[10] four major areas are covered by the term 'community': (1) community is 'a body of individuals organized into a unit or manifesting usually with awareness some unifying trait'; (2) community means 'society at large, people in general'; (3) community implies 'common or joint ownership, tenure, experience or pertinence; common character; shared activity, social intercourse, fellowship, communion, especially social activity marked by a feeling of unity but also individual participation completely willingly and not forced or coerced and without loss of individuality; frequent occurrence and a social or societal state', and (4) community also means 'a civil-law partnership or society of property between husband and wife arising by virtue of the fact of marriage or by contract'.

In the second version of *Webster's New Twentieth Century Dictionary of the English Language Unabridged* (William Collins Publishers 1979) community is mainly defined as: (1) 'common possession or enjoyment, as, a community of goods'; (2) 'a society of people having common rights and privileges or common interests, civil, political, etc., or living under the same laws and regulations'; (3)

'society at large'; (4) 'common character, similarity, likeness'; (5) 'commonness, frequency'; (6) 'the people living in the same district, city, etc., under the same laws'; (7) 'the district, city etc., where they live' and (8) 'a group of animals or plants living together in the same environment'.

We can synthesize the key aspects of the definitions of community given in the two editions of Webster as follows. First, a community is a unit composed of individuals, and a single individual cannot be called a community. Second, every member of a community often shares common interests including economic, political and social interests and enjoys common power. Therefore, people sharing common characteristics and common interests of pursuits are more likely to form a community. Third, generally speaking, the individuals of a community interact with each other; they do not exist in isolation and they must observe common rules or laws accordingly. Lastly, members of a community generally reside in the same area, though this is not essential. In other words, a community may consist of people living in different areas.

According to *English–Chinese Glossary of Terms in Housing, Urban Planning, and Construction Management* edited by a joint architecture team from US and China in the mid-1980s, the term of community applied in American English to a group of people, living together as a social unit and sharing common interests and goals related to activities and facilities that serve the public. 'Community' implies unity for certain purposes and willingness to provide mutual support for those purposes, formally through taxation and informally through volunteer efforts of group members. The term is usually used to describe towns or small cities as social rather than administrative units but may also be applied to larger units, including the 'community of nations' (United States of America Department of Housing and Urban Development, and Ministry of Urban and Rural Construction and Environmental Protection of The People's Republic of China, 1987).

Obviously, the concepts of community in natural and social sciences are very much identical in terms of both connotation and denotation. They convey, therefore, at least these messages: (1) community is a concept of group, not individuals; (2) every individual of the group shares common characteristics or interests; and (3) individuals of the group interact with each other.

In the research on community (apart from the debates about village community mentioned previously) Max Weber produced two more concepts of community to explain why the Chinese did not have general but only special trust in each other. He believed that the Chinese trusted each other on the basis of a community of blood relationships characterized by the family kinship or quasi-family kinship instead of a community of belief. He therefore concluded that, generally speaking, the Chinese had general distrust, not general trust, of those outside their community of blood (Weber 1951).

The concept of religious community is important and close to the concept of belief community. According to Benedict Anderson (1991), the region from Morocco to the Sulu Archipelago of the Philippines is an Islamic community; the region from Paraguay to Japan is a Christian community; and the region from southern Sri Lanka to the Korean Peninsula is a region of belief in Buddhism.

Anderson (1991) also defined ethnic group (nation-state) as an imagined political community. On the one hand, even in the smallest ethnic group, it is impossible for all people to know each other and it is even not possible for all of them to hear of each other. On the other hand, people's intent to connect with each other exists in everyone's heart (that is, everyone shares many common things in his/her heart). Therefore Anderson believes that, in a sense, ethnic groups are based on kinship or are similar to religion. In his opinion, all communities that are bigger than a primitive village, whose members have face-to-face contacts are imagined and at the same time real because an ethnic group has boundaries no matter how big it is.

After early Europeans migrated to the continents of America, Africa and Asia, they developed the particular forms of overseas settlements of European immigrants and social groups. Although Benedict Anderson (1991) does not refer to settlements and social groups directly as communities, it is justifiable to call them overseas communities of migrants such as communities of Euramericans, Eurasians and Eurafricans.

In addition, we often see concepts such as science community, clan community, language community and knowledge community, etc. In the same way, these communities are whole social units which share common characteristics and interests and whose members interact with each other. This shows that communities are real and visible social entities; that is, you can often feel their existence. However, there are exceptions, such as belief communities, religious communities and nation-state communities, which are relatively abstract. The concept of *guanxi* community we are about to formulate has a nature similar to these communities.

Guanxi

As we pointed out at the beginning of this chapter, an important reason why the Chinese civilization has lasted several thousand years without interruption and Chinese society has been relatively stable during all these years is that China has been fairly successful in providing balanced development of formal and informal institutions, and man-made and natural order spontaneously. That is to say, ethics and moral principles are more powerful than legality. Consequently many people have held that China is a country without laws and government. Moreover, even after informal institutions, in which Confucian ideas played the dominant role, became increasingly formalized to serve as the country's 'great traditions', diversified 'little traditions' that existed in all aspects of real life and had not been formalized always played an important role. China has never been brought under unified institutions, formal or informal, or 'great traditions' or 'little traditions'. This is an important foundation of the survival and development of Chinese civilization and China throughout the past several thousand years.

What, then, is the common fundamental spirit shared by Confucian culture, the 'great traditions', and civilian culture, the 'little traditions'? In the opinion of Liang Shuming, a well-known Chinese thinker, the spirit is an ethics-based mentality. The core of this mentality is the interpersonal, interactive relationship formed in society in accordance with specific rules. According to Liang (1988), 'China is an ethics-based society' and 'ethics-based means *guanxi*-based'.

Generally speaking, *guanxi* means 'connection between persons' (Zhongguo Shehui Kexueyuan, Yuyan Yanjiusuo [Institute of Linguistics of the Chinese Academy of Social Sciences – CASS] 1987). The connection is mainly blood-related (family relationships), geographical (fellow-villager or fellow-townsman relationships), and work-related (colleague, occupation or membership relationships), etc. Blood and geographical relationships are typically strong relationships in informal organizations. Work-related relationships, however, are very much like the relationships in formal organizations. In this general sense, the Chinese people's explanation of relationships is not much different from that of other societies.

Obviously, Liang Shuming's '*guanxi*' (relationship) not only includes the connection between persons in the general sense which we often refer to, but also expresses more about the strong social and cultural meaning of the relationship envisaged in 'a general modern concept of social sciences' (Chiao 1987). For example, the meaning it expresses about the social order and structure is like this: compared to Western society, the order of Chinese society is neither group-based nor individual-based, but rather it is based on interpersonal relationships, full of human feelings (Jin 2002). In Talcott Parsons's words, China's social order and structure are prominently a specialized relationship structure (1968). It is precisely because Chinese society is full of human feelings and there is a certain relationship order formed between persons in accordance with certain rules. It is a complete society able to function normally. In this sense, it was correct for Chiao Chien to point out that the *guanxi* or relationship in Chinese society was 'a social institution'. Accordingly, Chinese society is a more *guanxi*-oriented society.

Making *guanxi* a research subject strongly reflects China's genius features on the one hand and on the other hand it can also be well explained by the theories of 'structural holes' as we discussed in Chapter 2. This is a very important concept created by Chinese scholars to explain the complicated interpersonal relationships in China, but which is also quite similar to the Western theory of social capital.

Tradition shows that Chinese society stresses interpersonal relationships. Confucian ethics also attaches great importance to the harmonious operation of these relationships. They stress the importance not only of harmonious relationships between individual persons but especially of the harmony and stability of the entire social order based on these relationships between individual persons.

What is similar to the concept and methods of Chinese analysis and research on *guanxi* from the perspective of international comparison, are the analysis of networks and social networks. Under the Western framework of network analysis, a network is a complete system of the interaction of social actors (including individuals, institutions and organizations). Therefore, in a sense, the social structure is a system of networks (Wellman and Berkowitz 1988). The contents of the various relationships between actors (such as information and resources) constitute different types of networks and the strength of the relationships between individuals in the networks constitutes the forms of their existence.

German sociologist Georg Simmel was the first to analyse networks and social networks (Simmel [1922] 1955). British anthropologist Alfred R. Radcliffe-Brown in 1940 formulated the concept of social networks on the basis of Simmel's concept of networks. Following the efforts of other scholars, research on social networks has been developed into a fairly complete system as an independent discipline. So research on social networks emerged as a new field of sociology. James S. Coleman, Mark Granovetter, Nan Lin, Ronald Burt and others all played an important role in recent years in promoting the formation and development of this area, as discussed in the previous chapter.

Guanxi *community*

WHAT IS *GUANXI* COMMUNITY?

Different relationships consist of relationship networks. For example, blood relationships often come together with clan relationships and fellow-townsmen relationships to form complicated related groups based on blood and geographical relationships. As individuals in everyday life, people often connect themselves with their acquaintances and friends through different channels to form their related groups. As a matter of fact, these different related groups are relationship networks. On the basis of our preliminary understanding and analysis of the concept of community, and with the knowledge we have gained from the village community, the new concept of *guanxi* community can be used to generalize the content and meaning of relationship networks or related groups and we take this as the basic theory of our analysis in this research.

From the perspective of methodology, *guanxi* community is based on the field theory in physics. Magnets and magnetic fields are relevant in explaining this relationship. The components of a *guanxi* community such as villages in a village community, ethnic groups in an ethnic group community, and religions in a religious community are somewhat like magnets; there are magnetic fields centring on them. The village, ethnic group and religion act like magnets to draw the villagers to the village, members of the ethnic group to the clan and believers to the religion. In this sense, Fox Butterfield was justified in calling this relationship circle a 'social magnet' (Butterfield 1983). Everybody involved in this social magnet is closely tied with an invisible rope. The scope of a social magnet depends on the size and attractiveness of the village, religion or clan that serves as a social magnet.

In accordance with the above definition of ethnic groups by Benedict Anderson, *guanxi* community is somewhat like the political community as embodied by the ethnic group community. The *guanxi* community (relationship networks and related groups) is like an ethnic group to some extent and it is also an imagined community. On the one hand, its boundaries are relatively vague. For example, the division of inside and outside groups in interpersonal contacts is never absolute and the conversion of insiders and outsiders is very elastic. On the other hand, it has boundaries just like an ethnic group; no matter how large an ethnic group is, it cannot cover the entire mankind; it has its boundaries. No matter how big a relationship network or related group is, it has its boundaries and cannot cover the entire mankind. Of course, people in a *guanxi* community are just like those in an ethnic group community and share the same feeling of belonging to the community.

In addition, it is believed that there are similarities between the *guanxi* community on the one hand and the belief community and the religious community on the other. All of them constitute mainly a cultural system. Individuals of the community all have strong feelings of belonging to their community (these feelings are usually stronger psychologically than in terms of entity).

In terms of the analytical level, the *guanxi* community is a concept of community that is at the middle level but is inclined to be macroscopic. To be more specific, it is a community between very macroscopic communities such as the language community and the belief community and the relatively microscopic communities such as the clan community, the village community and the grass-roots market community.

In real life in China, the concept of *guanxi* community set out here is actually similar to the concept of a 'group of friends' (groups of people who accept one another) widely used among the Chinese people. These friends are not merely those friends in the full sense of the term we have long referred to and who are based on clans and the circle of relatives in traditional society. How, then, should the boundaries of the groups of friends, or in other words the *guanxi* community, be defined?

DEFINING THE BOUNDARIES OF THE *GUANXI* COMMUNITY

The three main mature and influential methods for defining the boundaries of the *guanxi* circle are:

First, the method advocated by Confucius, Mencius and other Confucianists for defining related groups by the five cardinal relationships, that is, the theory for recognizing the related groups, formed on the basis of the five cardinal relationships between monarch and subject, father and son, husband and wife, among brothers and among friends. Confucianism also has rules of order, namely, 'There is love between father and son, courtesy between monarch and subject, different responsibilities between husband and wife, respect between the young and the old, and trust between friends' (*Mencius: Duke Tengwen [I]*).

The basis of these five cardinal relationships are the naturally formed family relationships because, in the traditional society of China, the relationships between monarch and subject and among friends are often an extension of the relationships between father and son (symbolizing all vertical interpersonal relationships) and among brothers (symbolizing all horizontal interpersonal relationships). Therefore, as long as the relationship structures are formed by the three family relationships (the relationship between husband and wife usually symbolizes all the relationships between the sexes in traditional Chinese society), they will be stable with a solid foundation and the order of the entire society will be stable and orderly.

Theoretically speaking, the thinking of Confucius, Mencius and other Confucianists about the five cardinal relationships is, in essence, about the primary relationship pattern of mankind, namely, the system of blood relationship (family relationships). Generally speaking, when we talk about the system of blood relationships, we do not only mean the clan groups on the paternal side, but also extended groups related by marriage.

Second, the theory of the differential mode of association was formulated by Fei Xiaotong (Fei Hsiao-tung), a well-known Chinese sociologist. This theory is a good model for defining the different levels of interpersonal relationships. According to Fei's ideas, unlike the Western social pattern consisting of bundles of firewood bound together, China's social pattern is just like different myriads of ripples sent out by a stone thrown in the water. Everybody is the centre of the circle created by his social influence. Those affected by the ripples of the circle are connected with each other (Fei 1947). As a matter of fact, by social pattern, Fei means the pattern of interpersonal relationships in society. It is also the issue of 'human relations', that is, in his own words, 'the differential mode of the myriad of ripples among the group of people centred on oneself and having social relations with oneself' (Fei 1947).

Fei Xiaotong believes that under the differential mode of association, the Chinese definition of groups of friends is very unclear and elastic. Everyone has a circle centring on his/her role, but the size of the circle is not fixed. If necessary, anyone in the centre of the circle can include all those of his group of friends who want to do so to join the circle. However, one thing is very clear: under the differential mode of association, as a person's private relations increase, there emerge 'networks formed by private relations' in his/her social relations (Fei 1947).

Finally, the *guanxi*-making method. This means forming, in many ways, one's new *guanxi* community, where one does not already have natural blood or geographical relationships. This new *guanxi* community is generally based on some existing relationships, but it can also be an entirely new structure of *guanxi* community.

The *guanxi*-making theory is involved in the work of many researchers but is not so evolved as the two methods and theories outlined earlier. Generally speaking, the main aim of this method is to create or expand the *guanxi* community outside established relationships. There are many ways of creating and expanding relationships, including forming marriage relationships and simulating blood relationships as well as trying to establish personal connections by various means (Chiao 1987). Simulating blood relationships has a long history in China and it is done in many ways. These typically include adopting someone as one's father, mother, etc., acknowledging someone as one's fellow-townsman, becoming sworn brothers, and seeking common clans and ancestors.

THE MAIN MANIFESTATIONS OF *GUANXI* COMMUNITY

Obviously, the 'circle of friends' formed through various relationships, that is, the social order reflected in the concept of *guanxi* community we mentioned earlier, is a special community based on and transcending 'small communities' in real life (we have touched upon many 'small communities'). As things stand in China now, this community structurally takes the following forms:

First, the blood-relationship circle, which may also be called 'the blood-relationship community'. Members of this community are connected with each other by their blood relationships. Organizationally, it is extended gradually centring on the family and, eventually, often forms a clan community. In traditional Chinese society, this community consists of only paternal relationships (such as uncle and nephew), not maternal relationships in the family. However, there is a tendency to constantly extend the community to maternal relationships.

Second, the geographical-relationship circle, which is generally called 'the circle of fellow-townsmen'. In this study we called this 'the geographical-relationship community'. Usually this type of community originally evolves from the clan community. When a clan becomes very large, clan members living together will inevitably lead to the formation of natural villages. As a result, villages of people with the same surname or of many people with the same surname emerge to become geographical relationship communities based on natural villages. In this sense, the village community is a special form of the geographical community. As time passes, the boundaries of the geographical community become very blurred. However, one thing is very clear: the scope of the geographical community has expanded greatly. It has extended to the township, the county, the city, and the province and even to the country and the continent. For example, there are such special geographical communities we have mentioned above as the communities of Euramericans, Eurasians and Eurafricans as well as the European Union, etc.

Third, there is the occupation relationship circle, which may also be called the 'occupational relationship community'. This refers normally to colleagues or former colleagues working in the same organization, classmates who graduated from the same school or institutes, business partners or clients in the same area, etc.

Finally, there is the 'Chinese network society', which, in the concept of Benedict Anderson, may be called the group of overseas immigrants of Chinese origin. If we use the concept of *guanxi* community formulated in this book, then we can call this the Chinese network community which includes the typical communities of Chinese Americans, Chinese Europeans, Chinese Filipinos and so on.

Of course, the closeness of the relationships between people varies from one *guanxi* community to another; in the analysis of the social structure this is termed the intensity of the relationship. China's rural society has developed from a fairly closed one to a relatively open one, but generally speaking, members of communities based on blood relationships maintain closer relationships with one another than those of other communities. That is to say, the blood-relationship community has the highest intensity of relationships. This is especially true in rural society and has been proved in the results of many research projects on contemporary interpersonal relationships in China (Zhang 1999).

Being a member of a good *guanxi* community is of great significance for Chinese people in their real life. Different *guanxi* communities have very different resources, thus determining how members of a community use the community's shared resources for self-development. The boundaries of a community are not absolute, on the contrary they are very elastic and flexible. This makes it possible for people to operate relationships.

However, it is not easy to operate relationships or even to maintain them appropriately. To this end, the many rules related to the operation of relationships and relationship networks have to be mastered. From studies already carried out, we have found that the basic rules concerning the operation of relationships and the existence and development of *guanxi* communities can be roughly summarized as the four theoretical models (that is, the four fundamental rules governing the interpersonal contacts of the Chinese):

Model 1: the model (rule) of favour and face   In both traditional and modern Chinese society, the establishment of *guanxi* and *guanxi* networks is closely connected with favour. Basically *guanxi* or *guanxi* networks cannot exist in China without favour and favour is connected with face. So favour, face and *guanxi* networks constitute an integral whole. This is why the combination of these three things is usually referred to as the characteristic of the behaviour of the Chinese (Hwang 1987). No wonder Lin Yutang (1939) once said that the social life of the Chinese was under the joint control of the three goddesses of favour, face and fate. This is usually summarized as the *3F theory*.

According to the *Contemporary Chinese Dictionary*, the Chinese term '*renqing*' (favour) has five main meanings (CASS 1987): (1) human feelings (according to my understanding this should include joy, anger, sorrow, happiness, love and hate etc.); (2) obligations or responsibilities in feelings (which I think means a social resource used in exchange of gifts and an interpersonal obligation based on economic exchanges); (3) friendship; (4) etiquette and custom; and (5) gifts. When people combine favour, face and *guanxi* networks, favour mainly means (2), (3) and (4) above. That is to say, under this circumstance, by favour people mainly mean feelings of obligation and friendship, etiquette and custom in interpersonal relationships.

From the perspective of sociology, favour means the relationships between people. According to a study by Hwang Kwang-kuo, the Chinese have three types of favour relationships: affective favour relationships, instrumental favour relationships (mutually beneficial relationships based on business dealings and exchange), and mixed favour relationships (mutually beneficial relationships that are both affective and based on business dealings) (Hwang 1987).[11]

Although favour is more of a cultural concept in China and does not have any legal meaning, it has a strong moral meaning (popularized loyalty and forbearance). It is a very typical social norm with prominent characteristics of informal institutions (rules). It is a means for disciplining not only others but also oneself. The most important restrictive norm therein is 'reciprocity'.[12] The category of 'reciprocity' is clearly about the cause-effect relationships between people in their contacts, that is, the relationships characterized by the notion that good will be rewarded with good, and evil with evil.[13] Therefore, a series of obligations, trust, beliefs and expectations formed as a result of the cause-effect relationship plays an important role in promoting the connection and contacts between people. It is precisely because of this that some hold that 'reciprocity' is the foundation of social relationships in China (Yang 1957). Moreover, the foundation of the *guanxi* community formed on the basis of favour is more solid and this is especially true with traditional society.

Mianzi is also a major relevant concept. In a general sense in China, *mianzi* means 'reputation' and 'feelings' (Zhongguo Shehui Kexueyuan, Yuyan Yanjiusuo [Institute of Linguistics of the Chinese Academy of Social Sciences – CASS] 1987). However, as a carrier of culture and informal institutions, *mianzi* has a more complicated meaning. To use the words of Lu Xun, China's literary giant at the beginning of the twentieth century, in the cultural context, the concept of *mianzi* actually represents the programme of the Chinese spirit. American missionary Arthur H. Smith (1894) was the first to point out that *mianzi* was an important characteristic of the Chinese. All this shows that as a major component of Chinese culture, *mianzi* is of great significance.

From the perspective of culture, most scholars tend to interpret *mianzi* as *lian-mian*, and the term should be interpreted separately as *lian* and *mian* and should not be defined in generalities. After studying the discussion of *lian* and *mianzi* by many famous Chinese and Western scholars (Hu 1944; Ho 1975; Jin 2002; Goffman 1955),[14] Zhai Xuewei had these definitions: *lian* is the special image established by a Chinese person in other people's hearts (mind) through impression management and for the improvement of oneself or relevant to others; and *mianzi* is the position a Chinese person estimates he/she occupies or should occupy in other people's hearts (minds) by evaluating his/her *lian* (Zhai 1994).[15] However, as a matter of fact, both *lian* and *mian* are the appearances of people, so the *mian* of the Chinese is often connected with their *lian*: *lian* is manifested through the image while *mianzi* is displayed mainly through social contacts. Generally speaking, *lian* is the first manifestation of *mianzi*, and *mianzi* is the second manifestation of *lian*. Therefore, Chinese scholars share the view that the English word 'face' cannot fully express the complicated meaning of the Chinese term *lianmian* (Zhai 1994).

Just like favour, *mianzi* can also be used to condition others as well as oneself. An important factor therein is 'shame'. Because of the sense of shame, *lianmian* has a strong, positive moral meaning.

Whether it is favour or *mianzi*, and whether 'reciprocity' or 'shame' plays a role, in the final analysis, much of the fundamental spirit of these rules is an extension of Confucian rites. As pointed out in earlier sections of this chapter, 'rite' is the leading factor of all behavioural norms accepted in traditional Chinese society (including much of modern society); so it includes 'reciprocity', 'shame' and other norms. This shows that the important ideological and spiritual source of the *guanxi* community is still Confucian ethical doctrines because, in the final analysis, they are out-and-out doctrines about interpersonal relationships. The reason why Confucianists advocate 'rites' is that they want to use the rules derived from rites to establish harmonious interpersonal relationships in society as a whole.[16] For example, Confucian statements represent the most classical spirit for handling interpersonal relationships: 'Harmony receives the priority in applying the rites', 'the Master's Dao is to be loyal and forbearing', and 'virtue and morality are essential'.

Self (self personality) → *lian-mianzi* (conditioned by 'shame') → favour (conditioned by 'reciprocity') → *guanxi* community (group rules) (Figure 3.1).

However, we have also noticed it is far from sufficient only to have Confucian doctrines. The 'little tradition' that exists extensively among the Chinese people and has not been institutionalized by these doctrines and the behavioural norms observed by people in their daily lives are equally important. This can be clearly seen in our analysis of informal finance in Chapter 5. The utilitarianism under the influence of Chen Liang and Ye Shi has a very positive influence over the development of informal finance in Wenzhou today but the thinking is obviously at odds with the Confucian thinking of Confucius, Mencius and Zhu Xi. Therefore, we say that Confucianism lays the theoretical foundation of our concept of *guanxi*

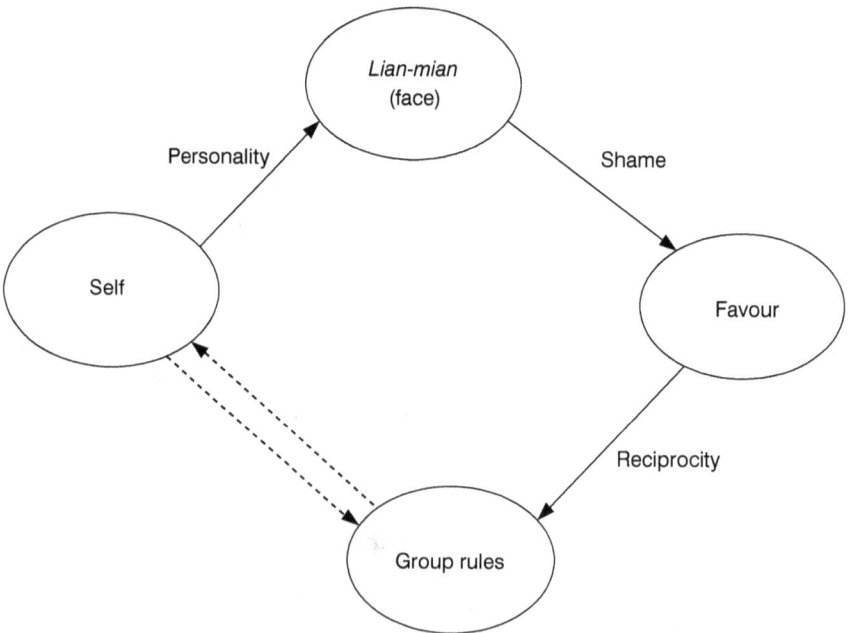

Figure 3.1 Value chain of face and favour in *guanxi* community

community to some extent but it does not lay the entire foundation. A large part of the foundation comes from people's traditions and the life of the general public. This is an important purpose of our research.

Model 2: the model of the differential mode of association   This is a theoretical model formulated by the famous Chinese sociologist Fei Xiaotong (1947) to explain the structure of the traditional rural society of China. We mentioned this theory earlier when we discussed the structural acceptance of *guanxi* networks. It is not only a model to explain the *guanxi* structure but also a very good theoretical model for the formation and development of *guanxi* networks. The model is valuable because it points out the differential mode of association of *guanxi* networks (for details, see the above discussion) on the one hand, and, it is fully aware of the open nature of these networks on the other.

Model 3: the model of social exchange   As an important economic activity, exchange has long been a common behaviour and action in economic life. Exchange in the economic sense is a rational act and is carried out at equal value and at real time. Therefore, economic exchanges do not have the flavour of affection, nor do they have much social meaning. This shows that, although economic exchanges are common and have a long history, they do not play a prominent social role in establishing a group or a community.

Cultural anthropologist Malinowski ([1922] 1967) studied the Kula exchange model (or Kula system)[17] among the Trobriand Islanders and discovered that Kula was not only an article exchange network of local tribes but also, more importantly, it played a prominent role in increasing the social connection between people and strengthening interpersonal contacts. Therefore, it became a symbol and sign of the social relationships of local people. In this sense, exchange is more of social significance. This is why Malinowski referred to this exchange as social exchange.

According to Malinowski, the following manifests the socio-psychological significance of the Kula Ring exchange: (1) The exchange is full of non-economic and non-material factors such as those that reflect obvious affection and social obligations. It also embodies the social reputation factor because only talented people with the highest prestige can have the Kula exchange articles with the highest social reputation. Therefore, the process of the Kula exchange is a process of giving social reputation to the exchangers. Accordingly, the exchange has the feature of 'showing off one's prestige'. It also has shared factors and expresses people's hope to increase their ties through this form. Therefore, the Kula Ring exchange is, in essence, a social interpersonal exchange and not mainly an economic exchange. (2) The desire of the people for social contacts is the driving force and foundation of their contacts in real life. They do not mainly use exchange to obtain economic efficacy and they do not care what is of higher value – bracelets or necklaces. (3) From (1) and (2), we can see that in the Kula Ring exchange, what counts is not the articles of exchange but the people who participate in the exchange because this process helps individuals become social. (4) The Kula Ring exchange helps to safeguard and expand social connections. (5) When it is of symbolic significance, social exchange organizes social order to some extent (or divides or consolidates it).[18]

George Caspar Homans (1961) devised a theory of social exchange. He was the first to use the principle of group dynamics in psychology to explain the behaviour of small groups and established a preliminary theoretical foundation of social exchange. His main views in this field are that people's behaviour is closely connected with the benefits they receive from their behaviour; the higher and more frequent the benefits of the activities are, the more willing people are to carry them out; people tend to choose the behaviour that benefits them the most.

In addition, Georg Simmel ([1907] 1990) formulated the principles for the materialization of social exchange, which are the attraction principle, the value principle, the power principle and the tension principle. Peter M. Blau (1964) developed Simmel's views. To be more specific, first, he noted that social exchange originated in social attraction and that, without attraction, there would be no value in exchange. Second, he stressed the importance of adjusting one's role play and doing well in impression management or facework, so as to boost the confidence of the other party in the transaction (Goffman 1955). Third, there are many forms of remuneration (returns) involved in social exchange. Money and goods are only part of it. Other returns include people's respect, higher status and access to more information and service which are also very valuable (Foa and Foa 1976). Social exchange must be carried out in accordance with mutually beneficial and fair principles. Otherwise, there will be social conflict.

In short, according to the theory of social exchange, the purpose of people's social life is to look for the resources that meet their needs. In order to obtain these resources, and especially to win social recognition, everyone is willing to carry out exchange at an appropriate cost. When they believe their exchange is fair, their interaction relationships are maintained amidst balance (Thibaut and Kelley 1959). In contrast to affective-neutrality and impersonality in economic exchange, favour plays an intermediate role in social exchange. Therefore social exchange relationships occupy a more important position in interpersonal relationships in traditional society. Moreover, mutual benefit (mutually related transactions between groups) and the principle of fairness are of great significance during social exchange.

Model 4: the model of the dramaturgy theory   The dramaturgy theory was formulated by Goffman (1955) to explain interpersonal relationship behaviour. Goffman's main views, using research of his theory by Chan Chi-chao (1987), Cathy Ruey-ling Chu (1987) and others, are summarized as follows:

First, Goffman believed that society is a stage, and life is just like putting on a show. The process of interpersonal interaction is a process of putting on a show.

The role in the show is given by society and the success or failure determines the face of individuals and their relevant groups (like *guanxi* communities).

Second, face is the main social indicator of the success or failure of an individual. In order to be successful in a show, it is necessary to do facework.[19] Facework has become a ceremonial manifestation of social interactive behaviour.

Third, an individual has two stages for his/her social interaction. They are the front stage and the back stage.

Fourth, all that an individual does in the process of contacts with others, that is, his/her behaviour in the front stage, is a falsified behaviour for others to see and is all facework behaviour. The real behaviour is on the back stage and invisible to others. In order to behave in accordance with social norms, everyone in society has his/her own facework tactics for social recognition.

Fifth, there are two types of facework. One is avoidance process and the other is corrective process. The tactics of the former are to protect one's own and others' face. The priority of the latter is to correct and restore the damaged face of one party or both parties. The concept of interchange is of great importance for the latter.

Finally, nobody plays only one role, so a person has many sources of face. But a person's main role provides the most important source of his/her face, thus forming the 'trinity' of agents, social roles and face.

Although Goffman's theory covers a lot of areas, its focal point is that, in order to maintain one's social relations and keep one's harmonious ties with certain social groups, one must protect one's face through impression management and win as many favourable social comments as possible. If everyone does this, there will be harmonious relations between them and their group and between groups and there will be harmonious order in society as a whole. Thus Goffman's dramaturgy theory provides theoretical support for explaining the researcher's analysis of *guanxi* community.

In addition, the ingratiation model of Jones (1964), the interpersonal model of Heider (1958) and the group theory model in its general sense also help the researcher deepen the understanding of the *guanxi* community model.

In his study of trust, Luhman (1979) said trust was a functional social mechanism embedded in the social structure and system. In fact, *guanxi* community has the same characteristics as trust. That is, they are a functional social mechanism embedded in a certain social structure and system under certain historical conditions. In the above discussion we have mentioned that *guanxi* community is an intermediate level concept. This concept echoes the macro judgements we have made at the beginning of this chapter such as the effective succession of China's modernization and traditions, and the social orientation and collectivism of Chinese society. In addition, the concept is also connected with our real life. The reason we have explored the definition of *guanxi* community, its form and content and then its basic theory and model is that *guanxi* and *guanxi* community are embedded in our real society and in many areas are also playing many important functional roles. Two of these areas are people's mobility or migration and TVE development. Therefore, on the basis of the above theoretical analysis and in accordance with the information collected from our on-the-spot investigations of villages in China, we will discuss more details relating to people's mobility in Chapter 6 and TVE development in Chapter 7.

4 Selection of research areas

After the broad discussion of theoretical and indigenous conceptual aspects of informal institutions and networks in the preceding chapters, we will now turn the focus of the discussion to the field survey. This will start in this chapter with an introduction to the research areas. More specific analyses of different issues will follow in Chapters 5 to 8; the final chapter, Chapter 9, draws the conclusions to the research.

This research focuses on informal institutions which link directly and closely with cultural and historical issues. This is especially true and more important when we extend our research to fieldwork. Therefore the introduction to the field research areas has to include the introduction of the local history and indigenous cultures of the research areas, and not only an introduction to the local economic development, simply because we cannot correctly understand the local economic and social development models or people's different behaviours in different places without linking with the historic and cultural backgrounds of the research areas. We could look at international migration of ethnic groups, for example, comparing Chinese-Americans with African-Americans. At a surface level, they have many common characteristics: they are all immigrants; they are all coloured races and so on. But if we look deeply into their behaviour, we will find many differences among these groups arising from their different cultural backgrounds. For instance, Chinese-Americans usually spend much more time and money on study than African-Americans. As a result, many young people from Chinese-American groups now work in scientific research and higher educational institutes or in the capital markets or open their own businesses; but the situation for African-Americans is different. As previously mentioned, different results have been achieved by the different transitional approaches adopted by China and countries in Eastern and Central Europe. These examples all demonstrate the need to discuss the topics of the present research in their historical and cultural contexts. This is even more important for research in big countries with a long history and diversified economic, social and cultural structures among different areas of the country, such as China.

Issues of interest in the fieldwork

Specific issues need to be taken into consideration at the relevant level of discussion. Based on the experience derived from long-term fieldwork and data available from the five selected villages in China, empirical discussions of this research will be focused on specific problems that examine how informal institutions such as trust, social networks and local governance affect people's actions in various areas of their real life as well as rural development in China.

First, as the biggest developing country in the world in terms of population, China continues to lag behind. How to finance rural development is therefore a key question. Since China follows principles of strict controls on capital markets and financial operations, small farmers in rural areas find it difficult to raise capital from government-controlled financial institutions such as state banks, capital markets, etc. Farmers, therefore, have to organize credit themselves to solve the problem of financing the process of development. In reality, informal institutions and tradition help farmers to create a kind of self-financing arrangement. Based on the local traditions of trust, Xiangdong villagers in Zhejiang Province raise funds efficiently through self-organized informal financing institutions, ROSCAs, and the systemic risk is also well managed. How trust works in this case and, as a kind of informal institution, how ROSCAs help villagers to make trust work well in the village are the key questions that arise (see Chapter 5).

Second, more than 100 million farmers moved to urban areas as people's mobility increased, to a large extent as a direct result of the implementation of China's new reform and opening up policies. This is unprecedented in Chinese history. No doubt, this is a very important issue and even a very significant event in the history of the world. Interestingly, intensive fieldwork in rural areas has found that in the absence of government support (in some cases government even became an obstacle in the 1990s), rural people have not only managed their movement to China's cities but also have been able to find job opportunities in these cities through personal channels. *Guanxi*, as a kind of informal institution as well as a kind of traditional cultural resource, plays a very important role in the process of rural people's movement into urban areas. In the case of one of the study villages in Shanxi Province, what is of interest is how the behaviour of migrating farmers through the use of *guanxi* networks has been well embedded into the social trust system (see Chapter 6).

Third, as mentioned in Chapter 1, is the importance of TVEs to rural development and rural industrialization in China. Of interest in past years is the question of how Chinese farmers were capable of building up such a large non-farm sector by stepping outside the state planning system during the era of shortage. Also of interest is the question of how rural people managed these enterprises well in opposition to the state-owned industrial and service sectors once market principles were introduced into China. The development of TVEs is sometimes linked to politics, but if we look at the development of TVEs as a whole, the most decisive factor is the previously lost long-held tradition in the history of rural areas of 'agriculture and handicrafts complementary to each other', and the deeply rooted *guanxi* rule in rural areas. Depending mainly on the tradition of 'agriculture and handicrafts complementary to each other' and the development of *guanxi* resources, Chinese farmers have created a legend in the world of the high growth and sustainable development of TVEs. Trust and *guanxi* played an extremely important role in the whole process; their use by farmers in China particularly provides a sense of how *guanxi* networks have been fostered and engineered (Chapter 7).

Fourth, in this period of historic transformation in China, both the market and government are not in the right place to manage development at the grass roots. This provides good opportunities for the community and local entrepreneurs to play larger roles in rural development. Of interest in this regard is how rural people are able to create new ideas to combine together modern enterprise and traditional village work to develop themselves based on community principles and how informal institutions are involved in the process. This is examined through the case study of the village-based Fuxing Science & Technology Co. Ltd., and Fuxing village in Hubei Province (see Chapter 8).

Regional backgrounds among the selected provinces

Although China is the largest country in the world in terms of population (the country's population was 1.29 billion at the end of 2003, 20 per cent of the world's total), it is only the third in the world after Russia and Canada in terms of land area. China covers 9.6 million square km or just 7.2 per cent of the world's total land area. Based mainly on its geographical features and economic development, China is divided into three development regions: the eastern, the central and the western regions.[1]

As we pointed out in Chapter 1, many studies have indicated that the south and north of China (this is also true of east, central and western China) have different cultural backgrounds (Huang 1985, 1990; Cohen 1990; Nee and Su 1990; Potter and Potter 1990; Friedman *et al.* 1991; Nee 1992; Lin 1995). Accordingly, they would show different characteristics in people's economic, social and cultural behaviour. In order to better reflect regional discrepancies in social, economic and cultural development, our study intentionally employed a method of purposive site selection to balance regional differences. That is, we selected two villages from the south and the north respectively and one village from the central region between the north and the south.

In selecting sample villages, apart from cultural factors, the difference in the economic development of these villages and their respective representativeness among their peer villages in the country was also taken into account. The economic development of the villages selected from the south is not the most developed in China but well represents the relatively high standard of economic development in the southeast coastal areas. The villages selected from the north, while not the lowest in China, can well represent the below-medium economic development level of the country. The village selected from the central region can well represent the economic development level of rural areas in central China (Figure 4.1).

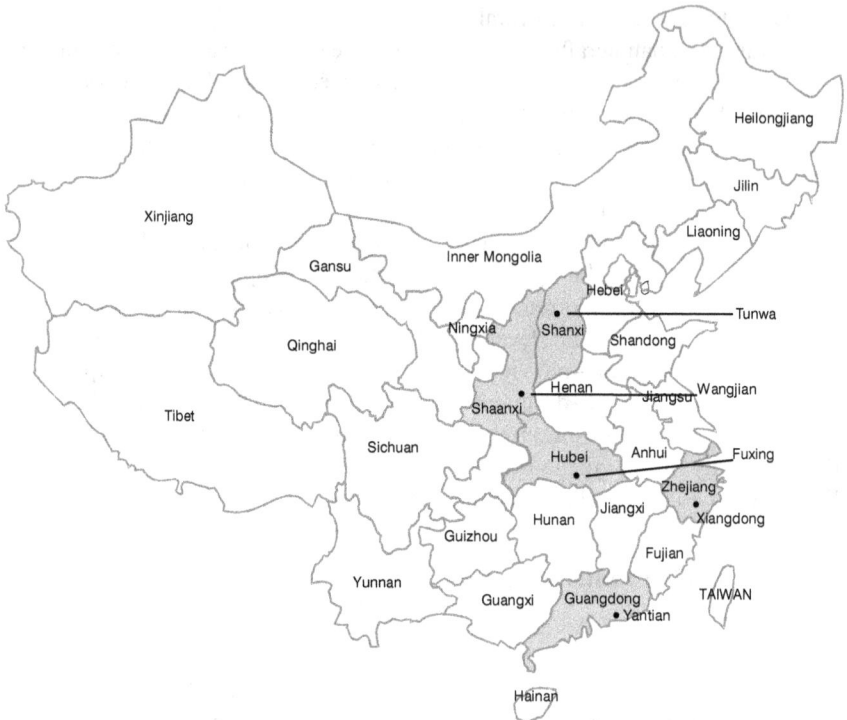

Figure 4.1 Sketch map of survey areas and villages

Tunwa village is in Shanxi Province and belongs to the central region, but it is located in the north and its economy is undeveloped and very similar to most of the western provinces. Fuxing village is in Hubei Province which is located exactly in the centre of the country. Xiangdong village and Yantian village are in the well-developed eastern coastal region in Zhejiang and Guangdong provinces respectively. Wangjian village in Shaanxi Province while not discussed in this present study, is looked at in other related research into the five villages.

Shanxi Province

Shanxi Province is located on the loess plateau of the north China plain on the northern side of central China. As it is on the western side of Taihang Mountains (*taihang shan*), it is called Shanxi, meaning in the west of the mountains. But, as it is on the eastern side of the Yellow River (*huanghe*), it is also referred to as Hedong, meaning east of the river. The official name of the administrative territory (the province) is Shanxi and not Hedong. Covering an area of 156,000 square km or 1.6 per cent of the country's total, it has a population of 32 million making it a lower medium-sized province in China (the average area and population of the Chinese mainland's provinces, municipalities and autonomous regions are 300,000 square km and 41 million people respectively). As 80 per cent of the land area is hilly and the flat areas only 20 per cent, it is regarded as a mountainous province. Judging from its geographical location, it is not located in a far-flung corner as it is only 500 km away from Beijing – the capital of China – and separated from it by Hebei Province.

Shanxi is a province very rich in mineral resources. There are presently 117 varieties of proven underground mineral reserves with a total potential value of about 13.7 trillion yuan, ranking it second in the country. Among them, the deposits of coal, bauxite ores and laterite rank first in terms of potential value, especially coal, with reserves estimated at 871 billion tons. The 94 counties with coal deposits that make up 39.6 per cent of the province's total area (Liang 1999: 4) account for 26 per cent of the total coal deposits in China. Presently, the output of coal in the province accounts for about one-third of the country's total production; hence, over many years it has earned the title of 'Coal Capital' in China.

Along with the rich mineral resources, iron smelting is also well developed. Historically, the local salt industry was of great importance to China; hence, the province was also known to be rich in both salt and iron.

Shanxi business people were also very successful. During the Ming and Qing dynasties (1368–1911), there were three major commercial conglomerates[2] in China and the Shanxi conglomerate was the strongest of all. From a historical point of view, China's commerce began with the salt industry. As Shanxi was the most important salt producer in ancient China, so the first business people in Chinese history could be said to be Shanxi salt merchants. By the Qing Dynasty (1644–1911), recognizing Shanxi business people's commercial capacity, the government gave them privileges to conduct border trade with Korea, Russia and Japan. Thus, Shanxi business people became ever more influential in the Qing Dynasty. This was especially true from 1823 onwards when the business people in Pingyao, Qixian and Taigu counties gradually developed bill exchanges (running remittance exchange services including money order, mail and telegraphic transfers), rapidly setting up an extensive network of bill exchange shops (*piaohao*) which basically monopolized the national money and fund regulation, and even stretched to branches in Japan and Korea. Because of this, Shanxi was also well known as the 'Capital of Universal Remittance'.

Shanxi was one of the original sites of ancient Chinese civilization. Chinese archaeology has shown that the history of Shanxi civilization can be traced back to the remotest periods 1.8 million years ago (demonstrated by evidence of primitive man's activity in the province). There is recorded history of about 4,000 years. The first dynasty in ancient China (the Xia Dynasty from 2070–1600 BC) was established by Qi (the son of Yu) in an area that currently belongs to Shanxi Province (Liang 1999: 5). Furthermore, according to historical evidence, the place nowadays referred to as China first arose in the southern part (Linfen prefecture) of Shanxi Province. That prefecture was precisely at the centre of activity of the legendary emperors Yao, Shun and Yu in ancient Chinese history before the establishment of the Xia Dynasty (Li 2003: 22, 150).

Another important feature of Shanxi is that its culture of emigration was at one time the most developed in the country. In the early Ming years, the government organized the emigration of people from Shanxi to Hebei, Anhui, Shandong, Henan and Beijing to mitigate unfavourable conditions following war (Liang 1999: 18). Before departing, these emigrants would assemble under the Huge Locust Tree in Hongdong County. That is why many Chinese, when referring to their roots, say: 'If you ask me where my native place is, it is the Huge Locust Tree in Hongdong County'. The emigration of Shanxi natives throughout the country made the region one of the original sources of Chinese culture.

Precisely because of its critical role as the origin of ancient Chinese civilization, as well as its economic prosperity in ancient times, Shanxi was the source of ideologies that had an important impact on the blossoming of that civilization. There were two principal schools of thought. One was the Legalist School during the Spring and Autumn Period and the Warring States Period (770–221 BC). The basic tenets of this school were to develop the rule of legalism and oppose the rule of Confucian ritualism, supporting the ideological trend during the early period of ancient China. The other school of thought was the budding neo-Confucian ideology in the Sui and Tang dynasties and neo-Confucianism during the Song and Ming dynasties. In the history of Chinese philosophy, the neo-Confucianism created by Xue Xuan (1389–1464) in Shanxi is referred to as the Hedong School. After the Song Dynasty the province was the proponent of neo-Confucianism which aimed to restore the original features of Confucianism by reforming old Confucianism and Zhu Xi's neo-Confucian school.

From the Legalist School, the most important figures promoting legalism in what is now Shanxi Province included Li Kui, Wu Qi and Han Fei. From the neo-Confucian School, the main proponents in Shanxi were Wang Tong who lived in the later years of the Sui Dynasty (581–618) and Xue Xuan in the Ming Dynasty (1368–1644).

Though they lived in different periods, Wang Tong (584–617) and Xue Xuan were of the same school of thought. Living in the later Sui years, Wang Tong was the first to propose combining Confucianism, Buddhism and Taoism as the dominant ideology. He did so by repudiating the Han dynasty's (206 BC–220 AD) classic Confucian studies, especially using the Sui (581–618) and Tang (618–907) studies of Confucian 'renovation of the realities' to repudiate Dong Zhongshu's (one of the very important thinkers and philosophers in the West Han Dynasty during 206 BC–24 AD) Doctrine of Heavenly Decree and the proposition of substituting Heavenly Decree with the Taoist Way and Virtue, thus pioneering the renovation of Sui and Tang Confucianism. In practice, this laid the ideological basis for the formation of the impending Song and Ming neo-Confucian school of thought (Li 2003: 134). On the other hand, Xue Xuan directly created the Hedong School which became one of the two major ideological trends in the Ming neo-Confucian school, enjoying equal fame with Wang Yangming's (1472–1529) Yaojiang School. The Hedong School emerged in the historical context of neo-Confucianism which took shape in the Song Dynasty (960–1279), reached its climax, and then declined in the early Ming years. In this context, Xue Xuan repudiated apriorism of Zhu Xi's school of philosophy while defending the basic neo-Confucian tenets, advocating the return of Confucianism to the ideological tradition of running state affairs with practical knowledge. Xue Xuan set up a more practical theory to serve the ruling class, advocating practical rationale and practical application. This was referred to as the Xue Xuan School of Thought East of the Yellow River. Xue was the first to propose the concept of *Practical Learning* which laid the theoretical basis for the rise of the upcoming *Practical Learning* in the middle of the Ming Dynasty (Li 2003: 224). Judging from practical effects, the pragmatic Confucian School East of the Yellow River did play a certain role in restoring the social order based on the three cardinal guides (ruler guides subject, father guides son and husband guides wife) and five constant virtues (benevolence, righteousness, propriety, wisdom and fidelity) in the feudal ethical code through defending and tightening the patriarchal hierarchy system and the Confucian rituals. Of course, the general trend of historical development eventually rendered this school of thought rather insignificant.

This study selected Tunwa village to investigate how it developed and matured in this historical context. A detailed account of real-life conditions of the village is contained in later analysis.

Hubei Province

Fuxing, the village chosen to represent central China, lies within the territory of Hubei Province which is located in the central part of China. The province borders Dongting Lake (Hubei means north of the lake in Chinese). The province has 60 million residents, 4.6 per cent of the country's total population. Covering 186,000 square km, or 1.9 per cent of the country's total land area, Hubei is a typical medium-sized province. Topographically, Hubei is similar to Shanxi Province. Hills make up 80 per cent of the land. The remaining 20 per cent of the province is made up of plains and lakes. An important feature of the province is the multitude of rivers and lakes. Apart from the Yangtze River, 1,193 rivers and waterways run through Hubei Province, of which 41 are more than 100 km long. The province is dotted with hundreds of lakes, large and small; hence, the name 'a province with one thousand lakes' (Hu 2002: 14). Of these, 320 have an area of more than three square km. The fertile soil and warm climate in the Jianghan Plain and the plain along the Yangtze River in eastern Hubei are suited to paddy rice cultivation and have high yields. The province has a 6,000- to 7,000-year history of producing paddy rice (Wang and Liu 1992: 199), hence, its fame in China as 'a place of great abundance in rice and fish'.

Historically, Hubei Province, as it stands today, belonged to the core of the Kingdom of Chu in ancient China. Archaeological investigations showed that man lived here as early as 700,000 to 800,000 years ago. In recorded history, Emperor Zhou (Chengwang) of the Western Zhou Dynasty (1100–770 BC) bestowed a feudal estate on Xiong Yi, who was later regarded as the ancestor who founded the Kingdom of Chu. The fiefdom was very small in area at that time, merely 100 *li* (50 kilometres) in circumference. Over seven centuries, the ancient State of Chu struggled to expand its land area. At its prime, it once embraced the whole of current Hubei, Hunan, Henan, Anhui, Jiangsu and Zhejiang provinces as well as parts of Jiangxi and Shandong provinces (ibid: 177, 268). As it stands today, Hubei Province, especially the Jianghan Plain, was always the central belt of the ancient State of Chu. It was from this plain that the ancient State of Chu emerged as a powerful kingdom.

Apart from traditional agriculture, the economic basis of ancient Chu consisted of three major economic pillars of copper and iron smelting, lacquer and bamboo ware, and silk weaving and embroidery. Modern archaeology has shown that copperware in the State of Chu, especially ritual musical instruments, reached a very high standard in ancient times. From archaeological findings, it can be concluded that iron smelting appeared in the Kingdom of Chu before the later years of the Spring and Autumn Period (about 2,500–3,000 years ago). In other words, it was the first feudal dukedom in ancient China to smelt iron and steel and produce ironware (Zhang 1988: 58). This shows that the ancient Kingdom of Chu was a leader in all the main economic fields. It also accounts for the fact that the Hanyang Iron Mill, the first iron and steel mill to be set up in the Westernization Movement towards the end of the nineteenth century was located in Hanyang in Hubei Province. Of course, this level of economic sophistication also laid the foundation for the development of Hubei culture and Chu State ideology.

From the ideological and philosophical point of view, two theories dominated ancient Chu. One was the Philosophy of Chu which played an important role in Chinese culture about 2,500 years ago in the latter half of the Spring and Autumn Period. The other theory was the Hu-Xiang[3] School of Thought born in the Song Dynasty, which exerted quite an influence in the development of modern China.

The founder of Taoism was Lao Dan, known as Laozi. The gist of his tenets was embodied in his work *Laozi*, which basically crystallized the achievements of Chu philosophy at its maturity. The core of this philosophy comprised four main points: (1) The Tao (Dao or Way)[4] was regarded as the ultimate origin of everything in the world, assuming that everything under the sun was born out of the Tao: 'The Tao engenders one, one engenders two, two engenders three, and three engenders everything (Laozi, *Laozi*). From this angle, Laozi's Tao had transcended all other schools of thought in the pre-Qin periods as it resolved the question of the world's origin. (2) Virtue was raised on the basis of the Tao (Way) as well as Virtue of the Tao. If the Tao is the vehicle, then Virtue is the goal. If the Tao were the very origin of everything, then Virtue would be the outcome of everything. In everyday life, Virtue referred to the social norms of human behaviour (Wang and Liu 1992: 96). (3) The law governing the Tao was regarded as a natural spiritual law or the law of governing by doing nothing against nature, or in other words, the law was to follow the spontaneous rules and order, and to achieve the purpose of governing by non-interference[5] in such natural laws (Laozi, *Laozi*, Chapter 57). The government must not enslave the people in disregard of the natural laws ('The sages should have no aim, but take the aims of the people as their own aim' (Laozi, *Laozi*, Chapter 49)). 'Man must not sabotage nature in disregard of natural laws'. (4) The proposition was raised that 'man follows the Earth, the Earth follows Heaven, the Heaven follows the Tao (Way) and the Tao follows nature' (Laozi, *Laozi*, Chapter 25). In other words, Laozi considered Heaven, Earth and Man as a totality inseparably bound together. Thus explains the famous ancient Chinese ideology of the integration of Heaven and Man. Of course, the Laozi philosophical system eventually returned to the ideology of the Tao engendering everything, while Heaven, Earth and Man all have the same origin since the Tao engenders Heaven, the Earth and also Man.

About a century after Laozi, there appeared in the State of Chu another great philosopher and thinker, Zhuang Zhou (or Zhuangzi). He developed Laozi's philosophy by incorporating his basic tenets. That was why people would often speak of Laozi and Zhuangzi as an integrated whole when talking about ancient Chu culture.

By the Song Dynasty, there also emerged a famous school of thought called the Hu-Xiang School in the State of Chu. Created by Hu Anguo, the school paid great attention to: (1) running state affairs with practical knowledge while rejecting empty talk; (2) advocating the combination of Heavenly rationale with man's desire (Hu Hong) and opposing the oversimplified stress on eliminating man's desire to preserve the Heavenly rationale. In a certain sense, the ideology of the Hu-Xiang School was similar to the previously mentioned ideology of the Hedong School.

Summing up the various factors for economic and cultural development in the ancient State of Chu, where Hubei Province is located today, there were the following obvious special features:

1   The culture of Chu mixed many factors from other cultures, principally the Central China Plain culture, the Wuyue (present-day Jiangsu and Zhejiang) culture and the Bashu (present-day Sichuan and Chongqing) culture in an open environment. For example, the State of Chu incorporated many useful ideas from the copper smelting skills of the northern Central China Plain and the Wuyue regions in the southeast part of China into its own production and exceeded the Central Plain and Wuyue in the same field. In the course of upgrading its textile skills, Chu was, in practice, influenced by the states of Qi and Lu. With regard to lacquer ware, it was influenced by the state of Qin.

2   Chu had a tradition of working hard for the prosperity of the state. Historical records by historian Zuo Qiuming recorded (Zuo Zhuan) that, in the more than 400 years from Xiong Yi, the Founder King of Chu to King Ling of Chu, 'all the ruling kings of Chu personally took part in reclaiming (cultivating) wasteland in mountain areas' in the early stage of development of the ancient state. This spirit has been handed down over the years. It was precisely because of such a spirit that from a tiny fiefdom, granted by the Emperor of the Western Zhou Dynasty to the founding king, King Cheng (Zhou Chengwang), the Kingdom of Chu soon expanded. By the Spring and Autumn Period, 200 years or more later, Chu had become one of the five hegemonic states and by the Warring States Period, it had become one of the seven powerful states.

3   The culture of Chu was imbued with a very deep spirit of innovation. This spirit was expressed at its fullest in agricultural irrigation and monetary

systems (Chu was the only state using gold as money), in its administrative systems (Chu was the first to set up the county system in 689 BC), in national policy (the first to pursue the national policy of integrating the Chinese nation with the barbarous ethnic groups to the west and south of ancient China), in its romantic literature (Qu Yuan's long patriotic poem 'Li Sao'), in the Laozi and Chanzong philosophy and in the creative philosophical thinking pioneered by Zhou Dunyi as neo-Confucianism in the Song and Ming dynasties.

4   There prevailed in Chu a strong feeling of love for the state and the family. Qu Yuan was a typical example of this.

The State of Chu paid great attention to culture. After the Qin conquered Chu and other states, and unified ancient China, the people of Chu worked hard to regain the State of Chu. In the final days of the Qin Dynasty, Chu citizens Chen Sheng and Wu Guang launched a peasant uprising, which eventually achieved the success of Liu Bang and Xiang Yu, both citizens of Chu. Eventually, Liu Bang established the Han Dynasty following the fall of the Qin Dynasty. In all these eventualities, conviction and culture played a key role.

This provides us with the regional historical and cultural background for the Hubei village survey in Chapter 8.

One village in Zhejiang Province and another in Guangdong Province were selected for the survey of China's coastal southeast region. As macro background, these profiles may help to provide a better understanding of the two villages surveyed as well.

Zhejiang Province

Zhejiang Province forms the southern wing of the Yangtze River Delta and faces out to the East China Sea. With a more than 6,400 kilometre long coast, Zhejiang has the longest coastline of any Chinese province. Zhejiang means winding river in Chinese, reflecting the meandering course of the Qiantang River that flows through the province. Its 102,000 square km account for 1.1 per cent of the country's total land area. A total population of 46 million people makes Zhejiang a lower medium-sized province in China. Of the total land area, hilly regions make up 70 per cent; plains and basins make up 23 per cent and rivers the remaining 7 per cent (Pan and Tan 2002: 29). In prehistoric times, Zhejiang developed later than Shanxi and Hubei. Man only began to be active in this part of China about 50,000 years ago. Four to five thousand years ago, human activity became extensive in this area. Being a coastal province, the local salt industry was well developed. China (porcelain) making, silk making, printing and shipbuilding were also all of a relatively high standard.

From the point of view of China's modern economic development, Zhejiang is most characterized by its vigour and vitality. It is the most animated regional economic development zone in China. The most direct reason for this vitality and vigour is the high proportion of private economy due to the fairly early adoption of market-oriented reform in the province. That reform was very thoroughgoing. What began as the Wenzhou Model[6] of market reform in Wenzhou was soon adopted elsewhere in the province to become the Zhejiang Model. It has become one of the regional development models generally emulated by other provinces and municipalities in China. Be it the Wenzhou Model or the later Zhejiang Model, the core lies in the rapid development of the private economy and the genesis of this development model is closely connected with the unique cultural model in the region.

Ancient Zhejiang also produced many excellent philosophers and thinkers. Apart from the well-known Wang Chong and Wang Yangming, Zhejiang was also home to the Eastern Zhejiang School of Utilitarianism, an important school in the history of China's philosophical and social thinking.[7] The school consisted of two branches that shared similar ideas. One was the Yongjia School and the other, the Yongkang School. The main idea of the Eastern Zhejiang School of Utilitarianism was to advocate utilitarianism and the practical knowledge of managing state affairs strongly and to oppose the bias created by the school of Confucian thought by stressing righteousness to the neglect of profit, especially Neo-Confucianism with Zhu Xi as its representative.[8] Both the Yongjia School and the Yongkang School advocated a free economy, were opposed to government intervention in non-governmental economic activities and called on the government to allow individuals to carry out all kinds of economic activities to meet their desire for profit (as well as sensual pleasure and desire for wealth) and to protect them. The two schools also fully affirmed the role of the rich as the country's pillar (Ye 1961; Chen 1974).

Guangdong Province

Guangdong Province is located at the southernmost tip of the Chinese mainland facing the South China Sea in the south and bordering Hong Kong and Macao at the east and west of Pearl River mouth respectively. The province has a total land area of 180,000 square km, accounting for 1.9 per cent of the country's total land area. In terms of topography, apart from the plain that makes up 36 per cent of the land, the remaining 64 per cent consists of hilly areas. As the province has a big population (79 million, ranking third among the provinces in China), so the per capita land area is only 0.2 hectare (3 *mu* in Chinese terms), and the per capita farmland acreage is even as low as 0.05 hectare (0.75 *mu*), less than 50 per cent of the country's average (Lu 2002: 110).

Being short of agricultural resources, Guangdong is one of the provinces that must seek development opportunities other than in the agricultural sector. On the other hand, Guangdong Province has the most overseas Chinese as well as returned overseas Chinese and their dependents. According to official statistics, there are 20 million overseas Chinese and Chinese residents from Guangdong, plus the 6 million living in Hong Kong and Macao and 4 million living in Taiwan. The province therefore has a total of 30 million people living in more than 100 countries and regions. There are more than 20 million returned overseas

Chinese and their dependents living in the province. Because of these special links, Guangdong has attracted more of the investment and remittances since the introduction of the reform and opening up policy than any other province of China. By the end of 2001, the province had actually utilized total foreign direct investment (FDI) of US$135.7 billion, accounting for 34.5 per cent of the country's total actual FDI in the same period. During the same period, the province also received US$30.6 billion remittances from overseas (Lu 2002: 113). This established a solid foundation for Guangdong to take the lead in setting up an export-oriented economic development model in China.

Guangdong culture belongs to the same cultural circle as the Hong Kong and Macao, i.e., the Lingnan[9] or Pearl River cultural circle. Due to the gradual impact of Western countries on China in various forms from Hong Kong, Macao and Guangdong during the Ming and Qing periods, Chinese and Western cultures blended together here. Therefore the Lingnan Culture was internationalized earlier than other cultures in China. Thus, from the very beginning, due to its special geographic, international and open environment and despite its later eventual formation (Ming and Qing periods), Lingnan Culture developed its own special features with distinct differences from other Chinese cultures. In other words, it was less fettered by the traditional influence of Confucian culture and opted freely for its own ideological and cultural style. This embraced the features of being more open, diverse (pluralistic), export-oriented, international, compatible and innovative, freer and more democratic (such as Sun Yat-sen's ideology), more mercantile and utilitarian and less envious of pseudo-fame and cherishing a stronger sense of political mission. Among these, the Lingnan Culture is most remarkable for its utilitarianism,[10] openness and compatibility. That was precisely why revolution in mainland China always sprouted from the fertile land of Lingnan Culture, ranging from the Sun Yat-sen's revolution in the early twentieth century to the reform and opening up in the latter half of the same century based on Deng Xiaoping's theory.

Yantian village, in Fenggang Township of Dongguan City in Guangdong Province selected for this study, is one such village that, under such a resourceful economic and cultural environment, opted for its own unique development model.

Village profiles

Following the regional discussion, our focus now turns to the general introduction to each of the selected villages. A more detailed description of each village together with more specific issues will be elaborated in the later chapters.

Xiangdong village, Zhejiang Province

Xiangdong village in Zhejiang Province is under the jurisdiction of Qianku Town, Cangnan County of Wenzhou City. It is located at the centre of the area from where Wenzhou Model originally developed in China.

From a geographical point of view, the village is at the southernmost end of Zhejiang Province. It is about 10 km west-northwest of the East China Sea. It is not far from the Aojiang River to the north. So the village is situated on a plain enclosed by the river and the sea. A river, about 200 metres wide, passes by the village connecting it to the Jing-Hang Canal (from Beijing to Hangzhou) through other waterways. The two highways alongside the village have bus services to the Wenzhou Airport and to Beijing, Tianjin, Shanghai, Wuhan and other big cities. So the village is accessible by means of both water and land transport.

The village is under the jurisdiction of Qianku Town which developed early in history. There was human activity around the town area 4,000 years ago during the Neolithic period. From 907 through 960 during the Five Dynasties and Ten States period, Qian Hongchu, king of the Wuyue State (currently Jiangsu Province and Zhejiang Province), established a tax office in the town to collect the local tea, salt, cotton and silk taxes from neighbouring areas. Later, the area where the tax office was located was simply named Qianku which means King Qian's tax office (Liu and Yang 1996: 1, 601).

Most villagers in Xiangdong village are surnamed Xiang. According to the Xiang family tree, Xiang Zhao (also known as Xiang Guoming) was the family's first ancestor to settle in the village. He was a native of Changxi, Fujian Province, and was a local official there. Disappointed with government authorities for their brutality and corruption, he resigned as an official. After that, he and his family settled in Yingqiao (now Xiangdong village) in Qianku Town, Zhejiang Province in 941. So for 35 generations (1,062 years) the Xiang family has been settled in

Plate 4.1 Xiangdong village in eastern China's Zhejiang Province

Xiangdong village. Currently, members of the Xiangdong family in the village mostly range from the 30th to the 35th generation.

As Xiangdong village has an unobstructed river course and is rich in aquatic resources it enjoys advantages in producing agricultural products. Rice is the village's main crop accounting for 72 per cent of its total crop-growing area. Rice is harvested in summer and fall. Vegetables, peas and wheat are grown in winter. The rice yield is high, averaging seven to eight tons per hectare in a normal year.

However, Xiangdong village's agricultural resources are far from adequate for its population. By the end of 2002, the village had 318 households with a population of 1,200. Its arable land amounts to 355 *mu* (one *mu* equals one-fifteenth of a hectare). Of this, 255 *mu* are paddy fields, 27 *mu* are dry land and the remaining 73 *mu* are hillside plots. So the average per capita land is 0.3 *mu* and the land for each household is 1.1 *mu*. Xiangdong is a typical Chinese village with a large population and little land.

In addition to farmland, the village's houses, roads and land for schools, enterprises and other non-farming purposes are concentrated in an area of one square kilometre. This land used for private and public purposes stretches along the east bank of the river.

Probably because of its limited agricultural resources, Xiangdong village has attached great importance to village industry since the 1970s. In 1972 it established the Xiangqiao Factory of Articles of Daily Use, the first collective enterprise in its long history. The factory focused on producing bottle caps, plastic products and signs. More than two decades later in 1993, when first visited for this study, Xiangdong village had 18 factories of different sizes producing mainly printing and packaging materials.

Most members of the village are engaged in both farming and industrial production. In 1993 the village's industrial and agricultural output totalled 22 million yuan (equivalent to US$3.82 million at the official exchange rate at the time of US$1= 5.76 yuan). This comprises industrial output of 20 million yuan, accounting for 91 per cent of the total; and agricultural output accounting for less than 10 per cent (Wang and Zhu 1996: 39). In that year the per capita net income of Xiangdong villagers was 1,200 yuan (US$208), compared to the national figure of 921.6 yuan (US$160) for rural residents. So the annual per capita net income of Xiangdong villagers was 30 per cent higher than the national level. Our investigations show that Xiangdong's real figure was higher because, in most cases, the statistics did not include villagers' income from private businesses.

However, visited again a decade later, great changes had taken place. The village streets are not as busy as they had been ten years earlier. And there are not as many goods being transported to and from the village as before. Only six of the 18 enterprises remained open (Plate 4.2 shows one of the family firms in the village) and they are not as big as they were a decade ago. The annual per capita net income of villagers in 2002 was only 2,300 yuan (US$277), which was 7 per cent lower than China's national level of 2,476 yuan (US$299) in the same year (there can be no doubt that the level of 2,300 yuan was much lower than the actual

Plate 4.2 A family business in Xiangdong village

figure because villagers often under-report their income from non-agricultural activities and from urban areas).

Our investigations show that the main cause of the problem is the change in the village structure. To be more precise, over the past decade, most of the villagers who had become rich by developing non-agricultural industries had moved their enterprises to the nearby larger towns of Longgang and Wenzhou. Some villagers simply invested all their money in real estate in Hangzhou, Shanghai and other cities and in commerce and trade in Beijing. In addition, two types of new immigrants moved to the village for different reasons. These immigrants do not have land and capital and they are targets of government anti-poverty programmes. This naturally drags down the income level of the village.

According to our investigations at the end of September and in October 2002, 62 households with 238 people moved out of Xiangdong village in the 15 years from the mid-1980s to 2001. So, on average, four households with 16 people left the village a year. More people did so in the four years from 1988 to 1992 than in any other year. Their destinations were all towns of different sizes. Most of them relocated to Longgang, the town closest to Xiangdong village (17 km), accounting for 75.8 per cent of the 47 households that moved out. Many moved to Qianku Town, just two km from the village (nine households, accounting for 14.5 per cent of the total) and to the Cangnan County town of Lingxi (six households, accounting for 9.7 per cent of the total). The heads of the relocated households were mostly aged from 25 to 40 years old.

New immigrants settled in Xiangdong village for two reasons. One was the influence of ancestry and the other was the compulsory government policy.

About 200 years ago in the later period of the Qing Dynasty, one of Xiangdong villagers' dragon boats sank in a race and some people were drowned. As a result, some villagers did not believe that Xiangdong was an auspicious village. One of the three brothers of the Xiangdong family moved four kilometres from Xiangdong village to Xiangjia Mountain, Xikuo village, to become a forester.[11] After about ten generations, this part of the Xiang family had expanded to more than 400 members in 2000. As Xiangjia Mountain is quite mountainous, transportation was poor and the area was economically backward compared with Xiangdong village. In addition, children in Xiangjia Mountain found it difficult to go to school. So some members of the Xiang family from Xiangjia Mountain asked Xiangdong village for permission to move back. As 90 per cent of the official residents of Xiangdong village had the Xiang surname, as did most of the village leaders, it was not long before the leaders of the two villages reached consensus. Xiangdong villagers did not oppose the proposed immigration because there were no big policy obstacles; villagers surnamed Xiang began to move from Xikuo village to Xiangdong village in December 2000. By the end of the year, about half of the villagers surnamed Xiang in Xikuo village or 58 households with 213 people had voluntarily moved to Xiangdong village. With the approval of the people's governments of Qianku Town and Cangnan County, these immigrants were granted registered residence in Xiangdong village.

According to the agreement between the two villages, as Xiangdong village had very little per capita land, it would not allocate immigrants from Xikuo village any farmland or housing. The immigrants still had the right to use their contracted farming land (*chengbaodi*) in Xikuo village but most of them had subcontracted that to others. At present, the immigrants mostly live in old houses bought from those who had moved out of Xiangdong village. Half of the immigrants are now salesmen or saleswomen and the other half do odd jobs in the enterprises of Xiangdong village and the town of Qianku.

As the immigrants and the Xiangdong villagers with the Xiang surname share the same ancestor, they are tolerant of each other. In June 2002, in the first election in Xiangdong village after the arrival of the immigrants, 39-year-old immigrant Xiang Yancun was elected to the three-member Xiangdong Village Committee of the CPC. Xiangdong village has another group of immigrants. These immigrants were allocated to the village in accordance with government policy in the winter of 1997 to make way for the construction of Shanxi Reservoir in Taikou village, Hongkou Township, Taishun County, Zhejiang Province. In accordance with the government's unified arrangement, 60 households with 300 people needed to be moved to Xiangdong village (at the time the research in the village was conducted, 45 households with 203 people had moved in). The government built houses for the immigrants in Xiangdong village (Plate 4.3). A small family received a one-room house and bigger families were allocated two-room houses. In addition, each family received 10,000 yuan to 80,000 yuan in compensation. The government granted Xiangdong village urban dweller status to 300 of its villagers

Plate 4.3 New houses under construction for immigrants in Xiangdong village

which the village sold to villagers for 3,000 yuan each for a total compensation of 900,000 yuan. In return, the village guaranteed each immigrant 0.3 *mu* of land as contracting farming land.

Tunwa village, Shanxi Province

Tunwa village was chosen as the case study for our survey in Shanxi Province. The village is administratively part of Yuanping City in the north of the central part of Shanxi, a relatively poor province in China.

Major features of the village

Geographically, Tunwa village is located deep in the mountains (Plate 4.4). It is surrounded to the north and south by far-reaching mountain ranges. In the middle of the mountain range is a deep-cut valley where Tunwa village is nestled. The village has a sizeable total land area of 37,810 *mu* (equivalent to about 2,520 hectares). However, only 1,205 *mu* (about 80 hectares) are cultivated, accounting for a mere 3.2 per cent of the village's total land area. In other words, 96.8 per cent of the village's land is non-cultivable mountainous terrain. Fortunately, a spring runs all the year round from the mountains and flows through the middle of the village; as a result Tunwa village has no worries about water shortages. This river (called Yongxing River by local villagers) divides the entire settlement into

Plate 4.4 Tunwa is a typical mountain village in Shanxi Province

two natural villages known locally as 'Southern Tunwa' and 'Northern Tunwa'. Located deep in the mountains, the village has no convenient communication and its only link with the outside world is an unpaved, rugged path. Even on clear days, driving to the village is difficult. As such, Tunwa village provides a survey of a typical Chinese mountain village.

From an economic perspective, the structure of Tunwa village can be characterized as being in a very special state, i.e., farming has been secondary not only to the village as a collective but also to individual farmers. Indeed, the income of villagers working as migrant labourers outside the village has become an important source of income for the farmers themselves.

Agriculture in Tunwa village is mainly to grain cultivation in 1,205 *mu* of farming land of which 600 *mu* are paddy fields. The remainder is dry land. The pattern of agricultural operation is the same as in most other places in the country, as farmers are engaged in crop production with each family serving as a work unit. Each family has only an average of two *mu* of arable land available for farm production, normally paddy fields and dry land, each accounting for half of the allocated land, which is scattered in separate plots. Taking the production plan in 2003 as an example, the major crops grown by the farmers were corn (960 *mu* accounting for 79.7 per cent), foxtail millet (90 *mu*, 7.5 per cent), potatoes (60 *mu*, 5 per cent), sorghum (40 *mu*, 3.3 per cent), *proso* (25 *mu*, 2 per cent), white turnip (20 *mu*, 1.7 per cent) and husked millet (10 *mu*, 0.8 per cent). The total grain output in 2002, after conversion into staple food grain, was 243,150 kilograms or an average of 201 kilograms of staple food grain per *mu*. The yield in other years was more or less the same as this. Calculating on the basis of an average 2.12 yuan per kg in normal years, the total gross income of each family from crop production was only about 400 yuan. Allowing for the payment of various taxes (about 300 yuan for each family) and production costs, villagers earned nearly nothing from crop production. The main driving force for villagers to be engaged in crop production was that they could be self-sufficient in grain supply, which makes it unnecessary for them to buy grain from the market.

Apart from growing grain, villagers have also taken full advantage of the land to grow a small number of fruit trees in the fields on the hills. According to incomplete statistics, the total output of fruit grown by the villagers in 2003 may amount to about 30 tons, with each family having 51 kilograms. Among them, 80 per cent are apples and the rest are pears and other fruit.

Besides crop cultivation, there were also some farmers engaged in livestock breeding in the village, including 13 families who raised sheep (among them, villager Zhao Wenzhou had the largest flock totalling 610 sheep in 2003; villager Chen Cunyin raised the smallest number of sheep, with only 11 in his flock) (Plate 4.5). Fourteeen farmers raised chickens (villager Zhao Cuifeng had the largest

Plate 4.5 Some Tunwa villagers increased their income by raising livestock

number of hens, raising a total of 3,000 chickens in 2003; six other farmers had relatively small-scale operations with each family raising only 500 chickens), and two farmers raised cattle (14 and 15 heads respectively). Counting all kinds of livestock raised by the villagers, there was a total of 1,913 goats and sheep, 14,300 chickens, 107 head of cattle and 150 pigs in the village at the end of 2003. They have become an important source of income for the farmers.

Due to limited agricultural resources, the farmers of Tunwa village have long begun to do business in various places across the country. In particular, a number of Tunwa villagers went to do business in Beijing; this was the most obvious phenomenon in the early period of last century. For this reason, a lot of local people simply referred to Tunwa village as 'Mini-Beijing' (*xiao Beijing*) until the founding of New China in 1949. Under the traditional influence of commerce, Tunwa village naturally became the earliest leader of the Yuanping area during the boom period of cooperatives after 1949. A Supply and Marketing Cooperative as well as a Rural Credit Cooperative (RCC) were established there. By the early 1960s, Tunwa village began to launch by-product businesses and industrial production of considerable scale in the form of collectives. Before the introduction of the Family Responsibility System with Remuneration Linked to Output (FRSRLO) in 1981, Tunwa village had set up ten machine repair plants which were of a collective nature. After 20 years of hard work the ten plants were contracted to individuals during the implementation period of the family contract responsibility system or FRSRLO. Some technical, management and marketing personnel who previously worked at the machine repair plants established their own machine repair plants, one after another, in the downtown area of Yuanping City. They further converted those machine repair plants into boiler plants to meet changes in market demand. By early 1991, the number of boiler plants in the village had grown to 11. Another 20 boiler plants were set up by Tunwa villagers who relocated to Yuanping City for various reasons such as inconvenient communication, lack of information and difficult access to electricity. Later, more enterprises moved into urban areas to seek better development opportunities. By 2002 and 2003, all the enterprises in the village had relocated to urban areas. Not a single enterprise could be found in the village during the last two surveys conducted in 2002 and 2003.

The outflow of boiler plants triggered large-scale job losses in the village. Among the 31 families and 76 labourers surveyed, 24 people were now working in other places, accounting for 31.6 per cent of the labour force sampled.

With privately owned enterprises expanding outward, and more and more villagers seeking jobs in other places, the income of the villagers has improved by a large margin in recent years. Using 2002 as an example, the net income of all the villagers of Tunwa village reached 21,000 yuan, about 8.5 times more than the national average (2,476 yuan) in the same year. Taking this into consideration, Tunwa village, though a typical village in a mountainous area, is by no means a poor one. On the contrary, it can be viewed as being quite affluent under the current national conditions of China.

The most obvious feature, in terms of the population and labour force, in Tunwa village is the people's mobility. According to statistics submitted by the village to the government, the total population and labour force of Tunwa village should be 1,519 and 496 respectively. Village leaders told me that the total population of the village was nearly 2,000 in the 1960s. For example, the total population of the village in 1969 was 1,956. The village leaders insisted that the total population of the village would have hit 3,000 without constant emigration from the village by a large number of the population and labour force. However, the actual number of population in the village at present was a little more than 1,500. I was also told that the number of permanent residents and labour force in the village were fewer than they had reported to higher level authorities because of the frequent migration of a large number of the population and labour force and because the figure reported was based on whether the villagers were registered as permanent residents. But the reality was that quite a number of villagers had been working outside the village for many years even though they were registered as permanent residents of the village. Therefore, the real number of the village population registered as residing there permanently was far fewer than the figure of 1,519 reported to the higher authorities. Take for example, the 31 farmer families sampled randomly in my research. The number of population and labour force registered as residing in the village permanently (roughly defined as more than half year's residence in the village) was only 72.9 per cent and 68.4 per cent of the official statistics.

Major changes in Tunwa village over the ten years of the survey

It had been ten years since our survey team conducted the first fieldwork in the village. What are the major changes that have taken place in Tunwa village during that decade? When we compare the various aspects of the surveys we have conducted in the village in different years, we have found many changes but the following three points are the most prominent until now.

First, village enterprises have gradually moved from the village to nearby cities. Not a single plant is left in the village after ten years of outward migration. There were a total of 23 industrial enterprises in the village in 1992, of which 17 were machine-processing plants. By 1998 when we conducted a survey on rural finance in Tunwa village, only three enterprises remained in the village. When we conducted a survey on small town and rural market development in the village and nearby towns in 2000, we found only one enterprise remained. We paid two consecutive visits to Tunwa village between 2002 and 2003 and found no traces of any enterprises in the village at all. By that time, all the enterprises, particularly the boiler-processing plants characteristic of Tunwa village, had relocated from the village to nearby cities. Most of the enterprises moved to Yuanping City which is about 20 km from Tunwa village.

Of course, the occurrence of such a phenomenon was linked to various specific reasons, such as Tunwa village's location deep in the mountains, inconvenient transport and communication, lack of information and occasional shortage of electricity supply, etc. Viewed from a broader perspective, however, this is not a completely isolated phenomenon. We found very similar trends in the development process of Xiangdong village as mentioned previously. This is a common but unavoidable trend arising from the urbanization process of Chinese villages. What we are interested in is how this change (transition) has taken place. This is where this research will focus and this will be discussed in detail in a separate chapter.

Second, with the mass migration of enterprises, there is a corresponding increase in the exodus of population and labour force from the village. When Tunwa village went all out to develop its boiler industry ten years ago, the labour force was naturally united by a great cohesive force. As plants moved out of the village, some of the labour force naturally quit the village.

Finally, great changes have taken place in the economic structure of the village and the income structure of the villagers. These are natural results of the above two changes. Such results have two implications: on the one hand, the collective revenue of the village has dropped by a large amount; on the other hand, the income of individual villagers and families has risen considerably.

If we make a simple comparison of the situation in Tunwa village in 1993 with that of 2002, according to the official reports the total revenue of the village from various economic activities amounted to 13 million yuan in 1993 while the figure was only 3.8 million yuan in 2002. Among them, the income from non-agricultural sectors totalled 11.8 million yuan in 1993 but the figure was a mere 2.5 million yuan in 2002. At that time, more than 10 million yuan income was generated from collectively-owned activities but all the income generated in 2002, although less, was directly from the production of individual farmers.

Nevertheless, the real income of individual villagers has increased greatly during the ten years. In 1993, the net per capita income of the village was only 1,563 yuan and the figure jumped dramatically to 21,000 yuan in 2002 increasing by 12.4 times or an average of 33.5 per cent annually.

Obviously, these changes have taken place in close connection with the macro background as China began to implement its reform and opening up policy, particularly its efforts to integrate the Chinese economy with the world economy in recent years. This has been discussed by many economists both at home and abroad but how should we look at this issue from a micro perspective, especially in light of the combined economic, social and cultural factors? We will discuss this in one of the following chapters.

Fuxing village (Duanjia village[12]), Hubei Province

Fuxing village is located in the south-eastern part of Hubei Province in central China. The village is administratively under the jurisdiction of Hanchuan City (county-level city), but it is also located at the boundary of Xiantao City and Tianmen City, Hubei Province. The village is 42 km from Hanchuan City proper and about 100 km from Wuhan, the capital city of Hubei Province (Plate 4.6).

General situation of the village

Fuxing village is an entirely migrant village. Although there are 35 surnames and many different lineages in the village, all the villagers moved here from Jiangxi

Plate 4.6 Fuxing village in Hubei Province

Province during the Ming Dynasty (Table 4.1). It is more than 600 years since the earliest families moved to Fuxing area and even the latest generation of migrants has settled here for more than 300 years. At present, there are altogether 900 house-holds (of which, Villager Group No. 9[13] has 91 households), 3,350 villagers (of which, Villager Group No. 9 has 227 villagers) and 1,778 agricultural labourers (of which, Villager Group No. 9 has 150 agricultural labourers). The total area of the village is 3,418 *mu* (equivalent to 227.8 hectares). Apart from the land occupied by Fuxing Company and the village infrastructure, the total area of land contracted by the villagers is 2,233 *mu* (equivalent to 148.8 hectares). The per capita arable land area of the village is only 0.67 *mu* (equivalent to 0.04 hectares); so, like most villages across China, it is a village with a sizeable population and limited farmland.

Viewed from the perspective of natural resources, Hanchuan City, where Fuxing village is located, is an important part of Jianghan Plain. Of the total land area of the city, plains account for 82.4 per cent, 13.7 per cent is taken up by lakes and rivers, and low hills (generally of a height of 60 to 120 metres) occupy only 3.9 per cent. Therefore, Hanchuan City has always been important as 'a land of fish and rice' (*yumizhixiang*) in Hubei Province and even in China; it is an important national production base for grain, cotton and fish. Since 1989, the city has been defined by the Ministry of Agriculture as the only pilot area in China for comprehensive economic reform of inland freshwater aquaculture and fisheries.

Table 4.1 Migration of the various lineages of Fuxing village

Lineage (surname)	Family origin	Time of settlement	History	Source
Duan	Taihe County, Jiangxi Province	Early Ming Dynasty	'About 600 to 700 years'	*Genealogy of Duan*
Zhang	Taihe County, Jiangxi Province	Early Ming Dynasty	Over 600 years	*Genealogy of Zhang*
Feng	Qianfeng Township, Nanchang, Jiangxi Province	'6th year of Emperor Hongzhi, Ming Dynasty'	About 600 years	*Genealogy of Feng*
Hu	Yihetian, Xinshi Township, Taihe County, Jiangxi Province	--	'Already several hundred years'(over 500 years)	*Genealogy of Hu*
Xiao	Taihe County, Jiangxi Province	'Since Emperor Hongwu of Ming Dynasty'	About 600 years	*Genealogy of Xiao*
Wang	Wangjiazhuang, Jishui County, Jiangxi Province	—	'With a history of over 600 years'	*Genealogy of Wang*
Huang	Jishui County, Jiangxi Province	'2nd year of Emperor Hongwu, Ming Dynasty'	About 600 years	*Genealogy of Huang*
Tan	Nanchang, Jiangxi Province	2nd year of Emperor Hongwu, Ming Dynasty	About 600 years	*Genealogy of Tan*
Xiong	Jinjin, Jiangxi Province	1st year of Emperor Zhengtong, Ming Dynasty	Over 570 years	*Genealogy of Xiong*

Source: Hu and Hu 1996: 22.
Note: The status of Xiong lineage is the result of field work in November 2003.

Fuxing village is no exception; for a long time, it has been a major cotton and grain production area with an emphasis on cotton cultivation, together with wheat and rice. In 1966, for example, the acreage of cotton accounted for 65 per cent of the village's total. When this village was visited in 1993, crop production had the following structure: the area where wheat and cotton were intercropped accounted for 70 per cent, the rape–rice crop rotation area accounted for 15 per cent, the early rice–late rice crop rotation area accounted for 10 per cent and the semi-late rice area accounted for 5 per cent (Hu and Hu 1996: 27). Visiting Fuxing village a decade later (late October to early November 2003), a complete reversal of the farmers' pattern of crops had taken place: the area under cotton accounted for only 27 per cent of the total and the remaining 70 per cent was used to plant rice. However, as the price of cotton rose by a larger margin than that of grain in 2003, it could be expected that more farmers would shift from rice to cotton cultivation in the years ahead.

Besides farming, one important characteristic of Fuxing village is its time-honoured tradition of iron processing. Most villagers have much experience related to the iron business, and in particular, one of the most common activities is the forging of various types of iron nails (see Plate 4.7 for example) and making iron wire. According to the records of the villagers' genealogy, iron and nail forging handicrafts have been handed down here by the ancestors of Fuxing village from their native birthplaces in Jiangxi and has a history of about 600 years. The old folk of Fuxing village told the researchers of doggerel dating

Plate 4.7 The traditional way of making iron nails in Fuxing village

back to the Ming Dynasty on the iron business in the area where Fuxing was located at that time:

> The glowing fire extended for ten miles,
> Accompanied by the tinkling of hammers;
> In the morning the work begins with forging tools in both hands,
> In the evening the whole family happily get together.

So far, this tradition has not only been inherited but also carried forward by the villagers. The reason why we say this tradition has been carried forward is that we have seen the development of Fuxing area and its people in the following ways:

1 In terms of quantity, when a survey was conducted in this village ten years ago, many households in the village were engaged in various operations related to the iron industry – some households making nails, some drawing wire, some making simple ironware. Walking through the village, everywhere you would see piles of scrap material, such as scrap iron wire and steel wire collected from all over the country. At that time, a sample of 47 households were selected from the 785 households in the village on the basis of location in the village and income levels and a detailed survey of them was carried out. The survey results showed that, among the 47 sample households, 40 were engaged in household economic activities related to the iron industry such

as scrap wire processing, hammering iron wire, forging iron, making nails, carrying out iron wire business, etc., while also undertaking agricultural activities. If those villagers working in Fuxing Steel Wire Shareholding Co. Ltd. (the name of the present Fuxing Company at that time) were also taken into account, a majority of labourers in almost all the sample households were engaged to a certain extent in activities connected with the iron industry (Hu and Hu 1996: 76).

2   Based on the estimates made by the research team at that time, the scrap iron wire used in the village in individual and private iron-processing activities alone exceeded 4,000 tons in 1993, and the total income that the villagers made from iron-related activities was about 9 million yuan (Hu and Hu 1996: 128). Viewed from the situation of 28 sample households with complete earnings data, income from cotton cultivation accounted for only 9.3 per cent, income from various non-agricultural activities other than iron industry accounted for 13.2 per cent, but iron industry-related income was as high as 77.6 per cent (Hu and Hu 1996: 106). A detailed survey of the individual and private iron operating activities of Fuxing village was carried out once again in 2003, and found that there were 80 households engaged in iron processing and 8 households specializing in iron wire processing and relatively mature 'hot mills' of considerable scale. In 2003, scrap iron and steel used by individual household activities in the village was about 8,700 tons, roughly double that of ten years earlier.

After more than a decade of accumulation and development in iron processing, Fuxing village had produced a group of rich villagers who can be regarded as the local 'nouveau riche'. Based on the incomplete statistics available, by relying on iron processing, five to six households in the village had an accumulated total household income of up to or more than 10 million yuan each. Also, there were another five to six households whose total household income had also accumulated to about 5 million yuan each.

Fuxing Science & Technology Shareholding Co. Ltd. (FSTSC) based in Fuxing village is the only listed company in Xiaogan City of which Hanchuan City forms a part in administration terms. It is a large company for Hubei Province, and moreover, it has become one of the largest metal product companies in China. The Fuxing Company will be explored in more detail later.

Major changes in the last ten years

Tremendous changes have taken place to Fuxing village in the decade since the tracking survey. These changes can be summed up as follows:

First, by the end of 2003 collective enterprises had disappeared, but individual and private enterprises had enjoyed further development in quantity and in quality.

Ten years ago when this survey was first conducted, there were three collective enterprises in the village: the Steel Shuttering Factory, the Brick and Tile Factory and the Precast Slab Factory. In November 2003, when the village was re-visited for this survey, the Steel Shuttering Factory was closed through debt, the Brick and Tile Factory was contracted to the former factory director Xia Songshan, and the Precast Slab Factory no longer existed.

Whether ten years earlier or at the time of the survey, village-run collective enterprises had not played a positive role in developing the village economy and improving the villagers' living standards. Worse, they had dragged down the village's economic development. For example, debts incurred by the village collectives were one of the adverse economic impacts caused by these enterprises. The survey found that the cumulative debts of Fuxing village created by the Steel Shuttering Factory and the Brick and Tile Factory amounted to 1.176 million yuan. By November 2003, the village had only repaid 326,000 yuan after many years of cumulative effort and still had a debt of 850,000 yuan. This remaining debt was financed through borrowing by villagers through private channels of 560,000 yuan and the remaining 290,000 yuan was borrowed from local state banks, rural credit cooperatives (RCCs), rural credit foundations (RCFs) and the local government fiscal departments. From in-depth interviews with the village cadres, it appeared that they did not regard borrowings from the non-private channels such as the state banks as debt and they had no plans or intentions of repaying any of it. Of the non-governmental borrowings from private sources, it was estimated that only about half could be repaid and the time for repayment would be very uncertain.

Since the closure of the Steel Shuttering Factory and the Precast Slab Factory, the village still nominally owns two enterprises – the Brick and Tile Factory and the Disc Spool Factory. These two enterprises have been contracted to individuals: the Brick and Tile Factory has been contracted to the former director Xia Songshan for an annual contracting fee of 140,000 yuan (including the 300 *mu* of land used as the brick field, the site for excavating clay and a 250-*mu* pond used as a specialized intensive fishery). However, various taxes and fees involved in Xia Songshan's Brick and Tile Factory still need to be paid from the 140,000 yuan contracting fee. The Disc Spool Factory has been contracted to villager Li Guocai for an annual fee of 60,000 yuan. Again, the related taxes and fees still have to be deducted from the contracting fee by the village collectives.

Visited again for a special survey, the scene at the Brick and Tile Factory was busy yet very orderly (Plate 4.8); over 30 workers were involved in various types of work. Several tractors were seen waiting in front of the kiln to load bricks. This was, of course, closely related to good market conditions at the time: Fuxing Company was at the height of its development and the renovation of the village was also at its peak; so there was a tremendous demand for bricks and tiles. Xia Songshan, director of the Brick and Tile Factory, told the researcher frankly, 'I basically need not worry about the market; I am investing 1 million yuan to construct a new kiln with 18 gates so as to increase the production capacity as soon as possible'. At present, the tile factory has a kiln with 22 gates and its output in 2002 was 20 million bricks, all used by the Fuxing Company's village renovation project. In 2002, the average price per brick was 0.12 yuan, which means that Xia Songshan's gross income in 2002 reached 2.4 million

Plate 4.8 The prosperous Brick and Tile Factory in Fuxing village in 2003

yuan. In general, the profit margin on bricks is about 25 per cent which means that Xia's net profit in 2002 would be more than 500,000 yuan. In 2003, the output of the Brick and Tile Factory could possibly reach 25 million bricks and the price could possibly increase to 0.14 yuan per brick which means Xia's gross income in 2003 could potentially reach 3.5 million yuan, an increase of more than 40 per cent compared with the previous year. Accordingly, his net profit will also exceed 800,000 yuan. In 2004, the output of bricks from the two kilns is expected to reach about 40 million bricks and, even calculated on the basis of the average price in 2003, Xia Songshan's gross income and net profit will further increase to 5.6 million yuan and 1.4 million yuan respectively. In this way, it seems there are quite good prospects for Xia Songshan from contracting the collective Brick and Tile Factory. However, these benefits have been obtained by Xia Songshan himself and the village collective still only receives a fixed income from the contracting fee.

The survey at the Disc Spool Factory found a different situation: the size of the factory was small, there were not many people in the work place and only four people were actually working (Plate 4.9). The value of the annual output of the contractor Li Guocai was about 2 million yuan and his annual profit was about 150,000 yuan.

It can be seen that, as a collective unit, no collective enterprises actually completely belong to Fuxing village. The annual contracting fee of 140,000 yuan (including all taxes and fees) that Xia Songshan hands over to the village is a kind

Plate 4.9 The Disc Spool Factory in Fuxing village is supported by Fuxing Company

of rent for the collectively-owned village land occupied by his factory. It is the same with Li Guocai's Disc Spool Factory, only his contracting fee is more a form of compensation for the use of the collectively-owned machinery and equipment than a rental for the use of the land.

In contrast to the decline of village collective enterprises, the development of private and individual businesses in Fuxing village is very impressive. These businesses have maintained a momentum of continuous growth in quantity, and more importantly, the operating scale and development level of these private and individual enterprises have improved greatly compared to their situation ten years ago.

Although it was found that private and individual iron businesses had declined to six village groups (Villager Group Nos. 1, 2, 3, 4, 12 and 13) at present from 13 groups ten years ago, the number of individual households engaged in specialized small-scale iron processing businesses was still as large at 80. Specifically, Villager Group No. 1 has 14 households, No. 2 has 13 households, No. 3 has 12 households, No. 4 has 12 households, No. 12 has 14 households and No. 13 has 15 households. In addition, three households[14] in the village had good 'cold rolling' facilities, eight households[15] had good 'hot mills' and their scale of operation had improved greatly compared to ten years earlier. In particular, four private iron businesses had achieved a high level of mechanization. In response to developments and changes in the operation of the steel wire business, five individual and private steel product shops which specialize in trading steel products have emerged in recent years.

In addition to the iron business, more than ten households specializing in commerce and construction have emerged in Fuxing village in recent years. Industrial division in Fuxing village shows a good incipient tendency.

Second, the outward expansion of Fuxing Company and its workers' residential quarters from the central factory area has become increasingly rapid and an increasing number of villager groups have become covered by the company and its development area. When a survey was conducted ten years ago, Fuxing Steel Wire Shareholding Co. Ltd. was limited to the area of Villager Group Nos. 9 and 10. When the village was re-visited later (November 2003), Villager Group Nos. 5, 6, 7, 8, 9, 10 and 11 had all been included in the development planning of the current Fuxing Company. Most villagers in these groups had been absorbed by the company and had been transformed from farmers into workers. Therefore, we found that most villagers in these groups no longer undertook individual and private iron businesses but instead joined Fuxing Company to take up corresponding work. Most of their land was also transformed from farmland into non-agricultural land. Moreover, the majority of their old houses had been demolished and the villagers had relocated to new houses built in a uniform manner by the company.

Third, despite the reduction of land area per household, the farmers' real income has increased a great deal due to the acceleration of economic restructuring. Based on the survey of the village at the end of 1994, the total annual net income of 28 sample households was 239,250 yuan in that year; the per household annual net income was 8,544 yuan and the per capita annual net income was 1,616 yuan (Hu and Hu 1996: 105), 32.4 per cent higher than the national average farmers' per capita net income of 1,221 yuan in the same year. In 2000, Zhang Zhengqun, the deputy director of Fuxing Village Committee, conducted a sample survey on ten households in the village. Through detailed accounts of the households' income and expenditure, he reached the conclusion that the per capita net income of the ten households in that year was 2,062 yuan which indicates that the farmers' per capita net income in 2000 was 27.6 per cent higher than that in 1994. However, when the survey results of Zhang Zhengqun are compared with the national per capita net income level of the rural residents in the same year, the sample survey results of Fuxing village showed a per capita net income 8.5 per cent lower than the national average (the national average of that year was 2,253 yuan). We knew that the per capita net income of Fuxing village was definitely higher than the national average. Both our survey results in 1994 and Zhang Zhengqun's survey results in 2000 referred to the net cash income after the deduction of all their expenditure from their gross income but did not include income-in-kind that the farmers obtained from agricultural activities, i.e., their stated income was visible and tangible cash income. In other words, if we calculate the income of Fuxing villagers according to the accounting standards of the National Bureau of Statistics (NBS) of China, we would get a much higher figure than the present one.

Another indicator clearly shows the degree to which the farmers' income had increased and their quality of life had improved; this is the change in the farmers' housing. Ten years ago, households living in buildings of more than one storey accounted only for about 30 per cent of the total; this percentage has doubled ten years later, reaching about 60 per cent (the percentage for the villagers in Villager Group Nos. 1, 2, 3, 4, 12 and 13 is still only about 30 per cent).

Fourth, the gap between villager groups and between villagers has widened; this can be directly seen from the quality of the villagers' houses. If we analyse in depth the level and source of income for different villager groups and villagers, this problem appears prominent. As mentioned above, there are five to six households whose wealth exceeds 10 million yuan and at least several dozen households whose wealth exceeds 1 million yuan. However, villagers in Villager Group Nos. 1, 2, 3, 4, 12, and 13 who rely mainly on cotton cultivation supplemented with traditional nail making and wire drawing, have little income and live in poor conditions.

Finally, implementation of the new institution of 'Integrating the Village with the Company' (IVWC) is the focus of study in Chapter 8.

Yantian village,[16] Guangdong Province

Located to the south of Dongguan City, Guangdong Province, Yantian village is located close to Shenzhen, being only 30 km from downtown Shenzhen (Plate 4.10), no more than 50 km from Hong Kong and 65 km from Dongguan.

In the present circumstances in China, Yantian can be regarded as a medium-sized village. At present, there are 2,796 villagers, of whom 1,769 are of the Deng lineage (63 per cent). The total population of the other 40 non-Deng lineage

Plate 4.10 Yantian village in Guangdong Province

families accounts for the remaining 37 per cent. It can be seen from these statistics that the Deng lineage has great influence in this village.

In addition, due to the rapid development of enterprises and good job opportunities in the village, a large number of migrants have been attracted to work here. According to local Public Security Department statistics, by the end of 2002 there were about 70,000 migrants employed here. The village leaders told the researcher that the actual figure was more than the registered number of persons employed and was estimated to be about 100,000.

The Deng lineage of Yantian originally lived in Nanyang, Henan Province, migrated to Jiangxi Province and then a branch moved to Dongguan. In about the reign of Hongwu during the Ming Dynasty, Deng Zhentian from the Deng lineage settled down in the present Yantian area. From Deng Zhentian to the most recent times there have been roughly 23 generations. Of them, except for Deng Zhentian's youngest son (the fourth son) who moved to Bao'an in Shenzhen, all the other descendents lived in Yantian (Plate 4.11 shows the newly built Deng Lineage Museum in the village in 2003).

What is worth special emphasis is that during the 30 years from the founding of New China to the end of the Cultural Revolution, due to the impact of incessant political movements, people of the Deng lineage in Yantian frequently left for Hong Kong. In particular, there were three major exoduses to Hong Kong: in 1957, altogether more than 400 villagers of the Deng lineage in Yantian left for Hong Kong; in 1962 about 500 people of the Deng lineage also left for Hong

Plate 4.11 Deng Lineage Museum in Yantian

Kong because of relaxed border controls; and in 1979 the number of people of the Deng lineage leaving Yantian for Hong Kong reached a record high of more than 600. Including other people of the Deng lineage who moved to Hong Kong in other years, the total number of lineage members who went across the border during the 30 years after 1949 reached about 2,000. That number is almost the same as the Deng population currently living in Yantian. Thus, the descendents of Deng Zhentian are now concentrated in places of residence: Hong Kong, Yantian village of Dongguan and Bao'an in Shenzhen. For this reason many members of Deng lineage in Hong Kong started to invest in Yantian village in the 1990s, directly boosting the rapid development of TVEs in the village. We will discuss this issue more in Chapter 7.

5 Village trust and bidding ROSCAs[1]

Reforms in the Chinese financial system have been slow relative to other reforms and, therefore, difficulties continue to emerge in the financial sector of the formal system supporting Chinese economic development. Two of the most serious problems are first, formal financing structures are not able to provide sufficient capital for the development of private enterprises and the shortfall is significant; second, they provide capital even less adequately for the needs of development in rural areas. Access to funding by rural households/farmers for non-productive activities such as purchasing durable consumer goods, house building, schooling for children, funeral and wedding expenses, medical care, etc., is almost non-existent. Formal savings and loan structures are absent. As a result, with the rapid growth of the private and rural economy in recent years, informal finance has been gradually resuscitated in various forms in both rural and urban areas. It is playing a more and more important role as a key supplement to formal finance during the critical period of reform and opening up of the Chinese economy. Despite the many restrictions imposed on informal finance by the government, various informal financial institutions and organizations are playing a key role in real life.

Brief introduction to formal and informal financial systems in China

The Chinese formal financial system

China's formal financing system is a relatively complete system made up mainly of wholly state-owned commercial banks, state policy-related banks, shareholding commercial banks, urban commercial banks and rural credit cooperatives. Rural cooperative banks have been tried in selected places, such as in Jiangsu Province, during recent years. There are trust and investment companies established by state-owned banks and government at various levels. There are securities companies run by state-owned banks, government financial authorities and state-owned enterprises. There are also finance companies operated by large state-owned enterprises as well as state-owned or joint-stock insurance companies and other non-banking financial institutions. Wholly state-owned, shareholding and urban and rural cooperative banks (cooperatives) play the dominant role in this huge system.

At present, there are four state-controlled commercial banks. They are:

1   The Industrial and Commercial Bank of China (ICBC) which was established in September 1983 on the basis of the industrial and commercial credit and bank savings business of the People's Bank of China (PBOC). At the same time, PBOC began to function solely as the central bank;
2   The Agricultural Bank of China (ABC) which was restored in February 1979;
3   The Bank of China (BOC) which was established in March 1979 on the basis of the relevant business of PBOC;
4   The China Construction Bank (CCB) which was officially established by the Ministry of Finance (MOF) in 1985.

There are three policy-related banks (all of which were established in 1994).

1   The China Development Bank (CDB);
2   The Export & Import Bank of China (Exim-Bank);
3   The Agricultural Development Bank of China (ADBC).

Starting with the Bank of Communications, China began to restore its joint-stock banks in July 1987 and successively established the CITIC (China International Trust and Investment Corporation) Industrial Bank, China Everbright Bank (CEB), China Huaxia Bank (CHB), Guangdong Development Bank (GDB), Shenzhen Development Bank Co. Ltd. (SDB), Shanghai Pudong Development Bank (SPDB), China Merchant Bank (CMB), Fujian Industrial Bank (now simply called Industrial Bank), China Minsheng Banking Corp. Ltd., the Yantai Housing Saving Bank and the Bengbu Housing Saving Bank.

Credit cooperatives in large and medium-sized cities were transformed into urban cooperative banks (UCBs) from 1996 and then into city commercial banks (CCBs). Experiments began in 2001 to transform rural credit cooperatives (RCCs) into rural cooperative banks and these experiments are still under way now.

Generally speaking, the Chinese formal banking sector is still dominated by the state banks, including state commercial banks and policy banks. The latest official statistics (*China Financial Year Book* 2004) show that state banks control more than 60 per cent of the total assets as well as the total savings of the banking sector of the country, while they also provide more than 60 per cent of the total lending. State bank employees make up more than 60 per cent of the total employees in the sector.[2] Joint-stock banks (shareholding banks) and credit cooperatives, including urban credit cooperatives (UCCs), UCBs and RCCs and RCBs form the other 30 per cent plus of the total; roughly half for each of these two categories, in terms of the indicators mentioned above.[3] Looking at the overall situation of formal rural finance, i.e., RCCs and RCBs, it accounted for 10.5 per cent of the national total financial assets, 11.2 per cent of the total lending, 12 per cent of the total savings but 28.1 per cent of the total employees.

The Chinese informal financial system

In point of fact, Chinese experience is that informal financing is much more developed than formal financing. This is particularly true in rural areas. Informal financing in China takes many forms including interpersonal lending without interest, usury, pawnbroking, private money houses, rural cooperative foundations (RCFs), and many kinds of ROSCAs.

Interpersonal lending without interest is the oldest and the most extensive form of informal financing in China. This form involves a small amount of credit based on personal relationships between relatives, friends or neighbours. The most prominent feature of the lending is that no interest is required. It has been established that interpersonal lending without interest in China first began in the Western Zhou Dynasty about 3,000 years ago (Xu 1996). Even today, when formal financing is well developed, interpersonal lending without interest based on friendship remains a vital lending channel in China. As government statistics about this are not available, estimates of the level of lending vary considerably. According to one source, interpersonal lending accounts for more than 70 per cent of total lending in rural China (Ma 2001). Of this amount, 40 to 50 per cent comes from interpersonal lending without interest (He [Heufers] and Hu 2000).

Usury also has a long history in China and it is very influential. In many places in China, it is more influential than interpersonal lending without interest. Research results indicate that usury in China also began in the Western Zhou Dynasty more than 3,000 years ago (Liu 1992). Throughout the long period since, the practice of usury has always been active. Rural society before the founding of the People's Republic of China in 1949, in particular, was more or less dominated by usury in terms of lending. In 1943, for example, of borrowing by Chinese peasants, formal lending through banks and cooperatives accounted for only 5 per cent whereas informal financing made up 95 per cent; of this usury accounted for 67.6 per cent (Li, J. 2000: 26). It was not until the late 1920s that the CPC banned usury in its revolutionary base areas, replacing it with credit cooperatives. Following the founding of the People's Republic, usury gradually disappeared throughout the country. When rural China began implementing reform policy in the late 1970s, usury reappeared. Although the Chinese government has always taken a very tough policy against the practice of usury, no great practical achievements have been made.

Pawnbroking in ancient China was non-government (or informal) financing characterized by mortgaging movables. It originated in the Western Han Dynasty (206 BC–24 AD) (Liu 1995: 6). In the period of 1912–49, pawnbroking already had shown notable signs of decline (Li, J. 2000: 62). After CPC came to power, pawnbroking was put out of business in both urban and rural areas. However, since China introduced the reform and opening up policy in the late 1970s, pawnbroking reasserted itself to some extent.

Private money houses were also one of the forms of China's traditional informal financing. They appeared and developed relatively late. Such financial organizations did not appear until the Ming Dynasty (1368–1644). At first, they functioned only as a service for the exchange of silver and copper coins before the middle and later periods of the Qing Dynasty (1644–1911). Later on, they extended to businesses such as savings, loans, deposits, remittances and banknote issue (Zhang 1987).[4] They provided service to a very wide range of clients including businessmen and small entrepreneurs in cities, and rural peddlers and farmers. After the founding of New China in 1949, private money houses were banned. In September 1984, the Qianku Town government in Cangnan County, Wenzhou, Zhejiang Province, approved the town's resident Fang Peilin's application to establish the Fangxing Money House. This was the first private money house in the People's Republic. This money house mainly provided deposit and loan services. It accepted deposits from all parts of the country but limited its loans to its own town. It allowed its interest rates to float freely. Its monthly interest rates on deposits were generally more than 0.7 percentage points higher than those of local credit cooperatives. Its interest rates on loans were more than 0.5 percentage points higher but about one percentage point lower than usury in the area. The money house operated for four months involving 2.1 million yuan in deposits and loans before being forcibly closed by the state financial administrative authorities (Xiao 1997). Even today private money houses are still banned by the government and there is not a single one operating in the open in China.[5]

It should be said that RCFs which appeared around 1984 were a special administrative institutional arrangement. RCFs were neither entirely non-governmental financial organizations or institutions, nor a financial institutional option of the government in the true sense of the term. They were, however, community-based mutual aid cooperative organizations combining rural collective and individual shares.[6] The central authorities suggested that RCFs should be non-profit, should not provide deposit and loan services and should conduct financing from within. However, as financial institutions, RCFs found it hard to comply. Therefore, it was not long before they grew to a rather large scale.[7] They played a positive role in effectively managing rural collective funds, supporting agricultural production and the development of TVEs and curtailing rural usury. However, during the Asian financial crisis, the central government decided in January 1999 to close and ban RCFs nationwide. They merged good RCFs with RCCs. This was completed by the end of 2002 (Zhang and Heufers 2002: 11, 220).

As traditional mutual aid cooperative financial organizations, rotating savings and credit associations (ROSCAs) first appeared during the Tang (618–907) and Song (960–1279) dynasties (Wang 1935: 5; Chen 1996: 173; Li, J. 2000: 116). So they have a history of more than 1,000 years. As a matter of fact, ROSCAs take many forms but people more often relate them to non-governmental financing, especially rural financing.

Financing-oriented ROSCAs take different forms. They include rotating savings and credit associations in terms of whose money is used by its members on a rotating basis ('rotating associations'); 'dice-shaking associations' that shake dice to decide the order of granting loans; 'bidding associations' that decide the order of granting loans through bidding for the interest; and 'escalating associations' which are a mixture of large and small associations.

As escalating associations have caused problems in practice, central government is opposed to anyone taking part in any form of activity relating to escalating associations. The central government does not have a clear-cut attitude towards rotating associations, dice-shaking associations and bidding associations, but one thing is clear: it does not encourage the development of these non-governmental financial organizations. In reality, one more thing is also clear: no matter what attitude the government takes, the enthusiasm of the general public for ROSCAs will not diminish. Moreover, the positive role of ROSCAs cannot be denied. This is at least true in rural Wenzhou in southern Zhejiang Province.

A village in Zhejiang Province where we have been conducting follow-up research since 1993 can be taken as an example. This chapter will first analyse bidding ROSCAs as a type of ROSCA as it is an informal financial system with long historical traditions in China.

The development of ROSCAs in Xiangdong village

From the end of September to early October 2002, I undertook two weeks of research into ROSCAs in Xiangdong village (the village is attached to Qianku Town, Cangnan County of Zhejiang Province). In order to gain a better understanding of the situation, I even joined one of the ROSCAs in the village by becoming a formal member. This experience enabled me to understand better the specific operating rules and features of this private financial institution in rural China.

Through the research, the following features were found among the ROSCAs currently established in Xiangdong village. First, the number of ROSCAs is high and they have a wide range. Almost all the local residents have taken part in a ROSCA and most of them have been involved in more than one. Second, the format of the ROSCA is always very simple. Most of them, with very few exceptions, are bidding ROSCAs. Third, the ROSCAs are very clearly community based. Most of the members are from the same village; it is not common for somebody from another village to become a member. Fourth, the aim of the villagers in establishing or taking part in the ROSCAs is mainly to finance family emergencies in their daily lives. The percentage of villagers who try to raise funds for businesses through this means is relatively low. Fifth, the members are very trustworthy and bad debts rarely occur; the financial risk is very limited.

General background

When I arrived in Xiangdong village at the end of September 2002, many of the household heads were away from their homes on business trips. The choice of households to study was based on chance and opportunity. Households were visited in succession; if the head of the family was at home, that household was included in the sample. If only the elderly or children were at home and they were unable to give information regarding the economic situation of the family or the ROSCAs, there was no choice but to exclude that household. Given this limitation, a total of 29 families in the village were interviewed of whom 24 were involved in the ROSCAs (see Table 5.1). The percentage of households that were found to be part of a ROSCA was 82.8 per cent (but cadres in the village insisted that the actual percentage should be at least 90 per cent, higher than the sample result).

The number of ROSCAs is large; the scale of the finance is considerable

As there is no documented history of ROSCAs in Xiangdong village, information was collected from the elderly in the village. As far as they knew from oral history, the practice of Xiangdong villagers raising funds by way of self-organized financial associations was vague, i.e., ROSCAs predate the Qing dynasty, but nobody knew how far back the custom went. Even if counting just from the early years

Table 5.1 General information on Xiangdong village ROSCAs development

Household reference number	Number of ROSCAs involved in during the past 10 years	Number of ROSCAs currently involved in	The established duration of current ROSCA (months)	Maximum amount involved in participating in a ROSCA (yuan)
1	12	2	3	12,000
2	11	2	3	30,000
3	2	1	2	5,000
4	13	2	3	10,000
5	8	2	3	10,000
6	10	2	3	10,000
7	5	1	1	2,000
8	3	1	2	6,500
9	39	5	3	30,000
10	12	1	1	6,000
11	21	6	3	41,700
12	4	1	3	10,000
13	6	2	3	30,000
14	11	1	2	10,000
15	28	1	3	10,000
16	7	3	3	20,000
17	4	1	1	5,000
18	3	1	3	10,000
19	6	2	3	14,000
20	3	2	1	1,000
21	4	2	3	50,000
22	1	1	3	50,000
23	7	3	3	10,000
24	4	1	2	6,000
Average	9.3	1.7	2–3	14,133

Source: Field survey in Xiangdong village.

of the Qing dynasty, there would be a history of more than 350 years. During the Nationalist period, there was a sharp fall in the number of ROSCAs throughout the country. According to research by the Agricultural Economy Department of the Central Agricultural Research Institute,[8] there was an average of only two ROSCAs per county in 1934. The average number of ROSCAs in Zhejiang Province was slightly higher at 3.4 per county in the 46 counties of the province. In Jiangsu Province, the average number of ROSCAs was the highest, at 6.1 per county in the 47 counties within the province. The average was nearly twice that of Zhejiang Province. However, based on the personal experience of elderly villagers, Xiangdong village normally had two or three ROSCAs in any given year in the 1930s (most of the ROSCAs at that time were 'non-profit' ROSCAs that did not charge any interest). This suggests that the research by the Central Agricultural Research Institute did not include this county, of which Xiangdong village is a part. Xiangdong village was not in Cangnan county at that time.

During the early years of new China, due to the enormous political change in the country, ROSCAs became inactive in Xiangdong village. But a few years later, at the end of the 1950s and the beginning of the 1960s, they again became common in the village. Even during the Cultural Revolution, ROSCAs managed to survive in Xiangdong village. However, most of those ROSCAs were interest-free and were purely a financial system providing mutual support. Since the reform and opening up era, ROSCAs have multiplied in the village. In the 1980s, particularly, ROSCAs were at their most popular. Almost every family became the founder of a ROSCA and there were at least 100 ROSCAs in the village. Due to the ROSCAs' rapid and uncontrolled growth, several instances occurred of people absconding with the money they raised through the ROSCAs. But this was quickly self-corrected with responsible management of ROSCAs after 1990.

Based on our research during the ten years after 1990, the 24 households interviewed had taken part, on average, in nearly 10 (9.3) ROSCAs (Table 5.1). Almost all of them took part in a ROSCA each year. Taking into account that the duration for most ROSCAs is longer than one year, it is not surprising to learn that some people took part in two or more ROSCAs at the same time. During our research, we found that the sample households were involved in an average of nearly two (1.7) ROSCAs at the same time. However, the number of ROSCAs in which the households took part varied widely. Some households were involved in five or six ROSCAs at the same time while most of them were involved in only one or two (Table 5.1).

Extrapolating estimates based on the data collected from the village shows a ROSCA participation rate of 82.8 per cent which indicates that 263 out of 318 households in the whole village were involved in the ROSCAs. We were also aware that the 45 families from Taikou village, Hongkou Township, Taishun County, who had arrived in the village recently as a result of the new migration policy, did not enjoy the same credit facilities as established residents because they were new to the area and they were not related to the Xiang family. They had not established their creditworthiness with the local residents in their new settlement. They were able neither to join any ROSCA run by the villagers nor could they start any ROSCAs of their own.

Thus, we have had to exclude the newcomer households from our estimate. In this way, we can come to the conclusion that the number of households involved in ROSCAs was approximately 226. If the average number of households participating in one ROSCA is 13, then there are at least 17 ROSCAs running simultaneously in the village throughout the year. Since the average number of ROSCAs for each household is 1.7, the number of ROSCAs should be at least as many as $17 \times 1.7 = 29$. Taking into account the overlap problem of villagers joining the ROSCA and others who join as out-of-village residents or friends and family of Xiangdong villagers, if this kind of ROSCA accounts for 20 per cent of the total number of ROSCAs, then the total number of ROSCAs in the village should be $29 + 7$. That makes the total number of ROSCAs in Xiangdong village approximately 36.

Based on the information we collected from the sample households, the average amount of money in each large ROSCA each period (normally of two months duration) is 14,000 yuan, compared to 1,000–6,000 yuan for small ones. Taking both large and small ROSCAs together gives an average of 6,000 yuan. If the average duration of each ROSCA is two years, then the funds raised each year by ROSCAs alone as a means of private finance in Xiangdong village is as much as: 6,000 yuan per ROSCA each time $\times$ 36 ROSCAs $\times$ 6 times each year (the average times per year for a household to have access to the fund, the period for each ROSCA/fund being 2 years) = 1,296,000 yuan. Our estimate is a conservative one. The actual amount of finance is almost certainly higher than our estimate.[9]

The form of these ROSCAs is simple: most of them are bidding ROSCAs

From both our general household research and our interviews of villagers, we found that bidding ROSCAs are the commonest form in Xiangdong. This is closely related to another feature of finance in the village, even though village ROSCAs are in such an advanced state, private lending is still actively practised. As long as people do not need the money quickly for an emergency, a number of them will still choose to seek out a private loan as a means of raising money, but if an emergency occurs the chosen source is the bidding ROSCA. If you are willing to pay higher interest than others, you will almost certainly receive the required money in time. You do not need to rely on 'having access to the fund in turns' (rotating ROSCAs) or 'having access to the fund by chance' (dice-shaking ROSCAs). Above all, the most important feature of the bidding ROSCA is that it can solve emergencies. This also shows that the most important purpose of the Xiangdong villagers' mutual-aid fund is for family emergencies rather than for business. We will discuss this later in the chapter.

A bidding ROSCA is a rural private finance cooperative which allows registered members to rotate their access to collective funds through a bidding system. The higher the interest offered as a bid, the sooner the member gets to use the fund.

The founder of the ROSCA normally is the first to benefit from the collective fund. He/she is called 'the head of the association' and the rest of the members are called 'the feet of the association'. The following is the written statement given to me when I joined one of the common bidding ROSCAs in Xiangdong village as a 'villager' (Table 5.2). As I came from outside the village and had no local credit history, I could only join as part of the household of Xiang Fanghuai, the head of the village, and he shared the costs with me. To the other members, it was clear that any risk taken due to my membership would be borne by Xiang Fanghuai.

The reason villager Xiang Xianliang set up this ROSCA was to repay a loan for his medical treatment. He had undertaken a high-interest loan of 6,000 yuan and his interest was more than 100 yuan per month. With his family's financial situation, it would have been difficult for him to pay off his debt. After setting up his ROSCA, he was able to make a one-off payment and clear his debt. As the head of the ROSCA, he did not have to worry about interest. From the following analysis (Table 5.3), we can see clearly how the head benefits from setting up a ROSCA.

Table 5.3 shows how Xiang Xianliang, the head, can take advantage of being the first one to have access to the fund. On the day the ROSCA was founded, he was able to take 6,000 yuan cash from the other members of the ROSCA. It was not until two months later that he needed to pay the first 500 yuan. He could pay this 500 yuan with part of the money he had already got from the others. Another two months later, he needed to pay his second 500 yuan, and he had two years to pay the 6,000 yuan he gained from the others in instalments. It is clear that

Table 5.2 Statement for Xiang Xianliang's ROSCA

Member order	Name	Date of using the fund (lunar calendar equivalent)	Interest paid for gaining the fund (yuan)	Amount received (yuan)
Head	Xiang Xianliang	10 April 2002	0.0	6,000.0
1	Xiang Fangchong	10 June 2002	70.0	6,000.0
2	Xiang Fangwei	10 August 2002	80.5	6,070.0
3	Xiang Lixian	10 October 2002	65.8	6,150.5
4	Huang Yi	10 December 2002	60.5	6,216.3
5	Xiang Yanbin	10 February 2003	68.9	6,276.8
6	Zhang Lanfen	10 April 2003	48.2	6,345.7
7	Xiang Fangkeng	10 June 2003	58.0	6,393.9
8	Xiang Xianfeng	10 August 2003	62.8	6,451.9
9	Xiang Binshi	10 October 2003	58.0	6,514.7
10	Xiang Xianzang	10 December 2003	80.0	6,572.7
11	Xiang Xianxiang	10 February 2004	59.0	6,652.7
12	Xiang Fanghuai, Hu Biliang	10 April 2004	0.0	6,711.7

Source: Field survey in Xiangdong village.
Notes:
a 'The ROSCA was founded on 10 April 2002 (lunar calendar equivalent), with total shares of 13; the membership fee is payable once every other month and the amount for each share is 500 yuan per payment. After the bidding process, the interest will be added. The time for the bidding will be at 12 noon on the due date. The bidding will take place on time. If anybody is late, it is deemed to be an abstention from bidding. Thank you for your co-operation'.
b The head of the association has the right to first access to the fund without having to pay interest.

Table 5.3 A structural analysis of the author's ROSCA (Xiang Xianliang's ROSCA)

Bid order	Name	Amount paid to the ROSCA each time (yuan)													Total payable (yuan)	Total received amount (yuan)
		1	2	3	4	5	6	7	8	9	10	11	12	13		
Head	Xiang Xianliang	* 0.0	500.0	500.0	500.0	500.0	500.0	500.0	500.0	500.0	500.0	500.0	500.0	500.0	6,000.0	6,000.0
1	Xiang Fangchong	500.0	*70.0	570.0	570.0	570.0	570.0	570.0	570.0	570.0	570.0	570.0	570.0	570.0	6,770.0	6,000.0
2	Xiang Fangwei	500.0	500.0	*80.5	580.5	580.5	580.5	580.5	580.5	580.5	580.5	580.5	580.5	580.5	6,805.0	6,070.0
3	Xiang Lixian	500.0	500.0	500.0	*65.8	565.8	565.8	565.8	565.8	565.8	565.8	565.8	565.8	565.8	6,592.2	6,150.5
4	Huang Yi	500.0	500.0	500.0	500.0	*60.5	560.5	560.5	560.5	560.5	560.5	560.5	560.5	560.5	6,484.0	6,216.3
5	Xiang Yanbin	500.0	500.0	500.0	500.0	500.0	*68.9	568.9	568.9	568.9	568.9	568.9	568.9	568.9	6,482.3	6,276.8
6	Zhang Lanfen	500.0	500.0	500.0	500.0	500.0	500.0	*48.2	548.2	548.2	548.2	548.2	548.2	548.2	6,289.2	6,345.7
7	Xiang Fangkeng	500.0	500.0	500.0	500.0	500.0	500.0	500.0	*58.0	558.0	558.0	558.0	558.0	558.0	6,290.0	6,393.9
8	Xiang Xianfeng	500.0	500.0	500.0	500.0	500.0	500.0	500.0	500.0	*62.8	562.8	562.8	562.8	562.8	6,251.2	6,451.9
9	Xiang Binshi	500.0	500.0	500.0	500.0	500.0	500.0	500.0	500.0	500.0	*58	558.0	558.0	558.0	6,174.0	6,514.7
10	Xiang Xianzang	500.0	500.0	500.0	500.0	500.0	500.0	500.0	500.0	500.0	500.0	*80.0	580.0	580.0	6,160.0	6,572.7
11	Xiang Xianxiang	500.0	500.0	500.0	500.0	500.0	500.0	500.0	500.0	500.0	500.0	500.0	*59.0	559.0	6,059.0	6,652.7
12	Xiang Fanghuai, Hu Biliang	500.0	500.0	500.0	500.0	500.0	500.0	500.0	500.0	500.0	500.0	500.0	500.0	*0.0	6,000.0	6,711.7

Source: Field survey data from Xiangdong village.
Note: * Interest after winning the bid for using the fund (yuan).

Xiang Xianliang, as head, can use the 6,000 yuan from others without having to pay interest during the period of two years. This helps him to gain plenty of time and opportunity to solve other problems caused by a shortage of cash. This is his biggest benefit as the head of a ROSCA.

Of course, the other members (the 'feet') are not as lucky as he is: in order to gain access to the collective fund, they need to pay interest (i.e., the cost of capital). In each ROSCA, only one member, the founder of the ROSCA or using the jargon, 'the head', does not need to pay interest to use the fund and he/she has the first right to the fund. This helps us to understand why villagers are enthusiastic about organizing ROSCAs and acting as the head. It does not matter who organizes the ROSCA and acts as the head, the key is that there are at least ten members who want to take part in it and pay regularly and on time. The villager who wants to set up the ROSCA will need to have some basic resources, such as his/her reputation and credibility in the village, family influence, a wide enough circle of friends and family members, etc. These elements restrict the number of ROSCAs and heads. Under these circumstances, it is not an easy task to set up a ROSCA and to be 'the head'.

We use another completed ROSCA as an example to further analyse the ROSCA system in Xiangdong village (Table 5.4). As the head of this ROSCA was called Xiang Sujiao, we refer to this as Xiang Sujiao's ROSCA. It was set up on 17 December 1999 (lunar calendar) and it was reaching its completion when I arrived in the village for the research. It was wrapped up according to plan on 17 September 2002 (lunar calendar) after having run for two years and nine months.

Xiang Sujiao was born in Xiangdong village, but she married into a neighbouring village, the Li's village which is roughly 2 or 3 km away from Xiangdong. She

Table 5.4 Statement for Xiang Sujiao's ROSCA

Member order	Name	Date of using the fund (lunar year equivalent)	Bidding amount (yuan)	Amount received (yuan)
Head	Xiang Sujiao	17 December 1999	0.0	22,000.0
1	Xiang Yanshen	17 March 2002	252.0	24,396.6
2	Xiang Weiwei	17 September 2002	0.0	24,850.6
3	Fang Zongling	17 December 2000	310.0	23,034.6
4	Chen Rusheng	17 June 2001	258.0	23,632.6
5	Chen Rujian	17 September 2001	268.0	23,890.6
6	Xiang Yanlun	17 September 2000	295.8	22,738.8
7	Xiang Zhuxian	17 March 2000	438.8	22,000.0
8	Wu Xiaohua	17 June 2002	202.0	24,648.6
9	Xiang Qiuhua	17 June 2000	300.0	22,438.8
10	Xiang Xiaoli	17 March 2001	288.0	23,344.6
11	Li Xuebin	17 December 2001	238.0	24,158.6

Source: Field survey in Xiangdong village.
Note:
'The ROSCA was set up on 17 December1999 (lunar calendar equivalent) with a total of 12 shares (include the head). The period is 3 months and each share pays 2,000 yuan every three months to the ROSCA. The time for the bidding will be at 1pm on the due date. Let us hope we have a good start and a good outcome. Thank you for your co-operation'.

nevertheless managed to set up this ROSCA in Xiangdong. She set up the ROSCA because business losses by her husband had resulted in debts.

Based on the above basic data and the ROSCA's operating regulations, we have the following initial structural analysis findings. From Table 5.5, we can clearly see the order of the members having access to the fund, the interest bid by each member at each bidding interval, the total paid amount, and the total repaid amount for each member.

In a bidding ROSCA, the winning bidder at any bidding interval is the member willing to pay the highest rate of interest for the use of the funds of the ROSCA. The change of the interest rate during the running of a ROSCA is a key feature. The interest offered at each bidding interval varies. It is affected by interest rates set by the central bank authority and by local economic conditions. It is closely linked to how urgently the 'foot' members need the capital. Amongst the factors, the last is the most direct and important and this is the 'charm' of a bidding ROSCA: the 'foot' members who need money urgently are normally willing to offer higher interest for the capital in order to get the money as soon as possible; those who can set money aside can gain interest from their capital. Participants feel they are helping others meet their emergency needs and at the same time are making some money. Of course, from an economic point of view, participants mainly act as supporters to help the head of the association since they have to take the risk of not getting back their money including their principal, while they may also lose their capital liquidity for a period of time if they only get funds in the late phase of the ROSCA.

Taking Xiang Sujiao's ROSCA as the example, the easiest way to calculate interest rates is simply to ignore the impact of the factor of time on capital utilization. Thus, the average interest rate = total interest payment (income)/total funds received from the association (total funds paid to the association)/a certain period of time (annual, quarterly, monthly and so on, see Table 5.6).

If we take the time factor into consideration, we then need to calculate the current value of the cashflow of the ROSCA based on the benchmark interest rates of the banks.[10] If the comparative interest rates of savings and lending from the formal banking system are also considered, we then need to have the third method for the calculation.[11] The general conclusion from all these economic calculations shows that even the 'feet' who gain the most interest income from this practice are still losers according to capital market principles. This denotes that mutual help is the core of ROSCAs in Xiangdong village.

The range of the ROSCAs is limited to the villagers, nearby friends and family members

Inquiring into the identity of the ROSCAs' members in Xiangdong village, we found that almost all of them fell into one of three categories. First, residents of the village; second, family relations (some of them are relatives of the villagers who live in the same village or are from other villages); third, co-workers or friends who live nearby.

Table 5.5 A structural analysis of Xiang Sujiao's ROSCA

Order	Name	Amount paid to the ROSCA each time (yuan)												Total paid (yuan)	Total received (yuan)
		1	2	3	4	5	6	7	8	9	10	11	12		
Head	Xiang Sujiao	*0.0	2,000.0	2,000.0	2,000.0	2,000.0	2,000.0	2,000.0	2,000.0	2,000.0	2,000.0	2,000.0	2,000.0	22,000.0	22,000
1	Xiang Zhuxian	2,000.0	*438.8	2,438.8	2,438.8	2,438.8	2,438.8	2,438.8	2,438.8	2,438.8	2,438.8	2,438.8	2,438.8	26,388.0	22,000
2	Xiang Qiuhua	2,000.0	2,000.0	*300.0	2,000.0	2,300.0	2,300.0	2,300.0	2,300.0	2,300.0	2,300.0	2,300.0	2,300.0	24,700.0	22,438.8
3	Xiang Yanlun	2,000.0	2,000.0	2,000.0	*295.8	2,295.8	2,295.8	2,295.8	2,295.8	2,295.8	2,295.8	2,295.8	2,295.8	24,366.4	22,738.8
4	Fang Zongling	2,000.0	2,000.0	2,000.0	2,000.0	*310.0	2,310.0	2,310.0	2,310.0	2,310.0	2,310.0	2,310.0	2,310.0	24,170.0	23,034.6
5	Xiang Xiaoli	2,000.0	2,000.0	2,000.0	2,000.0	2,000.0	*288.0	2,288.0	2,288.0	2,288.0	2,288.0	2,288.0	2,288.0	23,728.0	23,344.6
6	Chen Rusheng	2,000.0	2,000.0	2,000.0	2,000.0	2,000.0	2,000.0	*258	2,258.0	2,258.0	2,258.0	2,258.0	2,258.0	23,290.0	23,632.6
7	Chen Rujian	2,000.0	2,000.0	2,000.0	2,000.0	2,000.0	2,000.0	2,000.0	*268	2,268.0	2,268.0	2,268.0	2,268.0	23,072.0	23,890.6
8	Li Xuebin	2,000.0	2,000.0	2,000.0	2,000.0	2,000.0	2,000.0	2,000.0	2,000.0	*238.0	2,238.0	2,238.0	2,238.0	22,714.0	24,158.6
9	Xiang Yanshen	2,000.0	2,000.0	2,000.0	2,000.0	2,000.0	2,000.0	2,000.0	2,000.0	2,000.0	*252.0	2 252.0	2 252.0	22,504.0	24,396.6
10	Wu Xiaohua	2,000.0	2,000.0	2,000.0	2,000.0	2,000.0	2,000.0	2,000.0	2,000.0	2,000.0	2,000.0	*202.0	2 202.0	22,202.0	24,648.6
11	Xiang Weiwei	2,000.0	2,000.0	2,000.0	2,000.0	2,000.0	2,000.0	2,000.0	2,000.0	2,000.0	2,000.0	2,000.0	*0.0	22,000.0	24,850.6

Source: Field survey in Xiangdong village.
Note: * indicates the interest for winning the bid to use the fund (yuan).

Table 5.6 Xiang Sujiao's ROSCA interest analysis

Order	Name	Date for access to funds (lunar calendar equivalent)	Bidding interest (yuan)	Amount received (yuan)	Amount paid (yuan)	Net interest paid (or received)	Annual interest rates (%)
Head	Xiang Sujiao	17 December 1999	0.0	22,000.0	22,000.0	0.0	0.00
1	Xiang Zhuxian	17 March 2000	438.8	22,000.0	26,388.0	− 4,388.0	7.24
2	Xiang Qiuhua	17 June 2000	300.0	22,438.8	24,700.0	− 2,261.2	3.68
3	Xiang Yanlun	17 September 2000	295.8	22,738.8	24,366.4	− 1,627.6	2.60
4	Fang Zongling	17 December 2000	310.0	23,034.6	24 ,170.0	− 1,135.4	1.80
5	Xiang Xiaoli	17 March 2001	288.0	23,344.6	23,728.0	− 383.4	0.15
6	Chen Rusheng	17 June 2001	258.0	23,632.6	23,290.0	342.6	0.60
7	Chen Rujian	17 September 2001	268.0	23,890.6	23,072.0	818.6	1.28
8	Li Xuebin	17 December 2001	238.0	24,158.6	22,714.0	1,444.6	2.32
9	Xiang Yanshen	17 March 2002	252.0	24,396.6	22,504.0	1,892.6	3.08
10	Wu Xiaohua	17 June 2002	202.0	24,648.6	22,202.0	2,446.6	4.00
11	Xiang Weiwei	17 September 2002	0.0	24,850.6	22,000.0	2,850.6	4.72

Source: Field survey in Xiangdong village.

Again, the two ROSCAs that we are familiar with will be used as examples. In the ROSCA I joined (Xiang Xianliang's ROSCA), I was the only sub-member who was from outside the village. I was accepted only because I was introduced and backed by the head of the village. The rest of the members were residents in the village, including two who had been residents in the village in the past and now worked in Qianku Town which is only 2 km away. Apart from the elder brother of the head of the ROSCA, the rest of the members are not directly related, just fellow villagers of Xiangdong. On the other hand, Xiang Sujiao's ROSCA consisted mainly of her co-workers and relations. Of the 11 members, four are relatives of the head (36 per cent of members), four were her co-workers (another 36 per cent), the remaining three were Xiangdong villagers and were her neighbours or friends back in her mother's home village. The main link in Xiang Xianliang's ROSCA was that there were only villagers from the same village, while Xiang Sujiao's is based on her close friends and relatives (Table 5.7).

In some ROSCAs, all members are relatives. To cite the current village party general-secretary Xiang Zujian's ROSCA as an example, it was set up on 3 August 2001 (lunar calendar). The interval is three months and it was due to finish by 3 November 2004 (lunar calendar). The members who did not have access to the collective fund paid 3,000 yuan each time. For those who did, the one-off payment for the fund was more than 36,000 yuan: this is a relatively large ROSCA in the village.

Of the members of this ROSCA, apart from one village cadre and a co-worker of the head, the others were all direct relatives of the head (Table 5.8). All of them were close family members including his own children, brothers, cousins and his

Table 5.7 Relationships between members and the head of ROSCAs

Xiang Xianliang's ROSCA		Xiang Sujiao's ROSCA	
Member	Relationship to ROSCA head	Member	Relationship to ROSCA head
Xiang Xianxiang	Elder brother of the head, now living in Qianku town, a supply salesman	Xiang Weiwei	Sister
Xiang Fanghuai, Hu Biliang	Xiang Fanghuai and the head are neighbours	Fang Zongling	Brother-in-law, husband of Xiang Weiwei
Zhang Lanfen	Wife of Xiang Fanghuai, neighbour	Xiang Zuxian	Uncle on her parents' side, lives in Xiangdong village
Xiang Fangkeng	Elder brother of Xiang Fanghuai, lives in the same village as the head	Xiang Yanlun	Cousin on her parents' side, lives in Xiangdong village
Xiang Yanbin	Villager in the same village	Wu Xiaohua	Former co-worker, lives in Li village which the head married into
Xiang Xianzang	Villager in the same village	Li Xuebin	Former co-worker, lives in Li village
Xiang Fang-chong	Villager in the same village	Xiang Qiuhua	Former co-worker, lives in Xiangdong village where the head's parents reside
Huang Yi	Villager in the same village	Xiang Xiaoli	Former co-worker, lives in Xiangdong village where the head's parents reside
Xiang Binshi	Newly from Xikuo village, from the same clan family as the head	Chen Rusheng	Neighbour, lives in Xiangdong village where the head's parents reside
Xiang Xianfeng	Newly from Xikuo village, from the same clan family as the head	Chen Rujian	Neighbour, lives in Xiangdong village where the head's parents reside, brother of Chen Rusheng
Xiang Lixian	Newly from Xikuo Village, from the same clan family as the head	Xiang Yanshen	Friend, lives in Xiangdong village where the head's parents reside
Xiang Fangwei	Originally from Xiangdong village, now works in Qianku Town Hospital		

Source: Field survey in Xiangdong village.

Table 5.8 Relationships between members and the head in Xiang Zujian's ROSCA

Name	Relationship with the head
Xiang Zujian (general secretary of the party in the village)	The head
Wang Jinbu	Son, lives in Qianku town
Xiang Lijiao	Daughter, married into Xin'an Township, 2 km from Xiangdong village
Xiang Zuqing	Younger brother
Xiang Zuzhang	Cousin
Xiang Fangxuan	Son-in-law of the head's older brother, from same village
Xie Zuoguang	Cousin of the head's uncle
Xie Zuofang	Cousin of the head's uncle
Xie Zuoyin	Cousin of the head's uncle
Xie Zuokeng	Cousin of the head's uncle
Zhang Zongli	Younger brother-in-law
Su Xiaoying	Daughter of the head's wife's brother, married into nearby Jinxiang Town
Wang Fenyu	Cadre in the same village, colleague

Source: Field survey in Xiangdong village.

wife's relations. This was a closely related bidding ROSCA. During the research period in the village, the ROSCA held four bidding sessions and the winning bidders did not have to offer very high rates. They were low compared to interest rates of other ROSCAs during the same period of time. We might well infer that the closer the relationship, the lower the interest charged for using the capital, and the stronger is the co-operative spirit.

The purpose of the ROSCAs is to provide emergency funds for the villagers' daily lives, not to make a profit

The research on the ROSCAs in Xiangdong village indicates that the purpose for villagers of setting up a ROSCA or joining one is not to obtain loans for profitable activities but to provide emergency funds. This point is clearly shown in the data that was collected (Table 5.9).

The information in Table 5.9 covers a few of the ROSCAs in Xiangdong. Taking into account additional information from the research, it was found that there are four main purposes for Xiangdong villagers to set up ROSCAs:

1   Raising funds to meet family needs in emergencies or unexpected situations, for example, medical treatment for one of the family members, or tuition and other expenses to send a child to school. Generally speaking, families who do not have such funds are economically disadvantaged. The amount of share capital they can offer is small and consequently the size of the ROSCA they can join is also small. Most of their ROSCAs are limited to 1,000 yuan

Table 5.9 Reasons for setting up a ROSCA in Xiangdong village

ROSCA head	Reason for establishing the ROSCA	Size of the ROSCA (yuan)	
Xiang Zuchun	Poor health, in need of money for medical treatment	2,000	20 shares
Xiang Xianlai	Medical treatment for son	6,500	13 shares
Xiang Zumei	Their handicapped son and old age (73 years old and 66 for his wife)	6,000	25 shares
Xiang Yanyi	Medical treatment for his wife	5,000	10 shares
Xiang Yandang	Medical treatment for his wife	1,000	10 shares
Xiang Zuwei	Sending a child to university	5,000	10 shares
Guan Zhonglin	Sending a child to university	14,000	10 shares
Chen Ruishen	Sending a child to high school	10,000	10 shares
Lin Jinrong	Son's marriage	2,000	10 shares
Li Hongxiu	Buying a house in Xiangdong (working in Xiangdong most of the year, residency nearby Li village)	10,000	10 shares
Xiang Fanglian	Loss in his factory, raising money to pay his debt	10,000	10 shares
Xiang Yancun	Setting up a business in supplying goods	10,000	10 shares
Xiang Yanqian	Business	20,000	10 shares
Xiang Zurong	Frog farm business	30,000	10 shares
Zheng Jiashen	Business	50,000	10 shares

Source: Field survey in Xiangdong village.
Note: The number of shares in the ROSCAs does not include that of the head.

per fund payment for a period of 3 months. Members of their ROSCAs are mostly relatives of the head, neighbours and cadres in the village. Because the amount involved is small and members are willing to join for the sake of helping the poor and vulnerable, it is not difficult for them to set up a ROSCA. There are disadvantaged households in the village that set up ROSCAs every year. Some of them would have no alternative other than the benefits from ROSCAs; these villagers really depend on their ROSCAs. For example, for the previous six years, Xiang Zumei depended for his basic livelihood on setting up ROSCAs and being the head of them. Every year, he set up two or three ROSCAs. Disadvantaged villagers have tended to set up a great number of the ROSCAs in the village.

2   Raising funds for important family commitments. For example, building a new house for the family, the son or the daughter's wedding and children going to universities. The households who set up ROSCAs for these reasons are normally those who can manage their daily lives but they lack reserves for important family occasions and need the funds from their ROSCAs. The size of these ROSCAs must be sufficient for major purposes. In Xiangdong village, such ROSCAs normally can raise funds from 10,000 to 30,000 yuan.

3   Raising funds for business capital or setting up a factory. Members of such ROSCAs normally enjoy better financial conditions. The head wants more money injected into the business for expansion. Meanwhile, 'foot' members can also benefit from his/her business growth. Such ROSCAs normally can raise over 30,000 yuan from each member. A few of them can even raise 50,000 yuan from each member.

4   Raising funds for investment. It is possible to use the funds raised by establishing a ROSCA to invest in other ROSCAs and make a profit by way of interest, i.e., to gain capital through a ROSCA and make profits by using other people's funds. This is rarely, if ever, seen in Xiangdong village because nobody wants to join such a ROSCA or to support such a head.

These four reasons illustrate that ROSCAs in Xiangdong village exist for mutual aid and not for profit. Of the members interviewed, about 50 per cent were in the first group, 40 per cent in the second and 10 per cent in the third. The fourth group is a theoretical possibility rather than a reality in this village.

The risk in Xiangdong ROSCAs is so small that it can be discounted

Risk is a key factor for any financial institution. For a private financial organization such as a ROSCA, risk is even more important because in a ROSCA if any member breaches the agreement the ROSCA cannot survive. The welfare of all the members will be directly affected and their aims will not be realized. For this reason, every member of the ROSCA is fully aware of the importance of risk control and management. As the head, he/she faces even more serious responsibilities. Our research found that if any one of the members in a ROSCA fails to make his/her payment on time, the head will pay it out of his/her own pocket in order to maintain the running of the ROSCA. To prevent this from happening, the head must select his/her members carefully. Second, during the running of the ROSCA (normally for two to three years), he/she monitors the situation very closely to reduce any risks. If 'foot' members do not take the initiative to pay their share, he/she will often visit them and urge them to pay up, directly or indirectly, in order to ensure the smooth running of the ROSCA. It can be seen that it is not an easy task for a head of the ROSCA if he/she wants to achieve the benefits mentioned above.

The heads and members of ROSCAs interviewed in Xiangdong village said that in the period of more than ten years from the 1990s to the present, there have been only three cases of members breaching the agreement and failing to pay up their shares! The default rate was lower than one per cent. In fact, within this one per cent, none of the defaulters were simply lax in their behaviour. They failed because of serious family difficulties and could not make the payments on time. Under these circumstances, what normally happens in Xiangdong village is that the head will put up the money as a private loan for the member and gain repayment by transferring an appropriate portion of the share from the member to the head. In this way, the negative effects will be restricted and the ROSCA can continue to operate as usual. In fact, in the recent past, the default rate in Xiangdong village has reached the level of zero. Villagers told the researcher that the default rate for them is no longer an issue. This will be explained further in the following section.

Village trust: a theoretical explanation of bidding ROSCAs in Xiangdong

As a typical informal financial organization, bidding ROSCAs have played an important role in the economic and social development in Xiangdong village. Specifically, their role is concentrated in three areas:

- To help poor villagers raise funds for subsistence and practical emergencies in their families;
- To help villagers with an average income with major spending needs in their families; and
- To help well-to-do villagers raise more funds to seize an opportunity to expand their business.

In addition, lending through bidding ROSCAs does not involve much risk. Because of this, we cannot but ask ourselves this question: why is this non-governmental financial system operating so effectively in Xiangdong village? In this section, we will try initially to explain this question from a relatively comprehensive perspective in accordance with our understanding of Xiangdong village's bidding ROSCAs and by establishing this new framework of 'village trust'.

Formulating the concept of 'village trust'

As was pointed out in Chapter 2, village trust is a comprehensive concept. It refers to a community order (institution) whereby, within the village community framework, every individual in the village is embedded in the village system through certain social norms and community rules that are closely related with local culture and, therefore, has positive expectations of the others. Obviously, this is a self-organized order created by a set of informal institutions.

Existence of a village community is the prerequisite for the concept of village trust. Local customs, local laws, community rules, tacit knowledge and local traditions and trust are all important components of village trust.

As Figure 5.1 shows clearly, it is exactly because of the existence and role of this system in Xiangdong village that bidding ROSCAs emerged and have developed over a long period in the village.

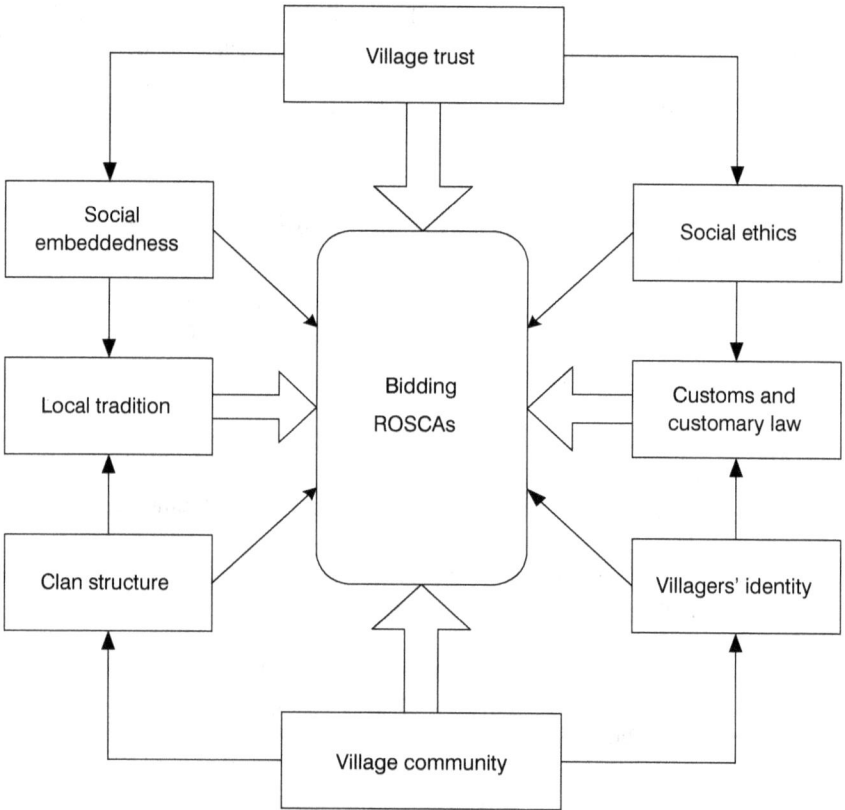

Figure 5.1 Village trust and bidding ROSCAs in Xiangdong village

Clan and village community

Village community has long been an academic topic related to research on rural development in China. Although G. William Skinner (1964–5), Prasenjit Duara (1988) and Philip C. Huang (1985, 1990) have different conclusions from their research in this area, their achievements are outstanding and all are landmarks in the subject.

The observation and analysis of the development of China's villages by our research team has been based on research conducted over a long period. They show in many cases the concept of the 'village community' is still of significance for research on China's villages. In particular, given the situation of Xiangdong village we are discussing now, we believe that it is still necessary to use the concept of village community to analyse questions for the following reasons:

1 Despite about 1,000 years of evolution and development, Xiangdong village still has many basic factors that constitute a village community. These include the fact that people with the Xiang surname are in an absolutely dominant position (more than 90 per cent of the villagers are surnamed Xiang), an ancestral hall has been expanded (Plate 5.1), there is a well-compiled genealogy, the association of elderly people (with a chairman, a vice-chairman and an accountant) still plays an important role as an advisory body on village management and the committee for compiling the genealogy,

Plate 5.1 Xiang ancestral hall in Xiangdong village

consisting of respected elderly people (with a president, a vice-president and several assistants) and different types of mutually beneficial organizations (such as ROSCAs), mainly within the borders of the natural village, are rather advanced.

2   The village boundary is quite clear. Xiangdong village has advanced water and land communications and it maintains very frequent contact with neighbouring villages and the neighbouring town of Qianku. However, in organizing economic activities such as ROSCAs, Xiangdong village is obviously a natural village. In our sample survey of more than 20 bidding ROSCAs, except for relatives, villagers from neighbouring villages seldom join each other's ROSCAs. Even villagers from Xiangxi village, which is across the river from Xiangdong village, do not join ROSCAs in Xiangdong village, and vice versa. A further example is that dragon-boat races during the Dragon Boat Festival in past years were all organized by the village.[12]

3   For historical and cultural reasons, the region where Xiangdong village is located has many dialects. In the surrounding area of 300 square km (that is, an area in the county with 11 towns and seven townships south of the Aojiang River), people speak several dialects. Generally speaking, in addition to Mandarin, there are four frequently used dialects, the Fujian dialect, the local dialect, the Ouyu dialect, and the Jinxiang dialect (Wang and Zhu 1996). People in the 20 square km around Qianku Town, where Xiangdong village is located, speak mainly the local dialect and the Fujian dialect. Villagers of Xiangdong village speak mainly the local dialect. Villagers from different villages speak the local dialect with different accents. Some have a northern accent whereas others have a southern accent. So, although the towns of Longgang, Yishan, Qianku and Jinxiang are close to each other, the local dialect is spoken differently. It is even the case that villagers from two neighbouring villages cannot understand each other. One of our research team members is a native of the area about ten km from Xiangdong village. However, during his research in the village, he could not understand those with a low level of education who could not speak Mandarin. Just like the other members of the team, he too needed a translator. This complicated language situation strengthens, to some extent, the independence of villages as single communities.

4   Historically, the area south of the Aojiang River in Cangnan County where Xiangdong village is located was an area where clans often fought each other with weapons. Generally, the direct causes of the fights were related to the ownership of land, forests and fisheries. According to incomplete statistics (Wang and Zhu 1996), this area with a population of 600,000, had more than 1,000 such incidents between 1967 and 1991 during which 20 people were killed, 39 others were injured, 218 houses were burnt down and 64 houses were destroyed, resulting in more than 3 million yuan of direct economic losses. In the fight between the Lin and the Chen families on 16 August 1992, there were five deaths and 18 were injured. Although Xiangdong village does not have many fights between clans, such fights did occur in the 1960s

and 1970s. In 1966 the village was involved in a fight with the Li family in neighbouring Lijiache village. It was not a big fight and did not have serious consequences. In 1975 Xiangdong village had a big fight with the Lü family in neighbouring Tongqiao village over a forestry dispute. Xiangdong village acted in collaboration with Xiangxi village and 300 villagers fought their rivals from Tongqiao village with guns. The fight was quelled by public security forces. Eight people from the two sides later received jail terms. Because of these fights, people fully understand the importance of their clans and villages. So they have gradually become heavily dependent on their clans and villages. Therefore, objectively speaking, these fights increased unity among villagers of the same village and especially those with the same surname (such as those surnamed Xiang in Xiangdong village) and they help to constantly foster a close system of village community based on clans. This shows that strictly speaking, Xiangdong village is a village clan community dominated by people surnamed Xiang (Wang and Zhu 1996).

Local culture and little tradition

Just as we mentioned at the beginning of this chapter, Xiangdong village is located in the middle of the Wenzhou Model region, an important model for regional economic development in China. To a great extent the characteristics the village has displayed constitute an important component of the Wenzhou model. Why, then, did the Wenzhou model, characterized mainly by private operations, emerge in this region and constantly develop historically? As a matter of fact, the fundamental reason is the influence of history and culture, and not the influence of the modern economic policy.

Under no circumstances should we overlook the ideas of the Eastern Zhejiang School of Utilitarianism in the history of China's philosophical and social thinking as we discussed in Chapter 4. The two founders of the Eastern Zhejiang School of Utilitarianism, Ye Shi and Chen Liang, were both from nearby in Zhejiang Province.

Ye Shi was a native of Yongjia County of Wenzhou, Zhejiang Province. He was born in 1150 in the Southern Song Dynasty. On the basis of a review of the academic achievements of the Nine Scholars in Yongjia County,[13] Ye Shi formulated a set of ideas on utilitarianism and social issues (Ye 1961).

Born in 1143, Chen Liang was a native of Yongkang County, Jinhua, Zhejiang Province. He became the representative of the Yongkang School of Thought because of his ideas on social utilitarianism and desire. He called for equal importance to be attached to righteousness and to profit. He also believed that it was necessary to use the achievements of fame and wealth to judge the level of benevolence, righteousness, virtue and morality. As he put it, 'success means virtue and whatever is right' (Chen 1974).

Many scholars note the significant impact of the philosophy of Ye Shi and Chen Liang on current regional economic development when talking about the Wenzhou Model (Yu 2002; Liu 2003). How do the ideas of Eastern Zhejiang

School of Utilitarianism influence present Wenzhou residents and what is the 'bridge' between the historical ideas and current experience of the people in the region? According to some scholars (Yu 2002; Zhuo forthcoming), understanding the mutual influence and interaction between the ideas of the School and people's practice in the region, as well as dynamic changes in the ideas of the School from the past to the present is the key to answer the question.

This implies that there are two 'bridges' between historic thought and current experience: one is the 'adaptation' between the theory of the School and the practice of local people; and the other is 'evolution' of ideas along with changes of time and environment through the historical dissemination and development of these ideas by local people.

As soon as Wenzhou was ready for its initial development in the Northern Song Dynasty, the Yongjia School emerged, led by Ye Shi in the Southern Song Dynasty. No doubt the local spirit of materialism and utilitarianism, and business orientation and hard work of the people in the area deeply influenced Ye Shi on the one hand (Zhuo forthcoming). On the other hand, Ye Shi's philosophy of utilitarianism influenced the people in the region further through the diffusion of his ideas from generation to generation.

The major milestone 'bridges' between Ye Shi's ideas, more than 700 years ago and the current practice include Huang Zongxi, Gu Yanwu and Yan Yuan, who were all native Zhejiang scholars in late Ming and early Qing dynasties; Sun Yiyan, Sun Qiangming, Huang Tifang, Song Shu, Huang Shaodi, Huang Qingcheng, Huang Qun, Zong Yuanhan, etc., in late Qing Dynasty, and Zhou Yutong, Xia Chengtao, Su Yuanlei, Lin Yin and Xia Nai in modern times (after 1949). Some of the major features of the current Wenzhou Model, such as the private economy and cooperative shareholding system had even been clearly proposed by some of the Wenzhou scholars in late Qing Dynasty (Liu 2003).

Customs and social norms

Although Xiangdong village is relatively open, under the framework of the village community it is still a small village society. In this society, ethics usually have great strength and influence, and customs and local traditional common laws still place great restrictions on people. These restrictions come partly from the influence of local religious forces (the village church in Xiangdong is shown in Plate 5.2) and partly from the institutionalised norms of behaviour of clans and villagers.

For example, as more than 90 per cent of the villagers of Xiangdong village are surnamed Xiang, the small number of people with other surnames are subject to pressure in their behaviour from those surnamed Xiang. An obvious example is that when Xiangdong village first began to establish village collective enterprises, villagers with other surnames found it difficult to find jobs in these enterprises. So they began to establish enterprises of their own. It is exactly because of this that the first private enterprise in Xiangdong village was established by people who were not surnamed Xiang. This is a positive example of innovation in the

Plate 5.2 The village church in Xiangdong

enterprise system due to the oppression through clan influence and is of positive significance in promoting the village economy.

Another example is that, following the establishment of the first private enterprise, several other private enterprises appeared. The composition of the shareholders of these enterprises shows that most of them were established jointly by members of the clan who are closely related; many of them were established jointly by parents, brothers or sisters. Generally speaking, enterprises employ mainly family members or close relatives. This is a factor that is derived from the traditional concept of clans that promotes the development of enterprises.

In addition, within the Xiang family, the family branches of the eldest sons are more powerful than other branches. So the branches of the eldest sons usually take control of the entire clan and even the whole village. This is true of Xiangdong village: before 1949, two major landlords in Xiangdong village came from the branches of the eldest sons and were much more powerful in the economy than others. After 1949, the first Secretary of the CPC Branch of the village came from the branch of the eldest son, and he was Secretary continuously for more than 30 years. Branches of the eldest sons produced most of the other cadres of the village. Our recent survey of the village shows no marked changes in this regard. The village cadres who had taken office the previous year still came from the branches of the eldest sons. Because of this, villagers from other branches of the Xiang family feel suppressed. This reflects the influence clan forces have on the political power in the village.

Moreover, the area where Xiangdong village is located has adopted the habit of swearing brotherhood (Wang and Zhu 1996). Generally speaking, parents help their young sons look for boys who could become their sworn brothers so as to expand their social connections. In the past this habit was followed by all the men in the village and it is still observed by half of the men. This local custom of expanding individual connection is to some extent cohesive.

As a matter of fact, villagers of the Xiangdong village regard the operation of different kinds of ROSCAs as a custom. The book entitled *Outline Annals of Zhejiang Customs* (1986) also discusses ROSCAs as a custom, especially all kinds of money-related associations (including the bidding ROSCAs we have discussed) that are prevalent throughout Zhejiang Province. From the perspective of economic development, ROSCAs are themselves a village norm that play a role within the village boundary. We will elaborate on this later.

Social embeddedness and the village

According to Liang Shuming (1992), a modern Chinese thinker, Chinese culture is basically rooted in villages because the country is generally based on and dominated by villages. He also considers the same situation to exist in the areas of legality, custom, and even in industry and commerce. That means villages are the foundation of Chinese culture and society. In accordance with Granovetter's theory (Granovetter 1985), if people as individuals or in organizations or institutions established for different purposes are embedded in a specific social context or structure, they will develop trust among each other and live in harmony. This is true with our research on bidding ROSCAs in Xiangdong village. It is exactly because these organizations and their members are integrated into the village that there is a foundation of culture in which both bidding ROSCAs and people's organizations which are non-governmental are trusted. The villagers involved in them are, therefore, deeply aware of the essence of the local culture. For example, one of the ways to encourage people's embeddedness into the village community more positively is to put examples of people's good behaviour, good manners, achievements, success stories etc. on display so that others can learn from these 'model people'; for example, in the Xiang ancestral temple a special hall for Xiang's 'Number One Scholar' (Xiang Guifa) has been built in recent years (Plate 5.3).

Plate 5.3 The 'Number One Scholar's Memorial Hall' in Xiangdong village

The application of game theory to bidding ROSCAs in Xiangdong village

Having formulated the concept of village trust and made a preliminary analysis of its framework and structure, we now need to return to the theme of bidding ROSCAs and make some specific analysis of them. We have just said that information in the village is basically full and transparent; so we can use game theory to explain the issue of bidding ROSCAs in Xiangdong village. Our field research and initial analysis show that the members of the bidding ROSCAs in Xiangdong village are acting not only in accordance with game theory but also social exchange theory (as they are also doing by taking part in various social activities in the village). As Xiangdong village is very much oriented towards clan and village community, both theories are applicable. The strategic alternatives for the ROSCA members taking part in multi-round bidding are: cooperation – repay the capital and interest/non-cooperation – refuse to repay the capital and interest.

Cost–benefit under cooperation

Cost under cooperation

For members who do not have access to the funds: C_{it}, $i = 1, 2, 3, \ldots, n-1$; (where C_{it} is the opportunity cost for putting money in the ROSCA, and t is the number of the ROSCA bidding rounds).

For members who have access to the funds: C_{nt} = interest payment; (where n is the person who is given access to the funds).

The overall benefit under cooperation

Under cooperation, members who do not have access to the funds have three advantages from their cooperation:

1 income from interest R_{it}, $i = 1, 2, 3, \ldots, n-1$, current value $= \Sigma \delta^t R_{it}$ (where δ is discounted rate);

2 expected future ROSCA income $E\left[\displaystyle\sum_{t=0}^{\infty} \delta^t M\right]$ (where t = bidding round; E = expected future ROSCA return under cooperation situation; M = return from the funds' utilization (interest return for members having no access to the funds, and investment return for members having access to the funds);

3 other gains from the public welfare of the village $\int_{0}^{\infty} \delta^t B_{st}(N) \, dt$ (where B = other benefits from the public welfare of the village; N = any member of the ROSCA).

Members who access funds can also benefit from three sources of income: i.e., capital from the ROSCA R_{nt} and the two other benefits shared with members with no access to the funds.

Income for members having no access to the funds:

$$R_{it} + E\left[\sum_{t=0}^{\infty} \delta^t M_t\right] + \int_{0}^{\infty} \delta^t B_{st}(N_t) \, dt$$

Income for members having access to the funds:

$$R_{nt} + E\left[\sum_{t=0}^{\infty} \delta^t M_t\right] + \int_{0}^{\infty} \delta^t B_{st}(N_t) \, dt$$

Net income under cooperation

Members having access to the funds:

$$\Pi_n = \sum \left[\delta^t (R_{it} - C_{nt})\right] R_{nt} + \left\{ E\left[\sum_{t=0}^{\infty} \delta^t M_t\right] + \int_{0}^{\infty} \delta^t B_{st}(N_t) \, dt \right\}$$

Members having no access to the funds:

$$\Pi_i = \sum \left[\delta^t \left(R_{it} - C_{it} \right) \right] R_{it} + \left\{ E\left[\sum_{t=0}^{\infty} \delta^t M_t \right] + \int_0^{\infty} \delta^t B_{st} \left(N_t \right) dt \right\},$$

$$i = 1, 2, 3, \ldots, n-1$$

Cost–benefit for non-cooperation

Cost of non-cooperation

Members having no access to the funds: $C_i = X \quad i = 1, 2, 3, \ldots, n-1$
  where X is principal loss.
  Members having access to the funds:

$$C_n = F + E\left[\sum_{t=0}^{\infty} \delta^t M_t \right] + \int_0^{\infty} \delta^t B_{st} \left(N_t \right) dt$$

  where F is future loss from other ROSCAs due to the reputation damage.
  The other two items in the formula are loss of expected income after a member loses his/her credibility and opportunity to join a ROSCA, and various potential gains now lost from village society due to losing his/her credibility.

	Non-cooperation	Cooperation
Non-cooperation	0, 0	$(n-1)X - \left\{ F + E\left[\sum_{t=0}^{\infty} \delta^t M_t \right] + \int_0^{\infty} \delta^t B_{st} \left(N_t \right) dt \right\}, \quad -X$
Cooperation	$-X_i, \quad (n-1)X - \left\{ F + E\left[\sum_{t=0}^{\infty} \delta^t M_t \right] + \int_0^{\infty} \delta^t B_{st} \left(N_t \right) dt \right\}$	$\left(\sum \delta^t R_{it} \right) - C_i + E\left[\sum_{t=0}^{\infty} \delta^t M_t \right] + \int_0^{\infty} \delta^t B_{st} \left(N_t \right) dt,$ $\sum \delta^t \left(R_{nt} - C_{nt} \right) + E\left[\sum_{t=0}^{\infty} \delta^t M_t \right] + \int_0^{\infty} \delta^t B_{st} \left(N_t \right) dt$

Benefit under non-cooperation

  Members having no access to the funds: 0.
  Members having access to the funds: $(n-1)X$
  where X represents the principal of the ROSCA member(s).

To sum up the above, the matrix for the game theory for Xiangdong villagers taking part in a ROSCA under the framework of the village is:
  If the game theory applies only for one round and the participants choose non-cooperation, it is impossible for the ROSCA to survive; if there is only ROSCA game theory operating, without village social exchange theory the ROSCAs cannot operate for long because of the absence of significant penalty to the member who breaches the agreement.
  Because of the infinite multilateral interactions that would be applicable in the village as a whole, the penalty to the member for lack of cooperation

$$P_n = F_n + E\left[\sum_{t=0}^{\infty} \delta^t M_t\right] + \int_0^{\infty} \delta^t B_{st}(N_t)\, dt$$

is not just limited to the short term economic loss but the complete loss of his/her long-term economic and social interests. Therefore, $P > (n-1)X$, and people will choose to cooperate. This is a strategic game.

When $P \le (n-1)X$, it is expected that there will be people who do not cooperate, therefore, the ROSCAs will not exist.

So, when X (size/scale of the ROSCA) is small, and $P > (n-1)X$, cooperation is the only way of reaching a Nash equilibrium. On the contrary, as the scale of a ROSCA becomes larger and larger, the probability for non-cooperation is increased. When it becomes very large, the likelihood of the ROSCA's failing is great.

Preliminary conclusions

After having carried out initial research and analysis on the ROSCAs in Xiangdong village, Cangnan County, Wenzhou City of Zhejiang Province we can come to the following conclusions:

First, as typical informal financial systems, the emergence and development of various fund-raising institutions, such as ROSCAs, is not only an economic but also a cultural, social and historical phenomenon. As a custom, it is rooted deeply in the whole social system of the local area. The ineffective operation of, or even the lack of, national formal financing systems in the rural area has strengthened the commitment of rural residents to self-help institutions based on the realities of their daily lives. We believe that private financial development is the trend for rural China and is unstoppable.

Second, a ROSCA, especially a bidding ROSCA in Xiangdong village, is a well-designed financial system, an easily operated and rational financial arrangement. This financial system, operated through interest-rate bidding for access to the collective fund, shows the importance of interest in the private capital market. Furthermore, the interest rate setting policy takes into account the price factor for the funds available in the local market. It reflects not only the trend of the domestic and global capital markets but also the principle of 'putting people first' and treating them individually. The interest varies depending on the structure of the ROSCAs: the ROSCAs having the lowest interest rates are formed by relatives in the same family. This arrangement combines economic interest and social and cultural factors. Thus, it is a highly competitive financial system.

Third, in Chinese rural society, given the close ties of the clan and the villagers, the low level of commercialization, limited mobility and the shared history of members from the same village or friends and family members, the aim of a ROSCA is largely to meet their daily needs and the size of the ROSCAs is small. Such financial institutions present very little risk.

6 *Guanxi* community and people's mobility

Following the theoretical discussion in previous chapters, we now turn our focus from the basic theories to one of the important extended forms of *guanxi* and *guanxi* community in relation to people's mobility in one of the villages surveyed.

We will, first of all, introduce briefly the general situation of people's mobility in Tunwa village. We will then discuss the channels or the issue of *guanxi* mentioned through which people's mobility in the village has taken place. Finally we will turn to the contents of in-depth interviews held with emigrants from Tunwa village and reach a preliminary conclusion. We hope that this may, to some extent, reveal how the model related to the establishment and development of the *guanxi* community mentioned in our theoretical discussions can be interpreted and illustrated in real life.

General situation of people's mobility in Tunwa village

Tunwa village can be described as a relatively large village in a mountainous area of northern and western China. The total number of registered residents in the village is currently 1,519 people in 588 families. The four-member survey team[1] visited the village between the end of July and early August 2003 to conduct a survey on the migration and mobility of its population and its labour force. As it is a sizeable village, sample surveys were used. We picked a sample of 123 out of 588 families randomly for our investigation. In other words, each of us was responsible for about 30 family interviews. While focusing our survey on those families, we also conducted a preliminary survey into the mobility of people in all of the village's labour force to be used as a reference when analysing the data from the sample survey from the perspective of overall investigations.

The research survey conducted by the author himself involved 31 families comprising a total of 107 people, which amounted to 7 per cent of the village population. Among them, 76 are physically able labourers making up 15.3 per cent of the total labour force in the village. According to the data collected from surveys of this population group, 29 were migrant or relocated persons, accounting for 27.1 per cent of the population surveyed. As migrant or relocated people represented the main labourers of families, the proportion was as high as 31.6 per cent (24 out of 76) when compared to the labour force of the migrant or relocated persons in the total labour force of the families surveyed. Looking just at the heads of household, those in this category who have migrated accounted for 77.4 per cent (31 heads) of the sample surveyed by the author. For whatever reason, even viewed from a very conservative perspective, this sample survey indicates that one-third of the labour force and more than a quarter of the population in the village are in a state of constant mobility (including outward relocation and migration): for detailed figures, see Table 6.1. Of these, 19.6 per cent of the migrant or relocated people moved from their village three years ago and spent most of their time (more than six months per year) in other places; while only 7.5 per cent of the migrant or relocated people had moved their village within three years or spent less than six months in other places each year. The situation for the labour force according to the same criteria are 22.4 per cent and 10.5 per cent respectively.

Table 6.1 People's mobility in Tunwa village

Head of family	Household members[a]	Family workforce	People with short-term mobility[b]	People with long-term mobility[c]	Remarks
Zhao Conggao	5	4	1	0	Village school teacher. Younger son is studying in Shanxi Mining Institute.
Chen Rushun	2	2	0	0	Younger son graduated from a Technical Secondary School in Taiyuan City, daughter married.
Zhang Wangshou	3	3	1	0	Two daughters working in other provinces after university graduation.
Zhao Huhu(1)	4	3	0	1	Son worked in a chemical plant for six years; youngest daughter finished her college education; two other daughters married.
Chen Quantang	2	2	0	1	Working in the township's power station, wife was a village school teacher. Daughter graduated from a college; son is a military cadre.
Chen Haizhu	2	2	1	0	Parents were sent to Tunwa from Hebei Science and Technology College in 1957. Two sons working in other provinces after graduation from university.
Chen Jianming	5	5	0	1	Several years in boiler business in Taiyuan. Younger brother is a truck driver.
Chen Guanliang	4	2	1	0	
Zhao Xihuai	4	2	0	0	
Zhang Yuesheng	3	2	0	1	Boiler salesman in a nearby county since 6 years ago.
Zhao Peicheng	3	2	1	0	Doing carpentry in Datong City from time to time.
Hu Guitian	4	2	1	0	Welder in a boiler manufacture plant in Yuanping City.
Chen Lantian	3	3	0	0	Two daughters are married.
Zhao Guizhong	4	2	0	0	Daughter is studying in Shanxi Agricultural University.
Xie Jianxin	5	2	0	0	

Table 6.1 continued

Head of family	Household members[a]	Family workforce	People with short-term mobility[b]	People with long-term mobility[c]	Remarks
Chen Shumao	4	3	0	1	Son is a casual worker in the museum of nearby Dai County.
Chen Kaoshun	3	3	1	1	Working in a local vegetable company. Younger son working in construction projects in Lishi City after 3 years in the army.
Zhao Luming	3	3	0	2	Working in a nearby coal mine. Son is working in the city all the year.
Zhao Genyu	4	3	0	0	
Zhao Fujun	3	2	1	0	One of the big chicken breeding households in the village.
Zhang Guohua	4	2	0	3	Running his own boiler plant in Yuanping City together with his brother.
Sun Cunshou	3	3	0	0	Two sons are married and live separately, he lives with his daughter.
Chen Yuxin	4	2	0	0	
Zhao Huhu(2)	4	2	0	0	
Chen Guoliang	3	2	0	0	
Duan Ermao	4	4	0	0	
Zhao Jutang	3	1	0	0	
Sun Peigang	3	2	0	3	A very experienced welder. His father is the Village Chief.
Zhao Yedong	3	2	0	3	Running a printing plant in Taiyuan City. He is also the son-in-law of the Village Chief.
Chen Jianye	3	2	0	3	Working in No.2 Chemical Plant of Yuanping City. He is the son of the Party's Secretary of the village.
Xie Yinwan	3	2	0	1	Working for a Tunwa entrepreneur in Beijing after leaving his village accountant job in early 2003.
	107	76	8	21	

Source: Field survey in Tunwa village.
Notes: (a) Does not include members of the workforce and population who moved out of the village through official channels of education, enrolment, or promotion to official cadres by the government departments.
(b) Short-term mobility is defined as those who had engaged in any kind of economic activity outside the village for more than 6 months every year in the past consecutive 3 years.
(c) Long-term mobility is defined as those who had been outside of the village for the whole year, including not only the workforce of the family but all the family members (include the eldery and children), but it does not include the people who moved out of the village for education, enrolment, government promotion and other official channels mentioned in (a).

It is interesting to look at this kind of structure of the mobility of the population and labour force. It showed that the mobility of the population and labour force in Tunwa village is relatively thorough with complete migration and relocation, displaying strong emigration characteristics. These results are not comparable to the features demonstrated by obviously temporary or visitor migration or the 'floating' population and labour force in most other rural areas in China. Particularly, Table 6.1 shows that most families in Tunwa village have one or more children who have received university education (including junior college education) or who are now studying in universities. For these people, it is impossible to ever return to Tunwa village. With more Tunwa villagers constantly venturing out to seek job opportunities elsewhere, the village population can be expected to drop further in the future.

Using the basic understanding of people's mobility derived from the data provided by the Tunwa village survey, the natural and closely related question to ask from a micro perspective is, besides such reasons as the overall environment and policy factors, what is the driving force that has prompted such tremendous changes in people's mobility in Tunwa village?

Our surveys show that people's mobility in Tunwa village took two forms: one was a result of marriage and the other was prompted by regional industrial and commercial development. Therefore, the issue can be looked at from two different dimensions.

Marriage-driven mobility and its *guanxi* networks in Tunwa village

Marriage is a universal phenomenon or we can call it a kind of institutional arrangement in relation to the family system. The normal situation in marriage in China means that a woman leaves her parents' home following the marriage ceremony and goes to live with her husband's parents or live with her husband independently if they can afford it. This is what Chinese people usually term 'men marry in and women marry out'. The cultural basis of this marriage arrangement is the traditional Chinese patriarchal marriage system (Christiansen and Zhang 1998: 18; Duncan and Li 2001) in which males are in the dominant position in the system.[2]

This simply implies that marriage triggers people's mobility (normally the women's movement) from one place to another (from the woman's village to her husband's in most of the cases). This kind of mobility can be called 'marriage-driven mobility'. No doubt, most of the marriage mobility for rural women is restricted to rural areas. However, marriage migration, as a special channel, once played a very important role for rural women moving to cities, because of government policies before the mid-1990s when urban–rural labour markets were not integrated. One study shows that the general situation before 1990 was that 40 per cent of rural women moving to cities did so because of marriage (Gu and Jian 1994). The focus of the discussion in this chapter is in relation to rural Tunwa village – one of the villages surveyed over the past ten years.

The subject of marriage-driven mobility of people in Tunwa village can be further divided into two categories – immigration and emigration. Immigration driven by marriage refers to the immigration into Tunwa village when men in the village married women from other villages. Emigration driven by marriage refers to the emigration of women of Tunwa village through marriage to men from other places. However, there is an exception, which was people's mobility involving no change in geographical location, despite a marriage. That was the case when the marriage was between villagers within the village itself.

Taking the 31 families sampled in the survey as an example, Table 6.2 shows the female members of the population who immigrated into Tunwa village through marriage. During the whole survey, our focal point was on the various relations emerging during the process of marriage-driven immigration. That is, how did people's mobility prompted by marriage take place?

Table 6.3 shows some of the female population covered in our sample survey who emigrated out of Tunwa village because of marriage. As already mentioned, when women were married to men of the same village there was no emigration or relocation among them for they were still living in the village. The focal point of our concern is not the act of emigration itself but the various factors behind this kind of population mobility.

Based on the above two survey tables, we can form the tabulation (Table 6.4) which clearly explains the three issues of most interest.

First, whatever the act of emigration or immigration resulting from marriage, the reason for this to happen lies in the various traditional *guanxi* networks which have existed for a long time and have played their role within rural society. In terms of immigration, 77.4 per cent of the people whose relocation was prompted by marriage took place as a result of the geo-relations (fellow villagers' *guanxi*), blood relations (relatives' *guanxi*) and partnership (or occupational) relations (*guanxi* of classmates, colleagues, etc.). Only 16.1 per cent of people married purely for love. A further 6.5 per cent of the female population was forced to seek refuge in Tunwa village because of famine (they are included in the 'others' column in Table 6.4). In terms of emigration, the results of the sample survey were almost the same as that of immigration. Marriage and marriage-driven mobility of 76.9 per cent of the women surveyed were based on traditional geo-relations, blood relations and partnership or occupational relations. Only 23.1 per cent of the women surveyed gave love as the reason for their mobility through marriage.

What is worth mentioning in particular is that the geo-relations bore special significance among various relations. Whatever the relations or *guanxi* of emigration or immigration prompted by marriage in Tunwa village, the marriages arranged by fellow villagers (men or women) as go-betweens comprised 43.5 and 46.1 per cent respectively, much greater than the impact of blood relations (27.4 per cent and 23.1 per cent). There was a typical instance: when a woman living in Jingle County, about 150 km from Tunwa village, married into Tunwa village in Yuanping City, there was an immediate wave of marriages to the village. Among the 31 families of Tunwa village in our survey alone, it was found that four wives came from Jingle County, accounting for 12.9 per cent of the sample. It was said that about 20 women in the entire village were married from Jingle County. From the social network theory point of view, the earlier comers of the Jingle women clearly acted as a 'bridge' in the social relations.

Second, viewed from the perspective of the marriages of both men and women, one-third of the women's marriages took place within the village or their spouses came from the same village. This indicated that the basis for people's *guanxi*

Table 6.2 Women moving to Tunwa village through marriage and guanxi networks

Name	Birthplace	Distance from birthplace to Tunwa (km)	Year of marriage	Introducer	Type of guanxi
Wang Payun	Nearby Wangjiaying village of the same township	5	1965	Husband's colleague (a village school teacher)	Colleague
Zhang Lihua	Wenzhi village of the same township	25	1994	Villager	Countryman
Liu Bianying	Yangerling village of Wangcun Township, Jingle County, Shanxi Province	150	1970	Countrymen of mistress who married to Tunwa earlier	Countryman
Wife of Chen Liangsheng	Bei'an village of the same township	10	1991	Countryman of master who is also the friend of mistress's father	Countryman + friend
Zhao Erchan	Tunwa village	0	1973	Aunt-in-law of the mistress	Relative
Zhou Jiner	Dongmafang village of Xincun Township in Jingle County, Shanxi Province	150	1981	Countrymen of mistress who married to Tunwa earlier	Countryman
Wu Heping	Tunwa village	0	1976	Master's aunt	Relative
Liu Aiping	Hou village of Ximafang Township of Jingle county, Shanxi Province	150	1968	Villager of neighbouring village (fled from famine to Tunwa village)	Countryman
Shang Yumei	Lijiagou village of Xingcun Township of Jingle County, Shanxi Province	150	Not clear	Fled from famine to Tunwa and knew each other with the master	
Fan Aihua	Shishunhui village of Liangcenhui Township of Lan County, Shanxi Province	150	1978	Cousins of the master who is also the mistress's countrymen	Relative + countryman
Wang Fengmei	Shanshui village of the same township	12	1991	Master's uncle	Relative
Zhu Xingping	Tunwa village	0	1988	Free choice	
Zhao Jianying	Same village	0	1986	Free choice	
Wang Lindeng	Dawangying village, Changlianggou Town of the same city	10	1969	Villager who is also the mistress' father's sister's husband	Countryman + relative
Chen Yueping	Tunwa village	0	1980	Free choice	
Guo Yinai	Huangsongdong village of Changlianggou Town of the same city	15	1989	Master's cousin who is also in the same village with the mistress	Relative + countryman
Chen Pingying	Tunwa village	0	1981	Villager	Countryman

Name	Place of origin	Number	Year	Description	Relationship
Chen Shuiping	Tunwa village	0	1972	Villager	Countryman
Nie Fenyu	Mairangou village of Huishungou Township in Ningwu County, Shanxi Province	45	1976	Master's uncle	Relative
Han Liangying	Jinliu village of Jinliu Township in Loufan County, Shanxi Province	150	1974	Countrymen of mistress who married to Tunwa village	Countryman
Zhao Shumei	Tunwa village	0	1988	Friend of master who is also in the same village	Countryman
Li Zehong	Tanglingang village, one of the suburban villages of Yuanping City	20	1999	Villager and colleague of the master who is also the friend of the mistress' family	Countryman + friend
Wang Qiaoyun	Nanguan village in Qiuzhou City, Hebei Province	600	1948	Fled from famine to Tunwa village	Countryman
Zhang Chanyu	Tunwa village	0	1971	Villager who is familiar with both the master and the mistress	Countryman
Chen Zhuqing	Tunwa village	0	1996	Villager who is familiar with both the master and the mistress	Countryman
Shang Shannu	Yuanping City town	20	Not clear	Master's aunt who is also the mistress' aunt-in-law	Relative
Zhu Cuihua	Zhujiagou village of Huishungou Township in Ningwu County, Shanxi Province	20	1995	Brother-in-law of the mistress	Relative
Shang Meiping	Baiyang village of the same township	5	1990	Free choice	
Chen Yongmei	Tunwa village	0	1999	Free choice	
Gao Aiwen	Dongliudu village of Loufan Township in Loufan County, Shanxi Province	150	1981	Villager who is also the brother-in-law of the mistress	Relative + countryman
Fan Yulian	Hekou Town in Lan County, Shanxi Province	150	1980	Villager who has relatives in Hekou Town	Relative + countryman

Source: Fieldwork in Tunwa village.

Table 6.3 Women moving out of Tunwa village through marriage and *guanxi* networks

Name	Moved to	Distance from Tunwa (km)	Introducer	Type of guanxi
Chen Xiaohua	Loubanzhai village of the same township	5	Master's cousin who is also in the same village with the mistress	Relative + countryman
Zhang Yanping	Yandi village, Yanzhuang Township of the same city	6	Free choice	
Chen Shufang	Xiying village of the same township	5	Cousin of mistress' father	Relative + countryman
Chen Shuxia	Shahuang village, Xizhen Township of the same city	20	Acquaintance of mistress' father who moved from the nearby Yang village to Tunwa	Countryman
Chen Chunlan	Tunwa village	0	Villager	Countryman
Zhao Meichuan	Jingjie village of the same towship	5	Mistress' younger sister who knew the master in Yuanping	Relative + friend
Zhao Aichuan	Tunwa village	0	Master's relative	Relative + countryman
Zhang Lala	Luxi village, Danudian Township of the same city	5	Villager who is the mistress' cousin	Relative + countryman
Zhang Chenhua	Tunwa village	0	Villager who is also the master's friend	Countryman
Chen Zhiping	Yuanping City	20	Free choice (knowing each other in the cement plant)	Colleague
Sun Peifang	Tunwa village	0	Mistress' friend who is also Tunwa villager	Countryman + friend
Sun Peizhi	Tunwa village	0	Mistress' aunt who is also Tunwa villager	Relative + countryman
Chen Jianping	Yuanping City	20	Free choice	

Source: Fieldwork in Tunwa village.

Table 6.4 Villagers' mobility caused by marriage and *guanxi* networks in Tunwa

	Moving in		Moving out	
	Number	*%*	*Number*	*%*
Number of people	31	100	13	100
From/to				
Same village	10	32.2	4	30.8
Other villages of same township	5	16.1	3	23.1
Other townships of the same city	4	12.9	6	46.1
Other counties of same province	10	32.3	0	0.0
Other provinces	2	6.5	0	0.0
Distance				
<2 km	10	32.2	5	38.5
5–15 km	6	19.4	5	38.5
16–25 km	4	12.9	3	23.0
26–50km	1	3.2	0	0.0
51–150 km	8	25.8	0	0.0
>150 km	2	6.5	0	0.0
Type of guanxi				
Countryman	13.5	43.5	6	46.1
Relative	8.5	27.4	3	23.1
Friends, colleagues	2	6.5	1	7.7
Free choice (love match)	5	16.1	3	23.1
Other	2	6.5	0	0.0
Date of marriage				
Before 1949	1	3.2		
1950–1978	11	35.4		
1979–1990	10	32.3		
1991–2003	7	22.6		
Unknown	2	6.5		

Source: Based on Table 6.2 and Table 6.3.

community building in Tunwa village, in terms of marriage-driven mobility, still shows close relations within and among surrounding villages. To date, no women from the 31 families in our random survey had been married into other counties (cities), let alone other provinces. Perhaps a village-wide survey might have found two or three instances of women marrying out of the cities (counties) of their origin. Of course, rare exceptions may exist. In the light of the marriage-driven immigration, one-third came from other counties but there were also exceptions, i.e., the group effect caused by the geo-relations of Jingle County.

From a comparative point of view, along with the expansion of service businesses in both urban areas as well as in rural market centres and the rapid development of urbanization in rural areas, more and more rural women seek job opportunities in a much wider range of areas away from the traditional village-centred small informal labour markets. Most of the women who migrate in this way are unmarried. According to sample investigations, more than a third of the total 'floating population' (of about 100 million in China) are women[3] (Roberts *et al.* 2004). One of the natural results is that, after some years working in cities and towns, rural women would become increasingly more likely to marry men who come from much further away from their native villages. But this situation has not happened among Tunwa women, except for the group of immigrant women from Jingle County.

Third, considering these two features, marriage-driven migration of women of Tunwa village has a relatively small radius. The home villages of 51.6 per cent of immigrant women were within 15 km to Tunwa village. Among them, the homes of 32.2 per cent of the women's parents were in the same village. Some 77 per cent of women born in Tunwa village were married within a radius of 15 km of whom 38.5 per cent were married within the village.

This represents the typical situation of the marriage radius (distance of marriage relations) in rural China. Historically speaking, the marriage radius in rural areas was about 5 km[4] during the 20 years from the 1920s to 1940s – in China marriage was within '*shili baxiang*' (five km and eight townships) which exactly matches the distance between the villages and the local 'primary market' of the area. Most of the villagers chose a marriage distance within the market radius in Old China (Gao forthcoming). However, the collectivization movements from the mid-1950s to the late 1970s helped people to get married within an even closer distance since such movements provided opportunities for young people to be involved in public activities within the village or surrounding villages; thus many women married their husbands within the same villages. A survey conducted in 1986 of marriage distance in rural areas of six provinces including 2,302 cases at different ages showed that 70.1 per cent of the people married spouses from within a distance of 10 km (Table 6.5); of them, the marriage distance of more than 51.7 per cent of the people was within 5 km[5] (Lei 1994). In Gao's judgment (Gao forthcoming) the optimal marriage distance for rural people would be between 1 and 3 km.

One of the villages in Shaanxi province (Wangjian village) which was surveyed also shows a similar situation in terms of marriage distance: 52 per cent of the married women in the village were from the villages less than 10 km away in the mid-1990s (Hu 1996: 191). Huo's case study from another northern village shows an even smaller marriage distance of only 4 km and it has decreased further in recent years (Huo 2002). According to his research, one of the important reasons is that intra-village or nearby village marriage strengthens mutual help amongst those connected by clan or kinship. Huang's study on modern kinship systems in rural China indicates that marriage becomes one of the very important

Table 6.5 Marriage distance of different age groups in 1986 (%)

Distance	18–35 years	36–55 years	56 and older	Total
0–1 km	18.3	15.8	21.2	17.5
2–5 km	34.4	34.9	31.6	34.2
6–10 km	18.9	18.1	18.6	18.4
> 10 km	28.4	31.2	28.6	29.9
Total	100.0	100.0	100.0	100.0
Number of marriages	693	1194	415	2302

Source: Lei 1994.

means of enhancing economic cooperation among co-villagers within a village or with neighbouring villagers. She therefore finds 'more marriages have begun to occur within a lineage or village and among kin members' (X. Huang 1998: 188). Odgaard and Christiansen also pointed out this trend in their earlier studies (Odgaard 1992a).

However, distant marriage has also been increasing in some rural areas. According to Gao again, about 100,000 women of Zhejiang Province had married into the province between 1982 and the first half of 1990 (Gao forthcoming).

One of the direct reasons, of course, is economic, but the cultural and social network factor is also crucial to the distant marriage. This is why we often heard that most of the *baomu* (nannies) in Beijing are from Wuwei County of Anhui Province, most of the private merchants are from Wenzhou of Zhejiang Province ('Zhejiang village' in Beijing as a typical example) etc., simply because the extension of their *guanxi* networks has reached the city. The networks have even formed different kinds of new *guanxi*-based communities (such as 'Zhejiang village' which is not really a true village but a new community formed among people who are all from Zhejiang Province and which acts as a locality network; it is the same for 'Xinjiang village' and 'Henan village' in Beijing); although others have not been formed at the moment.

Through such comparisons, we are not surprised to see both trends of intra-village marriage as well as distant marriage have been appearing in Tunwa village, the latter type being the large group of Jingle women married into the village. These two trends imply the development of two types of *guanxi* community forms, i.e., closely village-based local *guanxi* community as well as distant locality-based extended *guanxi* community across a longer distance have all been strengthened in Tunwa village.

Tunwa villagers' economic mobility and *guanxi* networks

Obviously the study of people's mobility in Tunwa village and their links with *guanxi* community must proceed from another perspective. That is to say, we need to shift our analysis from marriage-driven migration to mobility caused by the development of modern industrialization and urbanization in line with the significant changes happening in rural China after the reform and opening up policies implemented in the late 1970s.

Literature on rural people's mobility to urban areas or simply called rural–urban migration for economic reasons, rather than marriage, is becoming increasingly available. China has been experiencing since the mid-1980s the largest labour migration in history. As we know that migration is a selective process (Lee 1966), the following question arises: what are the major factors determining the selection? In other words, what are the critical characteristics of migrants, which help them to migrate from rural to urban areas successfully? Many scholars agree that educational attainment, gender, age, marital status and personal skills are important variables for the selection process with preferences on specific variable(s) in relation to different cases (Todaro 1969, 1976; DaVanzo 1981;

Greenwood 1985; Borjas 1987; Ma and Liaw 1994; Solinger 1995; Cai 1996; Davin 1996, 1999; Bailey and Cooke 1998; Hare 1999; Newbold 2001; Meng 2001).

Some scholars also insist that social networks – or what we called *guanxi* connections – also play a significant role in the migration selection process, both in other countries and in China (Greenwood 1969; Navril 1977; Montgomery 1991; Hatton and Williamson 1994; Massey *et al.* 1993; Rozelle *et al.* 1997; Chan *et al.* 1999; Lovett *et al.* 1999; Meng 2000; Zhang and Li 2001; S. Zhao 2000; Y. Zhao 2003). For example, Zhao conducted research in Shanghai and southern Jiangsu Province in 1995 by drawing on a random sample of 706 migrant workers; he showed that 75.6 per cent of the migrants were assisted by relatives and friends during their first trip from their villages (Zhao 2000; Y. Zhao 2003). Meng's survey of 15,000 migrants in Shandong Province in 1995 also indicates a similar result: 70 per cent of the migrants in the sample had jobs already arranged through the help of their relatives and friends before they had migrated (Meng 2000; Z. Zhao 2005). Zhao's observation on the general situation is that only 18 per cent of the migrants (rural–urban migrants) who find their jobs in urban areas rely on government help and more then 80 per cent of the migrants find their jobs through their own networks (Z. Zhao 2005).

Zhao's empirical study tells us that what is true in the case of the existence of migration networks is that all the material, information and psychological costs for migrants would be lowered[6] (by providing them with useful information to increase the probability of finding job opportunities and providing moral support at the destinations through the networks). Some of the studies on international migration of Chinese also show similar advantages; for example, Callahan's study on overseas Chinese in southeast Asia (Callahan 2002). More importantly, Zhao finds that rural–urban migration becomes a self-sustaining and self-enforcing process when migration networks are involved in the migration process (Y. Zhao 2003). Compared with the studies mentioned above, Zhang and Li's findings, from their study based on the 1995 North and Northeast China Living Standards Survey which covered 787 households from 30 villages of 18 townships in 6 counties in Hebei and Liaoning provinces, are even more conclusive:

> when *guanxi* is taken into account, the importance of other variables, such as human capital and rural institutions, becomes less significant. With limited non-farm job opportunities and imperfect market information, social networks play a key role in enabling rural workers to capitalize more fully on their education and skills. These findings help explain the clustering of rural migrants who come from the same rural areas that is observed in cities.
>
> (Zhang and Li 2001: 21)

Although all these studies show very clearly the significance of *guanxi* networks in rural–urban migration, the real situation of the correlation between people's economically orientated mobility and their *guanxi* networks in Tunwa village still needs to be carefully surveyed. We will discuss major findings by comparing other similar studies later in this chapter.

Our survey in this regard was conducted in two dimensions: on the one hand, we tried to get to know, through ordinary surveys among the villagers, the migration and relocation of population and labour force prompted by the industrial and commercial development in Tunwa village, as well as their causes; on the other hand, we arranged in-depth interviews with entrepreneurs originating from Tunwa village.

A brief introduction has already been given to the migration and the marriage-driven relocation of the 31 families sampled at random. By analysing the sample surveyed, a rough understanding can be made of the mobility of the labour force of Tunwa village. Consequently, some specific analysis of the movement of this labour force can be conducted.

Table 6.6 provides some information which the random survey revealed about the 92 members of the sample labour force who are mobile. This data may provide a preliminary answer from a micro perspective about the cause of their mobility, particularly from the viewpoint of the studies on *guanxi* community.

Tables 6.7 and 6.8 show in a more visible and clearer way the information about the mobility of people in Tunwa village as collated in Table 6.6. Table 6.7 contains some basic information about the 'floating labour force' of Tunwa village. Table 6.8 focuses on the root cause of the villagers' migration behaviour, i.e., the *guanxi* of each villager that helps determine his/her move.

Table 6.7 shows that the 92 migrant labourers surveyed in Tunwa village spent an average of nine months, or 270 days, a year working in cities. Of them, 68.5 per cent of labourers spent an average of more than six months a year working in cities. A further 22.8 per cent of them spent between three to six months working in cities. Only 8.7 per cent of labourers spent less than three months working in cities.

As to the type of work undertaken, 42.2 per cent found job opportunities in the boiler industry where they took up jobs related to the production (such as electric welders) or marketing of boilers. This shows that the traditional industry which characterized Tunwa played a vital and positive role in these villagers' transition to the city and to related industries. Apart from the boiler industry, 22.8 per cent of labourers found job opportunities in urban construction and service industries. Tunwa villagers working in the construction sector were not engaged in building skyscrapers, rather they worked on building inter-city expressways. From this point of view, the state's proactive fiscal policies implemented in recent years and the expansion of the state investment in building infrastructure in the western areas of China have had a positive impact on improving the job opportunities of farmers. In addition, 9.8 per cent of people found jobs in the manufacturing sector apart from the boiler industry. The villagers earned their living mainly as seasonal or contracted workers in urban chemical, cement and machinery plants. The remaining 2.2 per cent of labourers surveyed found jobs in the coal sector, mainly working as coal miners in nearby mines.

Table 6.6 Mobility of the workforce and *guanxi* networks in Tunwa village

Name	Gender	Age	Education	Time working away (months/year)	Where working	Start date	Industry/type of work	Channel and helper	Status of the helper	Type of guanxi
Chen Yaoshuang	M	44	SS	8.5	Taiyuan City	1994	Coal mine	Taking father's place	Worker at Xuangang Coal Mine	Relative
Sun Shaohua	M	24	SS	12	Yuanping City	1996	Service	Father's friend (Zhao Xianhong)	Director of Yuanping Textile Mill	Classmate
Zhao Shuangmao	M	39	SS	7.5	Yuanping City	1991	Boiler-making	Villager		Countryman
Sun Yueao	M	41	SSS	2	Yuanping City		Boiler-making	Relative		Relative
Zhao Quanniu	M	49	SS	12	Yuanping City	1990	Boiler-making	No	No	No
Sun Fulong	M	61	SS	6	Lishi City		Paving roads	Friend		Friend
Sun Jianyang	M	22	TSS	12	Taiyuan City	2001	Service	Father	Calligrapher, painter	Relative
Zhao Hongxing	M	32	ES	12	Yuanping City	1992	Cement plant	Half-brother (Chen Wenwen)	Worker	Relative
Chen Wenwen	M	47	ES	12	Yuanping City		Cement plant	Taking father's place	Father was working in the plant	Relative
Sun Xiaohong	M	28	SS	12	Taiyuan City	1998	Feed processing	Cousin	Worker at feed-maker plant	Relative
Sun Xiaolong	M	16	ES	12	Yuanping City	2002	Restaurant	In market, by himself	No	No
Sun Zhaosuo	M	47	SS	8.5	Yuanping City	1980	Construction	No	No	No
Sun Shuqing	M	39	ES	6	Yuanping City	1983	Boiler-maker plant	Cousin (Chen Erlai)		Relative
Chen shuwen	M	40	SS	12	Yuanping City	1984	Machinery making plant	Taking father's place	Worker at Yuanping machine plant	Relative
Wang Lansuo	M	42	SSS	12	Beijing City	2000	Plastic steel plant	Villager (Zhao Shutian) (in his plant)	Chairman of plastic steel plant	Countryman

Name	Sex	Age	Edu.	Years	Location	Year	Sector	Relationship	Current status	Type
Zhao Zhenwu	M	38	SS	2.5	Yuanping City	1982	Machinery making plant	Cousin (Zhao Renwu)	Running his own boiler-maker plant	Relative
Sun Bu'ao	M	55	ES	12	Changzhi City	1991	Transportation corporation	Wife's sister	Worker at transportation corporation in Changzhi City	Relative
Sun Shangzhong	M	51	SS	12	Yuanping City	1958	Restaurant	No	No	No
Zhao Zhijun	M	35	SS	6	Yuanping City	1986	Boiler-making	Villager		Countryman
Yang Jianli	M	29	ES	1.5	Xiangyuan City		Boiler-making	Friend		Friend
Yang Jianqin	M	25	SS	12	Lishi City	1999	Paving roads	Cousin (Chen Jugao)	Manager of road paving project in Lishi City	Relative
Chen Wenzhong	M	53	SSS	1.5	Yuanping City	1999	Boiler-making	Friend (Sun Wenxiu)	Running his own boiler-maker plant in Yuanping City	Friend
Sun Jianzu	M	41	SS	1.5	Lishi City		Paving roads	Countryman (SunWenxiu)	Cadre of Tunwa	Countryman
Sun Guicun	M	53	SS	3.5	Yuanping City		Boiler-making	By himself	No	No
Sun Huijun	M	32	SS	12	Yuanping City	1987	Boiler-making	Father	Contractor of boiler-maker plant	Relative
Xie Jianghai	M	64	ILL	3.5	In the village			Countryman		Countryman
Sun Fushuang	M	45	SSS	12	Yuanping City		Boiler-making			
Zhao Xinliang	M	17	SS	6	Yuanping City	2002	Construction	In market, by himself	No	No
Sun Hengli	M	63	ES	12	Datong City	1990	Boiler-making	Nephew (Zhao Huaiming)	Running his own boiler-maker plant in Datong City	Relative
Sun Guanping	M	39	ES	6	Yuanping City	1936	Boiler-making	Villager	No	Countryman
Sun Jinping	M	29	ES	12	Yuanping City	1936	Boiler-making	Father's friend (Yang Peiliang)	Running his own crane transporting plant	Friend
Zhao Xia	F	23	SS	12	Taiyuan City	1998	Service	Friend		Friend
Chen Xinming	M	22	SS	6	Taiyuan City	1999	Service	Friend		Friend

continued …

Table 6.6 continued

Name	Gender	Age	Education	Time working away (months/year)	Where working	Start date	Industry/type of work	Channel and helper	Status of the helper	Type of guanxi
Zhao Xinjun	M	29	SS	12	Lishi City	2003	Paving roads	Villager (Chen Jugao)	Manager of road paving project in Lishi City	Countryman
Zhao Xinjin	M	32	SS	12	Yuanping City	1998	Boiler-making			
Sun Changhua	M	28	SS	4.5	Lishi City	2001	Paving roads	Uncle (Sun Wenhui)	Principal of road paving project in Lishi City	Relative
Sun Yongqiang	M	28	SS	3.5	Lishi City	2003	Paving roads	Villager (Chen Jugao)	Manager of road paving project in Lishi City	Countryman
Sun Huiwen	M	40	SS	3.5	Lishi City	2001	Paving roads	Villager (Chen Jugao)	Manager of road paving project in Lishi City	Countryman
Sun Cunyi	M	51	SSS	6	Lishi City	2001	Paving roads	Villager	Manager of road paving project in Lishi City	Countryman
Sun Zhigang	M	24	TSS	6	Lishi City	2001	Paving roads	Villager	Manager of road paving project in Lishi City	Countryman
Sun Yinshuang	M	42	SSS	3.5	Xingtai City, Hebei	1989	Boiler-making			
Sun Jianwen	M	38	SS	6	Datong City	1981	Boiler-making	Brother-in-law (Zhao Huaiming)	Running his own boiler-maker plant in Datong City	Relative
Zhao Husheng	M	38	SS	12	Yuanping City	1997	Boiler-making	Neighbour (Zhang Tutu)	Foreman	Neighbour
Zhao Junsheng	M	32	SS	12	Yuanping City	1997	Boiler-making	By himself		No
Zhao Taisheng	M	41	SS	12	Yuanping City	1996	Boiler-making	By himself		No
Sun Xiaojun	M	21	SS	12	Taiyuan City	2000	Service	Uncle (Zhang Sanliang)	Manager of the store in Taiyuan City	Relative
Chen Qingjun	M	39	SS	3.5	Yuanping City	1993	Boiler-making	Acquaintance		Friend

Name	Sex	Age	Education		City	Year	Industry	Relation	Occupation	Type
Chen Shijun	M	33	SSS	4.5	Lishi City	2001	Paving roads	Villager (Chen Jugao)	Manager of road paving project in Lishi City	Countryman
Sun Haijun	M	23	SSS	12	Changzhi	2003	Boiler-making	Cousin	Running his own boiler-maker plant in Changzhi City	Relative
Sun Shuwen	M	43	SSS	6	Yuanping City	1991	Boiler-making	Brother-in-law (Sun Peigang)	Worker at boiler-maker plant in Yuanping City	Relative
Zhao Shuncai	M	57	SSS	6	Yuanping City	1985	Boiler-making	Brother-in-law (Zhao Wenzhou)	Running his own boiler-maker plant (formerly), shepherd (now)	Relative
Wang Shuangjin	M	32	SSS	4.5	Yuanping City	1992	Boiler-making	Villager (Zhao Furong)	Worker at recycling company in Yuanping City	Countryman
Chen Xinli	M	48	SSS	12	Yuanping City	1993	Boiler-making	By himself		No
Zhao Jigui	M	49	SS	12	Datong City	1995	Construction	Cousin (Sun Guobao)	Secretary of party committee of Datong real estate development	Relative
Sun Wenbao	M	50	SS	12	Datong City	1992	Boiler-making	Younger brother (Sun Guobao)	Party Secretary of Datong real estate development	Relative
Chen Fengli	M	33	SS	12	Yuanping City	1992	Boiler-making	Uncle (Zhao Haisheng)	Running his own boiler-maker plant in Yuanping City	Relative
Chen Fengfei	M	25	SS	12	Yuanping City	1996	Boiler-making	Older brother (Chen Fengli)	Worker at uncle's boiler-maker plant	Relative
Gao Jushuang	M	45	SS	12	Taiyuan City	1930	Service	Older brother (Gao Quanshuang)	Chief of HR section of Metallurgy Technology Institute of Taiyuan City	Relative
Wen Jiaoxin	F	45	SSS	12	Yuanping City	2032	Service	The Village Chief of Tunwa introduced her to the Township Chief to be a household helper	The Village Chief of Tunwa	Countryman

continued....

Table 6.6 continued

Name	Gender	Age	Education	Time working away (months/year)	Where working	Start date	Industry/type of work	Channel and helper	Status of the helper	Type of guanxi
Zhang Meiping	F	24	SS	12	Yuanping City	1998	Textile mill	Father's friend (Zhao Xianhong)	Director of Yuanping textile Mill	Friend
Chen Erren	M	46	SS	3	Yuanping City	1990	Boiler-making	Villager (Gao Xiheng)	Running his own business in Yuanping City	Countryman
Zhao Lijun	M	21	SS	12	Taiyuan City	1999	Service	In market, by himself	No	Market rules
Chen Ying	F	22	SS	12	Yuanping City	2000	Fertilizer plant	The acquaintance of uncle (Zhao Shuping)	Chairman of boiler-maker plant in Xinzhou City	Relative + countryman
Chen Junliang	M	38	SS	12	Yuanping City	1990	Car driver	Uncle (Yan Gaoxiang)	The deputy division commander of army section of Xinzhou City	Relative
Zhao Xiaojun	M	17	SS	12	Taiyuan City	1999	Service	In market, by himself	No	Market rules
Duan Maotu	M	50	SS	12	Yuanping City	1986	Boiler-making	Villager (Zhao Shutian)	Running his own constant-pressure boiler-maker plant in Xinzhou City	Countryman
Chen Guanzhong	M	49	SS	3	Yuanping City		Boiler-making	Villager (Zhao Shutian)	Running his own constant-pressure boiler-maker plant in Xinzhou City	Countryman
Zhao Zhengyi	M	26	SS	12	Yuanping City	1995	Service	Older sister (Zhao Lijing)	Married into Yuanping City	Relative
Chen Xiaoyan	F	33	SS	12	Taiyuan City	1988	Service	Her own business, since married into Taiyuan City	No	Marriage
Gao Ersuo	M	38	SS	12	Yuanping City	1982	Boiler-making	Brother-in-law (Chen Xinli)	Running his own boiler-maker plant in Xizhen Township	Relative + countryman

Xie Jie	M	20	SS	12	Taiyuan City	1998	Service	School, after graduation from cookery school	No	Market rules
Zhao Xuanping	M	36	SS	12	Yuanping City	1985	Boiler-making	Countryman (Chen Wenkai)	Running his own company – Dahua machine-making plant in Yuanping City	Countryman
Zhao Jili	M	37	SS	12	Yuanping City	1984	Boiler-making	Villager (Zhao Sanbao)		Countryman
Chen Fuyi	M	35	SSS	12	Yuanping City	1992	Boiler-making	In father-in-law's plant	Director of boiler-maker plant in Quiyu village	Relative
Chen Mingyi	M	32	ES	12	Yuanping City	1983	Construction	Older brother (Chen Jinyi)	Worker at Taiyuan No. 2 Construction Corporation	Relative
Chen Jinyi	M	41	ES	12	Yuanping City		Construction	Recruited by Taiyuan No.2 Construction Company		Market rules
Chen Qiaoping	F	22	SS	12	Beijing City		Service	Husband	Her husband has been working in Beijing for a long time	Relative
Zhao Peiyan	M	30	SS	12	Yuanping City	1998	Chemical plant	Brother-in-law	The section chief of chemical plant	
Zhao Yuesheng	M	45	SS	12	Mi County		Boiler-making	Villager (Gao Xiheng) (in his plant)	Running his own boiler-maker plant	Countryman
Zhao Peicheng	M	37	SS	12	Datong City	1997	Construction	By himself		Market rules
Xie Jianxin	M	40	SS	2.5	Taiyuan City			Nearby village friend		Friend
Chen Weiyu	M	25	SSS	12	Dai County	2002	Museum	Brother		Relative
Chen Yonggang	M	30	ES	12	Yuanping City	1998	Cement plant	The son of grandfather's friend		Friend
Chen Yongjie	M	25	SS	3.5	Lishi City		Paving roads	Villager (Chen Jugao)	Manager of road paving project in Lishi City	Countryman
Sun Jianguang	M	27	SS	6	Lishi City	1999	Paving roads	Villager (Chen Jugao)	Manager of road paving project in Lishi City	Countryman

continued....

Table 6.6 continued

Name	Gender	Age	Education	Time working away (months/year)	Where working	Start date	Industry/type of work	Channel and helper	Status of the helper	Type of guanxi
Zhao Meijun	M	22	SS	12	Yuanping City	1998	Construction	Brother-in-law's brother-in-law	Manager of decorating company	Relative
Zhang Guohua	M	38	SS	12	Yuanping City	2003	Boiler-making	Run business with younger brother Zhang Xinhua	Running own boiler-maker plant in Yuanping City	Relative
Zhang Xinhua	M	31	SS	12	Yuanping City	2003	Boiler-making	Running business with older brother (Zhang Guohua)	Running own boiler-maker plant in Yuanping City	Relative
Sun Quanshuang	M	37	SS	12	Yuanping City	1997	Boiler-making	Running business with older brother and brother-in-law together	Running own boiler-maker plant in Yuanping City	Relative
Sun Peigang	M	27	SSS	6	Yuanping City	1990	Boiler-making	Father (Sun Shuanggui)	Worker in father's friend's company in Yuanping City	Friend
Xie Yinwan	M	49	TSS	12	Beijing City	2003	Construction	Villager (Zhao Shutian) (into his plant)	Running his own plastic steel mill in Beijing City	Countryman
Xie Zhifeng	M	25	SS	12	Yuanping City	2002	Construction	Classmate who is the son of a boss	Running his own decorating material processing plant in Yuanping City	Friend

Source: Field survey in Tunwa village.
Note: M: male, F: female; ES: elementary school, SS: secondary school, SSS: senior secondary school, TSS: technical secondary school, ILL: illiteracy.

Table 6.7 Mobility of labour force in Tunwa village

	Number	Percentage
Time spent working in city each year		
more than 6 months	63	68.5
3–6 months	21	22.8
less than 3 months	8	8.7
Cities worked in		
Yuanping City	55	59.8
Other cities in Shanxi Province	33	35.9
Cities outside Shanxi Province	4	4.3
When started work outside Tunwa		
Before 1984	5	5.4
1984–1989	11	12.0
1990–1995	19	20.7
1996–2001	31	33.7
2002–2003	12	13.0
Not clear	14	15.2
Industry employed in		
Boiler making	39	42.4
Construction	21	22.8
Service sector (including transportations)	21	22.8
Fertilizer plant, cement plant, machinery plant	9	9.8
Coal mining	2	2.2
Age when starting work outside Tunwa		
Less than 18	3	3.2
19–25	18	19.6
26–30	11	12.0
31–35	12	13.0
36–40	17	18.5
41–45	11	12.0
Over 45	20	21.7
Education level		
Illiterate	1	1.1
Elementary education	12	13.0
Secondary education	64	69.6
Senior secondary education	12	13.0
Technical secondary education	3	3.3

Source: Based on Table 6.6.

In terms of the distribution of the labourers working in cities, Tunwa villagers chose Yuanping City (from where the village is administered) as their preferred working place, accounting for 59.8 per cent. Another 35.9 per cent of labourers worked in other cities within Shanxi Province. In other words, the proportion of the village labourers working in various cities of Shanxi Province amounted to 95.7 per cent with only 4.3 per cent of villagers finding jobs in cities outside the province. This clearly indicated a strong regional preference directing the mobility of people from Tunwa village.

In terms of the period during which workers from Tunwa village began to seek job opportunities outside the village, 54.4 per cent started to do so during the 12 years from 1990 to 2001 (Tunwa villagers started working outside since the early 1980s). This period witnessed the largest number of villagers looking for jobs in other places. Encouragingly, up to the time of the survey a good momentum had been maintained. During the one and a half year period from 2002 to the first half of 2003, the proportion of job seekers in other places accounted for 13 per cent of all those who sought job opportunities outside Tunwa since the early 1980s. Therefore, there is a strong impetus and great potential for Tunwa villagers to find jobs in other places.

In terms of the age of those seeking work in other places, unlike the results of most similar studies, Tunwa villagers seeking jobs in other places were mostly older. Of them, those aged 45 or above comprised the largest proportion, accounting for 21.7 per cent. This might be connected with the village's tradition of boiler production, as jobs such as boiler welding require expertise accumulated during many years of work. The age of those engaged in the marketing of boiler-related products was even more closely linked to the accumulation of experience in this trade and their subsequent marketing skills.

In terms of the educational background of job seekers, junior high school graduates accounted for the largest proportion, totalling 69.6 per cent. Graduates from senior high school and primary school each accounted for 13 per cent.

Of course, not only is the basic information about Tunwa people's mobility itself of interest, but more revealing is how this large-scale movement of villagers has taken place. Our concern about this issue carries more significance because of the widespread phenomenon of large numbers of laid-off workers in various cities across the country.

Table 6.8 provides a partial answer to this question from one important dimension. Of the 92 Tunwa labourers in the sample who had moved into cities for various jobs, 77 villagers found employment in cities through various *guanxi* connections, accounting for 83.7 per cent of the total. Only 16.3 per cent (15 people) found their jobs through the commercial job-seeking market.

Of the 77 Tunwa labourers who found outside work through the various *guanxi* connections available to them, we also found different types of relations had been used.

Table 6.8 Guanxi networks and mobility in Tunwa village

	Number	Percentage
Channels through which work outside Tunwa found		
Guanxi networks	77	83.7
Local job market	15	16.3
Type of guanxi *involved (77 people)*		
Blood *guanxi*	41	53.2
Geographic *guanxi*	25	32.5
Occupational, partners and business *guanxi*	11	14.3

Source: Based on Table 6.6.

First, blood relations or family ties through their relatives played a key role in helping them find jobs when migrating. Some 53.2 per cent of labourers found new jobs in cities by relying on their relatives. Such relative-based relations originate from not only their fathers' relatives, such as the brothers of their fathers or their cousins, but also their mothers' relatives, such as the husbands (wives) of their mothers' sisters (brothers), and the sons (daughters) of their mothers' sisters or brothers. Our study showed that there was no distinction between the relations from their fathers' or mothers' sides of the family in determining their mobility and employment in cities.

Second, 32.5 per cent of villagers were brought out of the village by people born in Tunwa village but who have now become wealthy and had lived in cities for some years. This was a more obvious feature of Tunwa people finding jobs in the boiler and road construction sectors outside of the village. The entire boiler industry in Yuanping City basically depended on those coming from Tunwa village. Similarly, as a few people had won road-building contracts, the managers of those projects usually awarded contracts for quite a number of construction tasks to the people from Tunwa village. Naturally, cultural factors such as trust and loyalty were taken into consideration in this regard. Of course, some labourers from Tunwa village were also brought out by their friends in nearby villages or townships which are not far from Tunwa village and who they knew very well.

In addition, occupational or partnership relations through colleagues (mainly fellow workers at previous or current workplaces), classmates and friends have also played a role in helping some villagers to find jobs in the cities. In our survey, 14.3 per cent of labourers found stable jobs in nearby towns and cities through this channel.

Indeed, the descriptive analysis of people's migration from Tunwa village shows very similar situations to other studies (such as the studies carried out by Zhao 2000; Y. Zhao 2003; Zhang and Li 2001; etc.) we discussed previously, which means that Tunwa people's mobility and their *guanxi* connections are directly linked to each other. This also confirms observations from investigations by other scholars in the area in the late 1980s. For example, what Christiansen found was that 'labour opportunities have increased much during the reform era' since the mid-1980s such as those for temporary workers and contract workers in urban areas on one hand; but on the other hand, 'in my interviews with people who have been recruited for work outside their home villages, I have never come across any people who had not been introduced to his employer through *guanxi* channels' (Christiansen, 1990b: 99–100). Huang tells several similar stories from her survey in Cangnan County, Zhejiang Province, that entrepreneurs there 'prefer hiring relatives', 'recruitment of non-relatives that needs skilled labour takes place only in the absence of kin members' (X. Huang 1998: 180). All these investigations indicate the importance of *guanxi* networks to rural–urban migrants. If they return home within only a short period of time in urban areas, then the selection in most of the cases, becomes negative[7] to them (Reyes 1997; Newbold 2000; Wang forthcoming). Therefore, we also need to look in more detail at how significant people's *guanxi* networks are to their mobility through multiple regression analysis, as well as at how the migrants' new communities based on their *guanxi* networks build up gradually, in the next two sections.

Regression analysis on Tunwa villagers' *guanxi* networks and their mobility

In order to further illustrate the links between Tunwa people's mobility and the various *guanxi* networks we have proposed, it is far from sufficient to rely solely on the data obtained from our random surveys of scores of farmers' families. Furthermore, we were unable to make quantitative analysis due to the small size of the samples. Therefore, while conducting more detailed sample surveys and in-depth interviews (discussed further below), we also carried out an overall survey into people's movement and the employment situation of the entire village labour force. We obtained relatively detailed information about the mobility and employment of all 496 labourers in the village.

Based on the detailed information obtained from the comprehensive surveys, we made a regression analysis of the issue by adopting the linear probability model. We chose this model instead of other more complicated models of regression analysis mainly because we considered that we had a reasonably large sample (496) and that the impact of heteroscedasticity would be less important. Besides, a more complicated model would have led to a more complicated calculation method and (probably) a large margin of error.

One feature of this regression model was that a large number of dichotomous variables (0, 1 variables) were employed. Specifically, we defined the variables involved in our analysis as follow:

EDU: years of education
SEX: gender variable, 1 = male; 0 = female.
X1 to X5 are the variables used in our analytical model:
X1 1 = finding jobs through the local market, 0 = finding jobs based on various special personal *guanxi*.
X2 1 = running their own business, 0 = working for others.
X3 1 = introduced by villagers from Tunwa or nearby, 0 = not introduced by villagers from Tunwa or nearby.
X4 1 = introduced by friends, 0 = introduced not by friends.
X5 1 = family or relatives, 0 = non-family or relative.

The regression results of the model showed that age has no obvious impact on whether or not Tunwa villagers will move to other places.[8] The details of the regression results are presented in Table 6.9.

The estimation equation is:

$$Y = (C(1) \times EDU) + (C(2) \times SEX) + (C(3) \times X1) + (C(4) \times X2) + (C(5) \times X3) + (C(6) \times X4) + (C(7) \times X5) + C(8)$$

Table 6.9 Relationship between people's mobility and *guanxi* networks in Tunwa village

Dependent variable: Y
Method: Least squares
Included observations: 594
Excluded observations: 2

Variable	Coefficient	Standard error	t-statistic	Probability
EDU	0.009396	0.003007	3.124996	0.0019
SEX	0.073303	0.022283	3.289581	0.0011
X1 (finding jobs through labour market)	0.700180	0.043587	16.06387	0.0000
X2 (running own business)	0.554426	0.069946	7.926442	0.0000
X3 (introduced by countryman)	0.879373	0.038656	22.74863	0.0000
X4 (introduced by friends)	0.911979	0.051997	17.53895	0.0000
X5 (introduced by relatives)	0.797086	0.031199	25.54857	0.0000
C	−0.052678	0.025884	−2.035155	0.0423
R-squared	0.751301	Mean dependent var		0.319865
Adjusted R-squared	0.748330	S.D. dependent var		0.466817
S.E. of regression	0.234187	Akaike info criterion		−0.052019
Sum squared resid	32.13825	Schwarz criterion		0.007063
Log likelihood	23.44976	F-statistic		252.8949
Durbin-Watson stat	1.758726	Prob (F-statistic)		0.000000

Source: Based on data collected from field survey in Tunwa village.

The results of the regression analysis indicate that the coefficient of each variable is significant and characterized by strong positive relations. Although the regression values of the constant term are negative, this is a normal phenomenon in the linear probability model. The impact of the length of schooling was also significant but it had a small coefficient. When the length of schooling increased by one more year, the probability of migration to other places grew a mere 0.94 percentage points. The variable of sex had a greater impact as the probability of male migration is on average 7.33 percentage points higher than that of females. What is noteworthy was that the variables of various relations were usually very significant and the numerical values were also large. This indicated that various relations exerted a huge impact on whether a Tunwa villager would move to a city. In other words, we have seen very clearly in the regression model that *guanxi* has played a decisive role in Tunwa people's mobility.

In the light of the value of *F*, the results of this regression model were reliable and have not been affected by heteroscedasticity, as frequently occurs in ordinary linear probability models. Meanwhile, it should be noted that the value of goodness of fit in the regression model was quite high, reaching 0.75.

How did the Tunwa entrepreneurs leave the village?

Two major reasons prevented us from completing our studies at this stage and compelled us to go deeper. On the one hand, in theory, our field surveys on the village and the regression model clearly demonstrated that *guanxi* had a decisive impact on Tunwa people's mobility. However, the random surveys we had conducted presented us with only part of the type of *guanxi* mentioned in the theoretical analysis outlined earlier in the chapter, namely, the role and impact of the more significant and traditional kin-based relations, geo-relations and occupational or partnership relations. It was still hard to discern such contents as 'making *guanxi* (relations)'. Therefore, more meticulous study was required in this regard; also, in terms of the actual situation, when we conducted the surveys on Tunwa people's mobility, we found that the movement of the villagers was closely linked with the entrepreneurs who left the village earlier to start businesses in the cities. Quite a number of villagers were brought by these entrepreneurs to work in their plants or on their projects. Thus, in order to have a deeper understanding of the relations between the villagers' mobility and the early-stage pioneers, we conducted more in-depth interviews with the entrepreneurs who had earlier left Tunwa village.

Furthermore, based on our long-term experience in conducting surveys in rural areas, our investigations were not confined to a simple questionnaire-like survey so far as those entrepreneurs were concerned. Instead, we conducted in-depth interviews. As they no longer lived in the village, we shifted the emphasis of our field work from Tunwa village to the cities. In Yuanping City, we found entrepreneurs who moved out of Tunwa village at an early date and then conducted in-depth interviews regarding their pioneering history.

In order to facilitate a clearer analysis of this issue, we will make a brief presentation of the basic information about some entrepreneurs from Tunwa village, the major subject of our survey, in the form of tabulation (Table 6.10) before discussing the contents in a more detailed way. Then a more detailed description and analysis of the three entrepreneurs with whom in-depth interviews were conducted will be presented.

Table 6.10 shows only two of the 12 entrepreneurs sampled from Tunwa village keep their household registration in the village while the remaining ten and their families have all moved permanently from Tunwa village to Yuanping City or other cities. Accordingly, only one person retained his contracted land in the village, and the other 11 had returned the families' contracted land to the village. Therefore, their family members, except aged members, have not lived in the village for years. Some even allowed other villagers to live free of charge in their houses in the village.

Table 6.11 shows that the 12 entrepreneurs have an average age of 48. Considering that they had become successful 15 years ago, they were roughly aged 33 on average when they first achieved success. In terms of education, six were graduates of senior high school or technical secondary school, accounting for half of the total. Five were graduates of junior high school and only one person was educated to primary school level only. Their educational background as such was much better than most ordinary Tunwa villagers working in the cities. Furthermore, each of the entrepreneurs had rich experience in doing business, taking the role of village leader, or managing their own enterprises. All these factors laid a good foundation for their eventual success.

In terms of timing, nine had emigrated during the period of five years from 1984 to 1988, accounting for 75 per cent. Only three migrated in the 1990s (Table

Table 6.10 Information about selected Tunwa entrepreneurs who have migrated to cities[a] (1)

Name[b]	Current residence	Registered permanent residential status (hukou)	Family contract land handed back to the village?	Any family members still live in the house in the village?	Wife and children living in village?	Parents living in village?
Gao Xiheng	Jiefang street, Yuanping City	The couple and older son's *hukou* are in Yuanping City, while that of the other two sons still in the village although they live and study in the city.	Yes	No, except for parents	No	Yes
Zhao Shuping[c] Zhao Shutian	Yuanping City	The whole family's *hukou* have been transferred to Yuanping City	Yes	No, the house is empty now	No	No
Sun Wenxiu	Yuanping City	The whole family's *hukou* have been transferred to Yuanping City	Yes	No, except for mother	No	Yes
Chen Jinsuo	Yuanping City	The whole family's *hukou* have been transferred to Yuanping City	Yes	No, except for mother	No	Yes
Chen Jugao	Yuanping City	The whole family's *hukou* have been transferred to Yuanping City	Yes	No, except for the father-in-law lives in the house	No	No (both dead)
Chen Wenkai	Ping'an street, Yuanping City	The whole family's *hukou* have been transferred to Yuanping City	Yes	No, except for wife's niece lives in the house	No	No (both dead)
Yang Wenzhu	Yuanping City	The whole family's *hukou* have been transferred to Yuanping City	Yes	No, one of the villagers lives in the house free of charge	No	No (both dead)
Zhao Shuanghu	Ruicheng county town, Shanxi Province	Still keeping rural *hukou* in the village, but has been in the city for 7 years.	Yes	Yes	Yes	Yes
Yan Gaoliang	Meiyuan Garden, Datong City, Shanxi Province	The whole family's *hukou* have been transferred to Datong City	Yes	No, except for father	No	Yes (father)
Wang Maosheng	Yuanping City	The whole family's *hukou* have been transferred to Yuanping City	Yes	No, one of the villagers lives in the house free of charge	No	Yes
Sun Guorong	Yuanping City	The couple's *hukou* is still in the village, while the children's have been transferred to Yuanping City	No, rented to a villager	Yes	Yes	Yes
Yang Peiliang	Yuanping City	The whole family's *hukou* have been transferred to Yuanping City	Yes	No, one of the villagers lives in the house free of charge	No	Yes (mother)

Source: Author's interviews.

Notes: (a) Information in the table is up to 10 August 2003 when the most recent study was conducted;

(b) The order of entries in the table is purely based on chronology of the interviews;

(c) Zhao Shuping has passed away, but his younger brother (Zhao Shutian) has kept and expanded his business.

Table 6.11 Information about selected Tunwa entrepreneurs who have migrated to cities[a] (2)

Name[b]	Gender	Age	Education[c]	Principal experiences
Gao Xiheng	M	46	SSS	• Salesman in village enterprises since graduation from high school (1977–84); • Since 1984, running business with Zhao Shuping, Sun Wenxiu and Chen Jinsuo together in Yuanping City; • Opened own business after separating from the three partners.
Zhao Shuping[d] Zhao Shutian	M M	44 43	SSS SSS	• Zhao Shuping's experience is very similar to Gao Xiheng's since they used to run their business together; • Zhao Shutian was a soldier after graduation from high school, then became a salesman of boilers in the village for a few years, joined his brother in 1986.
Sun Wenxiu	M	47	SS	• Had been in the army for 2 years after graduation from the middle school; • Created own business together with Gao Xiheng in Yuanping City in 1984.
Chen Jinsuo	M	48	SSS	• Boiler salesman for several years, then running business with Gao Xiheng together for a few years; • Started his new venture in coal and coke sector in 2000.
Chen Jugao	M	46	TSS	• Salesman for Tunwa village's boilers for 7 years before setting up his own company in Yuanping City.
Chen Wenkai	M	63	TSS	• Studied in Taiyuan Chemical Institute in 1959; • Taught in Tunwa village school from 1961–1969 after returning to the village as required by the government at the time; • Village leader in charge of village non-agricultural development issues from 1970 to 1981; • Opened a rolling mill with Yang Wenzhu and Yuanping Supply and Marketing Company in 1984; • Ran a rolling mill with Yang Wenzhu in Xiayuanping village in 1986; • Ran his own company since 1992 in Yuanping City.
Yang Wenzhu	M	67	SS (not completed)	• Working in one of the state-owned enterprises in Taiyuan City since 1958; • Returned to Tunwa village in 1970 due to a 'speculation mistake'; • One of the key persons for promoting Tunwa's boilers business during the period of 1970 to 1984; • Doing business with Chen Wenkai together from 1984 to 1986; • Started his own boiler-making business in Yuanping City in 1987.
Zhao Shuanghu	M	45	SS	• 25 years experience in manufacturing and marketing boilers and continued working in the area for a private boiler-making plant in Yuanping City.
Yan Gaoliang	M	48	SS	• 4 years experience of selling boilers for Tunwa village collective enterprise soon after his graduation from middle school; • 10 years experience in running his own boiler-maker plant in Yuanping City; • Migrated to Datong City, but retained his major business contacts in the Inner Mongolia.
Wang Maosheng	M	43	SS	• 6 years experience in selling boilers for the village collective enterprise; • Started his private company in Yuanping City in 1988; • Running a plastic weaving plant since 2002 in Yuanping City.

Name[b]	Gender	Age	Education[c]	Principal experiences
Sun Guorong	M	34	SS	• Opened a repair shop for home appliances for 2 years in Yuanping City soon after middle school graduation; • 2 years as an electrician, and another 2 years as the chief of Youth League Committee in the village; • 2 years as a salesman for a boiler company in Yuanping City; • Opened his own company in Yuanping cCty in 1995; • Became one of the deputy Party secretaries of the village as well as preparing for his new hotel business in Yuanping City since 2003.
Yang Peiliang	M	50	SSS	• Had been an accountant for 7 years in the RCC of Loubanzhai Township; • Started running his own boiler-making plant in 1986 in Yuanping City; • Changed his business to leasing equipments for paving road projects since 1988.

Source: Author's interviews.

Notes: (a) Information in the table is up to 10 August 2003 when the most recent study was conducted;

(b) The order of entries in the table is purely based on chronology of the interviews;

(c) SS: Secondary school; SSS: Senior secondary school; TSS: Technical secondary school;

(d) Zhao Shuping has passed away, but his younger brother (Zhao Shutian) has kept and expanded his business,

6.12). This has a great deal to do with the overall external environment at that time. After 1984, the central government began to relax restrictions on farmers moving to small towns and allowed farmers who were able to feed themselves to work in the industrial-commercial and services sectors. At that time, Yuanping County was one of the pilot counties in introducing comprehensive reforms at the county level as well as being one of the model counties in China. The county government adopted measures such as 'the government setting up a "stage" for farmers to perform', encouraging farmers to do business or open up enterprises in urban areas and then offering them preferential terms for land use or tax breaks. In this favourable climate, many Tunwa entrepreneurs began in 1984 to leave the village to settle in the county town of Yuanping County (currently changed to Yuanping City as approved by the State Council of China).

Possessing the resources of various special *guanxi* networks was very important for all the migrants. For instance, the relations of friends or relatives played key roles in promoting the development of their enterprises. The following stories of three entrepreneurs provide a more detailed analysis of this experience.

Interview 1: How Yang Wenzhu moved to Yuanping City

During the survey in Tunwa village, the villagers all agreed that Yang Wenzhu was one of the most successful and currently the wealthiest emigrant from Tunwa village. Growing from a small business into a large one, his enterprise has developed into a family venture of considerable size. Its business scope has expanded into many areas rather than being confined to its initial focus of making boilers. It was said the annual gross income of his business was about 5 million yuan with an average net profit of about 1 million yuan per year. Total assets held by his family was estimated to be about 10 million yuan or more. More than 70 people are now working regularly in his enterprise. Of these six are Tunwa villagers – electric welders who have mastered the basic welding skills. A study of his enterprise ten years ago in 1993 showed annual sales by his plant was more than 3 million yuan with a net profit of about half a million yuan per year (J. Li 1996: 109).

Yang Wenzhu's enterprise was visited on 6 August 2003. When we visited his plant (Plate 6.1), photos of the key leaders of Shanxi Province and Yuanping City were hanging in the upper part of the main wall in his office. However, Yang Wenzhu himself was not in any of those pictures.

Because our survey team had established a long-standing relationship of trust and understanding with him and Tunwa villagers during the past ten years, Yang Wenzhu and I had an agreeable conversation for nearly a whole day about the entrepreneur's pioneering business experience and history of migration.

> I was born in Tunwa village in 1936. I quit school after only one year in the middle school. When I was 17 (that was in 1953), my cousin (the son of my father's sister) working in Taiyuan City (who later became the director of the Supply and Marketing Cooperatives of the city) introduced me to work as a

Table 6.12 Information about selected Tunwa entrepreneurs who have migrated to cities[a] (3)

Name[b]	Enterprise	Date and city moved to	Position	How move to city and business success were achieved
Gao Xiheng	Yuanping No.1 Constant Pressure Boiler-making Plant	1984/Yuanping City	Founder/General Manager	• Yuanping government encouraged farmers to move into towns and cities to run their own businesses by providing land use, tax holiday etc. incentives in early 1980s; • Local Party Secretary of Ban village of Yuanping Town, Zhang Fuzhu, provided much help in the initial stages.
Zhao Shuping[c] Zhao Shutian	Xinzhou Prefecture Constant-pressure Boiler-making Plant;Beijing Daxing Plastic Steel Mill.	1984/1986:Yuanping; 2003: Beijing	Founder/General Manager	Similar to Gao Xiheng's case
Sun Wenxiu	Yuanping Jinsheng Constant-pressure Boiler-making Plant	1984/Yuanping City	Founder/General Manager	Similar to Gao Xiheng's case
Chen Jinsuo	Xinzhou Coal and Coke Co. Ltd.	1984/Yuanping City	Founder/General Manager	Similar to Gao Xiheng's case
Chen Jugao	Shanxi Yichen Co. Ltd.	1986/Yuanping City	Founder/Chairman	See interview summary Table 6.14
Chen Wenkai	Shanxi Yuanping Chuangda Machinery Co. Ltd.	1985/Yuanping City	Founder/Chairman	See interview summary Table 6.15
Yang Wenzhu	Xinzhou Prefecture Welfare Boiler-making Plant	1985/Yuanping City	Founder/Chairman	See interview summary Table 6.13
Zhao Shuanghu	Salesman for various boiler-making plants	1996/Ruicheng County town	Professional salesman	Many contacts and rich experience in the area
Yan Gaoliang	Salesman for various boiler-making plants	1998/Datong City	Professional salesman	Many contacts and rich experience in the area
Wang Maosheng	Yuanping Plastic Weaving Plant	1988/Yuanping City	Founder/General Manager	Many contacts and rich experience in the area
Sun Guorong	Xinzhou Saving-energy Boiler Co. Ltd.	1995/Yuanping City	Founder/General Manager	Many contacts and rich experience in the area
Yang Peiliang	Yuanping Chang'an Heavy Equipment Transit Service Company	1996/Yuanping City	Founder/General Manager	• Father was the Director of RCC of Yuanping City (formerly Yuanping County), then the President of ABC's Fanshi branch, which was helpful to having early access to capital when required.

Source: Author's interviews.

Notes: (a) Information in the table is up to 10 August 2003 when the most recent study was conducted;

(b) The order of entries in the table is purely based on chronology of the interviews;

(c) Zhao Shuping has passed away, but his younger brother (Zhao Shutian) has kept and expanded his business.

Plate 6.1   Yang Wenzhu's 'Xinzhou Welfare Boiler Plant of Shanxi Province' located in the centre of Yuanping City

casual labourer at a construction site in Taiyuan. I was doing mainly heavy manual work such as carrying bricks and stone as well as mixing mud and sand. Two years later, my cousin introduced me to the Taiyuan Machinery Plant to work as a rivet worker, where I worked until 1970. I was fired from the plant on charges of 'speculation', for I resold 70 pieces of silver coins (silver dollars used in old China) that I had bought from one of my fellow workers for six yuan each to nearby farmers at a price of seven yuan per coin earning 70 yuan all together.

Then I returned to the village. Upon the approval of Chen Youcai, the Party Secretary of the village at that time, the village took advantage of the welding skills I had learned at the Taiyuan Machinery Plant to begin running a farm tool repair plant, repairing farm machinery such as flat-bed trailers. With the help of Ren Hezhong and other Tunwa villagers who worked at Xuangang Mining Bureau (one of the state-run large-scale coal mine bases in China), the Tunwa-run plant obtained the opportunity to make rail spikes and check plates (a kind of claw plate used in coal mine tunnels) for Xuangang Mining Bureau. At that time, 25 kilograms of spikes and scores of pairs of check plates were made every day for the coal mine which earned a rough daily income of 90 yuan. After we became familiar with the leaders of the Xuangang Mining Bureau, the collective-owned plant of Tunwa village gradually began to repair coal scuttles and boilers and install pipelines.

After a period of business contacts, the leaders of Xuangang Mining Bureau told me that Datong Mining Bureau also had similar business needs. I had been considering for quite a long period of time through what kind of *guanxi* should I obtain the business contract there. I learned from multiple channels that the vice mayor of Datong City, whose surname is Guo and called Guo Datang in full name, came from Loubanzhai village, which is adjacent to Tunwa village. So that's half done, for my grandmother also came from the Loubanzhai village, having the same surname. They shared the same surname and home village. Then, I went to the General Office of Datong Municipal Government for information about Guo Datang. I was told that Guo Datang indeed was the vice mayor but had been newly assigned as Party Secretary at a state-owned factory. I went immediately to the factory and, using tips from others, luckily found Guo Datang. At the first sight of him, I called loudly: "Uncle!". Guo was taken aback at such a sudden "hello". However, Guo soon understood why I referred to him in that way after I told him about my grandmother's origin and my own purpose. He told me that Datong Cement Factory and Locomotive Plant also were in demand of similar businesses and that he had friends working in those plants as directors. Upon my request, he wrote to the leaders of different plants.

With his letters in my pocket, I first went to Datong Cement Plant and met the plant director. The director gave me a letter for the plant's business section. The section chief told me that they needed a huge amount of ball bearings (also informally called 'iron balls') and asked me to sign an initial contract for 10 tons. Worried about the limited production capacity of Tunwa village, I dared not sign that contract. Later I signed a contract to make two drying machines. The cement plant would provide all the raw materials and the Tunwa-run collective enterprises would be responsible for the processing. Each drying machine was charged a processing fee of 50,000 yuan. That contract earned Tunwa village a net profit of 56,000 yuan that year.

Later, by a very chance accident, I came across a man from Hebei Province buying oil tanks in Yuanping City and received a few errands to do at the Second Light Industry Bureau of Yuanping City. He told me that diesel fuel had been kept in underground cement pits for quite a long period of time in the rural areas in Hebei. People now wanted to store the fuel in oil tanks which were much needed. After receiving the news, I immediately went to Shijiazhuang City, the capital of Hebei Province. I contacted a few units and successfully negotiated some orders.

When I was staying in a hotel in Shijiazhuang City, I became acquainted with a man staying there who was working in the grain management department of Liu'an Prefecture of Anhui Province. He said they also needed oil tanks back home. So I went to some places in Anhui Province, such as Liu'an, Feidong, Feixi and Hefei, where I signed more than 20 contracts for making oil tanks. After I returned to the village, I discussed the issue with village leaders and it was decided that all the six production teams in the entire village would quickly set up machinery plants to manufacture oil tanks. Therefore, the industrial production boomed immediately in the whole village. By 1982, the collective economy in Tunwa village became quite well developed and the villagers' income reached a relatively high level. The value of ten work-points for a farmer increased from 0.3 yuan in 1970 to 5 yuan, increased by 15.7 times. In 1983, the household responsibility system for agriculture based on land was introduced to the village which led to the dissolution of collective enterprises. Individual farmers began to start their own private enterprises.

In 1984, my fellow villager Chen Wenkai and I were employed as salesmen by the Supply and Marketing Company of the Yuanping Bureau of Township Enterprises. In 1985, when I was staying in a hotel in Taiyuan City, the capital of Shanxi Province, I learnt in my chats with a salesman from Lin County (Linxian) of Henan Province (who was also a business partner of Chen Wenkai for many years) that his purpose in Shanxi was to buy waste steel and coal from Shanxi Province and ship the steel to his hometown, roll them into various types of wire rods in its rolling mill and sell them for quite a considerable profit. Working in collaboration with Chen Wenkai, we thus cooperated with the Supply and Marketing Company to establish Yuanping County Rolling Mill. We earned 400,000 yuan in profits that year.

In 1986, village Party Secretary Xing Renhai and Village Chief Wu Manyin of the Xiayuanping village on the outskirts of Yuanping City learnt from their friends that Chen Wenkai and I were good at running businesses. They then came to meet both of us, hoping to cooperate with us in setting up a rolling mill in their village. Besides the fact that both of us would have some private shares in the new venture, they also promised us two more conditions: one was that the household registration books (*hukou*) of all the members of our two families would be transferred from Tunwa village to Xiayuanping village of Yuanping City, i.e., our agricultural household registrations status (*nongye hukou*) would be converted into that of non-agricultural household registration status (*feinongye hukou*) (for the Xiayuanping village was located in the suburbs of the city); the other condition was that each of our families would be freely given a piece of land to build houses for our convenience. The two conditions were very attractive at that time and we agreed. However, the plant did not earn much money that year due to swift changes in the market. In 1987, we separated and each of us began our own businesses. I myself then established my own business – Xinzhou Welfare Boiler Plant of Shanxi Province located in Xiayuanping village, which is very close to the centre of Yuanping City.

In order to solve the housing issue at my plant, I took advantage of my private *guanxi* with the leaders of Xiayuanping village cultivated two years ago and bought half of the plot of land where the rolling mill was built (altogether 12 *mu* of land at a cost of 320,000 yuan). When our business boomed and the shortage in workshop space became acute, we rented houses as workshops. Generally, I rented the workshops from my relative by marriage (the father-in-law of my younger son who was from the Xiayuanping village. He was previously the labour contractor at the railway station of Yuanping City).

Between 1990 and 1995, my plant was able to earn more than 1 million yuan (of net profit) every year. However, it was hard to remain profitable in the following years. Therefore, I decided to diversify my business. I began to build Yuanping Hotel in the downtown area in 1995, which is presently the only star rated hotel (two stars) in Yuanping City. The hotel, located in the downtown area, has a land area of 4 *mu*. As my friends in the city government helped me in acquiring the land, the land price was fairly cheap (86,000 yuan per *mu*). I'm now thinking of establishing a coal washery to expand my business to a larger scale as well.

(Yang Wenzhu)

From the story Yang Wenzhu told me about his pioneering and migration process, we can see that various *guanxi* were employed in many places. We can sum up the links of various *guanxi* and their stages of development in the following brief table (Table 6.13).

Interview 2: How did Chen Jugao develop from a Tunwa villager into an entrepreneur and local politician?

While conducting surveys in Tunwa village, it was found that a lot of villagers were working at Chen Jugao's plants. They told the researcher that, after more than ten years of development, Chen Jugao's undertaking had grown from a single enterprise into multiple enterprises which had now become an enterprise group with diversified business in different areas. His fixed assets were said to have reached more than 20 million yuan with an annual gross income of about 10 million yuan.

Through my contact with the leaders of the local government, I knew that Chen was not only an excellent entrepreneur but also an excellent local politician. He had been a member of Standing Committees of the People's Political Consultative Conferences of Yuanping City. He was also President of the Yuanping Chambers of Industry and Commerce, charged with the responsibility of guiding and coordinating the development of local private enterprises in Yuanping City.

Therefore, Chen Jugao's enterprise in Yuanping City was visited on 5 August 2003. At first sight there were three business licences hanging on the wall of his office – Shanxi Yichen Industrial Co. Ltd., the Spark Boiler Plant of Shanxi Yichen Industrial Co. Ltd., and Yuanping Jianda Machinery Engineering Co. Ltd. of Shanxi Province.[9]

Unfortunately, it was not possible to have an interview with Chen Jugao himself because he was on a business trip. Luckily, the key leaders in charge of his enterprise (who were also his relatives) were all available. So, I discussed with Zhao Furong, his elder brother-in-law who was also deputy general manager in charge of financial affairs and Lü Huaizhong, the husband of his elder sister who was the director of the boiler plant, the man in charge of the key business of Chen

Table 6.13 Yang Wenzhu's experiences and his *guanxi* networks

Experience	Help from others	Helpers	Types of guanxi
Casual labourer in Taiyuan construction building site	Getting a job	Cousin	Relative
Riveting worker in the Taiyuan Machinery Factory	Finding a better job	Cousin	Relative
Salesman for Tunwa village-run firms	Getting orders from Xuangang Mining Bureau	Former Tunwa villagers (Ren Hezhong etc.)	Countrymen
Salesman for Tunwa village-run firms	Getting orders from Datong Cement Factory	Grandmother's clan family member, from Tunwa's neighbourhood village (Guo Datang)	Relative + Countryman
Salesman for Tunwa village-run firms	Signing contracts with several local grain management departments in Hebei and Anhui provinces	Guests staying in the same hotel	Business relations + *Guanxi* making
Working with the Supply and Sales Company of Yuanping Bureau of Township and Village Enterprises	Seeking orders	Guests staying in the same hotel	Business relations + *Guanxi* making
Running a company jointly with Xiayuanping village in suburban area of Yuanping City	Household registration status (hukou) changed to non-agricultural from agricultural, whole family moved into city from Tunwa village.	Major leaders of Xiayuanping village of Yuanping City	Mutual benefit + recommendation of a friend
Setting up own firm in Yuanping City	Land purchase for workshops	Major leaders of Xiayuanping village	Former business partner
Running own business	Renting workshop (low rent)	Son's father-in-law	Friend + Relative
Building his private hotel in the centre of Yuanping City	Purchasing land	A friend working in the city government	Friend

Source: Interview with Yang Wenzhu in Yuanping City.

Jugao's enterprise. These discussions revealed the course of the success of Chen and his enterprises.

Chen Jugao was born in 1957 in Tunwa village. After graduating from high school at Loubanzhai Middle School, he took up farming for several years before joining the collective enterprise in the village as a salesman. His main task was to sell products such as oil tanks and drinking-water boilers. After the introduction of the family household responsibility system in the village, Chen, together with four other villagers, jointly set up a plant in partnership making drinking-water boilers. As the plant was not that successful, they dissolved the partnership and began their own businesses half a year later.

In 1984, he tried by all means (including loans) to raise 20,000 yuan and rented a few old houses from a military camp on Yongkang Nanlu (Yongkang South Road) in Yuanping City, where he established the Yuanping County New Star Drinking-Water Boiler Plant. In less than four years of establishing the business, he gradually enhanced his ties with some leaders of the city government (one of the leaders, formerly the director of the General Office of the CPC Yuanping City Committee, who was from the Shangmodu village in the Daniudian Town not far from Tunwa village and Chen's friend), as well as the leaders of the suburban areas. As Yuanping City had also adopted flexible policies and measures encouraging farmers to begin private businesses in urban areas, Chen Jugao and the Party Secretary of the Shangyuan village in Yuanping's suburbs agreed that Chen would move his enterprise to Qianjin Xijie (Qianjin West Street). The leaders of the Shangyuan village hoped to take advantage of Chen's power to develop their village-run enterprises, so they sold him five *mu* of land at a fairly favourable price. Chen then had his own workshops built and renamed his plant 'Yuanping Spark Boiler Plant', which specially engaged in manufacturing various types of boilers and drinking-water boilers. Later, when an iron plant run by the government of Xizhen Township closed down, Chen bought the whole piece of land on which the bankrupt enterprise was located (about 7.5 *mu* of land) plus some old workshops, at a cost of 500,000 yuan. He then moved his plants to that location, i.e., the current site at Yuanma Lu (Yuanma Road), Yuanping City from Qianjin Xijie.

The enterprise has achieved a steady development since 1995 when it relocated to the current Yuanma site. While continuously exploring the traditional boiler market, Chen Jugao added quite a few new products such as steam boilers and pressure vessels. However, it became more and more difficult for the enterprise to collect payment for sales. Beginning in 1998, Chen acted swiftly to begin implementing a strategy of diversified development of the enterprise and entered the highway-related construction sector.

The most vital factor leading to the strategy of diversified development in 1998 was Shanxi Province's decision to begin building the Taiyuan–Jiuguan Expressway (simply called Tai–Jiu Express). One of the leaders in charge of provincial highway and transportation happened to be a friend of Chen's for nearly 20 years (Chen established fairly good *guanxi* with this leader when he was working as a salesman for the collective enterprise of Tunwa village in the early 1980s). Therefore, it was quite natural for the leader to help Chen win some contracts for the Tai–Jiu Express construction project, making road edge plates for both sides of the expressway.

With the help of the leader in 1999, Chen won a contract worth more than 1 million yuan to build toll stations on the road section between Yuanping to Taiyuan. In 2000, Chen again obtained contracts with a value of more than 14 million yuan to construct a five-storey office building and two toll stations on the road section between Fenyang to Xiajiaying. Between 2001 and 2002, Chen successfully contracted to build toll stations, office buildings and road beds on the sections of expressway between Changzhi of Shanxi Province to Handan of Hebei Province, Yuncheng of Shanxi Province to Sanmenxia of Henan Province, and Datong to Xinguangwu of Shanxi Province. It could be said that Chen had made initial successful attempts to expand his business scope to the highway construction sector from 1998 to 2002. Nevertheless, it must be noted that without the help of his long-standing friendship with the leader, who had access to abundant construction resources, it would have simply been unbelievable for Chen to achieve so quickly such great success in the new business.

In 2003, Beijing Urban Construction Group won a contract to dig tunnels in the Fenyang–Liulin section of the highway within Shanxi Province, which was part of the main arterial road from Qingdao in Shandong Province to Ningxia in China's remote west. Owing to the achievements of Chen's enterprises in the previous years and particularly due to the fact that one of the key leaders of Beijing Urban Construction Group used to be Chen's classmate in the Senior Section of the Loubanzhai Middle School, the firm was given the opportunity to cooperate with the Beijing Construction Company in this project, winning half of the 12 million yuan contract.

(Zhao Furong and Lü Huaizhong)

Obviously, Chen's path to success and his experience of emigrating from Tunwa village to Yuanping City have explicitly reflected his own pioneering course as well as that of his family, colleagues and employees in the past 20 years. We clearly found that the various personal relations (*guanxi*) that Chen had established over the years played a key role at every vital stage of development of his enterprises (see Table 6.14).

Interview 3: How did Chen Wenkai get out of Tunwa village and pioneer his way to today's success?

Chen Wenkai is a person that can be hardly ignored in any reference to surveys conducted in Tunwa village and this was the case for us as far as this survey was concerned. This was not only because his plants in Yuanping City have attracted a large number of villagers from Tunwa village but also because for many years

Table 6.14 Chen Jugao's success and his *guanxi* networks

	Help from others	Helpers	Types of guanxi
The initial stage of his business moving to Yuanping City from Tunwa village	Land purchase	Friend working in the city government	Friend + Countryman (neighbourhood villager)
Expanding business area to road construction from boiler making	Signing contracts on building toll station and toll road management department's offices	Key person is in charge of transportation issues in the government	Old friend
Further development in road construction area	Culvert construction project	The principal of a key state-owned construction company in Beijing	High school classmate

Source: Interview with Chen Jugao's brothers-in-law in Yuanping City.

he was the chief of the Tunwa village (then called 'Chief of Production Brigade') and, therefore, was very familiar with every aspect of the village. What is more, he is now regarded by the villagers as the wealthiest person from Tunwa village. When villagers were asked how much wealth Chen possessed, nobody could provide a definite estimate. Therefore, compared with other entrepreneurs from Tunwa village, he appears to be more of a mystery to the villagers.

A survey conducted by my colleague Li Jing ten years ago found Chen Wenkai had only 300,000 yuan in fixed assets and 420,000 yuan of working capital in 1993 and there were 20 employees in his plant (J. Li 1996: 105). Judging from this, if the villagers are correct in their estimation, Chen Wenkai must have had a period of abundant wealth accumulation during the past ten years.

In the afternoon of 5 August 2003, I visited Chen Wenkai's company and was first shown around his plant (see Plate 6.2) and then returned to his office where we conversed throughout the entire afternoon until dusk.

Some of Chen's pioneering history has overlapped with that of Yang Wenzhu's for both had previously worked together for many years to run a business in partnership. Besides this link, Chen and his family members shared the same mode, process and place of resettlement as Yang Wenzhu when they migrated from Tunwa village to Yuanping City. Therefore, that part of the interview has been omitted here.

Plate 6.2 Chen Wenkai's 'Yuanping Chuangda Machinery Co. Ltd. in the centre of Yuanping City

I was born in Tunwa village in 1940. I entered Yuanping Agriculture School (a secondary school of agriculture) in 1958 (aged 18) and was transferred to Taiyuan Chemical Industry School (a secondary technical school) in the following year. I returned to Tunwa village in 1961 when the state implemented a policy under which various types of the rural population and labour force who were then living in urban areas were compelled to go back to their native homes.

After returning to the village, I first taught mathematics in the middle school until 1969. In 1970, I served as deputy director of the Revolutionary Committee of the Tunwa Production Brigade, as well as the Production Brigade's Party Secretary in the following year. Three years later, I was dismissed from the post of Party Secretary because I concealed (under-reported) the grain output by 300,000 *jin* (150,000 kilogram) for fear that the villagers might suffer starvation and began working as the deputy brigade chief in charge of the brigade's collective enterprise development issues.

This was a tough assignment. After electricity was made available to Tunwa village in 1972, the village-run collective enterprises had a totally different mode of operation. They no longer took up simple jobs such as making farm tools or woodwork as they did in the 1960s. Instead, a machinery plant with a considerable scale was set up. It went beyond Tunwa village for job tasks and undertook contracts for making oil tanks, drinking-water boilers and boilers from all places nationwide (provinces such as Anhui, Hebei, Jiangsu, Inner Mongolia and Xinjiang, besides Shanxi province). I remember more than 50 workers (including a construction team) were doing sideline business in the village-run collective enterprises at that time. Later (in 1983), the decentralization policy of contracting farming land to each family was carried out and the collective enterprises were either contracted by individuals or dissolved. Thus, Yang Wenzhu from my village and I went to work at the Supply and Marketing Company under the county's Township and Village Enterprise Bureau.

In 1984, together with Yang Wenzhu, Li Jinshuo, Xing Shehui and the Supply and Market Company, a total of five shareholders including me, we established a rolled metal plant which was mainly engaged in rolling steel from waste metal.

The reason why this plant was born so smoothly was because we had conditions that had matured in all aspects: firstly, the county's Supply and Marketing Company provided land and workshop space; secondly, we 'headhunted' Li Jinshuo from a rolling mill in Henan Province, for he had expertise in this technology; thirdly, one of my distantly-related cousins, Xing Shehui, had some money and joined us by contributing 10,000 yuan. Yang Wenzhu was not only my old colleague once working in the same section at the village-run machinery plant but also he had riveting and forging skills plus good marketing skills. As for myself, I had quite a few relations in Taiyuan City. Under the then situation of a planned economy, I was able to obtain materials such as steel that was supplied only on a planning basis.

Furthermore, I was also able to receive advance payment from the other party (13,000 yuan paid in advance in the year the plant was established). Owing to our good operation, the plant was not only set up in a short period of time but also earned several hundred thousand yuan in that very year.

However, things changed drastically in 1986. As a large number of steel mills were put into operation, it became difficult to obtain raw materials. Since rolling mills had greatly polluted the environment, the government no longer allowed them to operate in urban areas. Under such twin pressures, we earned less money in 1986 – an amount of roughly 100,000 yuan only. Consequently, some shareholders were reluctant to continue the venture. Through the introduction of one of my classmates from Yuanping Middle School (who was then working in the Yuanping Taxation Bureau) and because the leaders of the Xiayuanping village needed people to help them run their enterprises, Yang Wenzhu and I moved our plant to Xiayuanping village. By collaborating for two years with the village's collective enterprises, it was possible to solve the problem of changing my family's agricultural household registration status into a non-agricultural one and moved to the city.

Later I had a rest for two years. By 1992, the government allowed land sales near urban areas to individuals setting up plants (which was previously prohibited). So I bought 4.5 *mu* of land at a cost of 16,000 yuan in the Xizhen Township within a very short distance of the city centre [by the side of the current Ping'an Avenue of Yuanping City – author's note], where I established a steel form plate plant, i.e., the Yuanping County Dahua Building Machinery Plant which was renamed in the following year as the Yuanping City Dahua Building Machinery Plant. This meant I had basically withdrawn from the boiler industry. My main concern was that too many people were engaged in boiler businesses and the number of entrepreneurs from Tunwa village engaged in this trade alone stood at about 30. There were reportedly about 100 boiler plants in Yuanping City, which led to extremely fierce competition. Therefore, I shifted priority to the construction sector, mainly the production of construction-related steel form plates (including those used in highway and railway construction projects). I have been in this sector since then until now. I have about 40 frontline workers in the plant all year round, with an average annual gross income of about 4 million yuan. However, the profit rate was not very high as the average annual net profit was less than 400,000 yuan.

As the state has increased investment in highway and railway construction in recent years, so my business has also grown to some extent. I then divided the entire business into three parts. One of them was what you saw just now which was the old business that I was responsible for. Another was a new business involving Golmud City of Qinghai Province. This was the business accorded to me by my old client, i.e., the No.20 Railway Bureau which was responsible for part of the Qinghai–Tibet railway construction project. No. 20 Railway Bureau began to use my products during the building of the Yuanping section of the Suzhou–Huanghua Harbour railway. As my products won the bid for materials supply for the Qinghai–Tibet railway construction project in 2002, my products were also used by No.17 Railway Bureau of Golmud City. This part of my business was managed by my younger son (Chen Yongsheng). The third part of my business was renting the overhauling workshop of a state-run auto repair plant in downtown Yuanping City (with a rent of 2,500 yuan per square metre annually) to produce steel form plates, so as to resolve a shortage of workshops in my plant. My elder son (Chen Shuangsheng) was in charge of this business.

We now have introduced a shareholding system. I, my two sons and my son-in-law are jointly entitled to this enterprise and the four of us each own a quarter of the shares, but the legal representative is my younger son Chen Yongsheng.[10]

I think I have benefited most from the help of my friends in running my enterprises. During my initial efforts to set up collective enterprises run by Tunwa village at the end of the 1970s and early 1980s, I often went on business trips to Taiyuan City because I was responsible for the purchase of raw materials. In those years when I stayed in hotels in Taiyuan, I became acquainted with salesmen of state-run enterprises who were in charge of purchasing materials under the state plan. I made friends with some of them. At that time, it was generally simple to make friends and I normally brought them some native products from our village such as eggs and walnuts or entertained them with a meal for about 170 or 180 yuan. I later benefited a lot from them (including my classmates of the Taiyuan Secondary Technical School) in such matters as raising loans. Now I no longer request loans. Instead, when in need of funds, I borrow from my friends, for we maintain very good credibility among ourselves.

(Chen Wenkai)

The key stages of Chen Wenkai's mobility from Tunwa village to Yuanping City and the development of his firms has been summarized in Table 6.15.

Preliminary conclusions

Two very interesting theoretical issues need to be emphasized in the preliminary part of the concluding discussion on *guanxi* community and people's mobility in relation to the survey from Tunwa village: one is what is the relationship between *guanxi* and *guanxi* community; and the other is why and how people's social mobility had happened simultaneously with the geographic mobility of Tunwa villagers.

Guanxi *and* guanxi *community*

Theoretically speaking, *guanxi* is more a kind of micro-level phenomenon which deals with interpersonal relations that focus more on the mutual interaction while *guanxi* community deals more with the intermediate structural issue; some special groups may finally emerge out of the *guanxi* as a consequence of people's

Table 6.15 Chen Wenkai's success and *guanxi* networks

	Help from others	Helpers	Types of guanxi
In charge of Tunwa village-run enterprise	Purchasing raw materials under the strict government controls at the time	Friends from state-owned enterprises	Friend + *guanxi* network
Running a rolling mill jointly with a suburban village of Yuanping City	Capital investment	Cousin invested part of the money and became one of the shareholders	Relative + business partner relationship
Running a rolling mill jointly with a suburban village of Yuanping City	Recommending Chen Wenkai and Yang Wenzhu to Xiayuanping village leaders	Middle school classmate	Classmates
Running a rolling mill jointly with a suburban village of Yuanping City	Household registration status (hukou) changed to non-agricultural from agricultural, all the family members moved into the city from the village.	Major leaders of Xiayuanping village of Yuanping City	Mutual benefit + recommendation of the friend mentioned above
Setting up own company	Access to loans	Mutual friends	Friends
Expanding business to Qinghai and Xizang (Tibet)	Bidding for order for providing steel moulding board for Qinghai-Xizang railway construction project	Former clients	Business relation

Source: Interview with Chen Wenkai in Yuanping City.

interaction. Our survey in Tunwa village has revealed an additional factor which is very important to understand better the relationship between *guanxi* and *guanxi* community, i.e. the change has been an evolutionary process; it simply means that it is a dynamic process of change from personal *guanxi* to *guanxi* community. Therefore, we should realize that *guanxi* community has different forms at different stages of its development: primary forms, extended forms, mature forms and so on.

Within the *guanxi* community framework, most of the *guanxi* that Tunwa people have built up so far are various primary forms of *guanxi*. One of the reasons which supports this point is that, if we borrow Granovetter's concepts of 'weak ties' and 'strong ties' (discussed earlier), we can say that *guanxi* communities forged by Tunwa villagers are built on strong ties and the role of weak ties is not visible at present. Maybe the inadequate education received by each individual in these relationship networks, as Burt (1992) pointed out, is the correct assumption in the case of Tunwa; maybe it is because the village is yet to be sufficiently open, because of its transportation constraints, etc.

However, we need to pay much more attention to the changing process or evolutionary process of the *guanxi* community at different stages of its development. Generally speaking, people's mobility out of village in Tunwa is based more on the strong ties such as the blood relation networks (kinship) which characterized 53.2 per cent of the total migrants; meanwhile, there are also several

(32.5 per cent of the total) who made their arrangements to migrate through former co-villagers who have been living in urban areas for some years, and 14.3 per cent of the migrants moved to cities with help from their former classmates, former co-workers, friends and so on. But the situation is different in the survey of 824 households from six provinces in China conducted in 1999 by Y. Zhao (2003). In Zhao's study, what is more important is the co-villager relations among current migrants, former migrants and non-migrants of the villages surveyed. Therefore, some new *guanxi* communities have been restructured based on the old villagers' relations. Thus Zhao measures the migration networks in the case by stressing very much the number of early migrants, since the new *guanxi* community is so important for subsequent migration,[11] not relying so much on personal kinship networks. Rozelle *et al.*'s study based on the village level data also shows how the new community has been efficient in supporting the villagers' mobility through the chain effect of migration (Rozelle *et al.* 1997).

Moreover, new communities can also be built up on a much bigger base crossing much longer distances, but rooted in some common *guanxi* resources. The famous 'Zhejiang village', 'Xinjiang village', 'Henan village' and 'Anhui village' in Beijing and similar villagers' communities and shanty town formation in Guangzhou, Shenzhen and in Shanghai's Pudong District (Solinger 1999) are all typical examples in the area (Ma and Xiang 1998; Davin 1999). Even from the international migration point of view, we can also find a similar situation; for example, Christiansen (2003) tells how the Chinese formed their own migration communities in Europe through the 'chain migration'[12] method, building up their new communities gradually. McKeown's research shows how Chinese in Peru, Chicago and Hawaii formed extensive systems that made cultural and commercial exchange possible in the early twentieth century (McKeown 2001).

What we learnt from the brief comparative studies, both domestically and internationally, is that new communities based on certain special *guanxi*, i.e., the new concept of *guanxi* community we discussed earlier, can be built up through different forms at different levels. Tunwa migrants' new *guanxi* community was set up mainly based on their personal kinship relations; the *guanxi* communities built up in both Zhao's case and Rozelle *et al.*'s case were much more based on the village-level grouping characteristics beyond immediate kinship. The 'floating villages' in cities like 'Zhejiang village' in Beijing became more like the real intermediate level *guanxi* community based on the various extended *guanxi* resources from certain localities, such as people from Zhejiang Province, Henan Province and so on; Chinese communities (some people called them 'Chinatowns') in Europe, studied by Christiansen, and many overseas Chinese communities in other countries, (for example, the Fujianese community in New York[13]) should be regarded as the mature forms of *guanxi* community. However, along with the further development of Tunwa people's business as well as their social networks in the city – mainly in Yuanping City – we can expect that some mature *guanxi* communities will be built up gradually. There are more than 30 Tunwa villagers who became managers in the boiler industry of the city and about 70 per cent of the business of the whole city is controlled by Tunwa migrants now.

This generates huge incentives for these people to be formed into more mature new communities based on their much expanded social networks.

Geographic mobility and social mobility

The Tunwa village survey also shows that people's geographic mobility has been very much positively linked with their social mobility in terms of both intra-generational mobility and inter-generational mobility. It means that migrants' social status has also improved along with their geographic move from the village into cities. All the three descriptive stories above show the situation very clearly. This is very different from the phenomenon of most other countries where professionals, managers and senior technical workers move from metropolitan areas of London, New York, etc., to suburban areas, semi-rural areas and rural areas on one hand, and many poor people such as refugees, students and new graduates move into big cities on the other hand. Even normal cases show that quite a number of rural–urban migrants immediately move into slums once they move into big cities in developing countries.

The key reason for people's geographic mobility being linked very positively with their social mobility is because of the existence of people's household registration system (*hukou* system) in China. Under the Chinese *hukou* system, people with urban *hukou* enjoy social welfare privileges provided by both the central government and local government, such as free education for their children, free health care services, assignment of job opportunities in the state units or state companies, etc. However, people who originate in rural areas cannot enjoy these kinds of conditions; they need to pay for everything themselves and the quality in all these areas is much worse than in urban areas. Therefore, in most cases, once rural people move out of their villages and settle in urban areas they achieve a certain upward social mobility since they become the members of another group in urban areas (although the urban *hukou* may not be available for them at all). This can also explain, from one of the many dimensions, why so many rural people have been moving into cities as soon as the Chinese government in recent years relaxed controls on people's geographic mobility between rural and urban areas.

Based on the experiences of social mobility from developed societies (Heath and Payne 2000; Aldridge 2001), one of the important pre-conditions for a society to increase social mobility is to build up a fair and just society where there is opportunity for all (equality of opportunity), social justice and individual freedom, etc. Clearly, some of the conditions are under-developed in China now which provides a lot of room for social networks to play a role. Thus, we are not surprised to see the extremely important role *guanxi* and *guanxi* community have been playing in China during both processes of rural people's geographic mobility as well as social mobility as shown by the sample studied in Tunwa village.

7 *Guanxi* community and TVE development in China

This chapter will focus on the importance attached to the development of town and village enterprises (TVEs) that received emphasis in the studies undertaken as a part of the 'European Project on Chinese Modernization: The Change of Cultural and Economic Patterns' which began in the early 1990s. Therefore, it is necessary to make an analysis of the development of TVEs by linking with the concept of *guanxi* community discussed in Chapters 2, 3 and 6 because *guanxi* rules and regulations play a significant role in supporting TVEs, especially in the initial stage of their development.

In research in the West, studies show increasingly clearly the importance of TVEs development to Chinese economic and social changes in post-reform China. Some of the research focuses on the contribution of TVEs to accelerating China's overall economic growth and generating job opportunities (Byrd and Lin 1990; Perotti *et al.* 1999; Garnaut and Huang 2001). Some of this research was focused on TVE contribution to promoting China's rural and social developments, including its role in poverty alleviation (Byrd and Lin 1990; Zhou *et al.* 1992). Some of this research emphasized TVE impact on pushing forward China's urbanization process (Kirkby 1985; Chang and Kwok 1990). Other research argues that the rise of TVEs has caused the change of property rights and diversion of political power in the countryside (Jin and Qian 1998; Odgaard 1992b; Naughton 1994) and so on. Generally speaking, most people take the emergence of TVEs in China as a positive factor to support the modernization of the country, especially to support modernization in rural areas of the country. However, some concerns about outdated technology, pollution and the sustainable development of TVEs have also been discussed (Garnaut and Huang 2001; Putterman 1997; Xu 1999).

What we are interested in analysing from this research is how TVEs in rural China have grown successfully, based on informal institutions and not from an official blueprint planned by the Chinese government. Although some of the research relating to informal contracting, informal governance of TVEs, etc., has been done by economists (Nee 1992; Qian and Xu 1993; Weitzman and Xu 1994; Goodhart and Xu 1996; David Li 1996), our analysis in this chapter will focus mainly on one of the new informal institutions – *guanxi* and *guanxi* community which we have discussed in Chapters 2, 3 and 6. The fieldwork we conducted in the sample villages has shown that they are related to the development of TVEs.

Background: rapid growth of the Chinese TVEs

After undergoing nearly half a century of unsteady progress, TVEs have not only played a vital role in promoting China's economic growth and social development, but have also attracted worldwide attention from the international community and have become another new hot spot in the study of China's modernization.

As defined in the Law of the People's Republic of China on Township Enterprises passed on 23 October 1996 by the Standing Committee of the People's Congress of the People's Republic of China, TVEs refer to 'the various enterprises set up by townships (including villages under their jurisdiction) and individual farmers in rural areas to assume the obligations of supporting agriculture, with major investment from collective economic organizations or from farmers'. Specifically, 'major investment' as defined in the law means 'the investment made by collective economic organizations in rural areas or from farmers accounts for more than 50 per cent of the total investment or although accounting for less than 50 per cent of the total investment, it plays a controlling or dominant role'.

This definition has three main implications: (1) the owner and manager of a TVE is a collective economic organization in a rural area or an individual farmer, i.e., the identity of a TVE is closely related to the identity of farmers; (2) TVEs are mainly located in rural areas and they are a kind of rural enterprise; and (3) TVEs are obligated to support agriculture. In short, a TVE is a kind of business set up by farmers, mainly located in rural areas and has the obligation of supporting local agriculture.

According to State Council's documents issued in 1984, 'township and village enterprises include enterprises set up by townships and villages, cooperative enterprises jointly run by some commune members as well as other forms of cooperative industrial and private enterprises' (Research Centre of the Secretariat of the Central Committee of the CPC 1987). The Law of the People's Republic of China on Township Enterprises follows such a categorization of TVEs. From a statistical point of view, TVEs include both enterprises set up by townships, towns, villages and villagers' production groups, shareholding cooperative enterprises and partnership enterprises by farmers, enterprises set up by family households or individual farmers and jointly invested enterprises set up by these enterprises with state-owned enterprises, urban collective enterprises, private enterprises and foreign investors.

Under that definition, all enterprises set up by rural collectives and individuals are covered by the concept of TVEs. Essentially, TVEs mainly refer to enterprises set up by farmers and, usually, the majority of these enterprises are located in a rural area. However, those enterprises invested in (or mainly invested in) by farmers or rural collective organizations into urban areas are also defined as TVEs. Generally speaking, the great majority of TVEs are manufacturing enterprises and other non-agricultural enterprises engaged in the tertiary sectors. However, some agricultural business activities are organized in rural areas in line with the operating pattern of an enterprise; though accounting for a small proportion in number, they are also usually classified as TVEs. At present, the number of TVEs that are engaged in agricultural business activities and the number of employees in such enterprises account for only 1.5 per cent of their respective totals and their added value accounts for about 1 per cent of the total added value of TVEs.

TVE was a special form of enterprise organization that emerged in China in 1958 and was marked by strong political influence, as its formation and early development were closely related to the political movements of 'the Great Leap Forward' and 'the People's Communization'. The wording, which had its earliest appearance in the documents of the CPC, was 'small-sized industry in rural areas' ('rural industry' for short), later changing into 'commune industry' and then 'commune-and-brigade-run enterprise' (CBE). The term remained the same until 1984 when 'commune' and 'production brigade' were replaced by 'township' and 'village' which took into consideration the development of private and individual enterprises following the implementation of China's rural reform policy in late 1978 and early 1979. The CPC Central Committee has changed CBE into TVE. They have enlarged its coverage from the previous 'commune-and-brigade-run collective enterprises' to various types of enterprises, including those private and individual enterprises in rural areas (Hu and Zheng 1996: 55).

Before 1984, the development of TVEs had been very unstable. During its emergence and initial development in 1958–59, rural industry had enjoyed rapid growth thanks to the strong push of the 'Mass Steel-making Movement'. During the subsequent period of 1960–5 however, its development had taken a downturn as the CPC Central Committee put forward the policy of terminating CBEs in 1962 in order to ensure grain production. Similarly, thanks to the continuous advocacy and support of the CPC Central Committee, the growth of CBEs had begun to recover slowly from 1965 until the eve of rural reform in 1978 and from 1979 to 1983. With the progress of rural reform, the development of CBEs enjoyed a new favourable turn and their stable growth and development began to be enhanced. After 1984, TVEs in China were experiencing a truly new stage of rapid growth and sustainable development (Hu and Zheng 1996: 35–77).

TVEs have generated one-third of China's GDP

Although TVEs experienced some twists and turns, an overview of the 45-year history of their development until now indicates that their rate of growth is quite rapid: in terms of the number of enterprises. There were only 260,000 CBEs across the country at the end of 1958 (Ma and Zhang 1989), whereas the number of TVEs reached 21.33 million by the end of 2002, growing by 81 times, with an annual growth rate of 10.5 per cent; in terms of gross production,[1] nationwide CBEs accounted for only 6.25 billion yuan in 1958 (Ma and Zhang 1989) but reached 14 trillion yuan in 2002, growing by 2,239 times, with an annual growth rate of 19.2 per cent. If we look at the value-added indicator, it has reached 3.2 trillion yuan at the end of 2002, accounting for 31.3 per cent of China's national GDP (Nongyebu Xiangzhenqiyeju 2003a; Guojia Tongjiju 2003).

TVEs have employed 27 per cent of the total rural labour force and 18 per cent of the total national labour force

In terms of employment, the number of workers employed in the CBEs were only 18 million even at the end of 1958 when the 'Mass Steel-making Movement' reached its peak, whereas the number of employees in the TVEs at the end of 2002 totalled 130 million, growing by 6.2 times and at an annual growth rate of 4.6 per cent. TVEs had absorbed 27.4 per cent of the total rural labour force and 18 per cent of the total national labour force (Nongyebu Xiangzhenqiyeju 2003a: 5; Guojia Tongjiju 2003: 411).

The value-added of TVEs has grown by 23.4 per cent annually during the 24 years since 1978

Even if the year 1978, when China embarked on rural reform, serves as the year for comparison, Chinese TVEs have clearly enjoyed a very high growth during the past 24 years (see Table 7.1). The number of TVEs, their value-added and number of employees increased respectively from 1.5 million, 20.8 billion yuan and 28.3 million at 1978-end to 21.3 million, 3.2 trillion yuan and 132.9 million in 2002 (Nongyebu Xiangzhenqiyeju 2003a: 3–8). Their gross growth rate reached 13 times, 154.5 times and 3.7 times respectively, with an annual growth rate of 11.6 per cent, 23.4 per cent and 6.7 per cent respectively.

Nearly half of the value-added of China's manufacturing sector comes from TVEs

The total value-added from the manufacturing sector of TVEs in 2002 had already reached 2.3 trillion yuan (Nongyebu Xiangzhenqiyeju 2003a: 7) accounting for 49 per cent of the total national manufacturing sector (4.65 trillion yuan) (Table 7.2) (Guojia Tongjiju 2003: 55).

By industry sector, in a normal year, the value-added of TVEs in the textile and garments industry accounts for more than 70 per cent of the national total in that sector. Their export delivery value usually accounts for half of the national export value in this sector and it also accounts for about 35 per cent and 15 per cent of the total textile export value of the whole of Asia and the world respectively. The value-added of TVEs in the food processing sector accounts for more than 60 per cent of the national total for the sector and also accounts for more than 60 per cent of the national total in the export value. The value-added of TVEs in the machine manufacturing industry accounts for about 60 per cent of China's total and the delivery value of its export products (mainly low-grade and primary products such as hand tools, general machine tools, bearings and standardized parts) accounts for about 15 per cent of the total export value of national machinery products. The value-added of TVEs in building materials also accounts for about 60 per cent of the national building materials industry but very little of this production is exported. However, the export value of

Table 7.1 TVE added value and employment and shares of the national total

Year	Total TVE added value (billion yuan)	National GDP (billion yuan)	Percentage of TVE added value of national GDP	TVE employees (million)	Total national labour force (million)	Percentage of TVE employees of national total labour force
1978	20.8	362.4	5.7	28.3	401.5	7.0
1979	22.8	403.8	5.7	29.1	405.8	7.2
1980	28.5	451.8	6.3	30.0	423.6	7.1
1981	32.2	486.0	6.6	29.7	432.8	6.9
1982	37.4	530.2	7.1	31.1	447.1	7.0
1983	40.8	595.7	6.9	32.4	460.0	7.0
1984	63.3	720.7	8.8	38.5	481.9	8.0
1985	77.2	898.9	8.6	69.8	498.7	14.0
1986	87.3	1,020.1	8.6	79.4	512.8	15.5
1987	141.6	1,195.5	11.8	88.1	527.8	16.7
1988	174.2	1,492.2	11.7	95.5	543.3	17.6
1989	208.3	1,691.8	12.3	93.7	553.3	16.9
1990	250.4	1,859.8	13.5	92.7	647.5	14.3
1991	297.2	2,166.3	13.7	96.1	654.9	14.7
1992	448.5	2,665.2	16.8	106.3	661.5	16.1
1993	800.7	3,456.1	23.2	123.5	668.1	18.5
1994	1,092.8	4,667.0	23.4	120.2	674.6	17.8
1995	1,459.5	5,749.5	25.4	128.6	680.7	18.9
1996	1,765.9	6,685.1	26.4	135.1	689.5	19.6
1997	2,074.0	7,314.3	28.4	130.5	698.2	18.7
1998	2,218.7	7,696.7	28.8	125.4	706.4	17.7
1999	2,488.3	8,057.9	30.9	127.0	713.9	17.8
2000	2,715.6	8,825.4	30.8	128.2	720.9	17.8
2001	2,935.6	9,572.8	30.7	130.9	730.3	17.9
2002	3,238.6	10,355.4	31.3	132.9	737.4	18.0

Source: Guojia Tongjiju 1985: 25; 1995: 83; 2003: 55, 126–7 and Nongyebu Xiangzhenqiyeju 2003a: 7.

household appliances manufactured by TVEs accounts for about 50 per cent of the total export value of this sector in China. Moreover, TVEs such as Midea, Galanz and Kelon have often been in the lead in the country in home appliances export. For example, Midea ranked No. 1 in the industry in China in terms of export value in 1997.

TVEs generate two-thirds of the rural aggregate GDP in China as well as 40 per cent of farmers' per capita net income

If we examine the relationship between TVEs and rural development, besides their role in employing a large number of rural labourers, these enterprises have become the most important promoter of rural economic development. The TVEs' total value-added has accounted for more than 60 per cent of the rural aggregate GDP in China (66.8 per cent in 2002, see Table 7.3) which indicates that the rural industrial structure of China has undergone material changes. That is, changing

Table 7.2 TVE manufacturing performance versus national manufacturing statistics

Year	Total value-added from TVE manufacturing sector (billion yuan)	Total value-added of the national manufacturing (billion yuan)	Percentage of TVE value-added from its manufacturing sector in the total of the national manufacturing	Employees in TVE manufacturing sector (million)	National total of employees in manufacturing sector (million)	Percentage of TVE employees in the national total in manufacturing sector
1978	15.9	160.7	9.9	19.7	69.5	28.4
1979	17.5	177.0	9.9	21.1	72.1	29.3
1980	20.9	199.7	10.5	22.8	77.1	29.5
1981	24.6	204.8	12.0	23.3	80.0	29.1
1982	27.2	216.2	12.6	24.9	83.5	29.9
1983	30.2	237.6	12.7	26.5	86.8	30.5
1984	41.8	278.9	15.0	32.3	95.9	33.7
1985	51.8	344.9	15.0	51.5	103.8	49.6
1986	59.6	396.7	15.0	60.3	112.2	53.8
1987	106.5	458.6	23.2	66.4	117.3	56.6
1988	130.6	577.7	22.6	71.9	121.5	59.2
1989	156.2	648.4	24.1	70.3	119.8	58.7
1990	185.5	685.8	27.1	69.2	138.6	49.9
1991	222.7	808.7	27.5	72.0	140.2	51.4
1992	335.0	1,028.5	32.6	78.9	143.6	55.0
1993	593.6	1,414.4	42.0	90.9	149.7	60.7
1994	808.7	1,935.9	41.8	85.8	153.1	56.1
1995	1,080.4	2,471.8	43.7	95.0	156.6	60.7
1996	1,262.8	2,908.3	43.4	98.1	162.0	60.5
1997	1,451.8	3,241.2	44.8	93.4	165.5	56.4
1998	1,553.0	3,338.8	46.5	89.7	166.0	54.0
1999	1,737.4	3,508.7	49.5	90.1	164.2	54.9
2000	1,881.2	3,904.7	48.2	90.5	162.2	55.8
2001	2,031.5	4,237.5	47.9	91.8	162.8	56.4
2002	2,277.3	4,653.6	48.9	91.3	157.8	57.8

Source: Guojia Tongjiju 2003: 55, 125 and Nongyebu Xiangzhenqiyeju 2003a: 5.

from a traditional agriculture-dominated structure into a non-agriculture-dominated structure.

Accordingly, the proportion of income generated from agriculture in farmers' total income has shown an increasingly declining trend. Meanwhile, farmers' income derived from TVEs has shown a significant rise. In 2002, 44 per cent of net farmers' income across the country was sourced from TVE wages (Table 7.3). This indicates that TVEs have now become a major income generating engine for Chinese farmers. Moreover, TVEs have also made a contribution toward supporting agricultural development. In recent years, about 30 billion yuan from TVEs has been used directly for agricultural purposes each year which is equivalent to about 15 per cent of the government budget allocation to the agricultural sector in a normal year (but 20.1 per cent in 2002, see Table 7.3).

Table 7.3 TVEs and agricultural and rural development in China

Year	Percentage of TVE value-added in the total value-added of rural society[a]	Percentage of TVE employees in total rural labour force	Percentage of farmers' per capita net income generated from TVEs[b] in total per capita net income	Percentage of TVE agricultural support funds in the government budget for agriculture
1978	17.0	9.2	8.2	20.1
1979	15.4	9.5	8.2	18.2
1980	17.3	9.4	7.9	19.7
1981	17.2	9.2	7.3	21.5
1982	17.5	9.4	7.1	19.8
1983	17.2	9.4	7.3	18.7
1984	21.6	10.7	8.4	32.3
1985	23.3	18.8	14.8	44.9
1986	24.0	20.9	17.1	42.3
1987	30.7	22.6	19.5	45.5
1988	31.3	23.8	21.5	48.6
1989	33.0	22.9	21.1	43.6
1990	33.3	22.1	19.6	44.9
1991	36.0	22.3	21.7	44.5
1992	43.6	24.3	26.3	45.6
1993	53.8	27.9	32.7	44.3
1994	53.6	26.9	28.8	41.2
1995	54.9	28.6	32.3	43.2
1996	56.1	29.8	31.5	38.3
1997	59.3	28.4	32.2	29.5
1998	60.4	27.0	33.3	16.1
1999	63.2	27.1	36.4	17.1
2000	65.0	26.7	38.8	13.6
2001	65.6	27.1	41.1	10.1
2002	66.8	27.4	44.0	20.1

Source: Based on Guojia Tongjiju 1985, 1990, 1995, 2000, 2003 and Nongyebu Xiangzhenqiyeju 2003a, 2003b.
Notes: a The total value-added of rural society in China is the total value-added of farming, forestry, animal husbandry, fishery plus the value-added of TVEs;
b Farmers' per capita net income generated from TVEs is equal to the total salary of TVEs divided by the total rural population.

The creation of industrial parks for TVEs has promoted the development of small towns in rural areas

The continuous growth and strengthening of TVEs in rural areas has also directly promoted the emergence of industrial parks in rural towns, the development of trading and marketing centres and the rise of small towns in rural areas. The latest survey results indicate that 'every village owns enterprises and every family household runs businesses' pattern as the general phenomenon in the early period of development of TVEs has been changed gradually by the emergence of industrial parks which concentrate TVEs in certain places, normally in rural towns. By the end of 2002, the number of TVE industrial parks across the country had grown to

8,699. In that same year, these parks hosted more than 1 million TVEs with a total export delivery value that accounted for one-third of the total export delivery value of all TVEs in China. In particular, these industrial parks had become the most important bases for foreign investment in Chinese TVEs. The contracted FDI and actually utilized FDI had reached US$33.5 billion and US$14.5 billion respectively by the end of 2002, amounting to 82.5 per cent and 81 per cent of China's total FDI in the TVEs sector (Nongyebu Xiangzhenqiyeju 2003b: 86).

TVEs have initially displayed a trend toward concentrating in industrial parks and opening up of international markets. Commensurate with the increasing concentration of TVEs, the development of small towns in rural areas, mainly designated towns, has undergone much improvement and progress from their original under-developed state. By the end of 2002, the number of designated towns in China had totalled 19,811 – nine times more than 25 years ago (2,173) when the reform policy was first introduced in rural areas. The total population in the designated towns has so far reached 110 million accounting for 14.1 per cent of China's total rural population (*Zhongguo Caijingbao*, October 30, 2003). On the one hand, this plays a significant role in transforming and absorbing China's agricultural population and labour force and, on the other, also helps to push forward the process of urbanization.

TVEs provide 15 per cent of China's national tax revenue

The constant development of TVEs has also directly added to the state's fiscal revenue. At present, taxes paid perennially to the state by TVEs are more than 200 billion yuan accounting for 15 per cent of the state's total tax revenue and for about 14 per cent of the state's total fiscal revenue (15.3 per cent and 14.2 per cent in 2002 respectively, see Table 7.4). Therefore, while bringing benefits to the farmers, the development of TVEs has, to a considerable extent, made a significant contribution to directly strengthening the nation's fiscal capacity.

In conclusion, TVEs in China have, through nearly half a century of zigzagging development, grown from a seedling into a towering tree. They are playing a vital role whether it is in the nation's economic growth, expanded tax revenue base and social development or in the generation of more income and more job opportunities for farmers and also providing political stability in rural areas. It is not an exaggeration to say that, in today's China, no mature statesman can afford to ignore the immense power and influence of TVEs. Without them, sustainable economic growth, social development and political stability in China would burst like a bubble. It can be said that the development of TVEs in China has been a great success. Then, how was this great success achieved? This is the issue of real concern in this chapter.

What factors determine the success of TVEs in China?

What factors determine the success of Chinese TVEs? According to the prevailing explanation and view in China, the success can be attributed to a package of good

Table 7.4 Contribution of TVEs to state tax revenue and fiscal income

Year	State tax from TVEs (billion yuan)	Percentage of TVE tax in the national total tax revenue	Percentage of TVE tax in the national total fiscal income
1978	2.2	4.2	1.9
1979	2.3	4.2	2.0
1980	2.6	4.0	2.2
1981	3.4	5.4	3.1
1982	4.5	6.4	4.0
1983	5.9	7.6	4.7
1984	7.9	8.3	5.3
1985	13.7	6.7	6.8
1986	17.7	8.5	7.8
1987	22.2	10.4	9.4
1988	25.0	10.5	9.5
1989	28.8	10.6	10.8
1990	31.3	11.1	10.6
1991	36.5	12.2	11.6
1992	49.4	15.0	14.2
1993	94.8	22.3	21.8
1994	103.5	20.2	19.8
1995	128.0	21.2	20.5
1996	130.7	18.9	17.6
1997	152.6	18.5	17.6
1998	158.3	17.1	16.0
1999	179.0	16.8	15.6
2000	199.7	15.9	14.9
2001	230.8	15.1	14.1
2002	269.4	15.3	14.2

Source: Guojia Tongjiju 1995: 215–8, 2003: 281–2 and Nongyebu Xiangzhenqiyeju 2003a: 17, 2003b.

policies such as reform, opening-up and revitalizing the economy carried out by the CPC Central Committee since the end of the 1970s. From the perspective of institutional economics, they are the changes in China's formal institutions that have induced the development and success of TVEs.

Such an explanation is reasonable to a certain extent. However, such an explanation is far from sufficient to account for the systemic and institutional changes encompassed by TVEs. The success of TVEs in China is a blend of both the successful transformation of formal institutions by the CPC during the last two decades of the previous century and the significant influence exerted in the new historical era by the informal institutions that are deep-rooted within Chinese culture and history. As there are so many study results relevant to the former, the emphasis of discussion in this chapter will be on the latter.

From the perspective of informal institutions, we have found that many rural areas in China have already formed a tradition of 'assisting agriculture with industry' and 'combining agriculture with industry' in business, during their long process of historical and cultural development. This tradition had spread throughout vast rural areas of China in the long history of the country. However, a full package of practices of closely combining agriculture and industry carried out by the CPC in the revolutionary bases in the remote rural areas are a full expression of the traditional Chinese business practice of 'mutual assistance of agriculture and industry'. The practice and success of contemporary TVEs have once again proved the great influence of business tradition from the historical to modern industrial development in China.

At the same time we have also discovered that, in the early stage of development of TVEs, the traditional Chinese *guanxi* community and its *guanxi* rules have played a directly supportive role in the process of the farmers' organizing and utilizing their limited resources to promote the development of TVEs. Thanks to the Chinese farmers whose wisdom has enabled their employment and interpretation of *guanxi* resources – one of China's traditional informal institutional resources – they have enabled TVEs to attain an insurmountable height. The TVEs have thus been able to overcome numerous difficulties and resistances to their development and finally achieve today's brilliant achievements.

Impacts of Chinese industrial traditions

In the early stages of primitive society (based on the Marxist view of the stages of societal formation) in ancient China, people made tools from wood and stones and used them for hunting, fishing and gathering food. Along with agricultural development, a few cottage industries such as pottery, spinning and weaving emerged. During slave society (also based on the Marxist classification), agriculture and manufacturing became so closely integrated, that within a household system, the main task of man was cultivation while that of woman was weaving. During the Xia Dynasty, which existed from the twenty-first to sixteenth century BC, other industries such as wine making, jade carving and building construction had developed. During the Shang Dynasty which succeeded the Xia Dynasty, bronze smelting emerged. The other industry which emerged during this period and made China world famous was silk processing. Tile manufacturing was developed during the Xizhou Dynasty (tenth century to 771 BC) and accelerated the pace of building construction. Iron making became popular in the Spring and Autumn (*Chunqiu*) Period about 2,500 years ago.

Around 475 BC, China developed into a feudal society which lasted for 2,315 years. Though property relations largely altered during this period, manufacturing activities flourished and developed. Some of the notable features in connection to this development were:

- steel making was discovered;
- export of silk to West Asian countries began;
- ceramic industry prospered to reach a high standard and a pottery production centre was set up in Jingdezhen in Jiangxi Province;
- diversified manufacturing was introduced in tea processing, sugar refining, paper making, printing and wood processing;

- categorization of the operation of manufacturing activities was introduced; in this regard, the operation of manufacturing activities was divided into four forms: (a) factories; (b) workshops; (c) household units and (d) independent units;
- organized efforts to diffuse manufacturing activities to all parts of the country began.

Out of the four categories of rural industry, factories and workshops were operated on capitalist principles which flourished especially during the Ming (1368–1644) and Qing (1644–1911) dynasties. Utilization of hired labour in some of the silk factories and workshops in the Yangtze (Changjiang) valley and the concept of middlemen, who processed the materials, were a few of the characteristic features that emerged during this period. These capitalist characteristics, however, were confined to the eastern coastal areas, whereas in the rest of the country, the mixture of small farming and household manufacturing remained the dominant feature of society.

While such a situation prevailed in China, certain changes took place after the 'Opium War' (1839–42):

> The intrusion of foreign capitalism influenced the Chinese socio-economic development in two ways. First, it had destroyed the self-supporting economy based on rural agriculture and urban and rural handicrafts. Second, it had accelerated the development of the market economy both in rural and urban areas in China.
>
> (Mao 1969)

Due to competition from foreign products, handicraft industries in China experienced a setback after 1840. The situation became worse after 1860. This can be seen from the decline in the proportion of the value of handicrafts in the total commodity circulation from 39 per cent in 1913 to 27 per cent in 1930 (Table 7.5).

Though their significance was reduced, handicrafts continued to hold an important position in the national economy. According to Wu Baoshan (1947), about three-quarters of the total value of manufacturing in 1933 came from handicrafts (Table 7.6).

The effects of foreign competition on rural industries were varied according to the geographical location. The damage was enormous in the eastern coastal zone, while in the interior areas it was less and it was negligible in the hill regions due to the problem of labyrinthine accessibility. Among various products, certain items such as cotton textiles, woollen products, metal products, candles and cigarettes faced strong competition. Goods such as wine, salt, bamboo products and minerals were unaffected.

In 1931, Japan invaded China prompting China to declare the 'War of Resistance' against Japan. The Japanese invasion and the subsequent war greatly disrupted the Chinese economy and rural industries. After occupying parts of China, Japan began exporting industrial goods into China and forced Chinese farmers to grow

Table 7.5 Structure of total commodity circulation value of products in China (per cent)

Products	1913	1920	1925	1930
Agriculture	36	38	39	36
Handicrafts	39	29	26	27
Modern industries	25	33	35	37
Total	100	100	100	100

Source: Wu 1932 quoted in Kong 1990.
Note: Total commodity circulation value is the total value of those products in circulation during the year surveyed (excluding the value of those products that had not been circulated through markets).

Table 7.6 Output share of handicrafts and factories in 1933 (per cent)

	GOVI [a]	NOVI [b]
Handicraft	73.05	73.18
Factory	26.95	26.82
Total manufacturing sector	100.00	100.00

Source: Wu 1947: 64 quoted in Kong 1990.
Notes: a GOVI: gross output value of industry;
b NOVI: net output value of industry.

crops (e.g., cotton) that could be used as inputs for 'strategic industries'. The cotton industry, for example, which stood as the backbone of a self-reliant economy was disrupted during the Japanese occupation. The production of cotton textiles in north China in 1940–1 declined to only one-third of output in 1937 (Kong 1990). The situation south of the Yangtze River was even worse where 58 per cent of the reeling mills were damaged and textile production dropped by 56 per cent. Similarly in Shanghai, 82.5 per cent of reeling mills were destroyed pushing down production by 78.6 per cent (Kong 1990).

At the end of the war against Japan, the Nationalist Party (Kuomingtang) led by Jiang Jieshi (Chiang Kai-shek) seized power in China. It imposed tight control on material supply, marketing, finance and tax. Through such measures, the country's economic power eventually concentrated in the hands of four families – Jiang Jieshi, Song Ziwen, Kong Xiangxi and the Chen brothers, Chen Lifu and Chen Guofu. These four families controlled about 60 per cent of fixed capital in the banking and industrial sector, 80 per cent of the fixed capital of the industrial and transport sector, 90 per cent of steel production and 67 per cent of electricity generation in the country (Zhu 1985). However, this did not affect household manufacturing very much. The proportion of total rural households engaged in manufacturing activities was 16.5 per cent and 16.4 per cent in 1938 and 1939 respectively and increased to 23.8 per cent and 24.7 per cent in 1946 and 1947 (Kong 1990).

The experience of CPC in the revolutionary bases

During the 1920s, all the cities and much of the countryside in China were under the control of Kuomintang and hence, the CPC had to retreat to remote areas of the country and establish revolutionary bases. The Kuomintang cut off food and other supplies to the CPC-controlled areas and hence they had to grow their own food and produce other necessities. They relied on the traditional Chinese principle of 'self-reliance' and they began growing their own food and producing manufactured goods. The CPC confiscated land from landlords, re-allocated them among peasants and encouraged them to grow grain, cotton, sugar cane and oil-bearing crops. These crops provided raw materials and induced the emergence of certain industries. The manufacturing activities were carried out by individuals as well as co-operative units include spinning and weaving, sewing, knitting, farm machines and tool making, boat manufacturing, woodwork and umbrella-making, straw-hat weaving, bean-cake processing, sugar refining, pottery, bricks and tile-making, paper-making, oil extraction, coal mining and iron smelting etc. (Kong 1990: 218). Towards the end of the 1920s, those who managed the bases established factories to produce iron, steel and weapons. Later products such as salt, sugar, textile, paper, machines and chemical products were also produced in factories. In 1941, the bases in Shaanxi, Gansu and Ningxia areas had 97 factories employing more than 7,000 workers (Kong 1990: 220).

In October 1949, the CPC led by Mao Zedong seized power by defeating the Kuomintang in a civil war and converted China into a socialist country. This change brought a new era for China and its rural industries. CPC used its experience in forming cooperatives during their revolutionary bases period to reform the industrial structure in urban as well as in rural areas. Therefore, it can be asserted that certain developments in rural industries during the pre-communist era had also some influence on the industrial development through TVEs in 'New China' under the communist system.

Influence of **guanxi** *community and* **guanxi** *rules*

From this brief discussion of the development of the household handicraft industry in China and the historical development process of its traditional link with agriculture, we can have a basic understanding of the Chinese long tradition and custom of integration of agriculture and household handicraft industries. To a certain extent this provides an important historical explanation about the rapid growth of contemporary Chinese TVEs from a macroscopic perspective. However, macro background alone is not enough and we must adequately and reasonably explain the rapid growth of TVEs from the micro perspective as well.

From a micro perspective, we can explain how the leaders of rural collective economic organizations or individual farmers as business operators have promoted the rapid and healthy development of TVEs through effective allocation of limited resources.

When talking of a resource allocation approach, people would naturally think of market rules (or a market-based system). In fact, market rules are not an absolute approach to resources allocation. For a long period of history, some socialist countries with highly centralized planning systems relied mainly on administrative planning instead of market rules. This demonstrates that market-based rules are not the only approach. Studies in recent years indicate that the economic success of some East Asian economies is mainly attributable to effective corporate organization and management. The factors determining whether an enterprise has effective organization and management are not only the result of market rules (the market approach) but also include the important influences and rules of culture (the cultural approach) and authority (the authority approach) (Hamilton and Biggart 1988; Herrmann-Pillath 1992). Some scholars attribute the improvement in the efficiency of economic resources allocation of Japanese enterprises to the managers themselves who integrate multiple factors (Johnson 1982). Other scholars, based on the successful experiences of overseas Chinese, propose the concept of economic culture, which is unique to the Chinese, to explain this issue (Redding 1993). All in all, there are some different options under which the resources allocation approach can function. One important point is to address this issue from the relationship between culture and economic development.

As we know, culture is very rich in content. Then where should we begin the analysis of the impact of culture upon economic development? As already touched upon briefly in previous chapters, Max Weber's attempt in this respect began with an analysis of Protestant ethics. Although people have different views on the conclusion of his study, people have generally accepted his approach and method. Prasenjit Duara began with an analysis of the culture nexus. However, many scholars have developed their studies by referring to Weber's approach to analyse China, as either for or against (Du 1993). Then, where should we begin this analysis of the impact of culture on the development of TVEs?

This issue could be summarized here by quoting two observations by Liang Shuming: 'China is an ethic-based society'; and 'ethic-based means *guanxi*-based' (Liang 1988: 262–77). These two remarks are very insightful and touch upon the essentials of this issue.

Incorporating the theoretical analysis of *guanxi* community in the previous chapters, this chapter has shifted the field of demonstrative analysis from people's mobility to TVEs. The *guanxi* analysis of this field is very significant, not only because TVEs are an economic sector in China with the fastest growth, but more importantly because TVEs were excluded from national development planning by the highly centralized central government at the early stage of their development. There was an extreme shortage of the resources they needed. How, then, have these enterprises survived this adverse environment and enjoyed rapid growth in a fairly short period? During their bumpy course of development, what is the relationship of *guanxi* and *guanxi* community to the organization of resources by the entrepreneurs of TVEs? The present chapter attempts to answer that question using material obtained from relevant surveys and studies conducted in China during recent years on TVEs in the villages the research team investigated.

Case studies on *guanxi* and *guanxi* community and TVE development

Detailed descriptions of the survey villages have already been given in Chapter 4. Based on the general methodology of village selection, that is to say regional differences of economic, social and culture developments among different villages are considered and the focus of this chapter is to see how, through case studies, these differences influence the entrepreneurs' behaviour in promoting TVE development in villages in the context of *guanxi*.

Enterprise development involves the multi-faceted organization and allocation of resources. The major resources include funds, technology, equipment, labour, raw material, market, etc. Except for labour, which is in ample supply, the supply and demand of other resources were unfavourable for the early development of TVEs. That is, there was a lack of funds, technology, mechanical equipment and raw materials, and no ready market for products, etc. One important reason for this scarcity of resources was that TVEs emerged and developed independently of the highly centralized economic planning system. Therefore, resources were not allocated to them within the central plan by the state. How, then, did the TVEs organize their allocation of resources in circumstances where the market was underdeveloped and central planning did not include them?

Yantian village of Guangdong Province: with investment mainly from people of the same clan in Hong Kong[2]

Following the implementation of China's rural reform policy, Yantian village began to develop TVEs just as other areas of the country did. In 1979, the village had set up ten brigade-run factories, mainly processing agricultural products and by-products. The scale was very small and the employees were only villagers of Yantian. By the end of that year, the village had barely made any profit from these factories.

In 1980, Z, who had 'fled' to Hong Kong from Huiyang (in Guangdong Province), planned to return to his hometown to invest and set up factories, but found that the place did not have the conditions necessary to make an investment there. Before his return to Hong Kong, Z went to Fenggang Township in Dongguan City to visit one of his comrades-in-arms who worked in the local military department. Z's comrade accompanied Z to Yantian village which is 6 km from Fenggang Township to visit a convention hall and tour the suburban rural area. Z found that Yantian had a favourable environment for investment; so he proposed to set up a factory based on the convention hall. As a result, the first overseas-funded enterprise in Yantian which engaged in 'three types of processing' (material processing, sample processing and part assembly) as well as 'complementary trades' was established.

In 1982, a number people of the Deng clan who left Yantian for Hong Kong also returned, planning to invest in their hometown. A few people invested in Yantian in that year, all from the Deng clan. Later, some of the Deng clan who were in Hong Kong, but who had left Yantian earlier, came back to visit and invest. In addition, Hong Kong members of the Deng clan were also constantly using their various connections to promote Yantian in Hong Kong. This had encouraged other Hong Kong people, including those outside the Deng clan, to invest in Yantian.

The leaders of Yantian village had also fully employed these connections and provided active support in various ways.

Through the efforts on both sides, investment in Yantian by Hong Kong business operators has shown a continuous upward trend and is of a considerable scale. By the end of 2002, there were 346 overseas-funded enterprises engaged in 'three types of processing and complementary trades', of which, 282 investors were Hong Kong entrepreneurs, accounting for 81.5 per cent of the total; 21 investors were Taiwanese entrepreneurs, accounting for 6 per cent; 12 investors were Japanese entrepreneurs, accounting for 3.5 per cent (see one of the Japanese enterprises in Yantian village as Plate 7.1 shows for instance); and the other investors were from other countries. Among the several dozen joint ventures, the major investment also came from Hong Kong. Of these joint ventures, 20 were partnered with Hong Kong, accounting for about half and the other enterprises were joint ventures with Taiwan, Japan, etc.

Among these overseas-funded enterprises, more than 20 investors were members of the Deng clan who had left Yantian village earlier and then returned to invest directly in the village. In addition, more than 100 Hong Kong investors were introduced to Yantian by these returnees through various connections and their total investment accounted for more than half of the total overseas investment.

At the early stage of Yantian's capital acquisition, the village had adopted the following methods in the main to cooperate with the Hong Kong members of the Deng clan and other overseas investors:

Plate 7.1 Shinano Kenshi, a Japanese company, set up its motor production as processor for its Hong Kong company in Yantian village in 1991

1 Transferring land to overseas businessmen and obtaining land rent from them. In order to encourage overseas businessmen to invest and set up factories in Yantian, the village had set a very cheap land rent of only 15,000 yuan per hectare per year. They signed land-use contracts with businessmen based on terms of not less than 15 years or as long as 30 years. In this way, during a period of more than a decade before 1994 when the village completed initial investment of capital, the village had rented altogether 73.3 hectares of land to overseas businessmen providing an annual income from land rent of more than 1 million yuan.

2 Leasing factory buildings set up by the village collectives to overseas investors. This provided much higher rental income than that derived from purely renting land. For example, in 1997, the rental income from factory buildings reached 29.44 million yuan. This alone accounted for 26 per cent of the total income of the village in that year. And over time, rental income has increased significantly. For instance, the annual rent for the factory shown in Plate 7.2, built by Yantian village and leased to Feng Chuan Tooling (Dongguan) Co. Ltd., a Hong Kong company in Yantian village, is now more than 200,000 yuan.

3 Leasing workers' dormitories to overseas companies. Overseas-funded enterprises were renting high-quality houses for their top executives, but some were also providing dormitories of a relatively low standard for their employees. This was mostly done by villagers but they had to pay 5–6 yuan

Plate 7.2 A whole factory built by Yantian village has been rented to Feng Chuan Tooling Co. Ltd., a Hong Kong company

per square metre to buy land from the village to build the dormitories and over 20 per cent of this rental income had to be handed back to the village. In this way, the village not only avoided the cost of housing but also gained some additional income. Villagers could also increase their income through this form of business; generally, rental income had accounted for more than 30 per cent of household annual income.

4   Obtaining funds from the transfer of the investment and the rights to operate some public utilities. For example, the transfer of rights to supply industrial water and sewage treatment and sub-contracting of construction projects, etc., have generated considerable income for the village (Plate 7.3 shows one of the sewage treatment plants transferred to a local entrepreneur).

5   Finally, more than 90 per cent of the initial investment of capital needed by the enterprises in Yantian village during their early development had come from overseas investment, especially by the members of the Deng clan in Hong Kong.

Now that Yantian village boasts great economic strength, the Village Committee has set up a special investment fund to encourage domestic and overseas Yantian people (mainly of the Deng clan) to further establish business, spending several dozen million yuan in the process. Thus, it can be predicted that TVEs in Yantian village will enjoy further expansion in the future.

Plate 7.3   The usage rights in one of the sewage treatment plants has been transferred to a local entrepreneur through contract arrangements

Fuxing village of Hubei Province: looking for 'ways' to purchase raw materials, secure loans and market products³

Detailed information about Fuxing village (which changed its name from Duanjia village on 24 December 1996) and Fuxing Company (FSTSC) will be given a special introduction in the next chapter. This village has many clans, most from Jiangxi Province. Their ancestors had brought with them a traditional iron forging handicraft industry and 'iron from Duanjia village' was well known, focusing on iron forging, nail making and wire drawing. Since the foundation of the PRC, Fuxing village has 'walked with both legs' – not only constantly exploring ways of developing collective village enterprises, but also making great efforts to promote the development of individual enterprises by farm households. However, both in the early stages and during the whole process of development, these enterprises have met a series of serious difficulties and problems. Based on local cultural traditions and by harnessing the spirit of that local culture, the people of Fuxing have developed some very interesting solutions. Some specific cases can illustrate the problem-solving process adopted by enterprises within the village.

Case 1: How the Steel Wire Factory managed to buy steel plates from Wuhan Iron & Steel Corporation

The Steel Wire Factory in Duanjia village (present-day Fuxing village) was officially set up in June 1985. Once operations began, the greatest difficulty faced was a shortage in supply of steel plate, its main raw material. The technical process used by the factory involved cutting steel plates into sheets of a certain size and then welding them with steel wire to form the clapboard used between floors in the construction of tall buildings. At that time, China's steel product market was not yet open and steel products were in short supply, making it difficult to obtain steel plates.

In early 1986, Zhang Zhengqun of the Steel Wire Factory was trying to purchase steel plates from Wuhan Iron & Steel Corporation (WISC). Zhang Zhengqun was later relating his personal experience in buying the steel plate from WISC:

> After arriving at WISC, I learned through inquiry from many sources that Chief *A* of the WISC Sales Section had the power to approve sales of steel plates. It was not a piece of work just to find him in his office, for I knew this matter could not be settled there; so I had to find out where he lived. It took me seven days to find out. At the noon of the first day, I saw him come out of the office building and ride on a bicycle. I immediately followed him by keeping some distance, first walking at a quick step, then trotting and finally running at great pace but still failing to catch up with him; so I had to give up. Before 5 o'clock in the afternoon, I went to the place where I had been left behind by Chief *A* when I followed him at noon and began to search for him among the crowds in the heavy traffic. When it was nearly

6 o'clock, I saw him coming by bicycle; so I immediately got ready to run. I ran in the sidewalk, with both my eyes focusing on him, while he rode in the bicycle lane. Before long, I was unable to keep pace with him, so I had to remember the place so as to come here the next day. In this way, I followed him twice a day, and on the evening of the seventh day, I followed him at last to his house. Shortly after he entered his house, I began to knock at his door. He opened the door and discovering he did not know me, he closed the door before I could explain to him my intentions. I fished out a cigarette, thinking of the way to go forward while smoking in the passageway. I told myself, I must not give up anyhow, since I have taken so much trouble to come this far.

While I was thinking, a woman passed by me. She went directly to the front of Chief *A*'s house, took out a key, opened the door and entered the house. So I pinned all of my hope on this woman; 'maybe a woman is more approachable', I thought. I plucked up my courage to knock at the door again. A good omen! It was the woman who opened the door. She asked me what was the matter, and I said I was looking for Chief *A*. She then asked me where I was from and in which unit I worked. I said I came from Hanchuan. 'Hanchuan?' the woman repeated subconsciously. I at once sensed that she must be in some way related to Hanchuan, so I immediately asked her where she was from. She said her native place was Makou Town of Hanchuan, and her grandfather moved to downtown Hanchuan, but she married Chief *A* in Wuhan. I was very pleased after hearing this, so I said, 'since we are fellow townspeople, would you please do me a favour? Our hometown has met some difficulties in running a factory, so I hope you would intercede with Chief *A* for me and ask him to sell us some steel plates'. *A*'s wife was very considerate and agreed right away to offer a hand. She said, 'you first find a place to live and then come here at tomorrow noon. I would talk with *A* on this matter after a while'.

At the next noon, I came to *A*'s home as agreed. After sitting down, I took out a 'Yongguang' brand cigarette and handed it to *A*. He accepted and quickly took out a cigarette which he offered to me. I felt this was another good omen. It appeared that his wife had played a very important role in the situation. While *A* sat easy, I stubbed out the cigarette he had given me and put it in my pocket. As his wife had already told *A* about the matter, I did not put forward my request, just chatted casually with him. After finishing her cooking, *A*'s wife insisted on my having lunch with them; so I had lunch in *A*'s home. After lunch, *A* asked me to come to his office the next morning.

Coming out of *A*'s home, I took out the cigarette *A* had given me, noticing that the cigarette was full of letters on it, without any Chinese characters. I came to know that Chief *A* liked smoking foreign cigarettes. Although I did not know foreign languages, after going to several cigarette stalls with this cigarette and consulting the young men who sold cigarettes, I finally managed to figure out it was a kind of cigarette imported from France. I searched through almost the whole Wuhan City for this type of cigarette. After going to many places around WISC and in Wuchang District of the city, I still couldn't find this brand. Finally I found this type of cigarette in Hankou District in the city and I bought three packs (6.8 yuan/pack at that time).

The next morning, one of my colleagues and I went together to Chief *A*'s office. We first placed on his office desk one pack of his favourite cigarettes according to the regular way of business conversation of my hometown and then we handed one cigarette to each person in the office. After smoking a few puffs, Chief *A* pointed to us and told Secretary *B*, 'sell their factory 50 tons of 2.0–2.5mm-thick sheet steel at the price of 730 yuan per ton'.

We succeeded after all; so both of us were very pleased. As a result, we treated Chief *A* and his wife, Chief *A*'s secretary *B* and *B*'s daughter to a dinner in a restaurant near WISC to show our gratitude.

After dinner, Chief *A* said, "now all the formalities are done, it's time for you to go back home and remit the payment". We went back to the factory and remitted the money. After a few days, I went to *A*'s home again to inquire about the goods. He said, 'you just rest assured and enjoy yourself in Wuhan for a few days and you need not care about other business'. I stayed in Wuhan for only one day. When I went back to my factory the next day, the steel plates had already arrived.

(Zhang Zhengqun)

This case clearly demonstrates how geographical relations (*guanxi*) – the *guanxi* of fellow townspeople – as well as kinship have worked together to influence people's decision-making behaviour. Just because *A*'s wife and Zhang Zhengqun were fellow townspeople of Hanchuan, *A* was willing to give 'face' to his wife and thus did Zhang a favour. It was by making use of such *guanxi* that Zhang managed to purchase for the fledgling TVE the raw materials that were in short supply and created conditions for the subsequent development of the enterprise.

This case also shows that contemporary Chinese farmers have at least the following three characteristics: first, perseverance in a goal until it is achieved. This shows that they are earnest and persistent. That Zhang had followed *A* for seven days until locating his home provides a good example. Second, they are very clever and are good at grasping any tiny opportunity for success in handling affairs. Zhang Zhengqun's buying of cigarettes and making a snap judgment from *A*'s wife's subconscious repetition of one sentence had demonstrated this point well. Third, they well-understand traditional Chinese culture and are able to make the best of some of its content to serve the development of an enterprise. This case, where Zhang had used fellow townspeople's relationships *(guanxi)* to purchase steel plates is an ultimate expression of this point.

Case 2: How Steel Wire Shareholding Co. Ltd. organized its first loan

When interviewed, Tan Xinzhi, the former deputy party secretary of the Steel Wire Shareholding Co., Ltd., related this story:

Within the first few years of the establishment of our factory, we did not make any formal application to the banks for a loan. Later, with expanding the scale of operation, we felt our own funds were inadequate to support the enterprise's development. So in the first half of 1988, together with Jiang Renben, Director of Chenhu Town Service Office of Agricultural Bank of China, I went to Hanchuan County Branch of Agricultural Bank of China and, on behalf of our factory, I applied for the first time to the bank for a loan of 200,000 yuan to purchase from Shanghai No. 2 Iron & Steel Plant imported steel products from Japan.

President *C* of Hanchuan Branch, Agricultural Bank of China, received us. After learning our intentions, he first explained to us that this loan had to be approved by the county Party Committee and the county government before being extended to us. Then President *C* made a few moderately critical remarks of Director Jiang (as they belonged to the same banking system and had a superior-inferior work relationship) and the matter came to a halt.

I planned to go back to our factory and report this matter to our factory Director, when it suddenly occurred to me that the person in charge of financial and economic affairs in the county government was deputy magistrate *D*, whose father had been my superior when I was a cadre in the production brigade. So I had the idea of asking my old superior to do me a favour. When I went to my old superior's home, he was very glad and after having lunch in his home, I told him my purpose. He promised to talk with his son about this matter, try to ensure its success and give me a reply the next day.

Sure enough, the next day I obtained a note of instruction written by Deputy Magistrate *D* to President *C*. The note read, 'Please ask President *C* to first conduct a field study and then make a decision.' In order to gain more certainty, I did not go directly to President *C* with the note of instruction; instead, I first went to old *E*, the former vice president of the bank's county office (now retired). He had frequently visited our village as a resident cadre and thus we bore each other fellowship. So *E* and I went together to visit President *C*. After seeing the note of instruction provided by Deputy Magistrate *D*, President *C* said he would make a decision after the completion of an investigation into the factory.

The next day, President *C*, accompanied by the Chief of the Credit Section and Director Jiang of Chenhu Town Service Office visited our factory and learned about some of its specific conditions. He thought we qualified for a loan. As a result, shortly after he returned to the county, he completed the formalities for extending a loan of 200,000 yuan. Soon, the loan was made available in two instalments within the year.

(Tan Xinzhi)

This is an example of a loan for a TVE being organized through the comprehensive employment of both business *guanxi* and kinship *guanxi* together. As in Case 1, Tan and Director Jiang had not succeeded when they approached

President *C* directly. When they took a roundabout way and let their old superior's son – Deputy Magistrate *D* – speak up for them (by writing a note of instruction) they quickly concluded the deal. In order to gain more certainty, Tan invited *E*, his old acquaintance and a former vice-president of the bank branch, to accompany him when he took Deputy Magistrate *D*'s note and visited President *C* again. By doing so, he once again had employed a business *guanxi*, which added to the weight of his 'face'. Of course, the successful approval of the loan was also closely related to the good economic performance and reputation of the enterprise. Nevertheless, however good the enterprise's performance and reputation might have been, President *C* would not have visited the factory but for Deputy Magistrate *D*'s note. Moreover, their application had already been turned down.

Case 3: How Steel Wire Shareholding Co. Ltd. managed to obtain a large amount of credit

When interviewed, Tan Xinzhi also explained how he handled the successful attempt to secure a large amount of credit for the company. Tan said it was an opportunity seized by chance.

In August 1988, at the handing over of our factory, I went to look up General Manager *F* of the Prefectural Metallurgy Corporation, an old friend of our factory, who was studying in the Provincial Party School. During the talk, she mentioned that she was studying together with President *G* of the prefectural branch of the People's Bank of China. This suddenly made me remember that President *G* had been a cadre in the countryside around our area and could be considered as my old superior and colleague. Despite this, it was still through General Manager *F* that I got together with President *G* again. President *G* inquired in detail about the operations and future plans of our factory. When he heard that our factory was striving towards a goal of lifting gross value to 100 million yuan, he became very excited and promised to extend loans to our factory.

In the first half of 1990, through our connection with President *G*, we obtained from the County Branch of the People's Bank a loan (with a term of three years) of 1 million yuan, which was used for a small scale steel wire development and production project. In 1991, again through President *G*, our factory obtained from the County Branch of the People's Bank a loan of 2 million yuan which was used to start up a small scale galvanized steel cable project. In 1992, President *G* helped our factory to obtain a loan of 4 million yuan to start a tempered tyre project ... If we add up all these loans, the total of loans obtained with the help of President *G* alone has reached about 20 million yuan.

(Tan Xinzhi)

This case study shows that friendship and *guanxi* between former colleagues played a decisive role in the Steel Wire Shareholding Co. Ltd., obtaining a relatively large amount of credit. Apart from the special relationship between Tan Xinzhi and President *G*, General Manager *F* also played a very important role in ensuring these loans were obtained so smoothly. At least her role was conducive to build up their mutual trust further.

Case 4: How the Steel Wire Shareholding Co. Ltd. solved the problem of power supply

Before 1986, the Steel Wire Factory had a very small scale of production and operation and mainly relied on manual labour; so it was not felt that power supply would be a constraint on the enterprise's development. After 1986, when the enterprise began to employ large-scale mechanical operations, the problem of power supply became quite important. It seemed very difficult to solve this problem which was a common one in China at that time; moreover, the enterprise was located in a remote rural area. It seemed impossible to solve this problem in a short period.

Fortunately, there was a military farm in this area – Chenhu Farm, under the administration of Wuhan Military Area. The power supply for military farms were usually reliable, so it might be possible to approach the army, using personal connections, to ask for help in solving this problem.

The person who directly helped the enterprise overcome this difficulty was Company Commander *H* who was in charge of electricity of the military farm. Originally, he did not have any special *guanxi* with the enterprise such as kinship, affinity and business relations. He was a native of Henan Province, and his wife and children had lived with him in Chenhu Town for many years. Although he lived not far from his hometown in Henan, he seldom went back there, as the whole family lived and was settled in Chenhu. Every year, when holidays or festivals came around, seeing that Commander *H* was an outsider, Tan Gongyan (Chairman and General Manager of the Steel Wire Shareholding Co., Ltd.) would invite *H*'s entire family to visit the enterprise. Through many years of cultivation, their personal relationship was constantly strengthened. Therefore, when the enterprise had difficulty with its power supply, Company Commander *H* at once interceded for Tan Gongyan with Station Master *I* of the army's power station. Very soon, the army increased its power capacity and laid transmission lines to the enterprise. When the enterprise encountered inadequate power supplies, the army would often first cut off power to other places and even to the farm itself before cutting the power supply to the Steel Wire Company.

In the summer of 1992, the enterprise added a large-capacity transformer by investing 500,000 yuan which could, on the whole, ensure power supply. However, with the continuous expansion of the scale of production and operation, the problem of power shortages was again likely to occur. So in order to prepare as early as possible for that likelihood, the company decided in 1994 to invest more than 3 million yuan to construct a 35 kv transformer substation in the village. This was put into operation from 1995, putting an end to the issue of power shortages.

This case not only demonstrates the influence exerted by several types of special human relationship, to which we have previously referred, in resolving real difficulties faced by enterprises. It also reflects a strong feature of Chinese culture. That is, the moral principle of 'returning the favour of a drop of water with a water spring'. As Tan Gongyan was very kind to the family of Company Commander *H*, so *H* did the enterprise favours in return, which seemed a very natural thing to the Chinese.

Case 5: How the Steel Wire Shareholding Co. Ltd. solved the problem of coal supply

Before 1990, the enterprise did not consume much coal, so the enterprise did not encounter any significant difficulties, even though China's coal market was not open at that time. But from 1990, the enterprise's consumption of coal increased greatly. With the coal fuel market still not open, the enterprise encountered a large obstacle. As a result, the leaders of the enterprise went to Manager *J* of the County Fuel Company and asked for the favour of obtaining a larger supply of coal from the annual plan – specifically a yearly supply of several hundred tons. Manager *J* said it was beyond his ability to grant that favour but suggested that the enterprise send people to buy coal directly from the coal mines. He had also offered to help the enterprise arrange train wagons for its transportation.

Later, upon repeated invitations from Tan Gongyan, the Chairman as well as the General Manager of the company, Manager *J* had paid a one-day visit to the factory. After talking with the host about the enterprise's situation and seeing the company's performance, Manager *J* promised to help overcome the current difficulty. He had decided, while on the site, to go together with one of the enterprise's leaders to the provincial authorities to bring back some coal.

On the next day, Manager *J* went to the Supply Section of the Provincial Coal Corporation and visited his close friend Chief *K*. On that very day, he secured 50 tons of coal.

Through the connection of Manager *J*, the relationship between the enterprise and Chief *K* had also gradually developed. This relationship continued till 1993 when China's coal market was fully opened to competition. During this period, the enterprise had basically secured the required quantity of coal at a negotiated price which ensured the smooth progress of production and operation activities of the enterprise.

In this case, the problem was also solved mainly through business relationships. If not for the business relationship between Manager *J* and Chief *K*, the 50 tons of coal that the enterprise urgently needed would not have been obtained in time. The relationship of the enterprise with Manager *J* and later with Chief *K* was not special but it was an expression of communication adopted by most Chinese.

Case 6: How Feng Gaocai solved the problem of the seizure of scrap steel wire

In 1983, several purchasers from the village had bought 11 tons of scrap steel wire in Bengbu City in Anhui Province which was seized during transportation by Bengbu City Administration of Industry and Commerce. It was imperative that the local government sent people to help solve this problem. So the township leaders appointed Feng Gaocai, who was in charge of TVE issues in the village at that time, to go to Anhui Province. Feng Gaocai later related his experience:

> When I arrived at the site where the goods were detained, I approached Director *L* of the local administration of industry and commerce and gave him a letter of introduction, asking him to help and give our goods a green light from the perspective of supporting the development of township and village enterprises. Director *L* said, 'according to the regulations of Anhui Province, outward transportation of local steel products is not allowed. We are only performing our official duties and cannot violate this regulation'. I found it very difficult to continue on this topic; so I shifted the conversation, asking about Director *L*'s age, where his hometown was, how long he had worked, etc. Later I discovered that we were born in the same year, entered primary school in the same year and graduated from junior middle school in the same year. In talking about these subjects, both of us became more talkative, and the tension at the beginning of the conversation became greatly relieved.
>
> The next day, we went to Director *L* again. After making a phone call to the Provincial Administration of Industry and Commerce, he let our goods pass.
>
> (Feng Gaocai)

This is a very interesting case which shows that, in Chinese *guanxi* culture, communication between people of the same age or of the same experience is easier. Director *L* in this case had identified himself through this special relationship which enabled Feng Gaocai to solve the problem smoothly.

Case 7: How the Steel Wire Shareholding Co. Ltd. sold its goods to a spring factory in Dongguan City in Guangdong Province

The person who had handled the business was Mr. Tu, the Sales Section Chief at the time. During an interview on this subject, he said:

> In September 1987, we heard a spring factory in Dongguan City in Guangdong Province needed to buy steel wire for making springs. So I went to that factory but the staff members in the Sales Section of that factory told me that they already had supply sources and did not need new suppliers. In order to clarify the truth, I visited Deputy Director *N* of the factory who was in charge of purchasing and marketing. Hearing that we were a township and

village enterprise in Hubei Province, he did not believe that we were able to produce the spring steel wire they needed. I offered to go to their warehouse and have a look at the quality of their stock and he agreed. From the quality of the stock in the warehouse, I could see that their stocks were a little better than our products. At the same time, I found that there was not much stock in the warehouse and they could make more purchases. I reported these to our factory leaders, and they said, 'we will control the quality by all technological means. We should take this opportunity and let them give us some orders'.

The next day, I went to Deputy Director N again, conveying to him the strong determination of our factory leaders. At first, N had let us bring some samples for inspection, and only after my repeated requests did he agree to order five tons for trial use.

To make things certain, our factory did not deliver five tons, but delivered initially only three tons of the highest quality goods. After the goods arrived at the Spring Factory, the technical staff had considered the spring steel wire from our factory a little weaker in strength; so it was difficult for them to purchase our goods in a batch.

It seemed that this business would fail. Just as I was at my wits' end, I heard by chance that O, one of the technical experts in this factory, was from P Metallurgy Research Institute. It immediately came to my mind that one of our friends in Shanghai, who was an expert, must know O, because this friend of ours had worked in P Metallurgy Research Institute. As a result, I called this friend at once and asked him to intercede for me when the Spring Factory conducted its technical testing. As expected, this friend of our factory had been a colleague of O, and he agreed to do this favour.

Later, thanks entirely to the help of O, our products had passed the quality inspection. The three tons of spring steel wire delivered here were all accepted. In November, this factory made another purchase of 10 tons of spring steel wire from our factory. Since then, this factory has made regular purchases of 50–60 tons of spring steel wire from our factory each month. After 1992, the quantity of purchases dropped a little but until 1995–6, it made monthly purchases of more than 10 tons.

(Mr Tu)

This is a case that demonstrates the employment of the *guanxi* with a friend's former colleague to get things done. This type of *guanxi* has an influence on business relations, both directly and indirectly.

Case 8: Why the prefabricated parts factory in Hanyang County accepted goods from Tan Shouqin

Human relationship is very subtle. Sometimes spending a little money or even no money can win others' understanding and support. Sometimes spending a lot of money would lead to just the opposite results. The key is to be 'honest to people and do things just right'.

When summarizing his many years' experience of doing business outside, Tan Shouqin told the research team:

> When first doing business in Xindi Township of Honghu County [now Honghu City] in 1983, I met Luo Laishi of Honghu No. 2 Construction Company. He was a person with great personal loyalty and I completed the business with only a few setbacks. Later, I was able to treat Luo to a simple meal.
>
> Also in 1983, I went to Ezhou City on 15 January of the lunar calendar to sell prefabricated parts made of scrap iron wire. I visited the home of Luo Kelin, Director of a Prefabricated Parts Factory and spent more than 30 yuan buying some gifts to give him as 'presents of our first meeting'. He refused to accept the gifts but the business was still a success.
>
> I met Manager Li Zhentian when doing business in Tianjin and told him I want to send him some small gifts but he got very angry.
>
> Of course, sometimes a 'small gift' can be of great help. In October 1982, I have helped my brothers to transport two trucks of steel wire to sell to a prefabricated parts factory in Hanyang County. When the goods were unloaded, the quality inspector refused to accept them. We believed there was no quality problem and furthermore, we had sold the same products before to many other prefabricated parts factories. Nevertheless, we respected his view and did not quarrel with the quality inspector. In the evening, we visited the home of this factory's director, saying we were coming to his factory to sell our goods. When we came here the first time, we had paid a special visit to him and gave him five bottles of sesame oil to show our regard for him. Then we told him what had happened during the day and hoped that he could help make clear the reason for the rejection of the prefabricated parts from our factory. We expressed that if our goods were not satisfactory, we could re-process them. The director said he would personally inspect the goods the next day. The next day, after seeing the goods, he said nothing and had accepted all the goods.

> (Tan Shouqin)

These few incidents related by Tan Shouqin have universal significance for interpersonal communication and relationship in China. Many people in China may have such an idea: treating somebody to a meal or giving somebody a small gift is not meant to offer help in economic terms to the other party but mainly serves to offer psychological comfort and to give 'face'; it is an expression of respect. From the perspective of the recipient, he does not expect to profit from the offering and his acceptance is only an expression of consideration for the other party and also serves to return 'face' to that party. This tacit interactive relationship has almost developed into a new *guanxi* culture in contemporary Chinese society.

Tunwa village in Shanxi Province: building up special marketing networks[4]

In 1976, the industrial and sideline gross (output) value of Tunwa village of Yuanping City, Shanxi Province exceeded agricultural output value for the first time because CBEs were relatively well developed at that time. After the implementation of the household contract responsibility system, the Food Processing Factory, the Mineral Product Processing Factory and the Wood Processing Factory had shut down. Not only was the Boiler Manufacturing Factory the sole survivor, but it also had become more prosperous. One important reason for this prosperity was the factory's access to steel product supplies from the local iron and steel base – Taiyuan Iron & Steel Plant. More importantly, they could sell their products through some special *guanxi* networks. This *guanxi* was derived from 'fellow villagers' who left the village to take jobs in numerous sectors all over the country.

More than 100 public officers or government officials were said to be from the village and many had been working since the 1930s and had, therefore, assumed important leadership positions.

Through these special relations, the people of Tunwa can call on their fellow villagers who are working elsewhere to contribute to the development of their home village TVEs. These fellow Tunwa villagers, who are strongly aware of Chinese culture, especially leaders from the older generation, are also very willing to do what they can for their hometown. Therefore, many people have done their best to introduce new business to the enterprises of Tunwa, to resolve technical difficulties, and in particular, directly promote the boiler products manufactured by the village. Moreover, many of them do not expect any remuneration for their efforts.

An investigation of more than 80 former Tunwa people (Table 7.7), who had helped promote Tunwa TVEs, shows that many were senior leaders in their field. No doubt, full employment of these relations plus the promotional efforts of a large number of sales people have played a very important role in supporting the development of TVEs in Tunwa village.

When we conducted research in Tunwa village, the village cadres and villagers told us that many of the persons listed in the table had whole-heartedly contributed to the development of TVEs of Tunwa village. In particular, many of them had promoted the boilers produced by Tunwa village in different places. Even very senior leaders such as Zhao Humao, a high-ranking military general, had made efforts to promote the boilers of Tunwa village and develop the TVEs of his hometown. Thanks to the role played by such special marketing networks, the boiler enterprises in Tunwa village have, in a period of a little over ten years, not only become a local brand name but also become a brand name in the whole of Shanxi Province.

Based on the analysis in the previous chapter, it is not difficult to argue that the special marketing network of Tunwa village is mainly founded on geographical *guanxi* community. This type of *guanxi* still applies although the persons listed

Table 7.7 Short list of Tunwa villagers who work outside the village

Name	Sex	Work unit	Position
Chen Shibin	M	Xi'an Aircraft Factory, Shaanxi Province	Machinist
Chen Wenbin	M	Xi'an Clothing Factory, Shaanxi Province	Director of the Auto Fleet
Chen Buwen	M	Beijing Airforce Command Headquarters	Senior Official
Chen Xugao	M	Beijing Coal School	Lecturer
Zhao Zenglong	M	Kelan County Grain Bureau, Shanxi Province	Senior Staff
Zhao Wancai	M	Duerping Mine, Xishan Mine Bureau, Shanxi Province	Party Secretary
Gao Quanshuang	M	Taiyuan Metallurgical Industry School, Shanxi Province	Senior Economist
Chen Jiji	M	Shandong Medical College	
Chen Yunfeng	M	Shanxi Provincial Architectural Design Institute	General Engineer
Chen Jianzu	M	Taiyuan Daily newspaper, Shanxi Province	Correspondent
Gao Lanheng	M	Taiyuan Xing'an Chemical Materials Factory, Shanxi Province	Director of General Office
Zhao Jihuai	M	Shijiazhuang Printing House, Hebei Province	Storeman
Chen Zengming	M	Hospital of Taiyuan Chemical Plant, Shanxi Province	Deputy Chief of General Affairs Section
Yang Manxi	M	Gujiao Grain Bureau, Taiyuan City, Shanxi Province	Director
Zhao Humao	M	Beijing Military Area	Commander-in-Chief
Zhao Erlao	M	Xinzhou Teachers' College, Shanxi Province	Lecturer
Xie Xianzhang	M	Shijiazhuang Military Hospital, Hebei Province	President
Chen Gaotian	M	Shanxi Tools Plant	Deputy Director
Sun Furong	M	Taiyuan Dongtaipu Brickfield, Shanxi Province	Team Leader
Yao Min	M	Shandong Auto Building & Repairing Factory	Section Chief
Zhao Yuangui	M	Ningwu County Grain Bureau, Shanxi Province	Director
Chen Zeyi	M	Linfen Civil Engineering Section, Shanxi Province	Section Chief
Chen Guiyu	F	Taiyuan University of Industry, Shanxi Province	Physician
Zhao Bin	M	Shanxi Provincial Food Service Corporation	Deputy General Manager
Chen Wenxiang	M	Taiyuan Municipal Disciplinary Inspection Commission, Shanxi Province	Director of General Office
Chen Wenjiu	M	Xi'an Public Security Bureau, Shaanxi Province	Director
Chen Baizhu	M	Xi'an Geological Bureau, Shaanxi Province	Team Leader
Chen Zhangzhu	M	Taiyuan Chemical School, Shanxi Province	President
Zhao Youguang	M	Xinzhou Auto Transportation Company, Shanxi Province	General Manager
Xie Bucai	M	Xinzhou Agricultural Mechanization School, Shanxi Province	Vice President
Xie Jiashu	M	Organization Department, Hunyuan County Party Committee, Shanxi Province	Director
Zhao Shengcai	M	Organization Department, Xinzhou Prefectural Party Committee, Shanxi Province	Director
Yang Fengchun	M	Fanshi County Branch of ABC, Shanxi Province	President
Zhao Pu	M	Shanxi Shentou Power Plant	Planning Section Chief
Yang Wenzhou	M	Taiyuan No. 4 Auto Transportation Company, Shanxi Province	Chief of Transportation Affairs Section
Zhao Puhui	F	Taiyuan Pest House, Shanxi Province	Accountant
Chen Quanren	M	Nanjiao Public Security Branch, Taiyuan, Shanxi Province	
Sun Junsheng	M	Taiyuan Architectural Design Institute, Shanxi Province	
Xie Buyu	F	Yuanping No. 2 Light Industry Management Department, Shanxi Province	
Zhao Fucai	M	Yuanping Auto Transportation Company, Shanxi Province	Manager
Zhao Youming	M	Xinzhou Prefectural Education Bureau, Shanxi Province	Deputy Chief of the Party Committee
Zhao Shengcai	M	Wutai County Party Committee, Shanxi Province	Party Secretary
Zhao Shengmao	M	Xinzhou Prefectural Party Committee, Shanxi Province	Deputy Chief of the Secretarial Office

Table 7.7 continued

Name	Sex	Work unit	Position
Zhao Ruigen	M	Yuanping Economic and Trade Commission, Shanxi Province	Senior Engineer
Zhao Ruhua	M	Yuanping Standard Batching Bureau, Shanxi Province	Director
Zhao Yucai	M	Yuanping Forestry Bureau, Shanxi Province	Party Secretary
Chen Bucai	M	Supply Department, Yuanping Fertilizer Plant, Shanxi Province	
Xie Xianliang	M	Yuanping No. 1 Chemical Plant, Shanxi Province	Deputy Director
Zhang Mingzhu	M	Yuanpin Chlorine Alkali Plant, Shanxi Province	Deputy Director
Zhao Junming	M	Yuanping Tax Administration, Shanxi Province	Staff
Zhao Wuhong	M	Yuanping Grain Bureau, Shanxi Province	Director
Chen Fengming	M	Xinzhou City, Shanxi Province	
Chen Fengli	M	Lanzhou City, Gansu Province	
Chen Jixiang	M	Datong City, Shanxi Province	
Chen Baolong	M	Wuda Coal Mine, Inner Mongolia Autonomous Region	
Zhao Wengao	M	Youyu County Public Security Bureau, Shanxi Province	
Zhao Chengxi	M	Chengdu City, Sichuan Province	
Zhao Yuexi	M	Taiyuan Trade Union, Shanxi Province	
Zhao Yuanlong	M	Taiyuan Dazhong Machine Making Factory, Shanxi Province	Purser
Chen Yunzhuo	M	Shijiazhuang Electromechanical Institute, Hebei Province	Lecturer
Zhao Gaoru	M	Taiyuan Locomotive Depot, Shanxi Province	Dispatcher
Zhao Yougen	M	Taiyuan Locomotive Depot, Shanxi Province	
Chen Yougang	M	Capital Construction Department, Renmin University of China, Beijing	Section Chief
Zhang Yongliang	M	Zhengzhou Diesel Engine Factory, Henan Province	Party Secretary
Zhang Tinghuai	M	Tianjin City	Engineer
Sun Chengzhong	M	Lanzhou City, Gansu Province	
Sun Liang	M	Taiyuan Municipal Party Committee, Shanxi Province	Accountant
Chen Xiuzhen	F	Chengdu City, Sichuan Province	
Sun Xiulan	F	Supply Section, Taiyuan Machine Tool Factory, Shanxi Province	
Sun Jun	M	Xi'an Clothing Factory, Shaanxi Province	Party Secretary
Sun Bingwen	M	Xianyang Machinery Factory, Shaanxi Province	Engineer
Sun Chao	M	Xinzhou Cultural Bureau, Shanxi Province	Deputy Director
Sun Haiyan	M	Greening Office, Xishan Mines Bureau, Shanxi Province	Party Secretary
Sun Yuhua	M	Xinzhou Teachers' College, Shanxi Province	Vice President
Chen Jushuang	M	Xinzhou Literature and Art Circles Federation, Shanxi Province	Vice Chairman
Zhao Yanyan	M	Dingxiang County Water Bureau, Shanxi Province	Deputy Director
Zhao Min'ao	M	Wuzhai County Forestry Bureau, Shanxi Province	
Sun Guobao	M	Datong Municipal Party Committee, Shanxi Province	Secretary
Sun Dongcai	M	Datong Civil Affairs Bureau, Shanxi Province	
Lü Wenxuan	M	Baijiazhuang Mine, Xishan Mines Bureau, Shanxi Province	
Sun Guicai	M	No. 1 Depot, Taiyuna Railway Engineering Bureau, Shanxi Province	Party Secretary
Zhao Xingzeng	M	Wuzhai County, Shanxi Province	
Sun Qi	M	Xinzhou Health School, Shanxi Province	Lecturer
Zhang Wantu	M	Taiyuan No. 4 Auto Transportation Company, Shanxi Province	Dispatcher
Chen Qi	M	Henan Province	
Chen Yi	M	Ningwu County Coal Sales Station, Shanxi Province	Manager

Source: Li Jing 1996: 126–9.

in Table 7.7 have worked for a long time in their respective areas and units and have developed their own new career and 'circles'. However, growing up under the influence of Chinese culture, and as fellow villagers born in the same village, these people have, to a large extent, the responsibility and obligation to do their best to contribute to the development of their hometown. This is where the mystique originating from geographical *guanxi* community lies. Naturally, this spiritual power has played a very important role in promoting the development of TVEs in Tunwa village.

Xiangdong village in Zhejiang Province: most of the migrant workers have special guanxi[5]

As the local enterprises grew to a certain scale, many immigrants were attracted by the development of Xiangdong village of Cangnan County, Zhejiang Province. But unlike Yantian village, immigrants were not allowed to work in this village without authorization. As early as the 1970s, when the Household Products Factory of the village began to recruit workers, the cadres of the village formulated special rules.

First priority was to be given to households with unemployed workers or to those who were suffering economic difficulty from having a large number of children and to those members of cadres' families.

Second, recruitment quotas were distributed to production brigades to allow those brigades to recommend recruits.

Third, under circumstances where the village itself was under employment pressure, some workers (about 20 people) living outside the village could be recruited so as to keep good relations with the outside. To facilitate outside business for the local enterprises, these immigrant workers should be members of the families of township officials or cadres in township government departments.

Now there are 50 immigrant households with a total number of about 200 people undertaking either non-agricultural work or farming-contracted land in Xiangdong village. Based on our survey of 36 householders, 11 people, accounting for 31 per cent, are members of the Xiang clan descended from those who had left the village but later returned. Another 19 are relatives of Xiangdong villagers; most of them are sons-in-law or nephews, brothers-in-law, etc., accounting for 53 per cent, and only five are immigrant workers who do not have any special *guanxi* with Xiangdong villagers, accounting for only 14 per cent. The list of immigrant households in Table 7.8 is not exhaustive but does include households who have lived in the village for a long time.

The *guanxi* reflected in Table 7.8 can be divided into two main categories: people of the same clan who had left Xiangdong in the past and later returned because of the rapid economic development and increasing job opportunities in the village; and people who are relatives of Xiangdong villagers. Furthermore, the formation of the majority of related families is through marriage.

As a matter of fact, the study of Fuxing village in Hubei Province also uncovered a similar phenomenon which has become quite normal in the countryside. That is, only through various personal *guanxi* are villagers more likely to find a job in

Table 7.8 Most of the immigrants in Xiangdong village have special *guanxi*

Name	Birthplace	Occupation	Relationship with Xiangdong villagers
Zheng Denglai	Dongkuo village of Kuoshan Township	Mason	Son-in-law of Chen Shigen
Wang Zhihua	Mountainous area	Mason	Prentice of Xiang Fanghuai
Li Yongjun	Lijiapu village of the same Township	Riding tricycle	Son-in-law of Chen Shixin
Chen Yixiang	Dongkuo village of Kuoshan Township	Factory salesman	Son-in-law of Xiang Yanqi
Xie Dao'an	Xikuo village of Kuoshan Township	Leasing land from Xiangdong village	Brother-in-law of Xiang Zujian
Xiang Bingcheng	Xikuo village of Kuoshan Township	Pig raising	Same clan
Zhu Defu	Dongkuo village of Kuoshan Township	Woodworker	Nephew of Xiang Zuyu
Zhu Deqiang	Dongkuo village of Kuoshan Township	Factory salesman	Nephew of Xiang Zuyu
Xiang Fangqiang	Dongkuo village of Kuoshan Township	Leasing land from Xiangdong village	Same clan
Xiang Yanmin	Xikuo village of Kuoshan Township	Leasing land from Xiangdong village	Same clan
Xiang Xianli	Jinxiang Town of the same county	Leasing land from Xiangdong village	Same clan
Li Pengsu	Lijiapu village of Xiangqiao Township	Factory salesman	Son-in-law of Xiang Xianzhi
Li Daojun	Lijia village of the same Township	Cartographer	Nephew of Xiang Yanhao
Li Daoli	Lijia village of the same Township	Factory salesman	Nephew of Xiang Yanhao
Zheng Jiashen	Dongkuo village of Kuoshan Township	Factory salesman	Cousin of Xiang Yanxiang
Xiang Yanheng	Xikuo village of Kuoshan Township	Leasing land from Xiangdong village	Same clan
Xiang Fahai	Xiangxi village of the same Township	Plastic processing	Uncle of Xiang Yancun
Wang Mufan	Sunjiahe village of the same Township	Factory salesman	Brother-in-law of Xiang Zukuai
Wang Mujuan	Sunjiahe village of the same Township	Leasing land from Xiangdong village	Introduced by Sunjiahe village Party Secretary
Ye Dehua	Mountainous area	Leasing land from Xiangdong village	Brother of Ye Deyi (married into Xiangdong village)
Xiang Haidong	Xikuo village of Kuoshan Township	Leasing land from Xiangdong village	Same clan
Luo Zhaoyi	Xikuo village of Kuoshan Township	Factory salesman	Nephew of Xiang Zuwei
Xiang Yance	Jinxiang Town of the same County	Factory salesman	Same clan
Xiang Yantiao	Jinxiang Town of the same County	Woodworker	Same clan
Lin Yuanwang	Yishan Town of the same County	Spinning	Uncle of Lin Zhansheng
Xiang Dahai	Xikuo village of Kuoshan Township	Factory salesman	Same clan

continued…

Table 7.8 continued

Name	Birthplace	Occupation	Relationship with Xiangdong villagers
Lü Jiaqi	Tongqiao village of the same Township	Leasing land from Xiangdong village	Son-in-law of Xiang Xianhua
Xiang Bingqi	Xikuo village of Kuoshan Township	Leasing land from Xiangdong village	Same clan
Guo Shuishen	Jinxiang Town of the same County	Woodworker	No special relation
Xiang Yanping	Xikuo village of Kuoshan Township	Factory salesman	Of the same clan
Zhu Dezeng	Yishan Town of the same County	Driver	No special relation
Dong Wendiao	Yishan Town of the same County	Photographing	Nephew of Xiang Yanhao
Xiang Peng'ou	Lihou village of the same Township	Factory salesman	Brother of Xiang Xianwu's wife
Xiang Defa	Kuoshan Township of the same County	Factory employee	Uncle of Xiang Zuban
Yang Zaisheng	Mountainous area	Factory employee	Son-in-law of Xiang Yanjie

Source: Wang and Zhu 1996: 172–3.
Note: Some revisions to Wang Xiaoyi and Zhu Chengbao's work have been made based on the survey of the village.

non-agricultural sectors. Table 7.9 is the result of research on the extent to which the main labourers of sample households in Fuxing village depended upon *guanxi* to find employment in non-agricultural sectors in the early stages of development in the village. It can serve as a comparison to the similar situation in Xiangdong village in Zhejiang Province.

Clan *guanxi* and kinship, as Table 7.9 shows, have a strong influence in the process of opening up job opportunities for villagers in Xiangdong and Fuxing. This bears a great similarity to the situation of people's mobility in Tunwa village, which was discussed in detail in the previous chapter.

Guanxi community and TVE development

As we pointed out in the earlier part of the discussion, the successful emergence and rapid development of TVEs in rural China can be explained by many different reasons. The focus of this research is to look at the issue mainly from one of the cultural factors, i.e., from the viewpoint of the impact of *guanxi* and *guanxi* community on the development of TVEs based on our fieldwork in the sample villages.

Guanxi *as a special supporting factor for TVE development*

In Chinese research, *guanxi* is not a new concept at all. Some studies, for example, Yan's field study from one of the northern Chinese villages focused on *guanxi* by linking closely with gift-giving. He shows that the major function of *guanxi* in the village he studied is quite different from the strategy of making economic

Table 7.9 Fuxing villagers' employment in non-agricultural sectors and their reliance on *guanxi*

Name	Sex	Education	Non-agricultural activity undertaken	Time entering non-agricultural sectors	Channel to entering non-agricultural sectors
Huang Xingfu	M	SS	Nail making	1960	Handed-down family handicraft
Zhang Gaoping	M	ES	Working in Fuxing Company	Oct. 1994	Good relationship of his father with the general manager of the company
Duan Xiaoping	M	ES	Helper (bricklayer)	Aug. 1993	Recommended by his relative
Chen Shangjun	M	SS	Working in Fuxing Comapny	1994	Recommended by his adopted father
Huang Hongbing	M	SSS	Working in Fuxing Company	1993	As a village cadre, his mother arranged for him to enter into the company
Xiao Jiangbing	M	SS	Wire drawing	1984	Handed-down family handicraft
Duan Shunxiang	M	ES	Iron wire processing	1983	Recommended by villagers
Zhang Fugui	M	ES	Construction helper	1994	Recommended by villagers
Zhang Zhizhong	M	SS	Wire drawing, nail making	1987	Led by his relatives and friends
Xu Shaoping	F	SS	Working in Fuxing Company	1992	Her uncle has good relationship with the general manager of the company
Nie Longguo	M	SS	Undertaking transportation in Tianjin City	1988	At his uncle's help
Nie Hanxian	F	ES	Doing needlework in Wuhan City	1994	Recommended by his sister-in-law
Tan Shouru	M	ES	Working in Fuxing Company	Jan. 1994	Close clan relation with the general manager of the company
Duan Yanxiang	M	SSS	Selling scrap iron wires	1981	Recommended by his brother-in-law
Feng Shizhong	M	ES	Working in Fuxing Company	1991	Recommended by his brother, who works in the company
Tang Tinghui	M	SS	Beancurd making	1987	Learned from his relative

Source: Hu and Hu 1996: 95–101.
Note: ES: Elementary school; SS: Secondary school; SSS: Senior secondary school.

use of *guanxi* among the people; it is more a kind of moral and social base for the people to maintain their stable social contacts and social order. That is, it plays more a social function in people's social life rather than an economic exchange function (Yan 1996a). On the other hand, Yang (1994, 2002) and others (Walder 1983; Y. Jin 1991; Hwang 1987) have shown clearly the importance of *guanxi*, as a kind of special resource for people to seize economic opportunities through various exchanges.

The cases we presented above show more the latter phenomenon. All the local entrepreneurs from the above stories have made the full use of *guanxi* connections as one of the most important instruments to support their enterprise development. From these stories, we have found the real value of *guanxi* as a special economic factor in what Yang (1994: 320) has called a 'particular instrumentalized and politicized form'.

Therefore, as Thøgersen (2002: 265) has correctly pointed out in his review article of our earlier work of *Village Economy and Culture in Contemporary China* (Chen and He 1996), *guanxi* research relating to the development of TVEs has been moved:

> from the primary form of guanxi, which works mainly within long and stable relationships inside the local moral world of the village, towards an extended form ... in the stage of transformation in which the networks of the entrepreneurs gradually expand from family, friends, and local cadres to wider geographical and social circles as enterprise development and markets expand.

This is very similar to the situation in China of building up private business links through gift-giving, where gift-giving and personal *guanxi* play significant roles in supporting private businesses (Yang 1989, 1994; Wank 1995). Clearly, without the facilitation of *guanxi*, as an instrument, in the process of TVE development, it would be difficult to see the success of TVEs in the villages we studied. This is one of the important findings we obtained from our village studies which is different from Yan's conclusion of his village study.

Guanxi *community: extended form of* guanxi

However, the major findings from Yan's and our research are not contradictory to each other, although they are different. One reason is that the pre-conditions of the two studies conducted are quite different: Yan's study has focused mainly on the internal relations among the villagers within a village based on the traditional farm economy (Yan used the term of 'moral economy'). However, the focus of our research is the *guanxi* between mainly rural local entrepreneurs and government officials based on the open and transitional non-agricultural economic activities and also on the *guanxi* between the villages and the outside world. Yan has focused mainly on the primary form of people's *guanxi* within a relatively closed community, say within a village, and he regards all forms of *guanxi* other than the primary form as extended forms of *guanxi* (Yan 1996b). This can be defined by the new concept of *guanxi* community as illustrated in Chapters 2 and 3.

According to our theoretical framework set up in Chapters 2 and 3, *guanxi* community is exactly what Yan (1996a) called 'extended forms of *guanxi*' which have included different forms of *guanxi* at a higher level of people's social connections. As we stressed in Chapters 2 and 3, one of the prominent features of *guanxi* community is its openness. As opposed to this, people's internal *guanxi* within a village as shown in the case Yan surveyed, is a kind of closed, micro and primary *guanxi* among the villagers inside the village. This means that Yan's studies and our studies have focused on different stages and levels of people's inter-connections, but there is no contradiction between the findings from both studies.

This will remind us to pay more attention to Yang's historical approach to *guanxi*. She argues that

> guanxi must be treated historically as a repertoire of cultural patterns and resources which are continuously transformed in their adaptation to as well as shaping of new social institutions and structures by the particular Chinese experience with globalization.
>
> (Yang 2002: 459)

She contests the idea of 'the declining significance of *guanxi* in China's economic transition' that was raised by Guthrie (1998: 254). Yang's idea is important simply because we cannot treat *guanxi* as a fixed phenomenon. Its social forms and expressions can be changed along with the changes of the cultural, economic and political environment of a society in a certain period of time. Actually, Yan's approach in his gift-giving study is also a historical approach since he also made much effort to compare different forms and functions of gifts in different periods of time in the history of the village he studied (Yan 1996b).[6] This is why we have to move the focus of our *guanxi* research ahead from the micro level (such as the researches conducted by Yan, Yang, Guthrie, etc.) to the meso level as proposed in Chapters 2 and 3 in order to understand better the changes and extension of different forms of *guanxi* in line with the changing environment.

Sanctions within the guanxi community relating to TVE development

As we know that sanctions are enforced by the *guanxi* system based mainly on its self-enforcement mechanism since *guanxi* is always closely linked with a set of moral constraints, such as face and favour, reciprocity, shame, etc., as we had discussed in Chapter 3, *guanxi* community has a similar sanctions mechanism, which is closely linked with value and moral principles shared by a certain group of people.

Along with the transformation of the rural economy from traditional household-based agriculture to a modern industrial economy and the rapid development of TVEs in some of the villages we studied, people's *guanxi* has also been extended both from inside of the village to outside the village and from the agricultural sector to non-agricultural sectors. What concerns us most is whether what Chinese people called *renqing* and what we have described as 'human feelings'[7] and the related moral values and principles will also be extended correspondingly. Otherwise, *guanxi* principles will not be working continuously in its extended forms; thus this is a direct challenge to the theory of *guanxi* community.

However, if we look at the reality in our cases, all the stories above show clearly that the success of all local rural entrepreneurs was due mainly to the self-enforced sanctions based continuously on the primary moral principles from the roots of the people who are involved in the deals. For example, in the case of 'How the Steel Wire Factory managed to buy steel plate from Wuhan Iron & Steel

Corporation', the major reason why Zhang Zhengqun could purchase steel plate successfully was because of the influence of Chief A's wife. The key question in the story is why Chief A's wife was willing to help Zhang. The answer to this is quite simple to most of the Chinese or people knowing Chinese culture – Chief A's wife was born in the same county as Zhang. This *guanxi*, from the viewpoint of Chinese culture, is a kind of *tongxiang guanxi* (fellow townspeople). Thus, Chief A's wife has an obligation (more precisely, it is a kind of informal obligation, not a formal obligation at all) to help Zhang if she understands the local culture well. There is no alternative other than to help Zhang to make the deal since Chief A is also from a nearby city. That also is his informal responsibility, although not really a formal responsibility. The situation is also true in the case of 'How Steel Wire Shareholding Co. Ltd. organized its first loan', where Deputy Magistrate D helped Tan Xinzhi to get the first loan from a state bank through the influence of D's father, due mainly to the special *guanxi* between D's father and Tan.

If Chief A's wife did not influence her husband and Deputy Magistrate D's father did not influence his son to help Zhang and Tan respectively, then Zhang and Tan would feel unhappy with the treatment from A's wife and D's father. Damage to the reputation of both A's wife and D's father as well as to the relatives or close friends of A's wife and D's father who are living in the nearby villages would result after the failure of the business. One of the negative impacts for A's wife and D's father is that their relatives or close friends would be gradually isolated in the area. These are typical self-enforcement constraints in relation to *guanxi* community and TVE development in these cases.

These stories tell us that the extended forms of *guanxi* or what we proposed as *guanxi* community works based on moral and cultural sanctions. But what is really important is that there must be 'bridge' building between the primary form of *guanxi* and its extended forms. In the case we discussed above, Chief A's wife is the 'bridge' between Zhang and Chief A. The 'bridge' in the case of 'most of the migrant workers have special *guanxi* in Xiangdong village' is the Xiangdong villagers since most of the migrant workers are their relatives or descended from people who lived in nearby places. Sometimes, the people involved in the 'game' are 'bridges' for themselves, just like a group of people who help Tunwa villagers to sell the boilers. Many Hong Kong members of the Deng clan investing in Yantian village, as we discussed above, are 'bridges' for themselves. Under all these kinds of situations, the sanctions are self-enforced within the moral framework; no formal enforcements from the outside are needed at all.

However, we must emphasize the extremely important role of the 'bridge' when we talk about sanctions, because the sanctions would be totally different under the conditions of the presence of the 'bridge' and the absence of the 'bridge'. Once the 'bridge' is there, then the sanctions for the people within certain *guanxi* communities will be self-enforced. This is also why we regard Putnam's latest development of the concept of 'bridging social capital' (Putnam 2000) as being valuable since he realized that certain social capital can play the 'bridge' function between the inside of the community and the outside world (see more details in Chapter 2).

The political function of **guanxi** *community in TVE development*

Once *guanxi* has developed into different extended forms, or forms different *guanxi* communities, then its political function has also been strengthened to a higher level.[8] *Guanxi* community has played two major political functions relating to TVE development from our survey villages. One in the villages with developed TVEs social stability has been improved more than that in the villages with less developed TVEs, because the relationship between village leaders, villagers, TVE workers and local government officials has been strengthened by the process of TVE development through various *guanxi* communities. The other is the economic performance in the villages with developed TVEs is much better than those villages with less developed TVEs. As we discussed above, one of the direct reasons for villages, village leaders and local entrepreneurs to achieve better TVE development is because they make good use of *guanxi* resources based on special communities which are being built up by themselves They obtain scarce resources such as credit and raw materials from the state-controlled formal channels as we discussed above.

As a natural result of the rapid development of TVEs in the area, the government officials involved in the *guanxi* communities relating to TVE development normally get promoted due to better economic and social development performance in the area. Village leaders or local entrepreneurs also benefit from the rapid development once they 'bridge' good relations with government officials who are taking TVEs as a medium through certain *guanxi* communities. One typical story is what happened to Tan Gongyan, a rural entrepreneur from Fuxing village in Hubei Province. In the late 1980s, once his Steel Wire Factory was achieving good results in sales, revenue, tax, etc., government officials started to visit his factory as one of the model factories in the area – county leaders came first, then came provincial leaders (including the Party Secretary of Hubei Province and the Provincial Governor). Therefore, Tan Gongyan seized the opportunity to get to know local politicians at all the levels within the province. He won the title of the provincial 'Farmer Entrepreneur' in 1988, the provincial 'Model Worker' in 1991. Further he became well known all over the country since the early 1990s: he was awarded the national 'May 1st Labour Model' in 1991 and has been one of the deputies to the National People's Congress from 1993 to the present.

Deng Yaohui, the Party Secretary of Yantian village also experienced a similar change in his political career.

From these cases, we see clearly how local entrepreneurs and leaders developed their political careers along with the extension of their *guanxi* communities. What is important for them is the acceleration of TVE development. This should help us to understand better the rapid growth of the economy in China, because of the natural result of the efforts made by people from the formal as well as the informal side.

Regional differences of **guanxi** *community phenomenon in TVE development*

Although *guanxi* networks and *guanxi* community has been a common phenomenon in TVE development in China, we cannot ignore the influence of the geographical location specific to TVE development in the country. Therefore, we will elaborate briefly the regional differences of *guanxi* networks and *guanxi* communities relating to TVE development in our survey villages.

Earlier research by Smyth (1997) taking TVEs as a specific example of regionalism argued that 'regional based economies are dependent on their local social and historical contexts'. That is, it was dependent on the 'region specific differences' (Smyth 1997: 258). What we also find important from our fieldwork on TVE development is that the foundation of different kinds of *guanxi* communities among different villages located in different regions of the country is quite varied. Most of the *guanxi* immigrants to Xiangdong village in Zhejiang Province are direct clanship or kinship *guanxi* with Xiangdong villagers; Yantian village in Guangdong Province show a similar situation. However, most of the *guanxi* between Fuxing entrepreneurs and the people controlling the material resources are indirect *guanxi*, and certain 'bridges' (middle persons) between the entrepreneurs and the government officials are required. Therefore, *guanxi* in Fuxing's case plays a more instrumental function than that in Xiangdong's case. This may explain to a certain extent why Fuxing entrepreneurs have finally made their company a public company (listed in one of the two domestic equity markets in China).[9] Yantian entrepreneurs who have developed their business are still relying on the village-based collective organizations, taking the Deng clan as the core of the structure, although, compared with Fuxing, they had enjoyed better conditions and resources to push forward its development through the marketization process.

Besides, we also find TVEs in different regions (villages) focused on different industries. For example, TVEs in Fuxing village focused on the iron and wire industry since the village has been well known in the area for this industry for hundreds of years (see Chapter 8 for more details). Most of the enterprises in Yantian village have focused their businesses on the manufacture of electronics, toys, clothes and garments, etc., due to the integration of the regional market with Hong Kong and other Asian economies. The key industry for Tunwa villagers has been boiler production and, for Xiangdong villagers, the printing industry due to their long time accumulation of specialized knowledge in those areas.

This shows clearly the significance of the impact of historical and cultural variations among different regions on the development of TVEs in different ways. This has proved that the development of TVEs is also embedded in the social and cultural environment of the 'regional web' (to borrow Smyth's term (1997)) where the TVEs are located. This simply demonstrates the policy of the Chinese government to always encourage people all over the country to set up a 'good model' by learning from a specific regional development approach such as Dazhai's agricultural development model (in the 1970s), Daqing's industrial development (in the 1970s), Sunan (southern Jiangsu Province) collective TVE development model (in 1980s), Wenzhou's private TVE development model (in the 1990s) etc. Just as the other way around, any specific regional development model will work only when the link between the development model and the regional web is well established. It is also true for the issue of *guanxi* community analysis linking it with TVE development in China.

8   The institution of 'integrating village with company' (IVWC)[1] and rural community development

Since the early 1980s, many very significant changes have taken place in the economic and social organization and management in rural China and the most important among them is the abolition of the People's Commune system. Many new forms of organization and management have since emerged and have been implemented in different areas. This shows a very clear trend of transition from a singular to multiple institutions in the course of organizing and managing rural development at the grass roots. This chapter will analyse these institutional changes, especially informal institutional changes, happening in one rural village in central China. The village is Fuxing village (the former Duanjia village) of Hanchuan City, Hubei Province, one of the five sample villages studied during the past decade by the author, and the new institution implemented in the village is what the local people call '*yichang daicun*' in Chinese which translates into English as 'integrating village with company' (IVWC).

The general situation of the transition from single management model to multiple management models in rural China will be introduced briefly as the background. Then the focus will turn to the new model of IVWC implemented in Fuxing village area. Considerable importance will also be attached to the impact of this institutional change upon the development of the local rural community.

Diversification of rural development models in post-reform China

Rural development in China is mainly manifested as the development of villages. Since the implementation of reform and opening-up policies in China, on the one hand, the number of villages has shown a decreasing trend. On the other, commensurate with the constant penetration and expansion of industrialization and urbanization into the rural areas, various types of profound changes have taken place in the organization and administration of the remaining villages.

In terms of number, there were 940,600 administrative villages in China in 1985; this number declined to 734,700 in 2000 and it fell further to only 709,300 in 2001 and 694,500 in 2002 (Guojia Tongjiju 2003: 411). In a period of 17 years, the total number of villages across the country fell by 246,100 with an annual reduction of 14,500.

In terms of form, organizational pattern and institutional structure, after undergoing unitary agricultural operation and People's Commune system characterized by 'integration of government administration with commune management', the villages in China in recent years have shown obvious differentiation and diversification. Based on two decades of village survey and research experience from the 1980s up to now, it has been found that the current development of Chinese villages show at least the following models of organization and management:

1   *The village as a whole is transformed into a group corporation.* This model of development can be called 'corporatization of village'. Huaxi village of Jiangyin City, Jiangsu Province and Daqiuzhuang village (it has since become a town) of Jinghai County, Tianjin, which were studied, belong to this type as they have changed into a group corporation and have been completely corporatized.

2   *A new city is formed from a village or a large number of villages which have been encompassed by the expansion of a metropolis or by metropolitan regions and been transformed into an important part of that metropolis or a metropolitan region.* This model can be called 'urbanization of village'. Yantian village of Dongguan City, Guangdong Province and many villages in the southern area of Jiangsu Province, which have been studied, belong to this type.

3   *The village has gradually 'drifted' from rural areas to cities.* After moving from the countryside into the city, the villagers congregate in specific areas of the city mainly based on regional (geographical) *guanxi* and have formed an 'in-city village'. The 'Zhejiang village', 'Henan village' and 'Xinjiang village' in Beijing are distinct examples.

4   *After accumulating a considerable amount of funds, the villagers in some villages have gradually invested in and moved to the nearby city, thus leading to a reduction in the village population and weakening the village's economic strength.* As this situation continues, it is possible for that village to decline gradually and eventually even die out. Tunwa village in Shanxi Province (see detailed discussion in Chapters 4 and 6), where a long-term survey and research has been conducted, belongs to this type.

5   *A powerful business partnership, private enterprise or individual enterprise has grown up in the village.* In order to solve conflicts in such issues as land occupation, the enterprise has taken the reverse action of gradually 'encroaching' upon the village and bringing under its leadership and control the village-level organization and the administration of the whole village. The village will exist in form but the village-level administrative body and organization such as Party Branch and the Village Committee have actually lost their roles of leadership and organization to the enterprise. Fuxing village of Hanchuan City, Hubei Province, 'encroached' upon by Fuxing Science & Technology Shareholding Co. Ltd. (FSTSC), which has been studied, belongs to this type. The local government, the village cadres and FSTSC, call this new system that they are practising 'yichang daicun' in Chinese, or

'integrating the village with company' by its English translation, referred to as IVWC in the following discussion.

Of course, the situation across rural China varies greatly, with strikingly different natural, social and economic development conditions. Therefore, different places have developed many innovative institutional choices adapted to their local characteristics. The aforementioned models are only a preliminary summary of the survey and research work conducted. There are many other relevant models. The emphasis of this chapter is not on the specific classification, comparison and discussion of different models and institutional changes in general, but on just one institutional form among them, i.e. IVWC.

Fuxing Science & Technology Shareholding Co. Ltd. (FSTSC or Fuxing Company) in Fuxing village

Before adopting the IVWC system in 1997, Fuxing village had been called Duanjia village, mainly because the surname 'Duan' is the commonest in the village accounting for 20.3 per cent of the village population (Hu and Hu 1996). FSTSC [2] was in essence a partnership enterprise which has grown up in the village. On 26 May 1999, the company had issued 55 million A-shares (the issue price per share was 5.43 yuan) on the Shenzhen Stock Exchange. The name of the stock at the time of listing was Hubei Chuansheng (Hubei Hanchuan Steel Wire) but was later renamed Fuxing Keji (Fuxing Science & Technology).

I first visited Duanjia village in July 1993 to conduct a preliminary survey of the village and many of its individual private enterprises, partnership enterprises and collective enterprises. The scene within the village was impressive with 'every family forging iron and every household drawing wire' I firmly believed that Duanjia would in the near future grow into a 'super village'.

Therefore, with the help of the local government officials Hu Shunyan, Cheng Zhengyan and Liu Daju, my colleague, Zhang Yuanhong and I spent a whole month of 18 October to 16 November of 1994 conducting a comprehensive and systematic survey on Duanjia village. We published this data in a survey report which later formed the book *Enterprise Organization and Community Development in Rural China: A Survey on Duanjia Village of Hubei Province* (Hu and Hu 1996). The book's emphasis was on the various aspects of Duanjia village but devoted little discussion to FSTSC (Fuxing Steel Wire Shareholding Co. Ltd. then).

About ten years had passed and great changes have taken place in both the village and the Steel Wire Shareholding Co. Ltd. Since the general village profile of Fuxing has already been introduced in Chapter 4, it is only necessary to provide some general introduction to Fuxing Company which still bases its headquarter in the village, before discussing the system of IVWC. This introduction will lead to an in-depth exploration on the related institutional changes.

Fuxing Company (see Plate 8.1) is a TVE set up by a group of Fuxing villagers, indigenous to the village, and listed in China's domestic A-share market. Its core

Plate 8.1 Fuxing Science & Technology Shareholding Co. Ltd., an A-share listed company, has grown in Fuxing village

business is producing various types of steel wire. By November 2003 when we conducted a survey of the company, the number of employees totalled 5,000, more than 20 items, and 830 specifications were produced and handled, and the total annual output of various metal products reached 120,000 tons, ranking it as one of the largest enterprises nationally in the metalwork industry.

The products of the company sold nationwide as well as to more than 30 other countries and regions such as the USA, Canada, Thailand, Indonesia, Singapore and Hong Kong. Since 1999, apart from continuing to be the national leader in the metalwork industry, the company has expanded its business scope into real estate and bio-pharmaceuticals and has had marked achievements within a very short time. In 2002, the company's gross income had totalled more than1 billion yuan of which, 430 million yuan came from metal products, accounting for more than 40 per cent of revenue, while income from real estate was about 500 million yuan accounting for nearly 50 per cent. As its bio-pharmaceutical initiatives have only just begun, little income had been generated in that year.

Based on our understanding of Fuxing Company, development has so far undergone four stages: start-up, preliminary expansion, restructuring, and diversification and rapid growth.

The start-up stage

The starting point of this stage in the company's development is basically concurrent with that of rural reform in China. With the formal inception of rural reform in the early 1980s which was marked by the redistribution of farmland to family households, Tan Gongyan, born in Villager Group No. 9 (called 'production team' at that time) and one of the founders of Fuxing Company, like his fellow villagers, had begun in early 1981 to purchase scrap iron wire from all over the country. This was then hammered straight, made into nails or auxiliary iron bars for pre-cast products, used in construction projects and then finally sold.

In November 1981, Tan Gongyan and his wife Feng Youying organized five fellow villagers plus a business partner from the neighbouring village to set up an eight-person partnership to establish an iron- and wood-processing factory (basically a cooperative handicraft industry workshop) which was based completely on 'free will and mutual benefit'. As it was organized neither by the village (called 'brigade' at that time) nor by villager groups (called 'production teams' at that time), its business activities did not receive any support from the village collective. However, this enterprise was, at that time, supported by the government of Fuxing Administrative Area (an agency of the commune) and, therefore, the iron- and wood-processing factory was named 'Fuxing Cooperative Iron and Wood Processing Factory', nominally a collective enterprise under direct administration of the Administrative Area but actually a partnership enterprise.

After the enterprise was set up, its major business during the three-year period from 1981 to 1983 comprised four parts: first, processing the scrap iron wire purchased from other places into iron nails; second, processing the scrap iron wire into auxiliary iron bars in pre-cast products which were used in construction projects; third, making some simple farm tools such as hoes, sickles, etc., which were based on the actual needs of the villagers; and fourth, producing a small quantity of tailor-made wood products such as furniture for the local villagers. During those three years, the enterprise had altogether made a net profit of 174,000 yuan. On the basis of considerable capital accumulation, the founders of the enterprise began to consider focusing on a specific direction of development with the aim of expanding its scale of operation. As a result, the enterprise embarked on the second stage of development.

The preliminary expansion stage

Eight years from 1984 to 1992 was the preliminary expansion stage for the enterprise. At this stage, two important issues were addressed in the development of the enterprise. First was the basic issue that was to define wire drawing and wire rope production as the core business of the enterprise and complete a transformation from manual to mechanical production (1986–7); the second was that the scale of the enterprise enjoyed much expansion: the number of employees increased from a little more than 20 in 1983 to 2,800 in 1993, and the gross income of the enterprise grew from only about 300,000 yuan in 1983 to 108 million yuan in 1993. These performance indicators have increased about 140 times and 360 times respectively during this period of expansion with an annual growth rate of 63.9 per cent and 80.1 per cent respectively. Thus, it can be seen that the expansion of the enterprise in these years was very fast.

The restructuring stage

This stage began in March 1993 when, upon the approval of Hubei Provincial Restructuring Commission, Hanchuan Steel Wire Factory[3] was formally reorganized into Hanchuan Steel Wire Shareholding Co. Ltd. of Hubei Province. Through this restructuring, the enterprise's original net assets of 41.5 million yuan, all of which were converted into share capital, plus the 2 million yuan worth of shares bought by the County Fiscal Bureau and the County Insurance Company (1 million yuan each) and the 20 million yuan worth of shares bought by the public, formed a total share capital of 63.5 million yuan. The 63.5 million shares, all common shares, were priced at one yuan per share. Of these shares, there were 1 million state shares (1 million yuan of the County Fiscal Bureau), accounting for 1.57 per cent of the total share capital. The 42.5 million corporate shares (altogether 42.5 million yuan, including 1 million yuan of the Insurance Company of the County), accounted for 66.9 per cent and 20 million individual shares (20 million yuan) accounted for 31.53 per cent. The individual shares were issued at a premium to the public based on a ratio of 1:1.5 and 30 million yuan was raised thereby (Hu and Hu 1996: 146).

The enterprise had applied all the funds obtained through this restructuring to the project of producing steel cord yarn and thus expanding its scale (Plate 8.2 shows inside the new workshop of the steel cord yarn branch factory of the company) and making necessary preparations for a further stock exchange listing. The restructuring stage had basically ended at the end of 1999 when Hanchuan Steel Wire Shareholding Co., Ltd. issued 55 million A-shares in RMB to the public on 26 May of that year and was listed on the Shenzhen Stock Exchange on 18 June of the same year which successfully raised 284.35 million yuan (the proceeds net of the issuance expense of 14 million yuan) from its public share offering.

The diversification and rapid development stage

Soon after the company was listed on the Shenzhen Stock Exchange, the leaders of the company, after careful analysis of the domestic and international economic situation, came to the conclusion that a new stage of high-speed growth would emerge in China and became aware of the need to spread risks.[4] Moreover, after being listed, the company had raised nearly 300 million yuan from the market. Therefore, the leadership of the company proposed the new development strategy of 'focusing on one industry and developing three industries'. Thus, they began to steadily enter the real estate and bio-pharmaceutical industries while adhering to the core business of metalwork. By so doing the company aimed at realizing

Plate 8.2 One of the workshops of the steel cord yarn branch factory of Fuxing Company

the common development of the three distinct businesses of metal work, bio-pharmaceuticals and real estate.

In August 1999, Fuxing Company had set up Wuhan Fuxing Huiyu Real Estate Development Co. Ltd.[5] to begin its real-estate operations based in the capital city of Hubei Province, Wuhan. During just four years of effort, Wuhan Fuxing Huiyu Real Estate Development Co. Ltd. has repaid its investors very well. Its average annual development capacity has reached about 300,000 m^2, its average annual sales income has reached about 500 million yuan and its profits and tax turnover has reached about 100 million yuan (Plate 8.3 shows one of the residential housing projects developed by Fuxing Company in Wuhan City in 2003 and 2004).

In order to join the worldwide trend of high-tech development in the new century and occupy a key position in this sector, the company leadership had decided from October 2000 to develop its own bio-pharmaceutical industry.[6] The company has set up its own 'bio-tech building' (Plate 8.4), purchased the necessary equipment and initially developed its own competitive products in the past three years by injecting nearly 200 million yuan in investment capital.

Through a series of restructurings and expansions, it is expected that the gross output value of Fuxing Company will exceed more than 3 billion yuan in 2006 of which the gross output value from metalwork will be 1.8 billion yuan. The real estate industry will account for 1 billion yuan and the bio-pharmaceutical industry will account for 300 million yuan. The company has planned to build Fuxing Area,[7] a new town centred on the Fuxing Company and Fuxing village with

Plate 8.3   One of the housing projects developed by the Fuxing Company in Wuhan City, the capital of Hubei Province

福
星
生
物

Plate 8.4   The 'Fuxing bio-tech' building in Fuxing village

metalwork as its mainstay industry and also have complementary enterprises to comprehensively develop the bio-pharmaceutical industry and service industries.

Through a decade of tracking Fuxing Company, it is felt deeply that the success of the Company is to a large extent dependent on one able man (Tan Gongyan) and based on the long history of a traditional industry (iron processing) and a familiar community (Fuxing village). As a company that has emerged out of a village and an indigenous farmer turned entrepreneur, their success will surely repay their patrons in various ways; such is the outcome determined by the spirit of Chinese culture. Moreover, if a modern enterprise surrounded by traditional villages does not establish a good cooperative relationship with the surrounding population, its further development will be greatly constrained.

Emergence and development of IVWC institution in Fuxing

With the rapid growth of Fuxing Company, many labourers living around Fuxing village and even in other cities and provinces have been attracted through various channels to work in the company. Many people have even moved their whole families to the Fuxing area. As a result, how best to organize the relationship between the enterprise and the increasing number of the incoming migrants and the relationship between the enterprise and the Fuxing villagers have become very realistic and large problems.

Therefore, taking the actual conditions as a starting point, the company leaders proposed two schemes in 1996 to solve these problems. One scheme has sought to respond to the changes in actual conditions, i.e., the constant increase of non-agricultural population, and suggested that the county government approve the establishment of Fuxing Residents' Committee of Chenhu Town, Hanchuan County.[8] The other scheme has suggested that the county government approve putting Duanjia village where Hanchuan Steel Wire Shareholding Co. Ltd. is located, under the direct administration and leadership of the company.

The two schemes proposed by the company were first approved by the local government, Chenhu Town People's Government, and was later approved by Hanchuan County People's Government on 2 September and 24 December 1996 respectively. The approved official names were respectively Fuxing Residents' Committee of Chenhu Town, Hanchuan County and Fuxing Village of Hubei Fuxing Science & Technology Shareholding Co. Ltd.

The latter name indicates that Fuxing village is indisputably under FSTSC, in terms of administration and leadership; yet the former implies Fuxing Residents' Committee is under Chenhu Town. According to the arrangement with Chenhu Town, however, 'The leadership of the Residents' Committee is proposed to consist of three members, to be elected by the general meeting of residents and the salary of the Committee members shall be borne by Hanchuan Steel Wire Shareholding Co. Ltd.'[9] This indicates that the Fuxing Residents' Committee, though nominally under Chenhu Town, was actually under the direct leadership and administration of Hanchuan Steel Wire Shareholding Co. Ltd. In this way, it is a brand-new administrative system and institution that an enterprise serves as an active administrative body and a township residents' committee and a rural administrative village have taken shape in Fuxing area. It should be said that this is a new institutional innovation in China. As urban administrative systems are not the subject of study here, focus of the discussion will be on Fuxing Company and its relationship to its host village.

The emergence of the issue of IVWC institution

As we mentioned in the above discussions, Hanchuan Steel Wire Shareholding Co. Ltd. had undergone much growth in terms of the scale of land occupation, number of employees and capital accumulation through the preliminary expansion and development stages from 1984 to 1993. In this way, the company leaders felt, to some extent, that at that time there was increasing conflict between the company and Duanjia village. The conflicts are mainly manifested in the following areas:

First of all, when the company had needed to increase its occupation of the village land during its rapid growth in 1993 and 1994, the negotiations of the company leaders with the village cadres and with the villagers did not go quite smoothly. On the contrary, there was much resistance. If the situation continued, the company's further expansion and development would certainly have been adversely constrained.

Second, when the company had carried out its residential development and expansion plan and needed to expand constantly the scope of the new village at the expense of the original old village, the expansion process was met with resistance and opposition from many villagers.

Third, some key leaders of the village at that time did not show due respect to the key leaders of the company. So the key leaders of the company had for a long time considered reorganizing the leadership of the village by virtue of their prestige and influence and that of the enterprise among the local villagers. But at the same time, the company leaders also considered another problem: if the new leaders of the village still do not cooperate with them, what should they do? Therefore, at that time the idea of designing and creating a new fundamental system and institution became a very practical solution for the company leaders.

Fourth, an increasing number of villagers complained that the rapid growth of the enterprise had led to more inconvenient communication and noise pollution from which they did not receive much benefit. So the relationship between the village and the villagers and the company and the company leaders began to become more and more subtle and sometimes even somewhat tense.

Finally, as a state-level outstanding entrepreneur always respected by local residents, Tan Gongyan, the chairman as well as the general manager of the company, also began to think of ways to work out a more reasonable mechanism to enable the local villagers to benefit from the process of the company's growth while integrating the resources of the company and the village in ways that would benefit the company.

For the above reasons, in the latter half of 1995, Tan Gongyan began to consider how best to set up a new administrative system to enable the effective integration of the resources of the company and the village. An incident took place at the end of that year which was very common for an entrepreneur and which had, to a certain extent, accelerated his promotion of this innovative concept of institutional reform. This incident had involved the village cadres pressing for repayment of borrowings at a time when the village did not have sufficient money. It should be said that it was not a problem for the company to repay the debts owed to the village as they were not a large sum, but rather that the relationship between the two parties had to be clarified before those obligations could be met.

On this occasion, Tan Gongyan, the general manager of the company, had called together 16 people including all the village cadres (Feng Gaocai, Duan Jikuan, Zhang Shoujiang, Zhang Xianbing, Zhang Zhengqun, Cai Zhongbo, Huang Xingfa, Hu Jianhua, Zhu Qiuzhen, Duan Jiyan, Feng Dequan, Xiao Zhexue and Tan Shoubiao) as well as the resident officials of Chenhu Town government in Duanjia village, namely, Zhao Yiyuan and Tu Peiyin, on 16 January 1996 of the lunar calendar to hold a meeting to discuss this issue at the home of Tan Shouren, the Village Party Secretary at the time (as Tan Shouren was ill at the time it was inconvenient for him to attend a meeting in the office).

At the very beginning of proceedings, Tan Gongyan had pointed out the various drawbacks of having separate administrations for the village and the enterprise. He suggested setting up a new system of 'integrating the village with the company' and then asked the participants to present their opinions and comments. According to Zhang Zhengqun, who attended that meeting and is now deputy director of the Village Committee, the expectations that the village cadres put on the company were mainly focused on how to help the village gradually pay off its debts and improve infrastructure such as village streets. Many people spoke at the meeting but finally the participants reached an agreement. That is, if the company and the village are well integrated into a new organizational institution, then it should be regarded as a new experiment in institution building that embodied Deng Xiaoping's idea of 'socialism with Chinese characteristics'. Therefore, all the participants agreed to implement gradually the new institution.

After this meeting, the company had formally brought the idea to Chenhu Town government and requested Hanchuan County People's Government to provide for instruction through the Chenhu Town government. The two factors considered by the county government were (1) that this was a new approach to promote rural economic development and (2) that this was a new way of accelerating rural urbanization and realizing integration of rural and urban areas.

Major contents of the IVWC institution

The official reply that was made on 24 December 1996 by Hanchuan County People's Government on implementing this new institution included four instructions.[10] They (1) approved putting Duanjia village of Chenhu Town, formerly under Fuxing Administrative Area, under the administration of Hanchuan Steel Wire Shareholding Co. Ltd., and implementing the system of 'integrating village with company'; (2) renamed Duanjia village as Fuxing village and the original assets and debts of Duanjia village to be borne by the renamed Fuxing village;[11] (3) instructed that the renamed Fuxing village assume various assignments of the former Duanjia village – the specific assignments to be sent down by Chenhu Town People's Government to Hanchuan Steel Wire Shareholding Co. Ltd., who will be responsible to Chenhu Town People's government; (4) implemented various tasks of 'integrating village with company' to be organized by Chenhu Town Party Committee and Chenhu Town People's Government.

Apparently, the practice of the institution of IVWC put the original Duanjia village, at least in form, under the direct administration and leadership of the company and its relationship to the company was entirely that of administrative subordination rather than guidance and assistance in the general sense. We can see this clearly from the public nameplate of the Village Committee and the Village Party Branch in adopting this new system and institution. Plate 8.5 shows that the new nameplate of the Village Committee is 'Fuxing Village Committee of Hubei Fuxing Science & Technology'. The new nameplate of the Village Party Branch was 'Communist Party of China's Fuxing Village Branch Committee of Hubei Fuxing Science & Technology'. The imprint produced by the new seal of the village reads as: 'Fuxing Village of Hubei Fuxing Science & Technology Shareholding Co. Ltd.'. All of which shows that the original Duanjia village has been integrated into Fuxing Science & Technology Shareholding Co. Ltd., and has become part of the company.

Plate 8.5 New name plates and new village leaders of Fuxing village

However, this has not been easy to achieve in actuality. It was learnt from discussion with Tan Gongyan, the current chairman and the president of FSTSC, that his company roughly reached the following common understanding regarding the division of responsibility and authority in the administration of Fuxing village. That the personnel and organization issues of the Village Committee and the Village Party Branch shall be addressed by the company and the issues with a strong social nature such as family planning, agricultural taxes and fees shall be addressed by the town government. President Tan Gongyan also reached some common understanding with the major village leaders: e.g., the secretary of the Village Party Branch is to be appointed by the company and not based on election by the village party members; the person for this position shall be determined through the collective discussion of the Party Committee of the company, etc.

As the institution of IVWC had continued to be in the experimental stage and without any written norms, let alone relevant rules and regulations, as part of the research two meeting were convened in the village with village cadres in order to understand accurately the essence of this issue. Based on the information they provided, it is possible to summarize the outlines of the system of IVWC as practised in Fuxing area as follows:

1   *Politically, the work of the Village Committee and the Village Party Branch must fully represent the will of the company.* This is first of all reflected in the appointment of village cadres. The secretary of the Village Party Branch must be appointed by the company and cannot be elected by the party members in the village. This means that the election of the Party Branch is basically impossible. Second, major decisions of the village, after being discussed by the village cadres, must be reported to the Party Committee of the company and the final decision shall be made by the Party Committee of the company, not by the village. For example, with regard to the issue of land-use rights, the Village Committee and the Village Party Branch do not have any decision-making power on any land. However, the village may make final decisions at the operational level relating to agricultural activities. By all accounts, the decisions of the village must be kept in line with the needs and interests of the company's development and shall not go against the interests of the company.

2   *Viewed from the perspective of economic relations, the village and the company are presently independent of each other.* The main source of income of the village collective is the very limited rent of 200,000 yuan from two contracted collective enterprises, plus land-use fees of 38,000 yuan from eight individual enterprises in the village. The village collective needs to hand over on behalf of the two contracted collective enterprises and eight individual enterprises, a land compensation fee of 46,000 yuan to households, agricultural tax and fees of 16,000 yuan, income tax of 25,000 yuan, an industrial and commercial administration fee of 5,000 yuan and an environmental protection fee and land management fee of 4,000 yuan. After deducting this expenditure, totalling about 100,000 yuan, the net income that the village collective receives is

only about 140,000 yuan a year. At present, the part of the village's annual agricultural tax and fees for social purposes of about 300,000 yuan is still paid by the villagers themselves, as the village collective does not have the ability to pay on their behalf and, as of 2003, the company has not borne these expenses.

3   *In terms of responsibilities and obligations, when the company needs to requisition land for development, the village must satisfy the demands of the company by all available means.* According to the stipulation of the company, there are two levels of compensation for villagers' farmland taken over by the company. One is basic land compensation of 300 yuan per *mu* per annum. In fact, this stipulation was not implemented before 2003; the company decided to implement this from 2004, so that the compensation can be paid directly to the households whose land has been taken over. The other is 'young crop compensation' usually based on a standard lump sum of 1,000 yuan per *mu* for vegetable fields, 800 yuan for cotton fields, and 600 yuan for rice and other grain crops. As for the company, it should give priority to employing Fuxing villagers to work in the company, do its best to improve the social welfare of all the villagers and help the village cadres to improve their salary and remuneration.

Evaluation of the effects of IVWC implementation

Although at the end of 1996 the county government approved the new system and institution of IVWC, the institution was not actually put into place during 1997. After 1998, the company and the village have made some effort to implement the new institution and have had some initial achievements. However, opinions differ in their evaluation of the effects of practising this new institution and system.

IVWC has become a relatively mature institution

From discussion with Tan Gongyan, chairman and president of the company, it was possible to learn his basic views about the practice of this new system and institution. According to him, IVWC in Fuxing area after several years has become a relatively mature institution. It can be said that the system has already completed its initial stages and the next step would be 'the full integration of the company and the village'.

According to Tan Gongyan's understanding, the following issues will be further addressed at the stage of 'full integration of the company and the village':

1   From 2004, the taxes and fees of all the villagers – such as the agricultural tax and irrigation and education fees (altogether more than 300,000 yuan) – would become the responsibility of the company and be paid by the company, and as a result, the villagers' burden from agricultural activities will be greatly alleviated.

2   From 2004, all the elderly people in Fuxing village would be covered by the company social welfare plan. At the time of the interview, only the elderly of Villager Groups Nos. 8, 9, 10 and 11 were covered by the company's social welfare plan such as pension insurance (a monthly pension of 90 yuan). However, the elderly of villager groups except the four mentioned are only entitled to low-level social welfare. Those who are in the other villager groups can only receive an annual pension of 300 yuan.

3   The company will further promote the village renovation project. Existing old houses will be replaced by new housing within the next two to three years.

The IVWC system has demonstrated many advantages as well as drawbacks during the past few years of implementation and needs to be improved in the future

According to the village cadres, the benefits that the villagers have experienced include:

1   The system of IVWC has played a positive role to a certain extent in alleviating village debts. So far the company has not directly helped the village collective to repay its debts, but the company has made effective efforts to help the village collective press for payment for various 'receivables' and coordinate with creditors to 'repay principal and cease interest'. The village has not only recouped most receivables, but almost all its creditors have accepted the repayment scheme of 'repaying principal, ceasing interest and making repayment year by year' proposed by the company. Through full cooperation between the village and the company and by adopting these measures, the village's debts have been reduced from more than 1 million yuan several years ago to the present level of a little over 800,000 yuan. Of this the village collective's debts to private individuals amount to 560,000 yuan and the remaining more than 200,000 yuan are owed to various financial institutions and local government departments.

2   With regard to the issue of employment, the company has conscientiously carried out the policy of 'priority for Fuxing village' since the institution of IVWC. In principle, there is no restriction on employing labourers from the village. Usually, like other workers, they can apply to become a regular contract worker after qualifying after a two-year probation period. According to company statistics, of the 5,000 workers currently at the company, 1,200 are from Fuxing village. This accounted for 24 per cent and a considerable portion of these workers were recruited into the company after the practice of the institution of IVWC. As the metalwork industry is characterized as heavy manual labour, the company prescribes that it generally does not recruit women over 30 years and men over 45 years. According to village statistics, of the more than 1,700 labourers in the village, 60 per cent of the male labourers under 45 years (more than 600 people) have been recruited by the company.

3   The small town in the area where the village is located has taken shape. This will directly promote the improvement of the availability of village infrastructure such as roads, electricity and drinking water. According to preliminary company statistics, the cumulative input of the company in constructing the small town and upgrading the living conditions of the village in the past few years has amounted to 94 million yuan, of which, planning and designing expenses alone have exceeded 1 million yuan. Currently, there are three levels of compensation for villagers' house relocation – 30 yuan per square metre, 45 yuan per square metre and 60 yuan per square metre.[12]

4   The villagers' social welfare has improved greatly. The company has set up a public auditorium with seating for more than 3,000. The auditorium is mainly used for performances of local dramas, singing and dancing, which are popular among local people and are open to all villagers free of charge; so they are warmly received. The company at its expense has built a brand-new middle school and primary school for the village, and moreover, the company has provided a tuition subsidy for the children of all its contract workers based on a standard 200 yuan per worker per annum (primary school), 400 yuan per worker per annum (junior middle school) and 1,000 yuan per worker per annum (senior high school). About 30 per cent of the villagers aged over 60 have begun to receive a pension from the company (the 300 yuan per annum for the elderly mentioned previously is not regarded as pension, but as a subsidy). This covered only those villager groups and households whose entire land has been taken over by the company but the company plans to gradually expand pension coverage. In addition, as FSTSC is located in the village, the long-standing harassment and disturbance of Fuxing by big surrounding villages has eventually disappeared. Furthermore, all the surrounding villages and villagers regard Fuxing villagers with a sense of respect and admiration. Fuxing village and its villagers enjoy a high social status among the surrounding villages and villagers which is beneficial, directly and indirectly, to the villagers in business dealings and in securing a spouse.

5   It has to a certain extent improved the income level of the village cadres. According to Chenhu Town People's Government stipulations only two cadres of Fuxing village, the Secretary of the Village Party Branch and the Director of the Village Committee, are entitled to receive salaries from town revenues. The Village Party Secretary's annual salary is 6,000 yuan and the Village Committee Director's annual salary is 5,500 yuan. At present, the salaries of other village cadres are paid by the village collective, while the Village Party Secretary receives his salary from FSTSC and the Director of the Village Committee receives his salary from the Town Fiscal Office. For other cadres, present salaries are: 5,000 yuan for the village accountant; 4,000 yuan for the Deputy Director of the Village Committee, and 3,500 yuan or 4,000 yuan for other village cadres. As the Village Party Secretary's salary is paid by the company, the village cadres distribute evenly between them the 6,000 yuan salary that the Village Party Secretary should receive from

the Town Fiscal Office, increasing their salary a little. In addition, Fuxing Company usually distributes bonuses (including awards) to the village cadres at the year-end. If the system of IVWC were not practised, the village cadres would not receive the bonus (awards) from the company.

On the other hand, the village cadres are much dissatisfied. According to them, the system currently implemented cannot be said to be a true system of 'integrating village with company' but rather only a system of 'administering village by the company'. If Fuxing Company does not work out ways, as soon as possible, to gradually improve the system of 'integrating village with company' in practice, the resistance to the implementation of this system would continue to increase. This is conducive neither to the development of the village nor to the development of the company.

The major problems put forward by the village cadres are mainly reflected in two ways. One problem is how the company can balance fairness and discrimination in practising the system of IVWC. If the relationship is not properly handled, it might lead to serious social conflict and dissent at some period in the future. It should be said that during the early days of the implementation of the new system of IVWC, the company has been scrupulous in the provision of preferential terms for the villager groups and villagers whose land had been taken over by the company, in providing better conditions for its own workers than for local villagers and for providing better conditions to regular contract workers than to temporary workers. However, the problem is that within one village and a small society where agricultural activities are not profitable or even make losses, if the company were to attach too much importance to the interests of one group of people and ignore the interests of other groups, it will definitely lead to a breakout of social dissent and social conflicts among villagers' groups as well as among villagers.

Marked disparities have emerged in the Fuxing area between the villagers whose land has been taken over and those whose land has not, between regular contract workers and temporary workers, and between men and women in the villagers' housing renovation. The renovation of housing for villagers whose lands have been taken over is fast, while that of the villagers whose lands were not taken over is very slow. In employment it is relatively easy for men whose lands have been taken over to have the opportunity to work for the company whereas it is difficult for the villagers whose lands were not taken over and it is difficult also for women. With regard to fringe benefits, elderly people in the villager groups whose lands have been taken over are entitled to the pension insurance provided by the company whereas those in the villager groups whose lands were not taken over are not entitled to pension insurance. With regard to schooling, contract workers are entitled to a child schooling subsidy whereas the temporary workers and the village cadres have to pay their children's tuition fees. Moreover, some disparities have even shown a tendency towards widening further.

The other problem is the village cadres' salary and fringe benefits. The village cadres generally complain that their salaries are low and they do not have social security such as pension insurance. As we mentioned above, the salary of a village cadre is roughly equal to only the basic salary[13] of an ordinary regular worker and moreover, it is not borne by the company but is paid out of the income of the village. This is neither conducive to bringing the village cadres' initiatives into play in handling village affairs nor to the unity and cooperation between the village and the company. Some village cadres told the research team that their present salary level was too low and they somewhat resembled 'a group of beggars'. Moreover, their remuneration did not match their workload. Other village cadres even told us that the company regarded them as 'housedogs' but at the same time was unwilling to feed them. These remarks strongly indicate that the village cadres are very dissatisfied with their low salary and welfare. They said that they did not necessarily demand a salary raise from the company but they hoped that the company would allow them to have the power to decide for themselves a reasonable margin for a salary raise on condition that the village collective's income increased. Village cadres are not entitled to company social benefits such as pension insurance. In the early days of the system of IVWC, company leaders had once decided to provide pension insurance to Duan Jikuan, the then Director of the Village Committee, and Zhu Qiuzhen and Zhang Shoujiang, the then Deputy Secretaries of the Village Party Branch, in the form of a lump sum compensation of 5,000 yuan, 5,000 yuan and 3,000 yuan respectively which were obtained by selling the village collective's Steel Shuttering Factory. Other village cadres have not so far received similar insurance compensation.

In addition to these two major problems, the employment of the women villagers is also a problem that is not easily solved. According to the company's stipulations, in households of which the farmland has been taken over, all women under 35 years may work for the company on a voluntary basis. In households of which the farmland has not yet been taken over, only the women under 30 years may be considered for work in the company. Because of this, a large number of women in the village who are over 35 years are unable to work for the company.

This situation was discussed with several villager groups. Generally speaking, the villagers in those groups whose lands were taken over early by the company received more benefits from the development of the company. In particular, the villagers of Villager Group No. 9 whose land was first taken over by the company were the first to receive good positions. A considerable number of middle-level officials of the company are the villagers from this group. They are entitled to good social benefits. The elderly in this group may live in houses for the elderly built by the company. They are also entitled to a monthly pension insurance of 90 yuan. Moreover, before the listing of the company, each villager had received 2,000 shares at the price of less than one yuan per share and thus, calculated on the basis of three members per household (the average number of members per household in Villager Group No. 9 has now dropped to 2.5 persons) every household could receive roughly 6,000 original shares at a cost of less than 6,000 yuan. When the shares of the company started to be officially traded on the Shenzhen Stock Exchange on 18 June 1999 at 5.43 yuan per share, these villagers' capital gains from the company shares appreciated by about five times. Furthermore, the company's share price has remained about 15 yuan for a long period after listing and was once as high as 23 yuan per share. Many villagers stated that quite a few people in Villager Group No. 9 had become millionaires as a result. Therefore, villagers of these privileged groups are generally in favour of IVWC.

The situation is totally different for those in other villager groups. They were neither able to receive original shares of the company nor able to attain top executive positions in the company. Moreover, their children cannot receive schooling subsidies nor are they entitled to receive various social security measures. Many villagers of Villager Group Nos. 2 and 3 told us that it was not easy for them even to become an ordinary worker in the company (see Plate 8.6).

Take for example Villager Group No. 2 which was part of the survey. There were 74 households and 346 people in this group. At present only 15 people (including three women) from this group work for the company which accounts for only 4 per cent of the total. According to the villagers, even these 15 people have some special *guanxi* with the company – 'they could not have been employed at all by the company if they did not have such *guanxi*'. Furthermore, the salary of these workers is not high, only 500–600 yuan per month. The situation of Villager Group No. 3 is similar to that of Villager Group No. 2. Of its total population of more than 340 people (representing more than 60 households), altogether only 20 people, accounting for 6 per cent, are working for the company. Of these

Plate 8.6 Some elderly villagers of Fuxing village evaluating the newly implemented IVWC institution

20 people, about half have special *guanxi* with different levels of leadership at the company.

According to the village cadres, no more than ten people each year from the village were employed by the company. Apart from the groups whose land has been used by the company (and who could work for the company based on company needs without quota restrictions), all the other groups only had two or three more employment opportunities with the company each year.

Therefore, each time we visited the village and talked with villagers, there were always some complaints: 'President Tan [Tan Gongyan] has set up such a big enterprise in our village but we have not benefited from our association with him. Instead we have fallen victim to him: the land has been occupied, the road is poor and there is much noise'; 'we have not received benefits from him [Tan Gongyan]. Only his relatives and the villagers of his villager group have received benefits', etc. According to them, even after adopting the system of IVWC, they did not feel they had received special benefits from this new institution. Of course, some remarks are somewhat general. It seems, at least, the implementation of this new system and institution still has much room for further improvement.

According to our initial observations, the impact of practising the IVWC system on the development of the company and the village has varied in different stages. However, in the long run, the practice of this system and institution should play a role in promoting the unification of the interests of the two parties. Otherwise, the implementation of this system will not be sustainable. In the present situation, putting the system and institution into practice has brought more benefits to the company than to the village. With regard to safeguarding the company's interests, the system of IVWC can at least solve the three practical problems, which are very important to the future development of the company:

First, it will help the company, through such institutional arrangements, to rationalize and legalize the requisitioning and use of villagers' land at low cost, which is important for the further expansion of the company.

Second, the implementation and execution of such a system and institution is conducive to the extension and dissemination of the influence of the company and its leaders in the village and to the whole area surrounding Fuxing village. This will allow the penetration of the authority of the company and its leaders into the whole community and will finally enable the further integration of the resources of the whole area and improve the company's competitiveness in future development.

Third, it will be conducive to setting up in Fuxing a regional community of interest centred on the Fuxing Company with the intention of safeguarding the political stability of the whole area, promoting the economic development of the whole area and finally materializing the grand objective of 'building Fuxing area into the largest metalwork city in China'.

From the viewpoint of the interests of the village and the villagers, as mentioned above, a considerable number of villagers have received very limited benefits from the practice of IVWC and some have not benefited from it at all; instead, they have been adversely affected. However, we should at the same time understand that this is not surprising in the early days of practising a new system. In the long run, the constant expansion of the company will help promote the incorporation as well as the urbanization of the village and will be conducive to the transformation of the whole village and all its villagers. This is a trend that now seems quite obvious. With the advancement and development of industrialization and urbanization, Fuxing village and the area where Fuxing Company is located will gradually be built up and transformed into a modern city with a reasonably large population in the near future. Then employment opportunities and villagers' social security will be greatly improved. Of course, this will be a relatively long process.

Industrial basis of the IVWC institution

The implementation of a new institution needs to be based on an industrial foundation. In theory, this at once reflects the Marxist requirement of economic base which will determine the social and cultural structure in a society and is consistent with the path dependency theory of the new institutional economics (NIE) and with the corresponding concept of the tacit knowledge. Viewed from the particular situation in the Fuxing area, which is a very important reason why the institution of IVWC has been proposed and implemented in this area, both FSTSC, as a modern corporate system and the village as a traditional organization in rural community have common characteristics. Both have a traditional industrial resource with local characteristics – the tradition, custom and craftsmanship of iron and metalwork processing. Because of this, the village and the company can, in general, find a mutually identifiable economic base in selecting the new institution of IVWC.

Modernization of the traditional industry

As mentioned in earlier parts of this chapter, as well as in Chapter 4, the area where Fuxing village is located historically boasts a tradition of iron processing activities, such as iron forging and nail making. With 600 years of experience, this traditional handicraft has been carried forward in Fuxing area into the largest comprehensive modern metalwork production base in China, which has considerable international competitiveness and covers multiple levels from low to high, from handwork to machine working, from traditional workshops to a modern listed company, and from local to international markets. Therefore, when a group of farmers from Fuxing village, led by Tan Gongyan, has gradually developed into a generation of outstanding entrepreneurs, they cannot but demonstrate in institutional innovation, their intrinsic local and traditional characteristics. Fuxing Company's success in metal products had proved this point.

Fuxing village is a migrant-based village. Iron processing is not the local industrial tradition of the village but an industrial tradition that the ancestors of Fuxing villagers brought here from their native place in Jiangxi Province. Elderly people in Fuxing village have said that they generally accept that this traditional handicraft was first brought to the Fuxing area by the ancestors of the Xiong clan. Then the Zhang clan followed in the iron forging business; later people of the Duan clan and other clans joined this area of work. When the pedigree of the Xiong clan was investigated, it was discovered that the ancestors of the Xiong clan here had moved from Jiangxi Province to Hubei Province during the reign of Yongkang in the Ming Dynasty (about 600 years ago). The first staging posts were Ziqing and Zihong. The first migrant ancestors of the Xiong clan, who had moved to Hubei Province, were Xiangyang. It was during the first year of the reign of Zhengtong in the Ming Dynasty (over 570 years ago) that they had relocated to the present Fuxing area.

According to the records of the pedigree of the Xiong clan, from its first migrant ancestors to the latest generation, the clan has been living in Fuxing area for 20 generations. In the early days of the development of the Fuxing area, the Xiong clan had the largest number of members, the largest number who forged iron and the largest number of furnaces; it was said that the Xiong clan had 48 furnaces in its heyday. In the early days, the iron-forging households were mainly concentrated in Villager Group No. 7 and later extended to Villager Group Nos. 5 and 6. Finally, all villager groups of Fuxing village took up iron forging. Even the villager group which was the last to take up iron forging has a history of more than 100 years. Recently, during the Fuxing Company's renovation of the village, layers of charcoal residue have been found at a depth of more than two metres underground. These residues are remnants of past iron forging over a long period and demonstrate the prosperity of the iron-forging industry in the Fuxing area.

Chen Liangou, 76 years old, of Villager Group No. 2 recalled that his father was engaged in iron forging, his grandfather was engaged in iron forging, and moreover, his father had told him that his grandfather's grandfather was also engaged in iron forging. In this way, by relying only on the old man's memory, we can reckon that his family has had an iron forging history of at least more than five generations. Duan Shulan, a 78-year-old villager of Villager Group No. 2, also stated that his family's iron forging history could be traced back eight to nine generations if his own memory is added to the memory passed down to him as a child from his grandfather. From these old men's recollections of past events, the author could deeply feel that they had a special sense of familiarity and intimacy with the latest 100 years of family iron forging history.

In the early days, the Fuxing villagers' iron forging had focused on three types of nails: hobnail, boat nail and clasp nail. Hobnails were a kind of small nail tailored to the needs of people living in the mountainous region who wore waterproof shoes and of many local people who wore getas (*youxie*) at that time; boat nails were a big nail tailored to the needs of people living in the lake area who made wooden boats; clasp nails were a kind of nail commonly used by rural residents in building houses. Therefore, hobnails and boat nails made at that time in the village were mainly for sale to other areas and clasp nails were sold equally locally and to other areas. The nails had good sales.

Iron processing was mainly organized as a household operation. Generally speaking, raw materials used to make nails are bought from big cities such as Wuhan. Usually a large distributor distributed these to specialized retail salesmen in the village for further distribution and retailing. According to elderly people in the village, in the 1930s and 1940s there were three relatively large iron firms in the village and there were also several other small iron firms. Before the founding of New China, the 1940s witnessed a booming iron industry in the village, with more than half the villagers engaged in some aspect of the iron business.

In fact, during the first few years after the founding of New China, the iron business in Fuxing village still existed and developed as individual operations. During the period of more than 20 years from 1956 to 1980, with the development of the collectivization movement, the iron business of Fuxing village also took the form of collective operations. At that time, the iron business was organized on the basis of production teams (under brigades), and generally each production team set up an iron business group. In each group, there were about 20 people regularly specializing in iron forging; during slack seasons in farming, more people would take up iron forging in each production team. The raw materials used in iron forging were bought by the village collective from big cities such as Wuhan. During this period the products made in the village were still mainly boat nails, hobnails and clasp nails, and also products to meet other needs in the village. These iron business groups had also tailor-made some simple farm tools and the furniture needed by the villagers. The various types of nails were mainly sold to the surrounding counties (such as Tianmen, Mianyang, Honghu, Qianjiang, Yingcheng, etc.). Usually, one person could make about 5 kg (10 *jin* – 1 *jin* being equivalent to 500g) nails per day which would be recorded as one standard workload.[14] At that time, the unit price of boat nails was about 0.8 yuan per *jin*. For villagers engaged in marketing, each sale of 50 kg (100 *jin*) nails would be recorded in the production brigade as 15 standard workloads.

At that time, Fuxing village had two major sources of income: one was cotton cultivation (accounting for more than half of the total cropped area) and the other was the iron nail business. Moreover, the two sources were roughly equal in terms of income. Because the iron forging industry served as an important supplement, Fuxing villagers had enjoyed adequate food and clothing during the more than 20 years of collectivization. At the end of every year, most households would receive some cash income (generally a little more than 100 yuan), and only about 20 per cent of the households were in a state of over expending (the overspend was also about 100 yuan).

In the early 1980s, like other areas in China, Fuxing village began to practise the household-based contract system with remuneration linked to output. Land was again distributed to farmers and iron furnaces were returned to their original owners. Naturally, many villagers again took up their former private iron business. Some villagers had discovered techniques related to the iron business when they had marketed iron nails to different places for the village collective during the collectivization period. An important technique was to buy back at a very low price the scrap iron and steel wire discarded by the large, state-owned enterprises and factories and then to make it into different types of wire through tempering or to make nails from this scrap wire. As a result, not long after the reform policy was carried out in rural areas, and farmers were free to use their time as they wished, many villagers had begun to purchase scrap iron and steel wire from all across the country and soon this became the trend in Fuxing village.

In this way, purchasing scrap iron and steel wires and making nails from them as a business, as well as gradually extending the use of scrap iron and steel wire in making auxiliary bars for pre-cast slabs which were used at construction sites, were vigorously carried out in Fuxing village. In 1994, of the 47 sample households that were selected when a survey was conducted in this village, 38 households were involved in iron-industry-related business activities (including those working in Fuxing Company) (Table 8.1). This accounted for 80.9 per cent of the sample households and only nine households (19.1 per cent) were not engaged in the iron business. The iron industry has almost become 'an industry participated by all people' (Hu and Hu 1996: 76–8).

Table 8.1 Fuxing villagers' involvement in iron industry (1994)

Head of household	Sex	Age	Education	No. of family members	General economic situation of the household	Economic acivities relating to iron industry
Huang Xingfu	M	47	SS	5	Medium	Making nails
Duan Xincai	M	48	SS	4	Medium	Helping others hammer iron wires
He Xiongcai	M	38	SSS	5	Medium	Selling and processing scrap iron wires
Zhang Zhengde	M	44	SSS	7	Superior	Iron forging, working in the Steel Wire Factory
Duan Bingyan	M	49	ES	5	Superior	Selling scrap iron wires, hammering iron wires and making nails
Chen Jinsong	M	45	SS	8	Medium	Processing iron wires, working in the Steel Wire Factory
Huang Xianxun	M	52	ES	5	Superior	working in the Steel Wire Factory, driving tractor
Chen Tiexiang	M	44	ES	4	Poor	Helping others hammer iron wires
Duan Zhicheng	M	44	ES	5	Superior	Drawing wires, hammering wires
Xiao Jiangbing	M	34	SS	5	Medium	Drawing wires, hammering wires
Duan Lianfang	M	45	SS	4	Medium	Forging iron
Xiao Mucheng	M	35	SSS	5	Poor	Buying/selling iron wires
Sun Shitou	M	37	ES	5	Medium	Forging iron
Duan Shunxiang	M	44	ES	4	Poor	Processing iron wires
Duan Shengde	M	60	ES	5	Superior	Forging iron, drawing wire, hammering wire and doing iron business
Sun Yanbin	M	37	SS	5	Poor	Hammering wire
Zhang Fugui	M	45	SS	5	Medium	Doing iron wire business
Zhang Zhizhong	M	37	SS	4	Medium	Drawing wire, making wire and doing iron wire business
Yan Jinbang	M	51	SS	6	Poor	Hammering iron wires
Xu Xianzao	M	45	SS	5	Medium	Working in the Steel Wire Factory
Tan Shouru	M	52	ES	10	Superior	Working in the Steel Wire Factory

continued…

Table 8.1 continued

Head of household	Sex	Age	Education	No. of family members	General economic situation of the household	Economic activities relating to iron industry
Tan Yongcai	M	50	ES	6	Medium	Welding iron wires and working temporarily in the Steel Wire Factory
Tan Shouqin	M	51	SS	9	Superior	Hammering iron wires, iron-material cutting, working in the Steel Wire Factory
Tan Gongfan	M	48	SS	5	Superior	Working in the Steel Wire Factory
Duan Yanxiang	M	44	SSS	4	Superior	Doing scrap iron wire business in other places all the year round
Wang Jincheng	M	34	SS	4	Medium to superior	Working in the Steel Wire Factory
Chen Dongxun	M	52	ES	7	Medium to superior	Working in the Steel Wire Factory
Xiao Zuoshu	M	38	SS	5	Superior	Household nail making
Feng Shizhong	M	37	ES		Medium	Working in the Steel Wire Factory
Feng Chengqing	M	38	SS	5	Medium	Working in the Steel Shutter Factory
Xiao Zhiming	M	37	SS	5	Superior	Drawing wires, making nails
Xiao Tongxiang	M	34	SS	5	Medium	Processing scrap iron wires
Duan Shuguo	M	48	SS	5	Poor	Forging iron
Duan Zhiguo	M	47	ES	4	Poor	Making nails, hammering iron wires and working in the Steel Wire Factory
Hu Tiancai	M	44	SS	7	Poor	Drawing wire, forging iron
Yin Zuosheng	M	37	SSS	13	Medium	Helping others forging iron
Hu Jinmao	M	40	SS	13	Medium	Forging iron
Hu Guoxiang	M	35	SS	13	Medium	Household nail making

Source: Hu and Hu 1996: 76–8.
Note: ES: Elementary school; SS: Secondary school; SSS: Senior secondary school.

As the whole village was engaged in the iron business, a large number of 'rich households' with a high level of income had already emerged: by the end of 1994, six households in the village had bank deposits of more than 1 million yuan, 19 households had bank deposits of more than 300,000 yuan, 54 households had bank deposits of more than 100,000 yuan and 260 households had bank deposits of more than 10,000 yuan (Hu and Hu 1996).

It was in this macro environment that Tan Gongyan and his partners had embarked on their business undertaking. Like most other Fuxing villagers in the early days, Tan Gongyan and his partners also took up the business of purchasing scrap iron and steel wire, drawing it into new usable wire and selling it at a considerable profit.

However, unlike other Fuxing villagers, Tan Gongyan and his partners did not stay at the stage of a small handwork business; instead, in spite of the immature conditions at the time, they moved in a very short period from manual operations to mechanical operations through continuous efforts and successful development of new products to meet market needs and by quickly responding to the constant changes in the market demand. The new products were based on traditional strengths and resources but, by going beyond tradition, they took a traditional industry with several hundred years' history in the Fuxing area into a modern stage and have made remarkable achievements on this basis:

1   *1986–7*, the company undertook the transition from manual wire drawing to mechanical wire drawing.
2   *In 1990*, the company had introduced a small-scale steel wire rope production line which was put into operation in that year to generate a new gross value of 5.97 million yuan.
3   *In 1991*, the company had invested 2.8 million yuan in a new galvanized wire rope project which had newly generated a gross value of 4.67 million yuan.
4   *In 1992*, seizing the opportunity of a production project of 300,000 'Fukang' (Citroën in China) cars being started in Hubei Province, the company had invested 2.8 million yuan in a new project for steel wire to be used in strengthening tyres to provide support products for the car production.
5   *In 1998*, the company continuously introduced several new projects, all of them successful; at the beginning of the year, the company had developed carbon steel wire for reinforcing fibre-optic cable with a production capacity of 3,500 tons. According to a provincial level appraisal, this product was at an advanced level for China. In May, the company had developed plastic-coated steel wire rope. In October, the company had developed 36-12-1FC round-strand wire rope. Without a comparable structure, either at home or abroad, the product was appraised by the State Intellectual Property Rights Bureau as being a practical patented product which filled a market gap in China.
6   *In the first half of 1999*, the company had developed a PC steel strand product with an annual production capacity of 12,000 tons. The total investment for this project was 25.4 million yuan and high-quality products were successfully produced in June of the same year. Under inspection by the State Construction Materials Testing Centre, the quality of this product had reached a leading level at home and an advanced level abroad, and the product had filled a market gap in Hubei Province.
7   *In October 1999*, in response to market demand, the company decided to develop linear contact-lay-wire rope. The company had invested 3.8 million yuan in purchasing manufacturing equipment from Kunming Heavy Machinery Plant; this was led by a senior engineer and was organized as a special group of development personnel. The company had successfully developed this variety of products into three structures and six specifications during more than two months of effort. All the products had passed the test of the State Testing Centre.
8   *Projects developed in 2000* included: bronze plating wire for tyre beds with an annual production capacity of 5,000 tons by introducing a complete set of equipment from TWTT Company of Italy and steel curtain wire with an annual production capacity of 5,000 tons.

242 'Integrating village with company'

In this way, by the end of 2002, the products that were produced by Fuxing Company included various steel wire and steel wire rope of more than 20 varieties and more than 830 specifications. The major products included steel curtain wire, pre-stressed PC steel strand for concrete (PC steel strand), bronze plating wire for tyre beds in tempering tyres, high-strength steel wire, galvanized wire, carbon steel wire for reinforcing fibre-optic cable, linear contact-lay-wire rope, multi-strand wire rope, etc.[15] These products have been widely used in such sectors as transport, aviation, navigation, electricity, petroleum, chemical, agriculture, construction, light industry, medicine and communication.

In the company's list of products and name brands were five varieties of the steel wire rope series which have won the title of ministry-level or province-level high quality products. In particular, the steel wire for tyre beds in tempering tyres had won the 3rd National Scientific & Technological Achievement gold award. Having achieved ISO9002 quality certification and been authorized to use the QCM-QCC quality mark, the company's leading products with 'Fuxing' as their registered trademark have become brand-name products renowned both at home and abroad. So far, the various products of Fuxing Company have been sold to more than 30 countries or regions including southeast Asia, Japan, USA, Europe, Hong Kong and Macau. In 2002, the Company's income from metal products reached 436 million yuan and the related assets reached 1.534 billion yuan. The company had a staff of 4,000 working in steel-wire-related operations. If the employees in the real estate and bio-pharmaceutical enterprises are included, Fuxing Company had 5,000 employees.

Thanks to the emergence of these positive technological innovations, the corresponding institutional change has become possible. IVWC is accordingly one of the important emerging institutional changes.

IVWC: integration of traditional industry and modern industry

The modernization of traditional industry alone is not adequate to account for the implementation and execution of the system of IVWC. It can only be explained by the one-way evolution process of an industry and its related technologies from traditional to modern. What it stands for is a centrifugal process. That is, it indicates that a more advanced technology and industry represented by a company breaks away from a relatively traditional former state and from its matrix – the village. Accordingly, Fuxing Company that was incubated in the village was born out of the original traditional village. We can use Figure 8.1 (modernization of traditional industry) to briefly define this process.

Apparently, if the process continues, it will ultimately lead to a widening gap between modern industry and technology, and tradition, and a widening gap between company and village. Therefore, this process of development can be called 'a centrifugal process'. If this were the case, the present institution of IVWC could not have been created at all, let alone the future emergence of the new system and institution of IVWC as put forward by Tan Gongyan, chairman and president of the Fuxing Company.

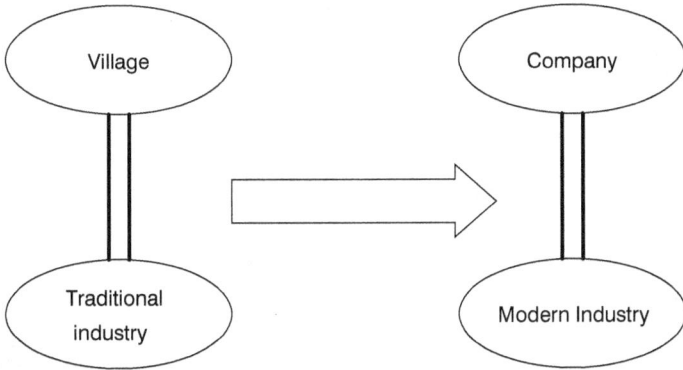

Figure 8.1 From tradition to modernization

From the perspective of industry and technology, what will enable the new system and institution of IVWC? There is another process, in addition to the modernization of traditional industry, which is in place, and that is the process of the integration of traditional and modern industry as shown in Figure 8.2. Behind the process of the integration of traditional and modern industry is actually the process of the integration of the traditional village and the modern corporation. Only in this way would it be possible to realize the system and institution of IVWC and even of 'the full integration of the village and the company'.

Figure 8.2 shows that the integration of traditional and modern industry is actually a two-way interactive process and a close combination of centrifugal and centripetal forces. Similarly, behind the interaction of industry and technology is actually the interaction and combination of corporation and village organizations, for which industrial and technological transformation has constituted an important basis for organizational and institutional change.

Viewed from the particular situation of the Fuxing area, some major characteristics and manifestations of the process of integrated development of traditional industry and modern industry can be understood from the following:

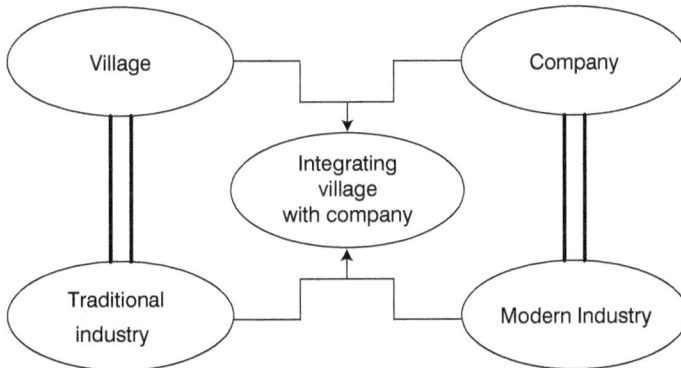

Figure 8.2 Integration of tradition and modernization

- First of all, in terms of industrial characteristics, the company and the village are of the same nature, i.e., both undertake metalwork focusing on wire drawing. Although the company's technical standard, degree of mechanization and level of management are much higher than those of the village, their manufacturing techniques and management processes are nevertheless the same. Therefore, the company and the village and its villagers all have in common the connections and communications of the industry and related technologies, which have laid a foundation for industrial cooperation between the company and the village and established a more in-depth institutional connection between the two parties based on this cooperation.

- Second, in terms of the human resources needed in industrial development, as the Fuxing villagers have for generations been engaged in the iron industry, people born here have since their childhood had a natural tie with and deep attachment to iron forging, wire drawing and related metalwork industries. Certainly, the villagers here have many generations' experience of the relevant techniques, and management and marketing methods. At a deeper level, the villagers have to varying degrees realized the economic value and cultural significance of operating an iron business. Because of this realization, whenever the Fuxing Company needed to recruit new employees because of its accelerating expansion, Fuxing villagers were naturally the most suitable candidates (most of them from the Villager Groups 7, 8, 9, 10 and 11). In fact, Fuxing villagers had accounted for 24 per cent of the company's employees at the end of 2003. In the early days of the company's development, this proportion was once higher than 70 per cent.

- Third, in terms of knowledge and skill needed for industrial development, traditional skills and implicit knowledge in the region have played a very important role. Due to the strong influence of the history of industrial development and traditional village culture (whether as a village collective, individuals in the village or the Fuxing Company), they have over a long period improved industrial operations and promoted the process of modernization on the basis of this knowledge and techniques. Neither the Fuxing villagers, nor Tan Gongyan, the leader of the company, would have embarked on the road to the development of modern metalwork industry without this history of industrial experience. In other words, the reasons why Fuxing village has become an 'iron industry village', famous far and wide, and why Tan Gongyan – who was born in the village – has been able to create what the local people call a legend in the development of metalwork industry, are not superficial, but actually have deep historical and cultural foundations. Here lies the significance of history and culture, and the local people's implicit knowledge in the industrial processes: it is technological and institutional selection.

- Finally, in terms of industrial relations, a relatively stable and long-term industrial cooperative relationship between the company, the village collective and the individual villagers' enterprises has taken shape. The enterprises administered by the village collective as well as a considerable number of villager-run enterprises have been conducted around the needs of the company. For example, the Disc Spool Factory which is administered by the village collective at present concentrates on producing a special product for the company: a kind of wooden wheel that is used to wind together the steel wire. This type of spool is an auxiliary product that serves the core production of the company. All the bricks produced by the Brick & Tile Factory under the administration of the village collective are supplied to the company at present, for use in the company's own expansion and renovation and as part of the village renovation project. All the non-agricultural activities of many villagers also are to provide pre-production and post-production products and services. In the long process of cooperation based on mutual benefit, the company and the village have actually shaped an industrial chain based on development of the metalwork industry and they have reached a stage of mutual dependence. Therefore, in these circumstances, the practice of the new institution and system of IVWC is at present a very natural result for both Fuxing village and the Fuxing Company.

Community-oriented[16] functional organization:[17] the organizational basis of IVWC

Institutional change must have an organizational basis in addition to a firm industrial and economic basis, if it is to work effectively. Based on observation and research, the organizational basis of practising the institution of IVWC is that, during more than a decade's rapid growth and since, the Fuxing Company has gradually begun to develop from a unitary functional organization towards a mixture of functional organizations and community-oriented organizations.

IVWC: transformation from a unitary functional organization to a mixed form

As we know, enterprises are some of the most common organizations in modern society. If an organization is classified, on the basis of its nature, as either a functional organization or a community organization, then enterprises are the most typical form of functional organizations (Sakaiya 1996). However, based on long-term research and observation of the Fuxing Company over ten years, the company has shown a strong tendency toward transforming from a functional organization into a community-oriented organization based on Fuxing village.

1   The controlling power of the Fuxing Company clearly has shown a constant tendency toward concentration based on kinship and geographical relations. The continuous development and mixing of these kinship and geographical relations within the scope of a small community is very likely to lead eventually to the emergence of an organization or institution with a strong communal nature.

2 From 1992, the company had moved Tan Shouren, one of its key officials, from the position of salesman in the company to the position of Party Secretary of Duanjia village. This has marked the formal beginning of an initial attempt to integrate the company with the village.

3 At the end of 1994, when we visited the Steel Wire Shareholding Co. Ltd., (predecessor to the present FSTSC) in Duanjia village (as it was called then) to conduct a survey, we found slogans posted on either side of the company's main entrance. On one side the slogan read 'Loyalty First, Ability Second' and on the other was 'Gambling Is the Source of All Evils'. This indicates that the values of the key leaders of the company leant more towards morality rather than ability. This mentality is to a large extent consistent with the principle of a community-oriented organization, but was inconsistent with the principles of functional organizations.

4 From 24 December 1996, the new institution and system of IVWC was officially carried out on the approval of Hanchuan County People's Government. Subsequently, the company has appointed Tan Yeliang, its high-calibre supply and marketing clerk, as the Party Secretary of the village and had begun to design the overall plan of complete integrated renovation of the Fuxing area. This included mainly Fuxing village and the area where the Fuxing Company was located but would later cover the surrounding villages.

5 In November 2003, when the next stage of development and planning for the company was discussed with Tan Gongyan, chairman and president of the Fuxing Company, he clearly put forward the idea of gradually implementing the full integration of the village and the factory and had the hope of achieving this aim in the coming three years.

As a large-sized public (listed) company, if it is overwhelmingly controlled by one clan or by a few people sharing close geographical connections and if it constantly expands in the direction of community-oriented development, then the company's functional nature will be weakened, at least in form, while its communal nature is strengthened. The Fuxing Company has exhibited exactly these features.

First of all, in terms of the controlling power, the leadership and delegation of power within the company were found to be controlled by the clan connections and they also had demonstrated a tendency towards further orienting the company towards the community. Of the 110 core leaders of the Fuxing Company, 23 are members of the Tan clan, mainly based on kinship (21 per cent). Members of the Zhang clan, the second largest clan assuming leadership of the company accounted for 9 per cent of the core leaders, followed by eight members of the Li clan (7 per cent of the key leaders). Moreover, the positions assumed by the members of the Tan clan are very important. In addition to providing the company's chairman and president, Tan Gongyan, the Tan clan had provided the vice-general manager in charge of external affairs, the assistant general manager in charge of equipment and technology, the executive vice-general manager of the Real Estate Company, the general manager of the Property Management Company, the deputy director of the financial department of the company, and the directors of Branch Factory Nos. 1, 3 and 5.

The Fuxing Company was initiated by Tan Gongyan and others from Villager Group No. 9 of Fuxing village. Consequently, villagers of Villager Group No. 9 have more and greater priority than those from other villager groups in various aspects of the company's development, in being placed in important positions and in being preferred for promotion. By the end of 2003, of the 110 important positions of the company, 33 were members of Villager Group No. 9 (30 per cent of the total). If we expand our analysis to the whole village, then 54 of the 110 important positions in the company were held by members of Fuxing village (49 per cent of the total).

Taking the analysis a step further, if we combine the Tan clan kinship with geographical connections to Fuxing village, these two accounted for 52 per cent of the 110 important positions in the company and they constituted the controlling power for the future development of the company (Table 8.2).

Generally speaking, of the company's six highest ranking leaders who comprised the management team, two were from the Tan clan and one from Villager Group No. 9. Together, half of the top ranking managers were from Villager Group No. 9. Moreover, the two highest leaders of the company were from Villager Group No. 9. Of departmental heads, the directors of three of the six branch factories as well as 11 of the 14 departmental heads were from the Tan clan or Fuxing village.

In addition to the direct kinship and geographical connections mentioned above, there are also some indirect yet very important relations. These are relations of people who have no direct clan or geographical connection themselves, but are related to key people from the Tan clan or Villager Group No. 9. The significance of this kind of relationship in accelerating the gradual transformation of Fuxing Company from a functional organization to a community-oriented organization cannot be ignored. Take for example the relationships to company President Tan Gongyan shown in the Table 8.3.

Viewed from the equity structure of the Fuxing Company, as of 31 December 2002, the company issued altogether more than 200 million shares (the precise number of shares is 266,695,000), which consisted of unlisted circulating shares and listed circulating shares of which, the employee shares in the company were listed and circulated on 8 July 2002. After the listing of internal employee shares, the total number of the company's shares did not change but the number of listed circulating shares in the equity structure had increased from the original 71,500,000 to 100,516,884 shares. The total number of shareholders in the company at the end of 2002 was 29,522. The top ten shareholders at the year-end report are shown in Table 8.4.

From this information about the shareholders, the controlling shareholder of the Fuxing Company is Hanchuan Steel Wire Factory of Hubei Province which is registered as an enterprise of collective ownership and its legal representative is Tan Caiwang. As it belongs to a collectively owned enterprise, the controller of

Table 8.2 Fuxing Company's political power distribution among different groups of people

Political power level	Member of Tan clan	Villagers of Villager Group No. 9	Other Fuxing villagers
Major leaders of the company	Chairman & President; Deputy General Manager; General Manager Assistant; Executive Deputy General Manager of the Real Estate Company; Deputy General Manager of the Real Estate Company; General Manager of Science & Technology Company; General Manager of the Property Management Company.	Chairman & President; Vice President & Executive Deputy General Manager; Deputy General Manager; Deputy General Manager; Executive Deputy General Manager of the Real Estate Company; General Manager of the Science & Technology Company; General Manager of the Property Management Company; Deputy General Manager of the Pharmaceutical Company.	Deputy General Manager; Deputy General Manager of the Real Estate Company.
Major leaders of departments	Directors of Branch Factory No. 1; Director of Branch Factory No. 3; Director of Branch Factory No. 8; Deputy Director of Financial Department; Deputy Director of Engineering Management Department; Director of Water and Electricity Company.	Director of Foreign Trade Department; Director of Operating Risk Control Department; Director of Enterprise Management Office; Deputy Director of Financial Department; Deputy Director of Technical Centre; Deputy Director of Investment Projects Management Department; Deputy Director of Production Planning Department; Deputy Director of Administrative Department; Leader of Company Cars Management Team; Director of Water & Electricity Company.	Director of Transportation Department; Director of Securities Department; Director of Production Planning Department; Directors of Branch Factory No. 3 and No. 8; Deputy Directors of Branch Factory No. 1, No. 3 and No. 5.
Other major officers	1 in Branch Factory No. 1; 1 in Branch Factory No. 5; 1 in Branch Factory No. 8; 1 in Branch Factory No. 9; 2 in Administrative Department; 1 in Water & Electricity; 1 in General Office.	2 in General Office; 1 in Labour & Human Resources Department; 1 in Materials Supply Department; 1 in Chief Engineer's Office; 1 in Enterprise Management Office; 2 in Production Planning Department; 1 in Administrative Department; 1 in Branch Factory No. 2; 1 in Branch Factory No. 5; 1 in Branch Factory No. 8.	1 in Materials Supply Department; 1 in Water & Electricity Department; 1 in Industrial Management Department; 2 in Branch Factory No. 1; 1 in Branch Factory No. 2; 2 in Branch Factory No. 3; 2 in Branch Factory No. 5; 1 in Branch Factory No. 1.

Source: Field survey in Fuxing village.

Table 8.3 Extension of Tan Gongyan's kinship and its political impact on the Fuxing Company

Name	Position	Relationship to Tan Gongyan and his clan	Remarks
Xia Muyang	Deputy General Manager	Husband of niece	From Xinzhou village of the same town
Hu Shuoshang	Assistant to General Manager & Chief Financial Officer	Husband of niece	From Mahe Town of the same city
Zhang Kaisong	Director of Branch Factory No. 2	Brother of great nephew's wife	From Zhangwan village of Maiwang Town of the same city
Li Longbiao	Director of Chief Engineer's Office	Brother of great nephew's wife	From Liukou village of Maiwang Town of the same city
Cao Dongcheng	Director of Materials Supply Department	Husband of niece	From Hongfeng village of the same town
Zhou Sufang	Director of Sales Department	Sister of great nephew's wife	From Yanglin Town of the same city
Liao Minghui	Cashier	Wife of great nephew	From Xiangfan City of the same province

Source: Field survey in Fuxing village.

Table 8.4 Top ten shareholders in the Fuxing Company in year-end 2002

Ranking	Shareholder	Shares held	Shareholding percentage	Type of share
1	Hubei Province Hanchuan Steel Wire Factory	144,5 88,000	54.21	Domestic legal person shares of sponsors
2	Hubei Shengsheng Investment Co. Ltd.	10,000,000	3.75	Domestic legal person shares of sponsors
3	Zhonggongmei Investment Co. Ltd.	5,000,000	1.87	Domestic legal person shares of sponsors
4	Xiaogan Municipal Property Rights Exchange Center	4,290,000	1.61	Designated legal person shares
5	Hubei Xincheng Industry & Trade Co. Ltd.	2,145,000	0.80	Domestic legal person shares of sponsors
6	Guotai Jinying Growth Securities Investment Fund	1,201,315	0.45	Circulating share
7	Great Wall Securities Co. Ltd.	664,759	0.25	Circulating share
8	Mr. Xie (individual shareholder)	444,200	0.17	Circulating share
9	Mr. Tao (individual shareholder)	343,640	0.13	Circulating share
10	Ms. Lin (individual shareholder)	302,912	0.13	Circulating share

Source: 2002 Annual Report of Hubei Fuxing Science & Technology Shareholding Co. Ltd.

the company should nominally be Chenhu Town Industrial Administration Station of Hanchuan City, which is an administrative entity of the government. However, as has been demonstrated repeatedly in the above discussion, the real controller of the Fuxing Company is the family and community interest group around Tan Gongyan and his family and centred on Villager Group No. 9, rather than the legal representative registered in the company's business licence or the Industrial Administration Station of the Chenhu Town Government.

How should we then understand the absence of an actual controller in the equity structure? From our experience over a long period of contact with Tan Gongyan, president of the company, two factors merit attention: first, Tan Gongyan himself is an entrepreneur of lofty aspirations and ambitions and his ultimate goal is to bring prosperity to local farmers through the development of the enterprise and to reach his grand aspiration of taking the lead in the central regions of China to achieve rural modernization and rural urbanization. President Tan does not pay much attention, therefore, to his personal interests (before the listing of the company, his annual salary was only 26,000 yuan for many years and since the listing of the company, his annual salary has only been 80,000 yuan), but rather he has attached great importance to his political value;[18] second, viewed from the developing prospects of the company, Tan Gongyan and his partners still worry about the political and economic consequences of privatizing the company and thus hope to reduce the transaction costs of enterprise development by continuing to wear the 'red hat'.

In terms of the company's employee structure, during a considerable part of the company's development, workers in the company were mainly recruited from Villager Group No. 9, where the president of the company lives. For example, at the company's inception, 75 per cent of workers were recruited from Villager Group No. 9; the percentage increased to 100 per cent in 1982, was 67 per cent in 1983, 48 per cent in 1984 and 62 per cent in 1985. As the company had developed very rapidly and its demand for human resources increased, far exceeding the capacity of Villager Group No. 9, recruitment of more new workers had to expand gradually from the core geographical connections to peripheral connections – from Villager Group No. 9 to other villager groups in Fuxing village and also to Lihua village and others near to Fuxing (Table 8.5). Therefore, by the end of 1993, of the 1,698 employees in the company, 127 were from Villager Group No. 9 of Fuxing village (only 7.5 per cent of the total), 376 were from the rest of Fuxing village (22.1 per cent of the total) and 228 from nearby Lihua village (13.4 per cent).

In terms of the clan structure of the company's employees, during the five-year period from 1982 to 1987, the Tan clan was the largest group among newly recruited employees compared with other clans (Table 8.6). After 1988, for the same reasons mentioned above, the demand for human resources generated by the company's development increased greatly and exceeded the capacity of the Tan clan. Moreover, a large number of villagers in nearby villages had various affinities and kinships with the Tan clan in Fuxing village; so the proportion of the employees from the Tan clan in the total employees had shown a downward trend. At the end of 1993, there were 89 employees with the surname Tan in the company accounting for 5.2 per cent of the total employees.

In addition, there is a similar kinship link when viewed from the perspective of persons designated by the Company as the Party Secretary of the village. While there is no denying that Tan Shouren, the first Village Party Secretary designated by the company, or Tan Yeliang, the later Village Party Secretary designated by the company, are very able men (according to our contact with them), at the same

Table 8.5 Geographical structure of the newly recruited employees of the Fuxing Company (1981–93)

Year	Number of new recruits	From Villager Group No. 9	Other villager groups of the village	Other villages of the town	Other towns of the county (city)	Other counties (cities) and other provinces	Percentage of those from Villager Group No. 9
1981	4	3	0	0	1	0	75.0
1982	5	5	0	0	0	0	100.0
1983	9	6	3	0	0	0	66.7
1984	21	10	2	3	6	0	47.6
1985	13	8	1	0	4	0	61.5
1986	52	14	13	10	14	1	26.9
1987	29	5	9	5	9	1	17.2
1988	40	7	13	6	12	2	17.5
1989	69	15	11	8	33	2	21.7
1990	95	9	27	20	38	1	9.5
1991	237	13	45	36	138	5	5.5
1992	329	14	77	194	19	25	4.3
1993	531	18	46	108	359	0	3.4

Source: Field survey in Fuxing village.

time it is possible to think that, besides their ability, their special background is to a certain extent related to their lineage, i.e., both of them have close kinship and clan relationships with Tan Gongyan, president of the company. Although their salaries are not large, we think that the president of the company places great trust in them, based on their appointment to major positions in the village being of great historical significance, whether to the development of the company, the development of the village or even to the whole Fuxing area.

Apparently, in circumstances where villagers with the surname Tan do not dominate Fuxing village,[19] the fact that the president of the company chooses cadres with the surname Tan to assume the most important positions in the village indicates that this behaviour involves certain factors of family concept and family awareness. Later, when the genealogy of the Tan clan was consulted, it was found that the early Tan clan had moved from Nanchang in Jiangxi to the present Fuxing village in the second year of the reign of Hongwu in the Ming Dynasty (about 600 years ago). It has generated four branches up to now, of which Tan Shouren is from the oldest branch and both Tan Gongyan and Tan Yeliang are from the second oldest branch. In terms of seniority in the clan, Tan Gongyan is one generation older than both Tan Shouren and Tan Yeliang. Tan Gongyan is of the 18th generation since the move from Nanchang, whereas both Tan Shouren and Tan Yeliang are of the 19th generation. Moreover, it was found that Tan Yeliang is relatively close to Tan Gongyan; if the relationship between Tan Gonghuan, who is Tan Yeliang's father, and Tan Gongyan is traced back four generations, they would have the same ancestor (i.e., they have a common great-great-grandfather). Tan Zhengtai had two sons, the elder was Tan Mingyuan and the younger Tan Mingpu. Tan Gongyan is the great-grandson of Tan Mingyuan whereas Tan Yeliang's father, Tan Gonghuan, is the great-grandson of Tan Mingpu. Therefore, Tan Gongyan's

Table 8.6 Surname structure of newly recruited employees at the Fuxing Company (1981–93)

Year	Number of newly recruited employees	Members of the Tan clan	Other surnames					Percentage from Tan clan
1981	4	1	Zhang (2)	Feng (1)	Tian (1)	Nie (1)		25.0
1982	5	1	Zhang (1)	Tu (1)	Zhang (1)			20.0
1983	9	3	Wang (2)	Tu (1)	Zhang (1)	Sheng (1)	Xiao (1)	33.3
1984	21	4	Zhang (3)	Chen (2)	Liu (2)	Nie (1)	Tu (1)	19.0
1985	13	3	Duan (2)	Zhang (1)	Li (1)	Qi (1)	Zhou (1)	23.1
1986	52	6	Li (6)	Zhang (5)	Liu (5)	Wu (4)	Chen (3)	11.5
1987	29	5	Zhang (5)	Chen (3)	Duan (3)	Tu (3)	Li (2)	17.2
1988	40	4	Zhang (5)	Li (4)	Chen (3)	Feng (3)	Wang (3)	10.0
1989	69	4	Chen (9)	Li (7)	Liu (5)	Tu (5)	Wang (5)	5.8
1990	95	10	Li (14)	Liu (10)	Chen (7)	Wu (7)	Zhang (5)	10.5
1991	237	12	Liu (20)	Li (17)	Zhang (17)	Chen (12)	Wu (10)	5.1
1992	329	22	Li (63)	Liu (57)	Zhang (45)	Wu (38)	Chen (30)	6.7
1993	531	14	Li (59)	Zhang (50)	Liu (42)	Chen (32)	Wu (27)	2.6

Source: Field survey in Fuxing village.

behaviour in selecting people to assume prominent positions in the village to a certain extent reflected the influence of the concept of family on him.

It can be seen that Fuxing Company and its leaders have a very clear long-term rather than a short-term idea of setting up a new and effective system by constantly pushing the family power outward and gradually integrating the forces of the grass-roots community within the scope of Fuxing village. Therefore, the gradual introduction of the institution of IVWC is a very natural result. All the theories about the nature of the firm, the coordination modes of the firm and governance that have been discussed in Chapter 2 can be employed to explain such a system and whether such an institutional selection is a rational choice and so on.

From an economic point of view, the Fuxing Company will gain quite a lot of benefit from this new institution. For example, the company has derived from the village many of the resources it needs, e.g., 2,233 *mu* of land and 1,778 labourers from the workforce of the village. The company has a need for further expansion through the local villagers' moral support for the company's development, through the positive impact of the cultural factors nourished by the local tradition of the company and through the leaders of the company who will provide stability to the corporate governance, etc.

If we put this special institution into an evolutionary framework, we find that it is a kind of institutional creation taking place in the historical period of China's transition from a centrally planned to a market economy. This implies that before the current market system of China becomes mature, the cost that the company pays for organizing and utilizing village resources can be controlled at a very low level. Thus the profit margin of the company can be improved. The point is most clearly demonstrated in the company's requisition of the villagers' land. At present the company's standard compensation for requisition of the villagers' land is almost zero. The company planned to make a lump sum compensation of 300 yuan per *mu* starting from the year 2004, whereas in the suburbs of such big cities as Beijing, the developers' standard compensation for requisition of farmers' land is usually not less than 400,000 yuan per *mu*, more than 1,200 times the Fuxing Company's compensation to Fuxing villagers. The cost of local labour is also very low; as a general standard, the temporary workers' monthly salary is 500 yuan and that of the contract workers is 600 yuan. Apparently the company can make a lot of marginal profits (or in other words surplus value) from the utilization and integration of the village resources. On the other hand, if Tan Gongyan and his company do not form a community within the village in the form of new governance, it would be very difficult for the company to obtain the land resources that it needs for its further development and, even if it could secure the land, the transaction cost would be very high.

In addition, moral support for the company and its leaders given by local people for such a community-based organization is also of great significance to the stable and sustainable development of the company.

Fuxing villagers' livelihoods have been gradually improving since the introduction of the IVWC governance structure in the area but there are still some concerns.

Community-based organization under the institutional framework of IVWC is different from that in the traditional agricultural society

As designed by Tan Gongyan, president of the Fuxing Company, the further development of the institution of IVWC will definitely promote its further transformation into the institution and system of full 'integration of village and company'. That is to say, theoretically, the mixed organization of functional organization and community-based organization that we have mentioned will further develop in Fuxing area towards creating a community in a rural area. The result of such in-depth development will ultimately promote the urbanization process in the area. To the Fuxing area, the emergence and development of a regional city will be an inevitable trend.

However, we must be aware that, with the development of the system of IVWC, the emergence and development of a regional community-based organization, brought about by the new institution and system of the full integration of the village and the company will not be the same as the village community in a traditional agricultural society. Quite the contrary, there is a great difference between them. Viewed from the actual situation in Fuxing area, these differences are mainly demonstrated in four ways:

- They are different in the industrial basis. The industrial basis of a traditional village community is agriculture, while the new community promoted by the system of IVWC is based on development of the modern metalwork industry of the Fuxing Company. Take the latest data for 2003 as an example. In the region of Fuxing village, total agricultural output was only 17.58 million yuan (13.4 million yuan in 2002) whereas total industrial output in 2003 was more than 1 billion yuan. Of this, the total output from two contracted enterprises and eight relatively large individual enterprises of the village was 6.67 million yuan. The output of 80 relatively small individual enterprises plus the income of villagers from steel wire and rolled steel processing reached nearly 100 million yuan. About 90 per cent of this was contributed by the Fuxing Company and the remaining about 10 per cent contributed by the collective enterprises and self-employed individuals in the village. On the whole, the total output of industry was about 60 times that of agriculture.
- They are different in their degree of openness to the outside. The traditional village community is basically a closed system with little substantive contact with the outside world and is marked internally by high homogeneity and self-sufficiency. But this new type of community ushered in by the system of IVWC and further by the full integration of the village and the company is a very open system and the internal contact and communication with the outside is very frequent; in particular, it has very close contact with external markets. At present, the metal products of Fuxing Company have been sold all over China and to more than 30 other countries and regions including the United States, Canada, Indonesia, etc., and its business activities can be said to have been fully internationalized.

- The new community has been built mainly on the basis of interest and profit, and does not exclude the role of a functional organization. On the contrary, the various functional organizations continuously play their role under a new overall community framework which is according to their own rational objectives. The community constructed with the system of IVWC represented mainly a kind of community taking interest as its driving force for further development and not the community as an all-embracing nature of common society. Therefore, such a community does not exclude concurrent roles of various subordinate functional organizations.
- The traditional geographical social structure will change accordingly and the confluence of the company and the village organization will directly promote the emergence and development of a new geographical social structure. Thus, it directly promotes the inception of the urbanization process in China from the rural grass roots in a new stage of historical development. Currently the restructuring project in Fuxing village carried out by the Fuxing Company is none other than the specific embodiment of this development trend.

Therefore this new form of Chinese rural community that is emerging in Fuxing area cannot be simply explained using traditional village community theory. In fact, commensurate with the accumulation and extension of the various factors in this new type of community, we can predict that, in the future, this community-based organization in Fuxing area which is promoted by the institution of IVWC and which aims at the full integration of the village and the company will increasingly show the characteristics of city/town community. Fuxing area will also gradually realize the transition and development from a rural to an urban area.

IVWC and rural modernization

The institution and system of IVWC has already brought about or will bring about some tremendous impacts on the economic, social, political, cultural and lifestyle aspects of the people in Fuxing area. Some impacts are positive but some others are relatively negative.

In terms of positive impacts, the implementation of the system of IVWC will promote the development of Fuxing area in the following main ways.

Under this new system, Fuxing Company would absorb as many labourers as possible from Fuxing village to work in the company

This is conducive to providing more job opportunities for villagers, accelerating the transfer of rural labourers into non-agricultural activities and helping villagers to increase their income. According to our survey, a considerable number of Fuxing villagers hope to work in Fuxing Company, but it is very difficult for them to get such an opportunity. At present, 1,200 workers of the Fuxing Company are Fuxing villagers, which accounts for 24 per cent of the total number of employees of the company. Of these 1,200 workers from Fuxing village, about 40 per cent are villagers from the Villager Group Nos. 8, 9, 10 and 11 whose lands have been completely taken over and about 60 per cent are villagers from other villager groups.

The system of IVWC has helped to promote the agricultural development of the Fuxing area by utilizing the force of the company resources

This is mainly manifested in three areas:

1. It is geared to the need for structural readjustment of agriculture. In 1996 the company built an aquatic breeding base with an investment of 500,000 yuan. The 15.6 *mu* base produced 20,000 soft-shelled turtles per year. In 2003, the Company had again invested 1.5 million yuan to help the villagers build a 100 *mu* base producing 100,000 soft-shelled turtles per year. It also invested 50,000 yuan in erecting a 12.6 *mu* vegetable shed.

2. To reduce the burden on farmers, the company is planning to help Fuxing villagers to settle tax and fee problems by paying in instalments by villager group starting from 2004. According to the plan from Tan Gongyan, beginning in 2004, the plan would invest more than 300,000 yuan per year to pay all taxes and fees for the villagers' contractual land and so reduce their burdens in a uniform manner.

3. The company has in the past few years invested some 1 million yuan to improve the village irrigation systems mainly by dredging water ditches and river channels. It is considering the possibility of increasing the economic efficiency of agriculture by adjusting the structure of agriculture to improve agricultural management skills and introduce high-quality crop varieties.

The company has greatly promoted infrastructure facilities in the Fuxing area

After successfully helping the local government to set up a 110,000 kW transformer station in Fuxing area, Fuxing Company had again independently set up a 35,000 kW transformer station (exclusively invested in by the Fuxing Company). This has directly helped the local people solve long-term problems of a stable supply of power. The company also financed the building of a gas station and a liquefied gas station in the village. In addition, it funded the building of a water plant and has helped the villagers to solve the problem of access to safe drinking water. A closed circuit TV system has now been installed to cover the company's residential area and the whole of Fuxing village. The company has also invested in linking village roads and adjacent villages to the outside world.

Social infrastructure construction has also made great headway

The company has invested 300,000 yuan in building the Fuxing primary school and more than 500,000 yuan in setting up the Fuxing middle school. It also has invested 100,000 yuan to support the middle school in purchasing teaching equipment. The company has also invested more than 1 million yuan in setting up study stipends for workers' children and outstanding teacher scholarships. Furthermore, the company has engaged good teachers from outside on high pay to teach children in the village, immensely enhancing quality of teaching in Fuxing village. Incomplete statistics show that the company has invested a total of more than 3 million yuan in education.

It has invested in helping the village restore the cooperative medical system and set up a village clinic

It has issued a monthly subsidy of 120 yuan to the parents of couples of which both husband and wife were employed by the company. It has set up a 12,000-yuan special fund to guarantee the 17 'five-guarantees' households (i.e. the aged, the infirm, old widows and widowers, and orphans, taken care of by the village in five ways – food, clothing, medical care, housing and burial expenses) a basic allowance of 55 yuan per month per capita. It has offered an annual special fund of 10,000 yuan to help people face difficulties due to natural disasters and accidents, etc.

The huge economic expansion of the Fuxing Company has played an important role in spurring the boom of the Fuxing village non-farm economy

At present, the village boasts of nearly 100 non-agricultural business owners including collective contract enterprises, and individual industrial and commercial businesses which employ a total of more than 800 people. The total gross value is estimated at about 100 million yuan based on the opportunities provided by the company in 2003 (compared with 70 million yuan in 1997). At a yearly profit rate of 10 per cent, the villagers will receive a net income of some 10 million yuan from non-agricultural activities related to the company's business.

Judging from our survey, there were three main categories of businesses contracted from the company to the villagers: (1) providing supplementary services for the Fuxing Company; (2) doing business with the outside by using the good name of the Fuxing Company and (3) running the various services for those coming to the Fuxing Company on business. We have already mentioned the village Brick & Tile Factory and the Disc Spool Factory.[20] They were all built and developed by means of support from the Fuxing Company. To promote and encourage the rapid and healthy development of village enterprises, the company created favourable conditions for them. For example, it invested 50,000 yuan in laying power lines for the village enterprises and provided them with direct power supplies at a preferential price.

The system of IVWC is conducive to promoting urbanization from the rural grass roots

In recent years, the company has stepped up the renovation of housing in the whole village as an important element and a step towards urbanization in Fuxing area. Before the implementation of the system of IVWC, the company's housing development plan was mainly concentrated on the housing needs of the company workers. The plan previously ignored the villager groups except those whose land had been completely used by the company. But after implementing the system of IVWC, the company expanded the original residential quarters development plan to the entire Fuxing area which included the whole of Fuxing village. By the end of 2003, the company had invested a total of 94 million yuan in the residents' housing renovation project. Apart from the company workers and the Villager Group Nos. 8, 9 and 10 whose lands had been totally requisitioned, the villagers of Villager Group Nos. 5, 6, 7 and 11 of Fuxing village have also entirely moved into the residential quarters built up in a uniform style by the company.

According to the company plan, all other villagers will also move into such new residential quarters within three years. Along with the completion of the whole village renovation project, taking all areas together which make up the construction of the Fuxing Company-led modern industrial area and the corresponding living quarters and residents' entertainment sub-area, the whole Fuxing area including the Fuxing Company and Fuxing village will be built into a sizable new and modern city within a rural area in the next five to ten years. The Hubei Provincial Planning Institute has already developed such a general plan which is now being implemented.

While presenting the positive side, we must not ignore the negative aspects that might be brought about by the system of IVWC

These negative impacts can be embodied in the likelihood that the villagers are denied their democratic rights as masters of village autonomy within the framework of the system of IVWC. For example, village elections seem to be meaningless now and Party branch elections have become utterly unnecessary and impossible. The company-led village system may probably lead to excessive company control of the village and may even lead to resentment and boycott by the village cadres and residents of the system and system of organization. Under the system of IVWC, inadequate external control would easily lead to the company infringing and exploiting the villagers' interests in the issue of utilizing village resources. This may trigger class and interest divisions within the special area and widen the gap between the rich and the poor. These are all noteworthy, important issues in the course of implementing the new system.

Preliminary summary

As rural modernization has become a major issue attracting widespread attention, whilst theoretical studies can be meaningful, practical experience will be even more valuable. The importance of this point is self-evident for a large agricultural country like China in the process of modernization and globalization. We should say that Chinese and foreign scholars have been discussing China's modernization and its corresponding rural modernization issue over many years. They have generated many valuable theories and ideas. It is not possible for me to pass judgment on any of these theories and ideas but I will relate my experience of practical research of an ordinary village that I have studied over the years. This story involves implicit knowledge, traditional technologies, traditional institutions as well as their historical evolution and inheritance within modern society. It has also involved innovations and abrupt changes.

Studies of the Fuxing area have shown that Chinese villagers can modernize the indigenous traditional technologies through self-evolution and integrate the traditional skills, technologies and industries with the modern ones. It is true that the selection of the new institution and the new system of IVWC that fits in with the local cultural and traditional development features has a strong reverse transition from functional organization to community-based organization. But with its integration of company development and community development, linking the traditional and the modern, the past and the present, this system is a suitable option in the Fuxing area in terms of its realistic and rational stage of development. The significance of functional organization is apparent in a sound market system and system of organization. But in an environment of interaction between tradition and modernity, a purely functional organization may not necessarily be the best option in the present process of transition now underway in China, where market rules are not sound. On the contrary, a community-based organization may be of greater importance to promote and encourage sustainable economic and social development in certain areas, under certain historical conditions, and at a given period of time.

9   Conclusion

Integration of tradition and modernity – towards understanding institutional arrangements in China's modernization

Based on the theories and the indigenous conceptions of networks which were developed in Chapters 2 and 3 respectively, and the general introduction to the research areas indicated in Chapter 4, we have examined in Chapters 5 through 8 how people in the survey villages were getting things done, such as raising funds, moving from villages to cities, accelerating TVE development and extending the entrepreneur's control and power from local firms to outside areas, through the application of 'network closure' village trust and ROSCAs, strategic brokering of the 'structural holes' among different *guanxi* communities, and IVWC governance structure. We find that the theory and the reality have interacted very well in the survey villages. As part of the conclusion, we will attempt to develop a more general theoretical framework to bring together these complicated situations of theories and practices by focusing on the more general concepts, i.e., the concepts of tradition and modernization.

Tradition and modernization reflect exactly what we have discussed throughout the whole study. Tradition is very closely related to the theme of this research, namely informal institutions. According to Hayek, informal institution refers to tradition (Hayek 1988). When Douglass North mentioned 'informal constraints' in his works, he meant the information from social communication, i.e., something as having its source in culture (North 1990: 37). This has also indicated that the culture he wanted to express when using this concept, mainly refers to the part of contents which are relatively traditional. Jon Elster (1989) has even regarded tradition and social norms as 'the vehicle of culture' which works as the 'cement of society'. Chinese indigenous culture and the related village trust and ROSCAs, and *guanxi* community are all Chinese tradition-based institutions.

On the other hand, if we were to look at reality, the process of evolution of the social structure[1] from the 'network closure' in the case of Xiangdong village and the ROSCAs within the village, proceeding to the mobile networks between rural and urban areas, such as a group of entrepreneurs and migrant workers from Tunwa village, and further into the integrated entity of a listed company and a village in Fuxing area, along with the changing environments, as we discussed in the theory chapter (Chapter 2), have all reflected the process of modernization in rural China during the country's period of transition.

Clearly, with 'closure' in the village community, ROSCA operation within the village has less risk since the villagers share the same village trust, which is a kind of 'collective trust' among all the members of the village. This is why almost all the villagers in Xiangdong village know how to make efficient use of this strategy. However, it is more difficult to apply *guanxi* community strategy (Burt used the term of 'brokerage strategy', see Burt 2000) by bridging structural holes among or between different social organizations, so there are only a few entrepreneurs from Tunwa village who successfully developed their *guanxi* as well as their businesses in the cities. Of course, expanding the function of a firm from the economic sphere to social and cultural areas, as well as extending the power of the entrepreneur to control by establishing a kind of new social structure such as IVWC, is the most difficult strategy and the practice goes even beyond the theories as we discussed in Chapter 2. Therefore, very few entrepreneurs are capable of managing this kind of special social structural change.

From an economic point of view, economic performance is a direct and very important force inducing social structural changes. As we discussed, closure structure is associated with performance because it lowers risks, while structural holes are associated with performance since more opportunities are generated, and an integrated social structure is associated with performance because more is gained from people's good behaviour such as loyalty, hard work, responsibility, etc. This is one important reason for us to link the evolution of social structures with the modernization process.

We have begun to develop a general theoretical framework about tradition and modernization in this chapter by linking with the contexts we analysed. The final conclusion from this discussion is still the idea mentioned previously, that tradition, informal institutions, customs, social norms, etc., always matter for the modernization, and they always mix and function together with formal institutions in all societies and tradition will not be superseded by modernization.

Village development and modernization in China

Through the survey and study of Yantian village, Tunwa village, Fuxing village, Xiangdong village and Wangjian village,[2] it was found that in each case there was a marked difference in the approach to development undertaken in the process of modernization, based on the individual characteristics of each village. To aid further analysis, the major characteristics of development among the different villages will be briefly summarized.

Industrialization and urbanization from the grass roots

Yantian village has vigorously promoted its process of industrialization mainly by introducing various types of overseas investments and has also gradually completed its own process of urbanization along with the rapid development of industrialization. The joint impetus of industrialization and urbanization has also promoted the building of a highly centralized and relatively complete village governance structure based on local conditions. From the perspective of its current stage of development and the potential of the village itself, the most important process of industrialization and urbanization of Yantian village has been completed. The next step in its development will mainly be brought about by further readjustment of its economic and social structure and local governance in line with overall socio-economic development in the Pearl River Delta and the development of regional integration of the hinterland rural villages into the major urban cities (such as Shenzhen) of the region.

Marketization and people's mobility

The increasing mobility of the population has been the greatest change in Tunwa village since the reform and opening up of China. As a result, skilled and educated villagers have constantly moved out of the village and set up their own enterprises in nearby towns and cities, and that has finally led to the complete disintegration of the village collective economy. Moreover, as this process continues the whole village in a crisis of decline.

Community development and social mobilization

What the entrepreneurs and village cadres in Fuxing village have explored is a comprehensive community development pattern with Chinese characteristics, that is, integrating a listed company – which is based on both the market principles as well as cultural rules – with the development of the traditional village. They have made use of traditional local knowledge and cultural and technical resources as well as agricultural resources such as land and labour. This has not only promoted the development of local industrialization and a process of urbanization at the grass-roots level, but has also accelerated the scale of the process of social mobilization and enabled local people to benefit gradually from the process of industrialization and urbanization.

Acceleration of social polarization and strengthened influence of tradition

Xiangdong village has faced a similar situation to Tunwa village in which social polarization has been accelerated in the village. On one hand, rich people from the village and well-run enterprises have moved to the nearby small towns (such as Qianku, Longgang or Lingxi) or even to the distant big cities (such as Hangzhou or Shanghai). On the other hand, many people of the Xiang clan have moved to the village from poor nearby mountain areas as well as migrants settling in the village because of government policy. The ancestral temple of the Xiang clan has been set up in Xiangdong and the traditional ROSCA is more active than ever.

'Alternate' contract system and industrialization

Although there is no special discussion in this book of Wangjian village in Shaanxi Province, our long-term survey and study of this village indicates that the industrialization process of even so poor a village located in the Qinling Mountain area in northern China has also begun to accelerate. The village has chosen tile and brick manufacturing as its main business, in which it has strengths and has adopted the system of individual contracted operation under village collective ownership – a system which has its own characteristics.

Village development and modernization

Considering, then, the individual characteristics shown in varied aspects of these villages, which theoretical framework should we use to generalize the common characteristics of their village development models? The concept of modernization should be an appropriate theoretical approach.

Although the concept of modernization is a relatively old analytical concept used to analyse new stages of development in human society and history dominated by the European and American societies since 1500, its application began to be gradually expanded from the end of the nineteenth century, especially after the beginning of the twentieth century. It has become a theoretical and analytical tool used to analyse all countries or regions as well as the different social formations of mankind. People usually borrow this theoretical concept when a series of issues in the process of macro change – covering economic development, institutional and social change, etc. – and development or changes of the characteristics of the age are involved.

Modernist theory can be understood from two perspectives, that of early proponents of modernist theory from the late eighteenth century to the early twentieth century (such as Saint-Simon (1760–1825), Herbert Spencer (1820–1903), Emile Durkheim (1858–1917), Max Weber (1864–1920)) and that of figures from the 1950s and 1960s to the present (such as Talcott Parsons, Walt Whitman Rostow, Cyril E. Black, Ronald Inglehart, Samuel P. Huntington, etc.).

Some approach modernization mainly from a narrow perspective. That is, regarding modernization mainly as a process of industrialization; here modernization basically refers to industrialization. As a result, modernization will lead to the transition from an agricultural to an industrial society. Wilbert Moore is a typical representative of those who are holding this view. However, more people approach modernization from a broad perspective, i.e., they regard modernization as a comprehensive process of all-encompassing change in economy, society, politics, culture and psychology, etc.

For example, Huntington's (1996) concept of modernization has covered such extensive elements as industrialization, urbanization, literacy, educational levels and improvements in the degree of social mobilization as well as more complex and diversified occupational structures.

Inglehart's (1997: 76) concept of modernization covered the aggregate of a group of changes such as urbanization, occupational specialization, formal education, development of mass media, secularization, individualization, mass production and the emergence of the modern nation-state, and at the same time he stressed the core function of industrialization in this process, i.e., according to him industrialization is the driving force of the whole process and the way toward creating wealth.

Giddens, though sometimes laying much emphasis on the great importance of industrialization in modern society and calling modern society an 'industrialized world' or a society of 'industrial civilization' (Giddens 1991), paid greater attention more often to the significance of comprehensive factors in the process of modernization such as institutional changes in various aspects and organization pattern, etc. (Giddens 1990). In addition, Max Weber's (1976) modernization theory also covers such ideas as hierarchical systems,[3] secularization,[4] etc.

All in all, modernization is a very sophisticated comprehensive process covering industrialization, urbanization, marketization, democratization, bureaucratization, secularization, social mobilization and nationalism, and it involves all aspects of human society, economy, politics, law, psychology, etc.

Obviously, whether from a narrow or broad perspective, a common characteristic shown by the different Chinese villages mentioned above is the ongoing modernization process, which can certainly be said to be a process of development. Whether it is the industrialization and urbanization of Yantian village, the marketization and increasing population mobility of Tunwa village, the unique community development model of Fuxing village based on extensive social mobilization, or the intensifying social polarization of Xiangdong village, all have clearly reflected the development path of rural modernization in the process of institutional change and social transition in China.

Therefore, in theory, we should put the development process of these villages into the macro framework of the theories on modernization, and only by this means can we completely understand and interpret this process; in practice, whether in China or in other developing countries, the issue of how to industrialize an agriculture-based country is the most significant issue of its modernization (Chang 1949). This point is of greater importance to China – the most populous developing country in the world, a country where about 800 million people still live in rural areas. In these circumstances, it is absolutely impossible to achieve the modernization of a whole nation without rural modernization.

Tradition, informal institutions and modernization

In terms of modernization, although there is marked difference between the villages that were studied, they have one point in common – in their modernization process – all the villages have brought into full play the role of traditional factors in their areas and have formed various informal institutions with different features by integrating traditional factors into the institutional framework. Furthermore, with the overall framework (formal institutions) of the reform and opening up policy already in place in China, tradition and informal institutions have played a much greater role than formal institutions in the modernization processes of the villages we studied.

In Chapter 5, we have discussed the issues of village trust and bidding ROSCAs. As mentioned in the discussion, the ROSCA has for a long time been regarded by the local people as a traditional custom in the area surveyed. In particular, the strict observance of the rules of the ROSCA by the members is a basic prerequisite for the continuation of this traditional informal institution. Both field investigation and theoretical analysis indicate that it is the mechanism of 'village trust' that has been the decisive factor. Detailed analysis was undertaken in Chapter 5 regarding this point. From a psychological perspective, according to the theories of psychologists Erik Erikson and D. W. Winnicott, 'village trust' can be regarded as a basic trust (Giddens 1990) as this trust is passed down from generation to generation among the villagers. Therefore, this form of informal financing carries very low risk.

Apart from the impact of basic trust as a factor in a community environment with a traditional trust culture, our previous discussions also showed the importance of 'embeddedness' as an acquired factor. This is an idea first put forward by Karl Polanyi (1944) and then developed by Granovetter (1985). In real life, it is not the case that trust will naturally occur as long as people's transaction behaviour is 'embedded' into a certain social structure. That is, mutual trust between people in an embedded state is more what Portes (1998) called 'enforceable trust' rather than a voluntary behaviour. Where does this coercive force come from? It comes mainly from the constraint of local traditional ethics, and violators are usually punished by ethics. In ancient China, as a punishment, those violating the regulations of the clan could even be forced to change their surname. In discussing the issue of 'ethics and social community', Baurmann has also touched upon this point from the perspective of why marketization may also foster morality based on the cultural roots. Thus the link between modernization and cultural traditions can also be built up (see Baurmann 2002 for more detail).

Of course, we should also be fully aware that any moral norm engendered in a relatively isolated community has a limited scope of application. Beyond their community, they are not likely to care about such 'enforceable trust'. In this sense, a remark by MacIntyre quoted by Baurmann is reasonable: if not living in a social community, people do not have to be moral persons (MacIntyre 1984). After much study of the process of the formation of spontaneous order related to public resources management, Ostrom (1990) drew the conclusion that, although people can absolutely find, at different times and in different places, various spontaneous orders that can reasonably and effectively solve the problem of public resources management, the formation of successful spontaneous order is not without conditions. According to her studies, these conditions included appropriate size, clear boundaries among the members from different communities, repeated interaction, prior norms establishing a common culture, etc.

Ostrom's conclusions have great significance. In some counties in Wenzhou in Zhejiang Province, members of ROSCAs did not know each other and did not share a mutual understanding and trust because the scale of the ROSCA was too large. Eventually several incidents of deliberately absconding with money had occurred there. Therefore, in our previous analyses, we also have stressed the importance of strict control of the scope and scale of ROSCAs, a clear understanding of the background of the members of the ROSCA and its financing purpose and internal monitoring coupled with the strengthening of 'self-enforcement' based on such internal monitoring.

Chapter 6 discussed the issues of *guanxi* community and people's mobility which purported to explain that people's mobility, as self-organized by the villagers of Tunwa village, is based on the traditional Chinese *guangxi* culture and interpersonal *guanxi* resources.

In order to explain this issue theoretically, we have borrowed the concept of *guanxi* which has strong local Chinese cultural characteristics; at the same time it has long been a kind of world outlook adopted by Chinese people. We have combined it with the concept of community, thus forming a unique new concept, i.e., the analytical framework of '*guanxi* community'. Which is, no doubt, a typical value of traditional Chinese culture as well as a typical Chinese informal institution. Through theoretical and empirical study, it has been found that the creation of a concept such as '*guanxi* community' is not only of vital theoretical but also of great practical significance.

Theoretically speaking, the creation of the concept of '*guanxi* community' can correct a long-standing, one-sided view of 'community' as being a closed concept, versus 'society' being an open concept and thus building a bridge between the so-called 'closed community' and 'open society'. Through this new analytical framework, what were regarded as very important past discoveries are, in fact, directly plugged (inserted) into a theoretical predicament (system).

No doubt many ideas in Baurmann's analysis of the conditions and environment in the establishment of the moral market can be said to be very insightful, but the high level of openness and strong flexibility of the Chinese '*guanxi* community' is quite different from Baurmann's judgments of communities in general. Therefore, his conclusion and action plan is quite sceptical to the concept of Chinese '*guanxi* community'. Even if all communities are, as Baurmann proposed, characterized by closure, the practical and feasible method of setting up a moral market is not necessarily to dismantle the community and establish an anonymous and mobile society. Is it not better to build ethical bridges of common values between different communities in the expectation of making use of these various existing community organizations, as we have discussed in previous chapters? The special values could be expected to exist permanently at some levels, which has been true and unalterable throughout the history of humanity.

The work of Max Weber (1951) and Parsons (1949: 550–1) has already touched on the issue of particularistic structure and criteria in Chinese inter-personal relationships. The problem is that '*guanxi* community' is an open system (for details, see the analysis in Chapters 2 and 3) and is fundamentally not a closed system; moreover, in the Chinese cultural tradition, good habits formed within a community can usually be used to deal with relationships with an outside community, which is, as advocated by Confucius, the universalization of the kinship-based family ethic by 'doing unto others as we would have others do unto ourselves' and 'honouring others' elders as we would honour our own and cherishing others' young as we would cherish our own' on the basis that 'benevolence is the characteristic element of humanity' (*The Doctrine of the Mean*).

Applying network theory to the analysis of people's mobility and migrant issues is not where the object of this book lies. There have been many empirical analyses on network theory which were made in combination with the development of the migrant economy. The study by Granovetter (1985) is a typical example. The significance of this study lies in the preliminarily discovery of the important role of the '*guanxi* community' as a traditional resource, which is unique to China in promoting the process of rural modernization in China. On the basis of this tradition and informal institutions which have emerged, a widely spread, large-scale population and labour movement has been taking place from rural to urban areas on a scale that has been constantly expanding.

The theoretical concept of '*guanxi* community' has been applied to analyse the emergence and development of TVEs in Chapter 7. It would not be exaggerating to say that, as special social capital, *guanxi* and '*guanxi* community' have played a vital role in promoting the development of TVEs in China, in particular at the early stage of enterprise development. The first-hand data obtained from our empirical research on the enterprise development in these villages have fully proved this point.

The emergence of a kind of new institutional arrangement is explained in Chapter 8 – a story of how a very successful entrepreneur in Fuxing village has pioneered ways to integrate gradually a public company listed on the A-share market of Shenzhen Stock Exchange with the village in which the company is located. In this we analysed an entrepreneur's institutional innovation through fusing modern market factors (IPO) with traditional factors (employment of the village and clan's 'specific' resources and organization strengths with the approach of IVWC) to promote the process of rural industrialization. This analysis indicated that the enterprises born in rural areas in China and those growing in urban areas, though facing the same competitive market, showed a marked difference in enterprise behaviour. The former followed mixed cultural, social and economic principles to a greater extent while the latter followed mainly the economic rules.

Not only are there many possible ways to design a community as an enterprise, but also community as an enterprise is not uncommon in reality (He 2000b: 424, 429). However, it is not common to fuse a public company with a community. So why, then, do the entrepreneurs of Fuxing village want to integrate their very much-modernized enterprise into a still very traditional village? Specific reasons have already been explored in the detailed analysis of the previous chapters; they will only be summarized here.

In the work of Ferdinand Tönnies (1955), Max Weber (1976) and Karl Marx (1973), views on community are basically traditional, i.e., considering a community as a small group of people (or families) connected by kinship and geographic relationships and considering the community principle to be different from the market principle of capitalism. In other words, the capitalist principle is to pursue personal interests whereas the community principle is to help each other in order to ensure the livelihood of members of the community. However, the results of empirical studies by T.W. Schultz (1964), Yujiro Hayami (2001), etc., do not support such traditional views. According to them, the community principle can be effective in improving economic efficiency and maintaining social stability.

Viewed from the survey results in Fuxing village, in a considerable number of areas in China, the rural community principle is indeed characterized by the close combination of economic efficiency and community welfare. This is mainly illustrated in three aspects: first, enterprises which are in the village must follow market principles and take an active part in market competition to maximize economic benefits; second, however, profit distribution must reflect to a considerable extent the principle of equity to the community members; the distribution of many benefits (such as land distribution, housing and income distribution) should reflect the principle of equitable distribution. The situation in Yantian village, which we surveyed, is a good example of this equitable distribution. Third, the exchange among the community members is mainly built on community trust and cooperation.

In addition, He (2000b: 429) has given the significance of community development and decision-making greater importance, i.e., he linked different patterns of community development with the building of a nation's democratic system. If a community has great authority, the nation might be 'democratic', because the exercise of this authority is transparent to the citizens and accords with the priority targets on which particular stress is laid. This also indicates that designing the role of community in the social system of a nation is the central task in the process of founding and maintaining a system of democracy. In this regard, practice in Fuxing village has already indicated that, compared with the state's long-term intense control of every aspect of rural lives at grass-roots level, Fuxing's independent selection of its unique pattern of community development and its recognition by the local government have demonstrated well that the rural democratic conditions in China have to a certain extent improved greatly compared with the central planning period. Furthermore, the threat that the emerging structure is always likely to be generalized and standardized across the country through state regulations in China that worried Herrmann-Pillath, does not seem a problem. However, we also noticed that within the new IVWC system the phenomenon of the enterprise and entrepreneurs' control of the village and villagers occurs, in other words, an improvement in the external democratic environment is accompanied by internal non-democracy. This is a problem that needs to be gradually overcome in the process of future development.

From an overall perspective, the results of our village studies indicate that traditional resources are very much supportive to rural development and rural modernization through various ways. The bidding ROSCAs in Xiangdong financed development in the village successfully. The '*guanxi* communities'

Conclusion 269

helped the villagers of Tunwa in finding job opportunities in the cities, also helped Yantian village in obtaining investment for TVEs' development as well as helped the enterprises in Fuxing village in overcoming lots of difficulties. The institution of IVWC has been leading the transition from a traditional village to a modern community in a rural area of central China. Some of the resources employed by the people are traditional organizational forms such as ROSCAs and '*guanxi* community', and some are traditional rules such as the institutional basis of the system of IVWC which is the principle of local community. Viewed from the course of the development of the villages in the survey – more than half a century from the 1930s to the beginning of this century (Chen and He 1996) – we have found that the various traditional factors have played a very important positive role in the modernization process in these villages (see the summary in Table 9.1). Moreover, it has also been seen that, under the macro circumstances of an under-developed market economy and incomplete market system in China, the influence of tradition and informal institutions far exceeds that of the modern formal institutions. This finds conspicuous expression in the new historical period of development in China since the implementation of the reform and opening up policy in the early 1980s.

These conspicuous manifestations include the following:

1   *Traditional organizations and informal institutions have provided a basis of trust for information sharing and for people's cooperation*, in particular for the mutual social aid and economic reciprocity of people living in a traditional rural society such as a village. The operation of bidding ROSCAs in Xiangdong village on the basis of village trust is a typical example of this aspect.

Table 9.1 Informal institutions and rural development in the survey villages

Village	Key factors promoting village development	Type of informal institutions	Theoretical basis for the informal institutions	New concepts developed
Xiangdong village, Zhejiang Province	ROSCAs provide finance for rural development at village level	Local trust, ROSCA and informal finance	Network closure	Village trust
Tunwa village, Shanxi Province	Social networks assist rural–urban mobility	Networks, social capital and Chinese *guanxi* arrangements	Structural holes	*Guanxi* community
Yantian village, Guangdong Province	Rural development at grass-roots level supported by overseas investment from *guanxi* channels	*Guanxi* investment, relational contract and investment	Entrepreneurial networks (or network entrepreneurs)	*Guanxi* community
Fuxing village, Hubei Province	Innovation in firm governance can influence local rural development	Integrating village with company (IVWC)	Firm theory and corporate governance	A firm as a mixed entity

2   *Traditional organizations and informal institutions have played a positive role to reduce transaction costs and utilize the limited resources effectively.* The '*guanxi* community' organizations and the system of IVWC function to a certain extent, as proposed by Coase and Williamson, to implement order and supervision of centralized management by integrating the various parties to the transaction through modern corporate organizations and thus would save transaction costs as we mentioned (Coase 1937; Williamson 1975, 1985).

3   *Traditional organizational forms and informal institutions can, to a certain extent, help people set up cross-boundary communities beyond small closed communities* and make people build up generally applicable trust on a long-distance, cross-boundary wide scope, thus enabling people to have a wider scope of cooperation across traditional communities, reducing cross-community and cross-boundary transaction costs. Regarding this point, the studies of Greif (1989, 1993) and Hayami and others (Hayami and Kawagoe 1993) have proved that the successful experience during the Middle Ages of Jewish merchants in Europe and Chinese merchants in southeast Asia in reducing transaction costs between distant commercial ports and between merchants and banks through the establishment of cross-regional ethnic communities that took a dominant position in commercial and financial activities (Hayami 2001: 22).

Modernization prospects in China

As we mentioned, China is still a large developing country based on rural traditional culture with farmers as the main body of its population (about 70 per cent of the total population in China still live in rural areas). Therefore, the direction and prospects of China's modernization is to a considerable extent still conditional on the extent of rural modernization. The empirical analysis above very clearly indicates that many traditional factors (in relation to culture, economy, social organization, politics, convention, psychology, etc.) and informal institutions are born out of the local environment (village, clan, etc.) and are of great significance in advancing the progress of rural modernization in China. This also means that the traditional factors and informal institutions we have analysed (and other factors and institutions we have not analysed) will directly exert an important influence on the modernization process throughout China. Therefore, before ending this book, it is important to make a preliminary analysis and assessment of the modernization prospects of China as a whole under the influence of informal institutions and traditional factors with reference to the above empirical studies.

Doubtless issues involving the subject of modernization of the whole of China are very complex and difficult to elucidate. Fortunately, a direct study of such a huge and topical issue as modernization is not the main task here, rather it is a study of informal institutions themselves and their impact upon rural development in China. However, because of the various reasons mentioned above, the issue of modernization in China is closely related to the issue of rural development, in particular, to the issue of tradition and informal institutions on which this discussion has focused. Therefore, it is natural and meaningful to elicit a view on China's modernization based on this analysis of informal institutions and rural development. This will not be a general discussion but will be based on various aspects of the empirical study above. Given this constraint, the discussion in this section on modernization is considerably limited in both scope and depth.

Modernization simply implies diversified modernization instead of unitary and universal modernization

There are many representative figures of the theory of modernization such as F. Tönnies, Emile Durkheim, Max Weber, Talcott Parsons, etc. In particular, the modernization theory of Parsons, an American sociologist, was greatly influential in the 1950s and 1960s.[5] The dualistic analysis framework of 'tradition versus modernity' has constituted the basic pattern of modernization in the sociological tradition of theoretical analysis of modernization. Furthermore, 'traditional society' and 'modern society' have constituted antithetic social structure frameworks. Based on the social evolution theory of the nineteenth century, society can only develop in the direction from simplicity to complexity and from low level to high level. Consequently, 'traditional society' cannot but develop and progress towards 'modern society'. This analytical approach has, since Francis Bacon (1561–1625), become a widely accepted misconception – using isolated and changeless principles of monistic methodology to look at the open and vast universe has resulted in the road ahead becoming narrower and narrower (Feyerabend 1975: 146). According to Feyerabend, this road has come to a dead end.

Based on such an approach and method, we can divide modernization theory into two major categories:

1 *The modernization process, with industrialization and emergence of the industrial society as its main elements, will ultimately erode various traditional values (tradition will be replaced by modernity), inevitably leading to the decline of religions, parochial ideas and cultural differences,* and finally making the whole world conform to the unitary modernization pattern modelled after contemporary European and American modernization. This view is best represented by Daniel Bell, an American sociologist (Tu 2001).[6] Modernization theorists holding this view include Max Weber, Emile Durkheim, Clark Kerr (the theory of convergence[7] – Kerr *et al.* 1960) and Inglehart (1977, 1997). According to Inglehart, Karl Marx also belongs to this category (Inglehart 2000). Taking a small step further, we can deduce and infer from this line of thinking that the process of globalization will also be the global popularization of the European and American modernization pattern, i.e., global Westernization and capitalization.

2 *Tradition will have a sustained influence on human lives in modern society and the advancement of modernization does not necessarily lead to the disappearance of tradition.* This means that the final result of global modernization cannot be Westernization or Euro-Americanization, i.e.,

Western modernization applies only to the modernization of the West itself, not to universal modernization. This means that the diversified culture of the world will also bring about diversified modernizations rather than a monistic modernization. Renowned scholars holding this view include Samuel P. Huntington (1996), Charles Taylor[8] (1992), Robert Putnam (1993), Lawrence E. Harrison (1985, 1998), S. N. Eisenstadt[9] (2000: 1–3), etc.

As Huntington said, on the precondition of not giving up their own culture nor entirely adopting Western values, institutions and practice, non-Western society is able to realize and has actually realized modernization (Huntington 1996). For example, the so-called 'modernization without the modern' in Japan is a typical non-Western modernization pattern with industrialization, democratization, individualism, etc., as its main elements, realized in an environment different from that of Western individualism – an environment characterized by a market system with strong government intervention and a democratic system with strong authoritarianism.[10] According to the study by Hayami, Thailand, which people call 'the fifth tiger cub', is also embarking on a unique modernization road consistent with its own cultural tradition (Hayami 2001: 330). Although Singapore is constantly criticized from various sides for its centralization of government power, its modernization has reached a high level. Taiwan and Hong Kong have also realized modernization through the so-called 'network capitalism', etc.

As a result, Tu Wei-ming inferred that since Confucianist east Asia can realize its own modernization without complete Westernization, it indicates that modernization may have different cultural forms. Therefore, it can be assumed that southeast Asia can also realize a modernization which is neither Westernization nor East Asianization, which is also true for the modernization of Islam and the modernization of Hinduism. In the same manner, there is no reason to doubt that Latin America, Central Asia, Africa and the various other places in the world have the potential to transform their inherent tradition and develop their modernization in a way that is different from that of the West. He also drew his own conclusion that this is a historical necessity (Tu 2000: 256–67). The study by Hayami also drew the same conclusion (Hayami 2001).

By referring to the experiences of Japan and Russia and after making an in-depth and detailed study on the economic history of China, Gilbert Rozman and others also drew the conclusion that different countries should have different patterns of modernization (Rozman 1981).

In fact, whether viewed from the perspective of the whole of the country or from different regions, the modernization road that China has taken since the reform and opening up process began has been different from Westernization, a road which can be called 'modernization with Chinese characteristics'.

Modernization with Chinese characteristics

According to the study by Rozman and others (1981: 6), the process of modernization is influenced by two factors, i.e., local factors and foreign factors. Generally speaking, foreign factors tend to lead to characteristics similar to the modernization pattern of other countries, whereas local factors would fuse a country's unique historical background into its pattern of modernization.

The results of the analysis of the various informal institutions in the foregoing chapters indicate that the future modernization realized in China is very likely to be a pattern of modernization with strong Chinese characteristics and is unlikely to adopt the Western pattern of modernization. This is mainly the result of the role of local factors in China. If this is the case, modernization with Chinese characteristics would be one of the manifestations of diversified modernization to emerge against the backdrop of globalization.

Apart from our empirical village studies, two other factors also support our judgement. First, whether it is the modernization methods in east Asian countries such as Japan, South Korea and Taiwan or the modernization explorations of southeast Asian countries, international experience clearly indicates that modernization patterns in different cultural backgrounds will take differing forms. In this regard, many world renowned scholars have expressed views, some of which we have touched on in the above discussions. Second, the extremely uneven practice of modernization in China throughout the twentieth century has shown that the country's modernization will be one built upon its own cultural foundation and that it will be difficult to achieve success by simply adopting wholesale the Western pattern of modernization.

The modernization of China originated from external pressures and could be seen as a kind of defensive modernization. From the Opium War in 1840 up to the present-day, the modernization process of China has lasted over one and a half centuries. However, this modernization process is still unfinished and, on the whole, China still belongs to the group of countries characterized by a slow process of modernization. There are three main reasons for this: first, political campaigns and movements in China are often interwoven with the modernization, but their goals are often inconsistent. So the adverse impact of political campaigns upon the modernization movement becomes inevitable and, on some occasions, has proved to be fatal. For example, the constant anti-imperialist and anti-feudal movements (including wars) from the late nineteenth to early twentieth century, the political struggle and finally the civil war between the CPC and Kuomintang in the late 1940s and the 'Cultural Revolution' from the mid-1960s to the mid-1970s, have all exerted a negative impact on the smooth progress of modernization. Second, politicians and intellectuals in China differed greatly on the issue of which path China should take towards modernization and a consensus on this issue was not reached, leading to the wavering direction of modernization. Third, in the modernization process in China, Western elements and Chinese elements cannot be fully reconciled which caused the country to always linger between two extremes, either wholesale

Westernization or wholesale traditionalization (such as Liang Suming's 'Rural Construction Campaign').

In the modernization process of more than 150 years, Chinese intellectuals' and politicians' understanding of modernization has roughly undergone the following major changes (Jin 2002 46–7):

1   *They were forced to learn from the West about techniques of 'powerful cannon and solid ship' after being defeated by the Western countries in warfare.* Therefore, the 'Westernization Movement' led by Zeng Guofan, Li Hongzhang and Zhang Zhidong had begun by adopting the approach to modernization of 'Chinese learning as the fundamental structure and Western learning for practical use' put forward in the late nineteenth century.

2   *With the design and guidance by Kang Youwei, Liang Qichao, Tan Sitong and others, the Reform Movement of 1898 was initiated at the top level of China* and touched some important issues of Chinese modernization from the level of formal institution, e.g., reforming the traditional imperial examination system, enacting new laws, etc.

3   *The Revolution of 1911 led by Sun Yat-sen was a major revolution that involved changing the political system as part of the modernization process.* It destroyed the feudal system which had lasted in China for more than 2,000 years and had established the new nation-state. This was a radical institutional transformation.

4   *The May 4th Movement* (also known as the *New Cultural Movement*) (1919) jointly started by Cheng Duxiu and Li Dazhao, the Marxists in China, Lu Xun, a radical and renowned writer, and Hu Shi, the representative figure of pragmatism, clearly put forward such modernization thoughts as 'Down with Confucius and Sons' and introducing 'science and democracy' from the West, which indicated that the leading figures of Chinese modernization had actually embarked on the road of 'wholesale Westernization'[11] (modernization had penetrated into the informal institutions, i.e., into the level of people's behaviour, belief and values).

5   *Not long after the founding of New China in 1949, the top leaders of the CPC had begun an all-round introduction of institutions, technologies, management systems and industrialization patterns imported from the Soviet Union* and had once again begun a new modernization upsurge (1953–8) of 'wholesale Westernization' (i.e., wholesale Soviet Unionization).

6   *The last large-scale modernization movement coupled with a political campaign in China was the 'Cultural Revolution (1966–76)',* which actually negated both the achievements of the European and American cultural modernization and the traditional Chinese culture modernization as well as the elements of the Soviet Union. The 'Cultural Revolution' negated the modernization achievements of every form except Marxism and Mao Zedong Thought.

It can be seen that, during more than 100 years, from the late Qing Dynasty to the 1970s, China had been exerting great efforts to explore its own path to modernization. Because of the various complicated reasons mentioned above, modernization in China remained at a low level of development until the end of the 1970s and the implementation of the Reform and Opening-up Policy.

In the quarter century from the end of 1978 to the present, with China's gradual relaxation of control on the economy and politics, the forces of the free market and democracy have begun to play their roles. To a considerable extent, this has promoted a transition from modernization and institutional change, dominated by the political and intellectual elite, to one that is driven by mass culture. In this way, the culture (the living culture of public society, especially the rural cultural elements of village life such as people's behaviour, folk religion, sacrificial obeisance, ceremonies, ghosts and gods, folklores, festivals, etc.) which Redfield (1960) called 'little traditions' began to play its role. People had begun to freely adjust their life attitudes and choose their own patterns of production, consumption and life styles. This is especially true in rural areas.

An important result of these changes in the macro environment is the slow revival of traditional Chinese culture which had taken heavy blows in previous modernization movements and political campaigns. The so-called 'old ethic, old religion, old literature and old arts' that Chen Duxiu advocated China to resolutely abandon and the 'four olds' (*sijiu*) (old ideas, old culture, old customs and old habits) which were toppled during the Cultural Revolution have slowly returned to people's real lives.

In the villages surveyed for this study, dismantled temples have basically been renovated or rebuilt. In particular, the renovated ancestral temples of the Deng clan in Yantian village and the Xiang clan in Xiangdong village are very resplendent and magnificent, and the rebuilt Catholic church in Xiangdong village is also quite brilliant. Various traditional ceremonies have been resumed in all the villages we surveyed; clan pedigrees are being revised in these villages and the new edition pedigrees are all beautifully printed; the traditional interpersonal relationships are continued and re-identified by people, traditional fairs and the various non-governmental informal financial institutions (such as ROSCAs) were again functioning in some villages.

This is also true for the whole economic development of China, according to Agarwala. His recent research (Agarwala 2002) shows very clearly that China's great economic achievements achieved in the past quarter century rely not on market forces alone, but also very much on the unique approaches of the 'socialist market system', 'gradualist reform', 'wide usage of social capital' etc., which are all based on informal institutions. Therefore, he expected that 'China will increase the range of valid options for development strategies. It will provide the world an opportunity for intellectual liberation from its present preoccupation with the *Washington Consensus*' (mainstream economic principles).

During the period when tradition was slowly reviving, China also gradually opened its door to the outside world culminating in China officially becoming a member of the World Trade Organization (WTO) in late 2001. As a consequence, a large number of foreign investors have entered China, more and more Chinese rural labourers have been absorbed into foreign-funded enterprises and, with the opening of the telecommunications, movie, cultural and financial sectors to the outside, Western values, culture and life styles have been gradually transmitted to China.

What course should the modernization of China follow under the combined action of these two forces (i.e., accelerated revival of local tradition and accelerated spread of Western culture) had constituted a new set of choices based on the country's new historical conditions. Those choices now facing China are also a new issue that we need to study at present. Viewed from the perception of more than two decades of rural studies, especially based on the long-term tracking survey of the five villages, as well as the results of above discussions, China's modernization in this new historical period should adopt a new pattern that fuses both local factors and non-local (not only Western) factors, and in so doing follow neither a simply Western form nor a purely local one.

In this new pattern of modernization, the elements at the implementation level will display more of the features of Western developed economies, but these Western elements will not be accepted passively, but will be transformed and then popularized. The elements at the formal institution level such as macro-economic policies, trade rules, banking regulatory guidelines, various specialized laws, etc., will show more and more features of the Western democracies. However, in the field of informal institutions such as values, ideologies, ethics, religious beliefs, etc., the background colour of this modernization and the overall cultural identity of a country with 5,000 years continuous civilization (based on written records) and with farmers forming the main body of its population, will definitely be its own hue, at least for a considerably long historical period of time, if not permanently.

First of all, theoretically speaking, Chinese culture and institutions as a whole are very complete, with at once rich and diverse systems of ideology (if we do not call it philosophy) and values serving as a guiding ideology. For example, there are the Confucian doctrines, the Taoist doctrines, the Legalist doctrines, etc., and a profound cultural tradition, a long-tested sovereign state, a set of highly developed administrative systems plus traditional processes and technologies different from those of the West such as traditional architecture, ship building, hydraulic engineering, spinning, acupuncture therapy, Chinese herbal medicine, etc. Even without the influence of foreign factors, these cultural and institutional values are not only sustainable but their pattern of development also leaves room for improvement based on the much emphasized proposition of 'integration of heaven and man'.

Second, viewed from the historical interaction between Chinese and foreign cultures, according to the studies by Gilbert Rozman and others, only three cultures have been successfully transplanted in China from outside the Chinese cultural circle in the 5,000-year history of China's development as a nation. First, the Buddhism of India entered China during the early days of the Eastern Han Dynasty, gradually took on strong Chinese characteristics and was controlled and used by the government. Second, Islam took root in the provinces in the north-western border areas and later spread across China as a religion and culture of ethnic minorities. Third, the natural sciences were introduced to China by European missionaries in the mid-1600s, and in particular, astronomy and the calendar system were once used by the imperial court as a tool to communicate between heaven and man (Rozman 1981: 28). According to studies by Tang Yijie, Western Nestorianism was introduced to China as early as the Tang Dynasty, later the action of Emperor Wuzong of the Tang Dynasty to exterminate Buddhism affected Nestorianism, and afterwards, Nestorianism had gradually disappeared in China. During the Yuan Dynasty other Western religions were also introduced to China, but all perished with the fall of that dynasty. The real impact of Western culture in China took place during the late Ming Dynasty in the 1500s. Some mainly Jesuit doctrines of Western Christianity were introduced to China at that time, although they were usually stretched over the framework of traditional Chinese culture (Tang Yijie 2003: 1–42).

Except for the period beginning from the mid-nineteenth century when the large-scale encroachment of the major Western powers put China in a passive position in regard to various aspects such as culture, politics and economy, the penetration of external cultures, sciences and technologies in other periods has been successfully assimilated into the traditional Chinese culture. Both Chinese culture and external culture have then developed through close integration. In particular, after integrating Buddhist culture, traditional Chinese culture to a certain extent altered its own form and content. From this altered form emerged the Neo-Confucianism of the Song and Ming Dynasties that had fused Confucianism, Buddhism and Taoism. This took the development of traditional Chinese culture to a new height. Meanwhile, Buddhism itself had altered its original form and content and became Sinofied Buddhism which had constituted an important part of traditional Chinese culture and is no longer Buddhism in its Indian sense. Therefore, the modernization taking place in these new historical conditions is in all probability a form that integrates Chinese and Western elements while still grounded in Chinese culture.

Third, top decision-makers and intellectuals and the common people have drawn many lessons after China went through three painful movements of cultural radicalism ('May 4th Movement', leaning completely on the Soviet Union and the 'Cultural Revolution') that sought the wholesale negation of the national culture. They had realized the true value of 'going down one's own road' and on this basis they had put forward some practical thoughts and policies such as 'taking the road of socialist market economy with Chinese characteristics', 'carrying out reforms gradually', 'closely combining the principles of ruling the country according to law with ruling the country with virtue', etc. This indicates that China has woken from the blind political fanaticism of the past and has become practical and mature. As a result, a pattern of 'modernization with Chinese characteristics' which is similar to the pattern of 'market economy with Chinese characteristics' will be more acceptable to the various stakeholder groups in China.

Finally and most importantly, the Chinese people have retrieved their tradition and have discovered the power of tradition in the environment of 'reform and opening-up' which is carried out by the state. In a sense, the success of reform and opening-up in China during the past 25 years is more the result of the positive impact of the role of traditional forces in China than the result of successful transformation of formal institutions. This is very clearly shown by the development process of the villages we surveyed. The significance of the formal institution is that it has created a more liberal macro-policy environment (including property rights, migration, private economy, financial system, taxation, etc.) than has existed before.

Therefore, the prospect of modernization in China is definite at present and that is modernization with Chinese characteristics. This is a special pattern of modernization, which can at once accommodate advanced Western civilizations including scientific and technological civilization and institutional civilization while still possessing strong Chinese characteristics. In this pattern, the traditional forces in China will be brought into better play and integrated with various modern forces.

Symbiosis, interaction and integration of tradition and modernity

Since Arthur H. Smith (1899: 266) and Max Weber (1951: 91) proposed the hypothesis that the Chinese village is a closed small-sized community with high autonomy, theoreticians have so far not come up with a commonly accepted argument. One fact is quite clear though, i.e., since the system of prefectures and counties was set up after the Qin Dynasty unified China until the Qing Dynasty, the reach of formal state authorities (the government bureaucratic system) only stretched as far as the county level. The various organizations under the county were only semi-official or purely informal and functioned to assist the formal authorities to collect taxes, provide corvée and maintain local public order. Only after 1939, when the new county system was implemented was the grass-roots political power in China transferred from the county to the township (Li 2002: 40–3). Despite this, before the implementation of the systems of Agricultural Production Cooperatives and the People's Commune in the 1950s, Chinese villages had enjoyed strong autonomy. Qin Hui once generalized the paradigm of traditional countryside in China as: the state power reached no lower than county; the power under county was only a clan; all the clans were autonomous; the autonomy relied on ethic; and the ethic shaped the country gentlemen (Qin 2003: 3). It should be said that this is a relatively succinct assessment of the traditional rural governance structure in China.

Viewed from this perspective, in most historical development periods in China, Chinese villages and villagers have lived in an environment of informal institutions and tradition which, in other words, can be described as an informal governance structure.

As formal institutions are basically absent at this level, the institutions regulating and binding the villages and villagers' behaviour are autonomous traditional ethic, customs and traditional local rules. After the launch of rural reform programmes in China, the villages have successfully implemented the system of the villagers' self-governance since the mid-1980s. Apart from receiving macro-policy guidance from various levels of CPC organizations and various levels of government, the villages still arrange their own economic, social and religious lives and consider and overcome the various problems they face mainly in accordance with the objectives, norms, religions, clan rules, customs, habits and regulations which have been passed down from their ancestors. Regarding this point, the village surveys and studies over the years have given us much food for thought. Edward Friedman and others have had the same feeling in their long-term observation of a Chinese village in Hebei Province (Friedman *et al.* 1991).

Viewed from the above case studies, in a small community with a strong autonomous nature, people's behaviours are basically expressed through various informal institutions, i.e., modern farmers are actually closer to tradition. According to the theory of Levenson, Wright and others, the authoritative Western theoreticians on modernization in the 1960s, tradition and modernity can by no means be in accord (Wang 2001: 27–64), which means it is almost impossible for either the traditional or contemporary Chinese village to realize modernization. Obviously, the surveyed villages do not represent all Chinese villages, but among four of those which have been discussed above, at least two have made considerable achievements in achieving modernization. They are Yantian village in Guangdong Province and Fuxing village in Hubei Province, and the other two are Xiangdong village in Zhejiang Province and Tunwa village in Shanxi Province. They are also marching towards modernization in different ways. Why is the distance between theory and reality so wide? Where does the problem lie?

The problem mainly lies in the understanding of the relationship between tradition and modernity. According to early modernization theories, such as the theories from Max Weber, Emile Durkheim, Walter W. Rostow, etc., the relationship between tradition and modernization is that of dualistic antithesis. The prerequisite for modernization is eradication of tradition, i.e., the two are incompatible as fire and water. Moreover, such modernization theory also holds that the transformation from tradition to modernity is a one-dimensional social evolution process (i.e., 'monistic evolutionism'), and therefore, all the traditions must be completely negated and demolished in order to realize modernization, – the more completely, the better. With the development of the modernization process, tradition (including folk culture and informal institutions) will also gradually disappear; otherwise, modernization will fail.

From the present perspective, such modernization theory is questionable. Many scholars have put forward entirely different views. For example, according to Marshall Sahlins (2001), the views regarding traditional culture as non-rational elements are problematic: traditional culture is not necessarily incompatible with capitalism nor necessarily the delicate object to be transformed; modernization practice of the non-Western nations has shaken the dichotomy of tradition versus change and of custom versus rationality that is widely accepted in the west, and in particular, it has toppled the well-known ideas of the antithesis of tradition versus development in the twentieth century.

S. N. Eisenstadt (1966) thought that tradition and modernity are closely integrated. Not only in Japan, but even in most European countries, we can also find many combinations that have merged traditional factors and tradition orientation into a modern structure with a high degree of differentiation.

The American anthropologist C. Kluckhohn once also pointed out that the modern development of a society is always linked with its past cultures. Any pursuit of change and innovation without the basis of cultural tradition is unimaginable and its result must be a failure (Kluckhohn 1962: 76).

According to Giddens, tradition is a custom that can organize belief and practice. It can play the role of linking the past, the present and the future and ensuring their continuity and can also provide a consolation mechanism for individual existence. It can provide a trust mechanism for interpersonal relationships in the region. Tradition is not invariable and tradition, in its pure sense, does not exist at all. The relationship between tradition and modernity is that of inter-dependence and interaction. On the one hand, modernization would dissolve tradition, and on the other, modernization is constantly repeating tradition (Yu *et al.* 2002: 355–6).

Tu Wei-ming (2000: 256-67) even thought that within the worldwide scope including Western Europe and North America, the expected complete trans-formation from tradition to modernity has not taken place. Tradition is still there and is an active factor influencing the various special forms of modernization which indicates that the modernization process itself has continued to adopt a great variety of cultural patterns rooted in tradition.

Jin Yaoji (2002: 19) also clearly pointed out that there is no clear-cut difference between modernity and tradition. He points out that tradition and modernity are in essence a 'continuum', and modernization should not and cannot root out tradition.

In order to make their analysis and theoretical study more pertinent to real social lives, many scholars have made many relevant empirical studies. According to the study by Ruth Benedict, the most important cultural basis for Japan's achievement of modernization is the 'shame' culture of the Japanese nation (corresponding to the 'sin' culture of the Western people) (Benedict 1946).

According to Hayami, in this 'shame' culture, the interpersonal relationship has made contracts perform more effectively. Therefore, the organization of Japan's industrialization is mainly based on individual interpersonal relationships, including community mechanisms such as the quasi-community organization and group moral values, and is almost without any reliance on explicitly provided formal laws and rules. After comparing the pattern of Japanese modernization with that of Western modernization, Hayami drew the conclusion that the important thing is not to determine which modernization system, the Western one or the Japanese one, is more advanced but to recognize that both systems, created under different cultural traditions, have been successful in employing modern industrial technologies to create high productivity and prosperity. The special significance of Japan's modernization lies only in that traditional culture or values are an important basis of modernization and the organizational forms of modernization will vary with the differences in the cultural tradition and historical path-dependency. It then follows that the Japanese modernization pattern is not suitable to China, even though it closely borders on Japan (Hayami 2001: 326–9).

Through studying Japan's modernization and its connection with tradition, R. E. Ward (1965) also drew the conclusion that the success of modernization in Japan, a non-Western country, is mainly attributed to the role of its traditional factors. In the whole process of Japan's modernization, tradition and modernization were not in contradiction; instead, they have showed strong symbiosis and mutual support. Traditional factors have always played a facilitating role in Japan's modernization.

Through his study, the Chinese scholar Zhang Lüping (1993) has listed some major traditional factors fully employed in Japan's modernization, such as (1) loyalty, (2) group departmentalism, (3) shame, (4) national spirit – *bushido*, diligence and frugality, (5) corporate culture of 'family departmentalism' ('lifelong employment system', 'closed community', 'enterprise as a family'), (6) corporate spirit – accumulation first and profits second, (7) 'Japan Joint-stock Corporation' which was associated with the government and its enterprises; economic development has always involved state and government intervention, establishing a mechanism which is in the middle of market and planning, etc. Of course, as a result of modernization, tradition itself was also gradually transformed into the process of modernization.

Another country used by many scholars for empirical study is China. As early as at the beginning of the twentieth century, in his book *The Problem of China* written after finishing a nearly year-long lecture tour of China (from October 1920 to July 1921), the British philosopher and thinker Bertrand Russell felt deeply that, if the Chinese could freely absorb the strengths of Western civilization and discard its weaknesses, they would definitely receive opportunities for growth from their own traditions and make splendid achievements that fuse the strengths of both the Chinese and the Western civilizations (Russell 1922: 42). John King Fairbank (1958) also told the American people clearly that their lifestyle in the USA is not the only lifestyle, nor even the future lifestyle of the majority of people. The Americans resort to legislation, contracts, jurisprudence and lawsuits, but the effect of this style is limited. China has nevertheless provided the world other styles.

Based on his study of the 100-year history of modernization in China, Jin Yaoji drew the conclusion that the modernization of China is basically the metabolization of the Chinese tradition and the renewal and reconstruction of the Chinese tradition. According to him, the modernization of China can by no means be built on the basis of nihilism but must be built on the basis of previously criticized tradition (Jin 2002: 19, 33). It should be said that these are deeply moving words from the bottom of his heart.

After long-term study of the economic, cultural and political issues of China, Herrmann-Pillath concluded that the market economy and modernization of China would take a pattern different from that of the West and even other economies in the

East. He also quoted the argument of Hayek that the nature of the market economy is a mechanism of processing knowledge. For this reason, as the knowledge and social sentiments vary with different societies, the functioning pattern of the market is also different. The greatest difference is that different societies have different cultural traditions. Therefore, he reminded the decision-makers in China that, in the process of carrying out the economic and social transition from planning to market, special attention should be paid to the structure of informal constraints and its changes in this period. He also had reiterated that the transition from planning to market in China and the corresponding institutional transition had required good management of the relationship between traditional and socialist culture (Herrmann-Pillath 1993: 39–41).

The study by Long (1997: 50) provided us with an interpretation from the perspective that tradition has determined the values of human rights in China. According to him, the great difference in the views on human rights between China and the West, especially the USA, is mainly caused by the difference in cultural tradition. In China, human rights have been traditionally viewed as the collective rights of a group of people, not the rights of the individual. This view is to a large extent determined by China's own tradition, as the social customs in traditional China had emphasized the superiority of the collective interests of the village over the individual interests of any person. Therefore, the concept of human rights in China is fundamentally different from the Western one, because the individual rights in the Western societies have been separated from the collective rights. As a result, the Western concept of human rights usually does not consider what ill consequences would be caused to the group.

In addition to the macro-empirical studies, many scholars, especially Chinese scholars, have undertaken many very good micro empirical studies. In particular, through studying the lives of Chinese villagers in the 1930s, Fei Xiaotong (1986: 1, 80) concluded that, in the process of modernization in China, it would seem ideal to replace the irregular traditional structure with a rational and unified one, but whether such replacement is necessary and the cost of implementing such a replacement should be considered. Moreover, viewed from the situation of China at that time, it is necessary to stress the equal importance of traditional forces and new forces [modern factors], because the real process of change to economic lives in China is neither the process of direct transplantation from the Western society nor merely the disturbance of the equilibrium of tradition. The general conclusion from Fei Xiaotong's research in the area is that the modernization process of China should be built on the basis of traditional, local and grass-roots culture, and various so-called 'modernizations' other than those are merely slogans (Wang 1996: 971).

A series of studies on Chinese villages by Wang Mingming indicated that the view that tradition 'is disappearing' within the progress of China's modernization is completely wrong. Tradition not only does not disappear in China's process of modernization, but rather traditional folk culture has been gradually revived along with the progressive realization of economic modernization. This is because local governments can utilize such traditional factors as temples, ancestral temples, clan pedigrees, ancestor worship, ritual, community identities, territorial identities, interpersonal relationships and social networks to attract overseas investors and tourists, especially investors and tourists from Hong Kong, Taiwan, Singapore, and Japan; also European and American Chinese, who have a common cultural background. This shows that tradition still plays a very important role in promoting modernization, especially in promoting regional and rural modernization (Wang 1996: 941, 953). On this basis, Wang Mingming proposed the concept of 'local tradition', i.e., a combination of many-sided community lives (including both modern aspects and traditional aspects) in a specific historical process. Such a combination is the intertwining and interaction of traditional and modern forces (Wang 1996: 964).

The results of studies on developed villages in China by Zhe Xiaoye and Chen Yingying (1996: 370) indicated that the features demonstrated by Chinese villages in the modernization process are not based on the dichotomy of 'tradition versus modernity' but based on the interaction and integration of the two. For example, the emergence and development of industrialization has not swept away the tradition of the rural society like a tempest and led to the gradual disintegration of villages; instead, it has penetrated into the original social structure and integrated with the tradition of rural society and regenerated a new and more vigorous structure and culture. The companies and enterprises in the village are modern institutions, but they are operated according to the traditional local rules of the rural society. The insurance and arbitration in the villages are modern institutions but they embody the traditional essentials of community protection. The declining role of agriculture in the villages has greatly changed the social relations of the farmers but the business relations are usually restricted by affinity and geographical relations. The formal rules related to law, market, enterprises, etc., are generally observed but informal rules such as personal promises, credibility or reputation, commitment, customs, *guanxi* network and ideology are also very important. The 'great tradition' and the 'little tradition' co-exist harmoniously in the daily lives of villagers.

Based on the above discussion, we can conclude that whether from a macro or micro perspective, informal institutions or tradition, as a notion of morality, ethic and an important source of social and economic organization, have played a positive role in promoting the modernization in China. More importantly, the combination of informal institutional factors and modern factors are at once harmonious and creative, i.e., through integration, they can not only co-exist and support each other but also innovatively generate new effective institutions and systems from this integration. This is consistent with the conclusions made in the previous discussions:

1 *the combination of FSTSC and the local traditional industry, traditional management ideas and patterns* and traditional business behaviour have created a new institution of IVWC;

2 *far from decaying and disintegrating, in the sample of villages studied, the extension of industrialization and urbanization to traditional villages has enabled modern group companies to grow up in Yantian village and Fuxing*

village, which has enabled small cities of considerable scale to emerge and grow in these two villages and has enabled regional urbanization to be achieved initially at the level of village;

3   guanxi *community has solved a very important problem, i.e., such an informal organization with strong Chinese characteristics enables the traditional closed community to be linked with the open modern society* and has enabled the application of traditional values and behaviour on the basis of closed community to be greatly extended;

4   *by virtue of the organizational features of clan and village, the functions of village trust in ensuring the smooth cooperation between community members and reducing transaction and management costs are clearly displayed in Xiangdong village.*

What is worth particular mention from a decade of observation and survey is that most villagers in the surveyed villages, after experiencing a great transitional period of what people called 'from tradition to modernity' and 'from planning to market', felt the meaning and the value of their lives. According to Herrmann-Pillath, this is the most important achievement (He 2000a: 238). This is significant not only to contemporary Chinese farmers who live in an age of drastic change but also to all people who need to face complex changes at every moment.

Theoretical implications of the research

Finally, the theoretical implication of this research is also worth to be emphasized in the final conclusion of the book.

This book has dealt with three major informal institutions that have been achieving modernization in the selected survey villages in the context of Chinese economic, social and cultural backgrounds. These are (1) village trust and ROSCAs, (2) *guanxi* community and (3) IVWC governance. Two major conclusions can be made through this research: one is that informal institutions, traditions, customs and so on play a facilitating role in social and economic development and overall modernization in China under its particular context as our analysis has shown; the other is that informal institutions always function together with formal institutions in the varying context of different social structures, not only in selective social networks as many scholars mentioned.

To reach the goals of this research, five major contributions have been made through this research to the related literature in the social sciences: (1) developed some new theoretical concepts; (2) built up a systematic theoretical framework for the research at different levels by filling the gap of intermediate level theories; (3) bridged the gap between Western theories and the Chinese contexts by developing the indigenous concepts of networks linking strongly with Confucian ethics; (4) bridged the gap between Confucian ethics and people's real practices by allocating the *guanxi* community in between, and (5) constituted an interdisciplinary approach for institutional analysis as well as for rural studies, especially for village studies by introducing theories and concepts from sociology, anthropology, political science, philosophy, law and cultural studies, etc., into the economic system of the social structures.

1   Some new theoretical concepts have been developed to specially explain the behaviour of Chinese people under their real and unique formal and informal contexts. Based on 'network closure' theory, the 'village trust' theoretical concept was developed to explain how ROSCAs work in the network closure condition. Based on the theory of 'structural holes', the '*guanxi* community' theoretical concept was developed to explain how rural Chinese entrepreneurs search for new opportunities between rural society and urban society by linking rural-urban migration and TVEs development in the survey villages. These new theoretical concepts will enrich the literature on similar research in the area.

2   A systematic analytical framework comprising micro/meso/macro levels for social sciences research has been built up by inserting the meso level analysis into current popular micro/macro research framework. The two major intermediate theoretical concepts developed in this research are '*guanxi* community' and 'village trust'. The former has been inserted into the current social capital theory at the macro level and people's practices through various ways in various areas at the micro level, especially linking with Chinese context; and the latter has been adopted into trust theory as a general phenomenon at the macro level and people's activities involving trust behaviour such as ROSCAs in the rural Chinese village. This kind of 'embeddedness' of intermediate level theoretical concepts is useful to avoid misunderstanding among people coming from different cultural, social and historical backgrounds and it is extremely important for international dialogue on academic research as well as political negotiation and business cooperation.

3   Indigenous concepts of networks has been developed to distinguish cultural differences between the West and China, which is useful for us to put the Western universal cultural and moral value into perspective when we deal with Chinese issues. Although people are quite knowledgeable about Confucian ethics, it is still important for us to establish its framework by linking it with issues of social networks about which we are concerned.

4   The long-missing bridge between the abstract Confucian ethics on social networks and the people's practical behaviours has been built up through '*guanxi* community' concept. Through this approach, the path between the Confucian doctrine originated from the past and people's alternatives in various ways in the present has been paved which makes Confucian ethics practicable today as well as for the future.

5   Theories, concepts, terminologies from other social science areas such as from sociology, anthropology, political sciences, philosophy, history and so on have been employed into this analysis of institutions and rural development. This provides reference to the interdisciplinary approach on institutions and rural development research for the future studies in the areas.

Glossary of Chinese terms

baiji	拜祭	sacrificial obeisance
bao	报	reciprocity (cause–effect relationships between people)
baomu	保姆	nannies
bashu wenhua	巴蜀文化	Bashu culture
bendi dakuan	本地"大款"	the local 'nouveau riche'
biaohui	标会	bidding associations (bidding ROSCAs)
biezi weizu	别子为祖	younger sons served as clan founders
chaoji cunzhuang	超级村庄	super villages
chaxu geju	差序格局	differential mode of association
chengbaodi	承包地	contracting farming land
chengxiang yimin	城乡移民	rural–urban migration
chi	耻	shame
chuanding	船钉	boat nail
chunqiu wuba	春秋五霸	the five hegemonic states in the Spring and Autumn Period
chuwenhua	楚文化	the culture of Chu
citang	祠堂	ancestral hall
cunluo gongtongti	村落共同体	village community
cuntianli, mierenyu	存天理，灭人欲	eliminating man's desire to preserve the Heavenly rationale
dadao kongjiadian	打倒孔家店	down with Confucius and sons
daihongmao	戴红帽	wear the 'red hat'
dalian gangtie	大炼钢铁	mass steel-making

dao	道	Tao (Dao or Way)
daode guifan	道德规范	moral standards
daofaziran	道法自然	the Tao follows nature
daojia xueshuo	道家学说	Taoism (Taoist doctrines)
dayuejin	大跃进	the Great Leap Forward
dazhong wenhua	大众文化	mass culture
difang wenhua	地方文化	local culture
dengji mingfen zhidu	等级名分制度	the social estate and status system
Deng Xiaoping lilun	邓小平理论	Deng Xiaoping Theory
dezheng	德政	virtuous government
dezhi	德治	the rule of virtue
diandang	典当	pawn-brokering
difatian	地法天	the Earth follows Heaven
dishuizhien, yongquanxiangbao	滴水之恩，涌泉相报	turning the favour of a drop of water with a water spring
dixia qianzhuang	地下钱庄	underground private money house
diyuan guanxi	地缘关系	geographical relationship
dongyahua	东亚化	East Asianization
dushiqun diqu	都市群地区	metropolitan region
eyouebao	恶有恶报	evil will be returned with evil
fajia xueshuo	法家学说	Legalist doctrines
fangyan	方言	dialect
feinongye huko	非农业户口	non-agricultural household registration status
fenfengzhi	分封制	the system of enfeoffment
fenshu kengru	焚书坑儒	having books burnt and Confucian scholars buried alive
Gangao tongbao	港澳同胞	Hong Kong and Macao compatriots
ganhui	干会	non-profit (interest-free) ROSCAs
gaolidai	高利贷	usury
geming genjudi	革命根据地	the revolutionary bases
gongxiao hezuoshe	供销合作社	Supply and Marketing Cooperative
guanxi benwei shehui	关系本位社会	guanxi-based society

guanxi he guanxi wangluo	关系和关系网络	guanxi and guanxi networks
gufen hezuo qiye	股份合作企业	shareholding cooperative enterprise
guiqiao yu qiaojuan	归侨与侨眷	returned overseas Chinese and their dependents
guishen	鬼神	ghosts and gods
hanyang tiechang	汉阳铁厂	Hanyang Iron Mill
hedong xuepai	河东学派	Hedong School of Thought
hehui	合会（钱会）	rotating savings and credit associations (ROSCAs)
hehuo qiye	合伙企业	partnership enterprise
hetonggong	合同工	contract worker
Hongdong dahuaishu	洪洞大槐树	huge locust tree in Hongdong County (in Shanxi Province)
huanben fuxi	还本付息	repay principal and cease interests
huaqiao	华侨	overseas Chinese
huaren wangluo shehui	华人网络社会	Chinese network society
huijiao	会脚	the 'feet' of a ROSCA (members of a ROSCA)
huishou	会首	head of a ROSCA
hukou	户口	household registration (book)
hunyin banjing	婚姻半径	marriage radius (distance of marriage relations)
huxiang xuepai	湖湘学派	Hu-Xiang School of Thought
jianjinshi gaige	渐进式改革	gradualist reform
jianzhizhen	建制镇	designated town
jiaose yu wei	角色与位	people's social roles and position in the society
jiazu xiedou	家族械斗	clan fight
jiebai xiongdi (jiemei)	结拜兄弟(姐妹)	becoming sworn brothers (sisters)
jieshaoren	介绍人	go-betweens
jin	斤	measure of Chinese weight equal to half a kilogram
jingshi zhiyong	经世致用	running state affairs with practical knowledge

jinshang	晋商	Shanxi conglomerate (Shanxi merchants)
juntong	君统	monarch's rule
keju zhidu	科举制度	imperial examination system
laoren xiehui	老人协会	the association of elderly people
li yi lian chi	礼义廉耻	propriety, righteousness, honesty and shame
li	里	a unit of Chinese length equal to half a kilometre
lingnan wenhua	岭南文化	Lingnan cultural (Pearl River cultural)
linshigong	临时工	temporary (seasonal) worker
lisao	《离骚》	Li Sao: Qu Yuan's long patriotic poem
liyizhibang	礼仪之邦	land of ceremony and propriety
lizhi zhidu	礼治制度	the system of rule of rites
lizhi	礼治	the rule of rites
lizhiyong, heweigui	礼之用，和为贵	harmony receives the priority in applying the rites
longzhousai	龙舟赛	dragon-boat race
lunhui	轮会	rotating associations (rotating ROSCAs)
lunli benwei shehui	伦理本位社会	ethics-based society
lunyu	论语	The Analects of Confucius
Mao Zedong sixiang	毛泽东思想	Mao Zedong Thought
mianzi	面子	face
minjian jinrong	民间金融	informal finance
minjian zongjiao	民间宗教	folk religion
mu	亩	measure of area equal to 1/15 (0.0667) hectare
nanhun nüjia	男婚女嫁	men marry in and women marry out
ni qinyuan guanxi	拟亲缘关系	simulating blood relationships
nongcun hezou jijinhui	农村合作基金会	Rural Cooperative Foundation (RCF)
nongcun renjun chunshouru	农村人均纯收入	annual per capita net income of rural residents

nongcun xinyongshe	农村信用社	Rural Credit Cooperative (RCC)
nonggong jiehe	农工结合	combining agriculture with industry
nonggong xiangfu	农工相辅	agriculture and handicraft complementary to each other
nongmin qiyi	农民起义	peasant uprising
nongye hukou	农业户口	agricultural household registrations status
nongye jitihua yundong	农业集体化运动	agriculture collectivization movement
nongye shengchan huzhuzu	农业生产互助组	farmers' mutual help groups in production
paoli chuanjian	炮利船坚	powerful cannon and solid ship
pingjun fenpei	平均分配	equitable distribution
qianzhong	钱中（钱背）	middlemen
quanpan chuangtong	全盘传统	wholesale traditionalization
quanpan xihua	全盘西化	wholesale Westernization
ren gandie (ganma)	认干爹（干妈）	adopting someone as one's father (mother)
ren yi li zhi xin	仁义礼智信	benevolence, righteousness, propriety, wisdom, credit (trust)
renfadi	人法地	man follows the Earth
renmin gongshe	人民公社	people's commune
renmin gongshehua	人民公社化	people's Communization
renqing	人情	favour
renzheng	仁政	benevolent government
rujia xueshuo	儒家学说	Confucian doctrines
sancong side	三从四德	three obediences and four virtues
sangang wuchang	三纲五常	three cardinal guides and five constant virtues
sanlai yibu	三来一补	three types of processing and complementary trades
sannian kunnan shiqi	三年困难时期	Three Difficult Years (of 1960, 1961 and 1962)
Shanxi piaohao	山西票号	Shanxi bill exchange shops
shanyoushanbao	善有善报	good will be rewarded with good

shedui qiye	社队企业	commune-and-brigade-run enterprise (CBE)
shehui gongli lun	社会功利论	thought on social utilitarianism
shehui liudong	社会流动	social mobility
shehuizhuyi shichang tizhi	社会主义市场体制	socialist market system
shengchan dadui	生产大队	production brigade
shengchan dui	生产队	production team
shichang banjing	市场半径	market radius
shichanghua	市场化	marketization
shili baxiang	十里八乡	five kilometres and eight townships
shixue	实学	practical learning
shoutu shoumin	授土授民	investing both territories and slaves
sijiu	四旧	'four olds' (old ideas, old culture, old customs and old habits)
siren qianzhuang	私人钱庄	private money house
songming lixue	宋明理学	Neo-Confucianism of the Song and Ming dynasties
Sun Zhongshan geming	孙中山革命	Sun Yat-sen's revolution
taihui	抬会	escalating associations (escalating ROSCAs)
Taiwan tongbao	台湾同胞	Taiwan compatriots
tianfadao	天法道	the Heaven follows the Tao (Way)
tianminglun	天命论	Doctrine of Heavenly Decree
tianren heyi	天人合一	integration of Heaven and man
tongxiang	同乡	fellow villagers (fellow townsmen, fellow townspeople, fellow provincials)
tuiji jiren	推己及人	doing unto others as we would have others do unto ourselves
wangluo zibenzhuyi	网络资本主义	network capitalism
wenhua dageming	文化大革命	the Cultural Revolution
Wenzhou moshi	温州模式	Wenzhou model

wubaohu	五保户	'five guarantees' (food, clothing, medical care, housing and burial expenses) households
wulun guanxi	"五伦"关系	five cardinal relationships (between monarch and subject, father and son, husband and wife, among brothers and among friends)
wusi yundong	五四运动	the May 4th Movement (New Cultural Movement)
wuwei erzhi	无为而治	to achieve the purpose of governing by non-interference
wuxi jiedai	无息借贷	interpersonal lending without interest
wuxiao gongye	五小工业	the five small industries (small iron and steel, small coal, small chemical fertilizer, small cement and small machinery)
wuxu bianfa	戊戌变法	the Reform Movement of 1898
wuyue wenhua	吴越文化	Wuyue culture
xiangcun jianshe yundong	乡村建设运动	Rural Construction Campaign
xiangzhen qiye gongyeyuan	乡镇企业工业园	TVE industrial park
xiangzhen qiye	乡镇企业	township and village enterprise (TVE)
xianjishi	县级市	county-level city
xianzhi	县制	the county system
xieding	鞋钉	hobnail
xiupu weiyuanhui	修谱委员会	the committee for compiling the genealogy
xixueweiyong	西学为用	Western learning for practical use
xueyuan guanxi	血缘关系	blood relationship
yangwu yundong	洋务运动	Westernization Movement
yaohui	摇会	dice-shaking associations (dice-shaking ROSCAs)
yaojiang xuepai	姚江学派	Yaojiang School of Thought

yeyuan guanxi	业缘关系	occupational (partnership) relationship
yichangdaicun	以厂带村	integrating village with company (IVWC)
yide zhiguo	以德治国	ruling the country by virtue
yifa zhiguo	依法治国	ruling the country by law
yigong bunong	以工补农	assisting agriculture with industry
yili zhiguo	以礼治国	ruling the country by rites
yilishuangxing	义利双行	equal importance to be attached to righteousness and profit
yiren weiben	以人为本	putting people first
yongjia jiu xiansheng	永嘉九先生	Nine Scholars of Yongjia County
yongjia xuepai	永嘉学派	Yongjia School of Thought
yongkang xuepai	永康学派	Yongkang School of Thought
yuan	元	measure of Chinese currency equal to US$0.125
yumi zhixiang	鱼米之乡	a place of great abundance in rice and fish
zhangfang	长房	the branch of the eldest son
zhanguo qixiong	战国七雄	the seven powerful states in the Warring States Period
zhedong gonglizhuyi xuepai	浙东功利主义学派	Eastern Zhejiang School of Utilitarianism
zhengshe heyi	政社合一	integration of government administration with commune management
zhengzhi jingying	政治精英	political elite
zhenjiu liaofa	针灸疗法	acupuncture therapy
zhihe	致和	bringing about social harmony
zhishi fenzi jingying	知识分子精英	intellectual elite
zhong xiao jie yi	忠孝节义	loyalty, filial piety, chastity and righteousness
zhongcaoyao liaofa	中草药疗法	Chinese herbal medicine
zhongguo tese xiandaihua	中国特色现代化	modernization with Chinese characteristics
zhongxue weiti	中学为体	Chinese learning as the fundamental structure

zhongyuan wenhua	中原文化	the Central China Plain culture
Zhu Xi lixue	朱熹理学	Zhu Xi's Neo-Confucian School
zhuading	抓钉	clasp nail
zhuizong renzu	追宗认祖	seeking common clans and ancestors
zhujiang sanjiaozhou	珠江三角洲	the Pearl River Delta
ziji zizu de jingji	自给自足的经济	self-reliant economy
zili gengshen	自力更生	self-reliance
ziyou lianai	自由恋爱	freedom of love
ziyuan huli	自愿互利	free will and mutual benefit
zongfa zhidu	宗法制度	the patriarchal clan system
zongtong	宗统	clan rule
zou ziji de lu	走自己的路	going down one's own road
zupu	族谱	clan pedigree

Places

Cangnan county	苍南县
Chenhu town	沉湖镇
Dongguan city	东莞市
Fenggang town	凤岗镇
Fuxing village	福星村
Guangdong province	广东省
Hanchuan city	汉川市
Hubei province	湖北省
Loubanzhai township	楼板寨乡
Qianku town	钱库镇
Shaanxi province	陕西省
Shangzhou city	商州市
Shanxi province	山西省
Tunwa village	屯瓦村
Wangjian village	王墹村
Wenzhou city	温州市
Xiangdong village	项东村
Xiaogan city	孝感市
Yantian village	雁田村
Yuanping city	原平市
Zhejiang province	浙江省

Dynasties in Chinese history

Xia Dynasty (2070–1600BC)	夏
Shang Dynasty (1600–1100BC)	商
Western Zhou Dynasty (1100–771BC)	西周
Spring and Autumn Period (770–476BC)	春秋
Warring States Period (475–221BC)	战国
Qin Dynasty (221–207BC)	秦
Western Han Dynasty (206 BC–24 AD)	西汉
Eastern Han Dynasty (25–220)	东汉
Three Kingdom (220–280)	三国
Western Jin (266–316)	西晋
Eastern Jin (317–420)	东晋
Southern and Northern Dynasties (420–589)	南北朝
Sui Dynasty (581–618)	隋
Tang Dynasty (618–907)	唐
Five Dynasties and Ten States Period (907–960)	五代十国
Northern Song Dynasty (960–1126)	北宋
Southern Song Dynasty (1127–1279)	南宋
Yuan Dynasty (1279–1368)	元
Ming Dynasty (1368–1644)	明
Qing Dynasty (1644–1911)	清
Republic of China (1912–1949)	民国
People's Republic of China (after 1 October 1949)	中华人民共和国

Notes

1 Introduction: background to the research

1 One of the important reasons for Chinese government's implementing of extremely strict control of rural-urban mobility with the *hukou* (household registration) system starting in the late 1950s and the beginning of 1960s was because of 'the three years of natural disaster'. The Chinese government introduced food rationing (through food coupons) for urban residents based on the number of people, their age and occupation in the book of *hukou*. Consequently, the rural population had to be restricted from moving to urban areas to guarantee food supply for urban inhabitants (Qian 1996). This sounds reasonable since the government started in 1984 to allow peasants to move to cities on the condition of 'bringing their own grain' with them (Zhonggong Zhongyang Shujichu he Zhongyang Wenxian Yanjiushi 1987). These restrictions have been removed gradually since the early 1990s when food security became less of a concern.

2 In fact, farm land assigned to individual rural households is still legally owned by the village collective organization, but individual family households gained the right to use farm land after land re-distribution reform.

3 There was no such statistical item from 1985, which means that farm land re-distribution reform was fully completed by the end of 1984.

4 There were a total of 16,252 townships set up in 1983 and 91,171 by the end of 1984, which indicates that 28.9 per cent and 99.7 per cent of the communes were restructured as townships in those years (Guojia Tongjiju 1984, 1985).

5 Many works trace the changes in great detail. See Glaeser (1987), Nee (1989), Byrd and Lin (1990), Whyte (1992), Christiansen (1993), World Bank (1997, 1999, 2000), Ford Foundation (2001), etc.

6 The Eastern Coastal Region even made 45 per cent of its total exports, but 35 per cent for the Middle and the Western Regions (Nongyebu Xiangzhenqiyeju 2004).

7 See more references from the work of Lee (1989), Ebanks and Cheng (1990), Ginsburg, Kopple and McGee (1991), Guldin (1992), Laquian (1997).

8 This law was trialled in 1988 in some rural areas and after 10 years, i.e. in 1998, it was formally implemented nationwide after the Standing Committee of the National People's Congress voted to approve it at the fifth meeting of the ninth session.

9 The main subjects of villagers' self-governing system include: democratic election of village leaders, formulating management rules and regulations to govern the village affairs according to villagers' wishes, and carrying on transparent village issues, particularly the village budget.

10 North (1990) assumes that norms and informal institutions are rooted in cultural traditions. Wang Dingding (1996) and Hayek (1988) look at tradition as the institution without conscious design or planning made by formal organizations, that is to say, tradition means informal institutions to a certain extent.

11 More detailed background of the research project will be given in the following section.

12 See Chen Jiyuan and He Mengbi (1996) for more details.

13 Other research members include Zhu Qiuxia, Rainer Heufers, Li Jing, Wang Xiaoyi, Zhang Jun, Yao Mei, Zhang Yuanhong and Li Renqing.

14 Based on our research focus, modernization here is defined as the overall economic, social and cultural changes and developments (Chen and He 1996).

15 See Koentjaraningrat (1967), Dasgupta (1977), Murray (1977), Poffenberger and Zurbuchen (1980), Hayami and Kikuchi (1981) for more details.

16 See more works in the area by Freedman (1958, 1966), Skinner (1964/65), Hinton (1966), Baker (1968), Parish and Whyte (1978), Philip Huang (1985, 1990), S. M. Huang (1989), Friedman, Pickowicz and Selden (1991), and Yan (1996b) for further information.

17 More detailed information about the selection of the fieldwork samples will be discussed in Chapter 4.

18 This research wasdirected by Carsten Herrmann-Pillath and Chen Jiyuan. Major research members included the author, Rainer Heufers, Li Jing, Wang Xiaoyi, Zhang Jun, Zhang Yuanhong, Li Renqing, Feng Xingyuan and Liu Qiang.

19 This research was directed by the author. The major research members include Zhang Jun, Li Renqing, Dang Guoying, Li Guoxiang, Weng Ming, Wang Xiujie and Wu Lishan.

20 From 2003, the author and his research team initially carried out fieldwork in social services governance in the five sample villages.

21 This is clearly shown in the two works published after fieldwork in the two villages: *Institutional Change and Power Distribution in Rural China: A Survey on Wangjian Village, Shangzhou City, Shaanxi Province* (Hu 1996) and *Enterprise Organization and Community Development in Rural China: A Survey on Duanjia Village, Hanchuan City, Hubei Province* (Hu and Hu 1996).

2 Village trust, *guanxi* community and IVWC governance: an interdisciplinary approach to informal institutional analysis in rural China

1 The typical neoclassical theories here refer to what people usually call the standard economic theories or mainstream economics developed mainly by Edgeworth, Jevons, Walras, etc., where the transaction costs are absent and impersonal market system is the only way to realizing the exchange; see Jevons' idea in this regard, for example (Jevons 1871).

2 In many cases, people also use the terms 'formal institutions' and 'informal institutions'. However, this does not mean that 'market institutions' simply means 'formal institutions', while 'non-market institutions' means 'informal institutions'. It is very difficult to differentiate the two pairs exactly, but the general idea should be that there is quite a wide overlap between the two pairs of concepts. For the convenience of discussion in this research, I assume there is no great difference between the two pairs of concepts; consequently, they will be used interchangeably in this work.

3 This question is also very much in line with the definition of trust given by Sako (1992: 32) as '… a state of mind, an expectation held by one trading partner about another, that the other believes or responds in a predictable and mutually expected manner', and this is also similar to Luhmann's (1979) definition of trust as predictability (see also Nooteboom 2002).

4 For example, the Whiggish economists see trust as arising out of the transactions, as we mentioned, based on rational calculations and efficient 'rules of thumb' (Etzioni 1988: 8). The fundamental reason is that trust can be only understood when we recognize the concept of uncertainty, but uncertainty is not the basic assumption for conventional (mainstream) economics.

5 Herbert A. Simon (1976) regards organizations as institutions. According to him, organizations are an assembly of similar information and rules. Binswanger and Ruttan also consider organizations to be an important part of institutions (Binswanger and Ruttan 1978). Apart from John R. Commons' (1934) instincts and customs, Veblen's analysis of institutions even covers the meaning of the institutions in operation; by this concept, he mainly means the factory in operation (that is, the turnover of raw materials, machines and factory buildings) and the business in operation (organizing and using the equipment and materials to produce use value).

6 In Aoki's comparative study, Schotter is considered to be in favour of institutional game equilibrium. See Aoki (2001) for details.

7 According to Aoki (2001), Greif and Milgrom (1994) are thought to be advocating the repeated game approach.

8 Bowles is in favour of the evolutionary game approach according to Aoki's comparative analysis.

9 Veblen also said, from a psychological point view, institutions are 'A prevalent spiritual attitude or a prevalent theory of life. As regards to its generic features, this spiritual attitude or theory of life is in the last analysis reducible to terms of a prevalent type of character'. Thus, he defined institutions as 'the present accepted scheme of life' and 'social evolution is a process of selective adaptation of temperament and habits of thought under the stress of the circumstances of associated life' (Veblen [1899] 1934: 191, 239). In relation to evolution, he said: 'The situation of today shapes the institutions of tomorrow through a selective, coercive process, by acting upon men's habitual view of things, and so altering or fortifying a point of view or mental attitude handed down from the past. The institution – that is to say the habits of thought – under the guidance of which men live are in this way received from an earlier time; more or less remotely earlier, but in any event they have been elaborated in and received from the past' (Veblen [1899] 1934: 191).

10 Commons' 'collective action' here is not referring simply to the activities of organizations but also includes unorganized custom (Chamberlain 1962: 72).

11 For example, Commons ([1934] 1990: 705) regards informal institutions, 'custom and habitual assumptions are the underlying principle of all human relations'. Of course, it is also the foundation of various written laws. More importantly, what is often referred to as 'unwritten law' is actually a kind of 'living law' (Commons [1934] 1990: 707). In Commons' theory of institutional economics, different kinds of customs (including feudal, agricultural, commercial, industrial, family and religious customs) are unwritten laws. However, constitutions, laws, supplementary provisions, notices, administrative orders, legislative regulations, corporate franchise, employment contracts are written laws. In other words, customs refer to informal institutions; and written laws are formal institutions. Also according to Commons ([1934] 1990), in terms of depth, customs are usually more influential than individuals and even the state; and in terms of breadth, collective action is more common in unorganized customs than in organized groups.

12 That means that institutions created in this way evolve gradually along a stable path and the evolution is not designed by anyone, but takes place through the interaction of people as a whole. Language and good manners are typical examples of internal institutions. According to the research of Kasper and Streit (1998: 102), the philosophy of 'ritual' created by Confucius in China 2,500 years ago, the theory of the unwritten law system developed by the French social philosopher Charles de Montesquieu 300 years ago, and the notion that the internal institutions of evolution constitute the institutional foundation of the survival of a society put forward by Anglo-Saxon philosophers John Locke, David Hume and Adam Smith were all the results of earlier research on internal institutions. The main representative in this regard today is Friedrich A. Hayek.

13 Civil law and a traffic code are typical examples of external institutions. According to Kasper and Streit (1998), external institutions are formal institutions forever.

14 Generally speaking, all sanctions for violations of external institutions are always formal and all go through an organized system (such as police, courts and prisons, etc.) and sanctions for violations of internal institutions, for the most part, are not applied in an organized way but occur spontaneously.

15 Kasper and Streit (1998: 103–5) also divide internal institutions into four types of rules: conventions, internalized rules, customs and good manners, and formalized internal rules. They define the first three categories of internal institutions as informal institutions because of the different ways to impose sanctions. The latter internal institutions, however, are formal institutions because under them, sanctions are enforced through an organized mechanism.

16 North initiated his study on institutions from the mid- and late 1960s, when he studied world ocean transport in the 250 years from 1600 to 1850. He found that during the period no major improvements were made in ocean transport technology, but the productivity of ocean transport increased considerably because ocean transport became safer and the ocean transport market improved thanks to the introduction of some rules. This led to a reduction in ocean transport costs and an increase in productivity (North 1981, 1990, 1994; North and Thomas 1973). This prompted him to begin a series of studies on the relationship between institutional structure and its changes and economic growth.

17 The fundamental reason why institutions are able to determine economic performance is that 'if the basic institutional framework makes income redistribution the preferred economic opportunity, we can expect a very different development of knowledge and skills than a productivity increasing economic opportunity would entail' (North 1990: 78). People are then induced to seek these opportunities and the knowledge and skills to increase productivity rapidly. This means that the basic driving force for institutional changes is maximization of profits. As long as the expected returns exceed the expected cost, people will continue to promote institutional changes. In other words, if institutions are improper, they may in turn become vehicles for increasing transaction costs and hinder economic development. For example, the rules limiting market access, regulations for carrying out invalid inspection and policies leading to instability in property rights in some countries all play a negative role in this regard.

18 North argued that on one hand 'organizations incrementally alter the institutional structure' and on the other hand that 'competition, decentralized decision making, and well-specified contracts of property rights as well as bankruptcy laws are also crucial to effective organization' (North 1990: 73, 81).

19 Because efficient property rights help create a stimulus so that individuals' economic efforts make individuals' earning rate closer to the social earning rate, individuals should also have the right to possess land, manpower, capital and other property and to freely transfer them to others.

20 According to North, 'the major role of institutions in a society is to reduce uncertainty by establishing a stable (but not necessarily efficient) structure to human interaction'. Normally, 'formal institutions usually provide people with mechanism-like norms such as the voting system and hierarchical structure and informal institutions provide a set of customary rules' (North 1990: 6).

21 If a transaction cost does not exist, then the property rights structure will not have any effect on the allocation of resources. It is exactly because of the existence of transaction costs that information and markets are incomplete. With the emergence of increased returns, it is evident that institutions are important. Coase's theory has proved that transaction costs are not zero (Coase 1960, 1988). Therefore, the importance of institutions for reducing transaction costs is evident.

22 The major reason is because transaction costs exist and are not zero. One of the functions of the state is to formulate rules through various formal channels and basic services are the underlying rules of the game.

> Whether evolving as a body of unwritten customs (as in the feudal manor) or as a written constitution, they have two objectives: one, to specify the fundamental rules of competition and cooperation which will provide a structure of property rights for maximizing the rents accruing to the ruler; two, within the framework of the first objective, to reduce transaction costs in order to foster maximum output of the society and, therefore, increase tax revenues accruing to the state.
> (North 1981: 24)

However, due to the existence of certain conflicts between the two, it becomes more critical for the state to properly deal with the issue. If the state deals well with these conflicts, there will be some positive impacts from the state on economic growth and development; otherwise, the result is a negative impact from the state on economic performance.

23 Ideology provides people with a subjective spiritual concept to interpret the world and make choices. The concept has great significance on the resulting interaction of people and the eventuating social performance. Ideology greatly helps solve the 'free rider' problem. Otherwise, the transaction cost of any institutional changes will be high.

24 What has happened to these two ancient countries was that: in the first five centuries, Greece and Rome led the civilization of the world because:

> the Athenian structure of property rights was based on law, the contribution of Rome was the elaboration of a complete system of civil law ... and, codification of commercial law was a major economic achievement of Roman society ... also the laws of property which dealt with the ownership of slaves, the major source of the labour of the early Empire.
> (North 1981: 109, 123)

As the state no longer provided protection and enforcement of property rights once Rome's military advantages evaporated, the Roman Empire then declined.

25 Despite being a small Western country, The Netherlands became strong simply because its 'government encouraged an efficient economic organization by granting and protecting private property rights and discouraged restrictive practices' (North 1981: 154). In Britain, in addition to the world's first patent law encouraging technological innovation in the seventeenth century, parliament played an important role and was more powerful than the king. With the support of parliament, organizational innovation (such as the establishment of the Bank of England and securities markets, the rapid development of shareholding companies, etc.) in Britain evolved quickly.

26 The failure of France and Spain to develop as Western European economies in the sixteenth and seventeenth centuries was mainly due to overemphasis on centralization which put the interests of the king above all else and placed parliamentarism under the control of the monarchy. In addition, both countries permitted regional monopoly in return for taxes (North and Thomas 1973). This eventually hindered innovation and economic growth and led to the fall of these countries within those two centuries.

27 The emergence of Western Europe since 1500, 'was basically conditioned by the heritage of Greco-Roman civilization' (North 1981: 124). Naturally, the core of this cultural heritage is the protection of property rights through various laws.

28 In the United States, positive institutional factors include its 'federal political system, checks and balances, and a basic structure of property rights', and all these 'have encouraged the long-term contracting essential to the creation of capital markets and economic growth'. However, Latin-American economic performance was poor,

mainly because it perpetuated the Spanish/Portuguese institutional heritage of a centralized, bureaucratic system (North 1990: 116).

29 Also by many economists as we discussed above.

30 North found the direction of change and development in any society is determined by a combination of the adaptability of formal institutions and the continuity of informal institutions. Therefore:

> although formal rules may change overnight as the result of political or judicial decisions, informal constraints embodied in customs, traditions, and codes of conduct are much more impervious to deliberate policies. These cultural constraints not only connect the past with the present and future, but provide us with a key to explaining the path of historical change. This is why institutional changes always happen in an incremental way, 'even discontinuous changes (such as revolution and conquest) are never completely discontinuous. This implies informal institutions are 'a source of path dependence'.
>
> (North 1981: 44)

31 The influence and importance of informal institutions are universal and eternal: they always expand, complement and modify formal institutions. Therefore, informal institutions are highly stable, even if change often takes place within formal institutions. The long-term trend of economic development is still very clearly due to the existence of informal institutions in the society (North 1990: 38–43).

32 For example, customary laws are facilitating to reduce uncertainty to a certain extent (North 1990). Normally, informal institutions play a more critical role in cases with higher transaction costs. Due to the incompleteness character of most contracts, informal institutions normally play a major role in their enforcement in reality.

33 According to research by North and Thomas (1973), the manorial system in Western Europe in the Middle Ages was based on customary laws (manor customs – which was expressed orally on the basis of people's memories): on one hand, the manor owner had a monopoly of land and other resources and had the right of inheritance under the customary law; on the other hand, peasants of the manor enjoyed the right to use the land and pasture and had the obligations to pay wedding and burial taxes to the manor and do *corvée* labour. In a manor, a self-reliant economic community, the manor owner was the judge and enforced the customary law. However, manor customs played an important role in protecting the interests of peasants. In accordance with the generally accepted explanation of economics, the collapse of the manor system was caused by the rise of the free market economy. But according to North and Thomas, the disintegration of the manor system was mainly caused by the excessively high cost of enforcing manor contracts.

34 Initially, Paul David described the essence of this concept as:

> It is sometimes not possible to uncover the logic (or illogic) of the world around us except by understanding how it got that way. A path dependent sequence of economic change is one in which important influences upon the eventual outcome can be exerted by temporally remote events, including happenings dominated by chance elements rather than systematic forces.
>
> (David 1986: 30)

35 John Hicks (1969) has also found customs were of decisive significance to the village economy during the Neolithic Period and at the beginning of the Middle Ages and for economic forms that are based on traditions that are still found in many parts of the world. Hicks describes such economic forms as 'customs economies'. Under the customs economic system, economic organization is completely different from market economic organization. As the leader of a customs organization, the tribal chief or the *gerousia* has absolute authority in the decision-making of its tribal community. As

it took a long time for the customs organization to develop and evolve, it has great vitality. Hicks believes that customs were dominant throughout the whole of feudal economic society.

36 As we discussed above, Commons concluded, 'an institution is collective action inducing individual action'. He also emphasized, although 'there is a great variety of institutions and sanctions, and these are continually changing in the history of civilization', 'the general principle common to all of them is custom and derived habitual assumptions, hence, the principle of Custom is the Similarity of Compulsion that induces individuals to conform to standards'. He even stated that 'It is the totality of changing customs that is civilization' (Commons [1934] 1990: 710).

37 Why did the nobility in Europe in the seventeenth and eighteenth centuries maintain a showy conspicuous consumption, a fashionable habit at the time? According to Bourdieu (1984), the conspicuous consumption looked extravagant, but in fact it played a role in turning economic capital into political, social, cultural or symbolic capital. Burke (1992) believed that such kind of consumption helped the nobility appear nobler than other groups.

38 This is directly related to his understanding of human characteristics. According to Malthus, humans are not rational but are stupid animals manipulated by their feelings. Without customs and government coercion, it would be impossible for humans to treat each other peacefully. He tried to prove this with excessive population and war as evidence.

39 But, on the contrary, 'human agents are both rational and sub-rational at the same time' for their intentional actions (Hodgson 1988: 110). In people's decision-making process, habits play a very important role since 'they provide us with a means of retaining a pattern of behaviour without engaging in global rational calculations involving vast amounts of complex information' (Hodgson 1988: 126). Therefore, the processes of action, if Hodgson's judgement is correct, then become well organized in a hierarchical manner and can make adjustments along with changing incoming information. Aiming the argument that the formal, explicit side of the contract can or will gradually erode the customary and informal rules and regulations to the extent that they can be ignored, Hodgson very clearly and strongly contended that 'as uncertainty remains undiminished and dynamism of the capitalist system creates ever greater complexity for the decision-maker, reliance on some informal rules and customs can never decrease to insignificance'. He thought even the market system under capitalism, which tries to 'drive out all vestiges of habit and tradition is both theoretically implausible and unrealizable in practice' (Hodgson 1988: 160).

40 Quesnay believes that customs are the foundation of natural laws, rights and order. Only economic institutions that are based on customs are good institutions. State intervention or artificial order is not a good choice of economic institution (Vaggi 1987).

41 According to Thompson's research, by taking manor customs as a local law, he believes that as long as manor customs were not declared ineffective, they would always be legally binding (Thompson 1991).

42 The title of his book.

43 Customary law (accepted rights and practices) played a significant role in resisting the enclosure movement (which lasted from the fifteenth century to the beginning of the nineteenth century, although the most important were the 60 years from 1760 to 1820 (McCloskey 1972) especially for private enclosure). Although that resistance eventually failed, it delayed the completion of the enclosure process by many years. In addition, the struggle waged by villagers using customary law brought about many changes in the conditions of enclosure.

44 Although the divorce laws were introduced in the 1850s, as a custom, wife selling in London, Nottingham and other parts of Britain was still quite common during the period from 1660 to 1890 (Thompson 1991).

45 People were humiliated through 'rough music' (loud noises – noises from beating basins and plates) and other informal or non-legal means (this was in essence an informal ceremony for making a court decision or meting out punishments). For example, licentious women or prostitutes were paraded naked through the streets with loud noises as a punishment. Loud noises were also made against bigamists, thieves and those who beat their wives. All these helped safeguard the public order of communities (primarily village communities). In essence, it is a means of social control beyond the government.

46 According to Karl Polanyi's theory of economic organization (Polanyi 1944), in real society there exist three different kinds of economic organizations, namely, the market system, the mutual benefit system (an economic organization based on the exchange of gifts) and the redistribution system (social estate system). The market system is under the control of classical economic principles whereas the other two economic organizations do not function or exist on the basis of market laws.

47 When studying material civilization, economy and capitalism from the fifteenth to the eighteenth century, Fernand Braudel (1981) regarded customs, constraints and commitments as the main part of civilization or culture. He believes that civilization is heritage and that it is important because when a society is about to have cracks or fissures, culture can fill or at least cover them. He also believes that capitalism is actually a mixture of all cultural assets (Braudel 1981). He found much information to prove that as market and capitalist factors emerged and developed, many changes took place in the customs in Europe (Braudel 1981): the rich in France began to eat in dining rooms instead of in kitchens as they had done in the sixteenth century; at the beginning of the seventeenth century, Austria already had many requirements at banquets, for example, participants must be properly dressed, clean their beards and mouths before drinking wine, and refrain from spitting in plates, licking their fingers and clearing their noses with the tablecloth; in the middle of the eighteenth century, European men changed their longstanding habits and began to wear underclothes, which they changed daily. In my understanding, Braudel meant that capitalism is a special form of culture taking customs as one of the foundations.

48 According to John Locke's theory, habits directly constitute the foundation of people's tacit action. As a matter of fact, they also constitute the foundation of social and economic development because the private property in reality and their inheritance system had already been determined by habits before social organizations and relevant legislation took shape (Locke [1690] 1960). Therefore, Hayek also said this was a phenomenon in which laws come before legislation (Hayek 1973: 72).

49 George Katona's (1951: 230) research shows that customary and conventional actions are very useful to policy-making in commercial activities. There can be no doubt that characteristics such as honesty, punctuality, payment of due debts, and honesty with all customers, old and young, are important for all businessmen.

50 Interestingly, Elias looked at human civilization from the angle of changes in manners in people's daily life in Western countries in terms of having meals, clearing their noses, spitting, using toilets, sleeping, riding horses, nudity, sexual relations, etc. from old manners (people in the Middle Ages used their hands to clear their noses, cleaned their hands with their clothes, and ate with dirty hands) to modern manners (the nobility in Italy, France, Britain and Germany began in the sixteenth century to successively use knives and forks to eat meals, serve meals individually and use napkins) (Elias 1976). Although the customs and norms about eating, spitting, etc., are not formal institutions, they are of vital importance for progress in human civilization. In particular, by analyzing this gradual and irrationally devised process of civilization and rationalization by proceeding from people's experience in their real life instead of from a scientific and traditional angle, Elias gradually led us to the foundation of human civilization – a special order that was created during the interdependence of people (Elias 1976). Elias's conclusion is that human civilizations and the states did

not come into being and develop under pre-devised rational and spiritual guidance but in an unplanned way. However, as their development came in stages in a certain direction, it was not accidental and disorderly. On the contrary, these developments and changes were orderly. This orderly nature was determined by the relationship networks among people. Just as we have discussed above, the relationship networks are what we call customs and informal institutions, which charted the direction for human historical changes and served as the foundation of human civilization (Elias 1976).

51 Elias's investigation indicates that the word '*civilité*' in French originally meant noble customs in the royal court (Elias 1976).

52 Taking Williamson as an example, the trust issue is so closely linked to transaction costs. In his early work, Williamson quite closely accepted the notion of trust: 'trust is important and businessmen rely on it much more extensively than is commonly realized' (Williamson 1975: 108). However, he turned to neglect (1985) and even explicitly rejected (1993a) trust in his later analysis of transactions. According to Nooteboom (2002: 6), trust does not go beyond calculative self-interest; it does not add anything to existing economic analysis on one hand, yet on the other hand, if trust does go beyond calculative self-interest, it necessarily yields blind trust which is unwise and will not survive in markets, and is best limited to personal relations of friendship and family. This suggests that trust has nothing to do with economics and business.

53 'We must trust even without a basis in rational evaluation, affect or proven routines. This is due to radical uncertainty of behaviour and the incompleteness of language ('language and communication cannot work without trust that goes beyond reason and affect') or as what Quine called 'inscrutability of reference' and 'we must surrender to trust or die from inaction' to overcome the uncertainty (Nooteboom 2002: 83, 84; Quine 1960).

54 See Knight's research in the area for more details (Knight 1921).

55 High monitoring costs are due mainly to information asymmetry which makes people difficult to monitor based on formal institutions alone. Under this situation, informal institutions such as trust are of more importance than formal institutions.

56 Trust is rooted in the sources of ethics, emotional concern, justice, fairness, etc., (macro sources) and kinship, friendship, commitment to mutual interest, etc. (micro sources) (Nooteboom in Casson 2000: 55).

57 We can find various definitions of trust from different disciplines. For example, many sociologists simply treated trust as a kind of behaviour (Deutsch 1962; Zand 1972) i.e., trusting behaviour; some others treated trust as a type of expectation (Bradach and Ecceles 1989; Sako 1992) and so on. After very detailed comparative analysis on various definitions about trust, Nooteboom (2002: 18) defines trust as 'the expectation that things will not go wrong' in the broad sense that encompasses all the sources of trust, and 'to accept or neglect the possibility that a partner will utilize opportunities for opportunism even if it is in others' interest to do so' in the narrow sense that goes beyond self-interest (Nooteboom 1996, 2000: 54).

58 According to Luhmann (1979), a whole socio-economic system can be the object of trust on one hand; it can also be the source of trust on the other. This means, one can have trust in the system or an organization or the legal system of the society. Hence, system trust can provide part of the basis for personal trust. Conversely, personal behaviour and experience can also affect system trust. This shows that both system trust and personal trust mutually interact. See also Nooteboom (2002: 8).

59 Coleman, somehow, linked networks when he looked at the social capital issue (Coleman 1988). But the problem is that he neglected factors of value, norms and informal institutions in his analysis.

60 The detailed explanation about networks by Herrmann-Pillath is:

> We regard networks as patterns of transactions with triads as minimum units. The network emerges from positive externalities across transactions, and because of being perceived as a Gestalt by its members, with individual perceptions converging towards a common pattern. Network dynamics result from the interaction between divergent individual networking activities, giving rise to the distinction between weak and strong ties.
>
> (Herrmann-Pillath 2000a: 15)

In comparison, Granovetter's 'embeddedness' and Burt's 'structural holes' are two examples which define the underlying structure of a sequence of transactions, i.e., networks (Herrmann-Pillath 2000a: 11, 16).

61 A more detailed definition is:

> Social capital is a stock of knowledge about networks, namely, a kind of accumulated common knowledge about externalities within networks, that simultaneously draws boundaries between different networks and can, thus, also be called the 'culture' of the agents constituting the network. ... Individual social capital is also determined by the interplay between internal and external relations ... and the aggregate social capital of larger groups (societies) is the outcome of the interaction between a vast number of different networks and their cultures.
>
> (Herrmann-Pillath 2000a: 23)

62 Since a complete chapter in the book focuses on the discussion of community from both theories to practice linked by the empirical studies, we do not plan to discuss community theories in detail in this section.

63 The conventional community conceptual framework is more based on a traditional pattern of people's communication, i.e., the method of face-to-face contacts and communication.

64 It is mainly a type of place-based community.

65 Greif's research in this area is very often quoted in much of the recent literature. According to Greif's comparison, Genoese traders and Maghribi traders evolved different institutional frameworks in the late medieval Mediterranean trade process within the interpersonal markets of long-distance trade. The former evolved bilateral enforcement mechanisms which entailed the creation of formal legal and political organizations for monitoring and enforcing agreements, and an institutional framework that lent itself to the further evolution of increasingly complex trade, while the latter adopted the cultural and social attributes of Islamic society in perpetuating a personalized structure. The results derived from the two trading methods are quite different: the former went on to evolve more productive markets, and the latter eventually disappeared in the face of intensified competition (Greif 1994; North 1994).

66 Kroeber and Kluckhohn (1952) collected nearly 200 different definitions of the concept of 'culture' from various angles.

67 It is also true in other disciplines in that regard. For example, Boas ([1911] 1983) in which the image of pragmatism regarded culture as 'the totality of the mental and physical reactions and activities ... in a social group collectively and individually in relation to their natural environment'. Weber ([1904] 1949) simply defined culture as 'a value concept'; while Shweder defined culture as 'the intentional world and ... it is the constituted scheme of things for intending persons' (Shweder 1991).

68 Mead (1937) linked mainly the traditional behaviour with culture:

> culture means the whole complex of traditional behavior ... it can mean the forms of traditional behavior which are characteristics of a given society or of a group of societies, or of a certain race, or of a certain area, or of a certain period of time.

69 According to Geertz, culture 'denotes an historically transmitted pattern of meanings embodied in symbols, a system of inherited conceptions expressed in symbolic forms by means of which men communicate, perpetuate, and develop their knowledge about and attitudes toward life' (Geertz [1966] 1973: 89).

70 Again, as mentioned previously, 'informal institutions' here also refer to the terms of 'non-price exchange institutions' or 'non-market institutions' as many scholars used to a certain extent.

71 This argument is sometimes called 'Coleman's Prediction' (Burt 2000).

72 Coleman noted in his book: 'without a high degree of trustworthiness among the members of the group, the institution could not exist – for a person who receives a payout early in the sequence of meetings could abscond and leave the other with a loss (Coleman 1990, 306–7; see Burt 2000).

73 See repeated game theory from Kandori (1992).

74 Actually, Landa also mentioned very clearly that 'Trust and reciprocity is greatest among close kin within the household and decreases as social distance increases' (Landa 1997, 14).

75 La Ferrara (2003: 1731–2) takes reciprocity to explain why kinship bank networks work well as capital market institutions in Ghana. What is special comparing her model with others in the literature is that she employs the overlapping generation game in the process:

> it is possible to 'use the borrower's child' to enforce repayment, either by having the child deny support to a defaulting parent ('direct' punishment), or by having future lenders deny credit to the child of a defaulter.

Actually, this is a concept of 'generalized reciprocity', i.e., 'reciprocation can be carried out not only by the original beneficiaries but also by their offspring and can be directed to the original benefactors as well as to their offspring'. In La Ferrara's case, 'the scope for "social enforcement" is enlarged in a dynastic community because sanctions can fall upon the deviant members as well as upon his or her offspring'. This makes cooperation possible even in very short-term interactions.

76 Landa (1997: 130) pointed out that they are based on 'shared code of conduct' and 'shared genes' respectively.

77 One of the common efforts made by people in China to extend their genetic network is to create blood relations through adopting children from other families, setting up 'blood-brothers (sisters)' or 'sworn brothers (sisters)' relations among informal agreed people (see also Landa 1997).

78 The theoretical base of Burt's structural hole includes (1) Simmel ([1922] 1955) and Merton (1957)'s idea of autonomy generated by conflicting affiliation; (2) traditional economic ideas of monopoly power; (3) competitive advantage economics; (4) Granovetter's theory of the strength of weak ties (Granovetter 1973); (5) Freeman's argument of between-ness centrality (Freeman 1977) and (6) Cook and Emerson's idea of the benefits of having exclusive exchange partners (Burt 1980, 2000).

79 Holes here refer to the weaker connections between social groups (Burt 2000).

80 The exchange view of the firm, simply takes the firm as a kind of special market, where price system decides how to reward workers or punish workers based on their task assignments. Moral factors are not considered under this control mode: commitment is important under this control system, but not moral factors.

81 The command view of the firm depicts the way of controlling the firm through the order-obediance relations between owners and employees of the firm based on their contracts.

82 The custom (team) view of the firm takes custom and tradition as the major instrument for coordinating the firm's activities. Mutually perceived duties, responsibilities, entitlements, obligations, understanding, common value and shared history, etc.,

are all very important instruments to deal with the long-term contractual relations between the controller and the workers of the firm. According to Schlicht (1998: 224), all these social, cultural and moral elements are embodied in job descriptions and job assignments of the workers in the firm.

83 Heilbroner and Milberg use the terms 'market, command and tradition' in their work (Heilbroner and Milberg 1972); while Polanyi uses the terms 'exchange, redistribution and reciprocity' (Polanyi 1977).

84 The term is initially introduced and analysed by Polanyi (1958). He also sometimes uses the term 'personal knowledge' to express the meaning. For the same phenomenon, social psychology usually uses the terms 'procedural knowledge' and 'implicit knowledge' (Anderson 1980: 223–54; Greenwald and Banaji 1995). Organization theory refers to 'behavioural knowledge' (Barnard 1938), (see also Schlicht 1998).

85 This term originally used by Fuller (1954) and developed by Williamson links with his governance theory.

3 Indigenous conceptions of networks

1 In his attempt to rule the country by law, the First Emperor of the Qin Dynasty totally negated the role of ancient traditions, ethical codes and social ethics. He even committed such brutal acts as having books burnt and 460 Confucian scholars buried alive. Although the Qin Dynasty had very complete laws and regulations, it misused them and tried unscrupulously to destroy the traditional moral standards of benevolence, rightness (righteousness), rites and wisdom (wit) against the will of the people. This led to peasant uprisings which overthrew the 15-year Qin Dynasty (221– 207 BC).

2 As a matter of fact, when Confucius put forward this concept, the system of rule of rites was already on the decline after the Spring and Autumn Period (770–476 BC) and Warring States Period (475–221 BC). He, however, was fond of the traditional norms of conduct, especially Western Zhou rites. Consequently, he and his disciples made great efforts to promote those rites. His thoughts were not expounded and promoted by Dong Zhongshu during the reign of Emperor Wudi of the West Han Dynasty.

3 Etiquette actually appeared in the primitive clan commune mainly as rituals and proceedings at sacrificial ceremonies. Later on, they were expanded to include rituals and proceedings of war, harvesting, moving capital, holding public positions and hunting. They were regularized to become rules or norms to be observed by people and then became the tools and means for maintaining public order (D. Li 2000: 3).

4 These constitute the social estate and status system Confucius worked hard to create and are generally known as the core of Western Zhou rites. According to Confucius, 'If names are not rectified, what is said will not sound reasonable; if what is said does not sound reasonable, efforts cannot culminate in success; if efforts cannot culminate in success, the rites and music will not thrive; if the rites and music do not thrive, crimes cannot be punished properly; if crimes cannot be punished properly, the common people will have nothing to go by.' (*The Analects of Confucius: Zilu*). As long as the social estate and status system is in place, everyone will have his own social status, public order will be naturally established and there will be social stability.

5 In accordance with Mencius's moral concepts of benevolence, righteousness, propriety and wisdom, the Western Han philosopher Dong Zhongshu put forward the social norms of three cardinal principles and six regulations which governed the relationships between ruler and subject, between father and son, and between husband and wife and among father, brothers, clan members, uncles, teachers and friends. In the Song Dynasty, Zhu Xi categorically used the concept of the Three Cardinal Guides and the Five Constant Virtues, setting standards for eight interpersonal relations. The Three Cardinal Guides are: 'Ruler guides subject, father guides son, and husband guides wife (Zhu Xi, *General Book: Leshangjie*), and the Five Constant Virtues

are: 'love between father and son, courtesy between monarch and subject, different responsibilities between husband and wife, respect between the young and the elderly, and trust between friends' (Zhu Xi, *Remarks*, Vol. 57).

6   According to Confucius, to exercise self-constraint means to be benevolent. That is to say, everybody can be benevolent as long as he knows how to exercise self-constraint and acts in accordance with the principles of rites, making sure that everybody 'does not look, listen, speak and act regardless of rites' (*The Analects of Confucius: Yanyuan*).

7   Both Mencius and Xunzi argued that righteousness was the most important property of humans and the fundamental symbol differentiating humans from all other creatures and things in the world. Realizing it was impossible for him to restore Western Zhou rites, Mencius laid more emphasis on righteousness, not benevolence. Xunzi also said, 'Water and fire have vigour, but no life; grass and trees have life, but no perception; birds and beasts have perception, but no righteousness. Humans have vigour, life, perception and righteousness and are therefore the most superior of all under heaven' (Xunzi: *Wangzhi*).

8   At first credit meant what was said to the heaven and ancestors during sacrificial ceremonies. All these remarks were truths, not lies. In Confucius's ideas, credit is included as an important part of benevolence. In general, credit mainly emphasizes the way of making friends and is about things at a lower level than filial piety and loyalty.

9   According to Guanzi, 'Without the four cardinal virtues, the state will perish' (*Guanzi: Part Herdsmen*). The Qing historian Qian Daxin said, 'With a sense of propriety, you don't make hasty moves. With a sense of righteousness, you don't make friends carelessly. With a sense of honesty, you don't talk recklessly. With a sense of shame, you don't act recklessly' (*Shijia Study Moral Improvement: Honesty and Shame*).

10 The full definition of 'community' from *Webster's Third New International Dictionary of the English Language Unabridged* are as below (G. & C. Merriam Company, 1976):

1   A body of individuals organized into a unit or manifesting usually with awareness some unifying trait: **a:** state, commonwealth. **b:** the people living in a particular place or region and usually linked by common interests; broadly: the region itself: any population cluster (small, compact, homogeneous communities such as the Greek city-state or Elizabethan England – C. D. Lewis). **c:** a monastic body or other unified religious group. **d:** an interacting population of different kinds of individuals (as species) constituting a society or association or simply an aggregation of mutually related individuals in a given location 'a climax community'. **e:** a group of people marked by a common characteristic but living within a larger society that does not share that characteristic (the Chinese community in New York; the artists' community downtown; the Jewish community in London); especially such a group politically organized and recognized especially as a separate voting group for election purposes (Sikh and Muslim communities in India). **f:** a group sharing a particular economic or social belief and living communally. **g:** any group sharing interests or pursuits (a community of scholars; a group linked by a common policy; a tariff community of small nations). **h:** a body of persons or nations united by historical consciousness or by common social, economic, and political interests (the entire Christian cummunity; the European coal and steel community)

2   society at large: public: people in general –used with the definite article 'the interests of the community'.

3   **a:** common or joint ownership, tenure, experience, or pertinence: commonness, sharing participation (asserts that community of goods would be the ideal institution – G. L. Dickinson), (out of the atmosphere of controversy to the community of our love again – Mary Austin), (the essential community of interests shared by

all branches of learning – G. W. Cottrell). **b:** common character: fact of showing a trait or various traits in common: agreement, concord, likeness (although there are varieties, the community of style is still more evident – O. Elfrida Saunders). **c:** shared activity: social intercourse: fellowship, communion: especially social activity marked by a feeling of unity but also individual participation completely willing and not forced or coerced and without loss of individuality (in order that there may be a community, there must be conscious and purposive sharing – Ernest Barker). **d:** obs: frequent occurrence. **e:** a social or societal state (emerging from feral isolation into community).

4   a civil–law partnership or society of property between husband and wife arising by virtue of the fact of marriage or by contract.

11 This is similar to the four acts Marx Weber had for humans, namely, 1) carefully planned instrumental rational act that is carried out for one's short-term interests; 2) value rational act for conscious belief and acceptance; 3) affective act subject to feelings, emotion, mental desire or affective conditions; and 4) traditional act formed as a result of habits.

12 As a matter of fact, 'reciprocity' is not unique to China. Marcel Mauss and other Western scholars also use 'reciprocity' as an important category (Mauss [1950] 1954).

13 In Chinese tradition, 'reciprocity' has a dual meaning. To be more specific, one should do all he can to repay good for good and return evil for evil. In addition, there are two exceptions: to repay good for evil, and to return evil for good, although these do not comply with common sense.

14 As Hu Hsien-chin (Hu 1944) was the first to separate '*lian*' from '*mianzi*' and explain '*lianmian*' in terms of concept, it is necessary to give a summary of her views. She believes that '*mianzi*' means the prestige one has established in society on the basis of his/her achievements; and that '*lian*' is the reputation one enjoys as he/she is respected for his/her moral integrity. According to her research, '*mianzi*' was over 2,700 years older than '*lian*' (the fourteenth century BC vs the Yuan Dynasty in the thirteenth century) (Chan 1987).

15 Cathy Ruey-ling Chu (1987) of the Academia Sinica in Taiwan highly summarized '*lian*' and '*face*' as society's recognition of one's achievements in 'ethics' and 'ability' respectively. Chu believed that '*lianmian*' is a tool for maintaining social order. Hwang Kwang-kuo (1987) of Taiwan University believed that an individual's '*mianzi*' is the function of his/her social status and reputation.

16 'Human relations' advocated by Confucianists are actually the rite rules for the interaction between people in different types of interpersonal relationship networks.

17 Residents of the tribes on the island exchange only two fixed articles – bracelets made of white shells and necklaces made of red shells. The former are exchanged counter clockwise, and the latter are exchanged clockwise. This gives rise to a closed ring called the 'Kula Ring'. After a participant in the Kula obtains Kula articles, he keeps it for a short while before exchanging them again. So once you are in Kula, you will be in it forever. Consequently, there is a fixed 'partnership' between Kula participants that will last forever from generation to generation. As time goes on, the neighbouring tribes come close together through this system to form an integral whole. See Shi Lin (2002) for more explanation about this system.

18 Cf. Zhou Changcheng's comments on this issue in his works (2003).

19 According to Hwang Kwang-kuo (1987), as a matter of fact, Goffman's facework is a behaviour of impression management, a behaviour one deliberately carries out for others to see so that they will have a special impression of him or her. In Goffman's theory, facework is a front stage behaviour done for others to see in the mixed relationship networks (including arranging the setting of interpersonal contacts and improving one's appearances and manners in front of others). People's sincere

behaviour is the backstage behaviour designed only for 'friends' to see within their affection networks.

4 Selection of research areas

1 According to China's official definition, the Eastern Developed Region (area) includes Shanghai, Beijing, Jiangsu, Tianjin, Zhejiang, Shandong, Guangdong, Liaoning, Hebei, Fujian and Hainan, totalling 11 provinces (municipalities and autonomous regions); the Western Underdeveloped Region includes Guangxi, Sichuan, Xinjiang, Neimenggu (Inner Mongolia), Chongqing, Ningxia, Shaanxi, Qinghai, Gansu, Yunnan, Xizang (Tibet) and Guizhou, totalling 12 provinces (municipalities and autonomous regions) and 8 provinces of the Central Region are Jilin, Heilongjiang, Hubei, Hunan, Henan, Jiangxi, Anhui and Shanxi.

2 The three major commercial conglomerates in the Qing Dynasty were the merchants of *Jin Shang* (Shanxi merchants), *Hui Shang* (Anhui merchants) and *Chao Shang* (Chaozhou merchants from Guangdong). Among them, the Shanxi merchants were the earliest contingent that had prospered for more than 500 years, and were considered to be the best merchants in the world matching their Jewish and Venice counterparts.

3 Hu-Xiang is the simple way to call two neighbouring provinces of Hubei and Hunan (its simple name is *Xiang*) together.

4 The initial meaning of the Tao (Dao) was very simple. It means the Road. But later, it extended to be the origin of reasons and the universe or the world. The Tao as Laozi expounded it was precisely the philosophical exposition of the origin of the world.

5 By the period of Wei to Jin there prevailed the metaphysical ideas of everything ruling over itself and things of different nature playing their own roles. They were practically the re-manifestation of Laozi's doctrine of the Tao following nature and of doing nothing against nature.

6 This is a model of regional economic development. Represented by Wenzhou in southern Zhejiang Province, China, the market-oriented model is mainly characterized by private household operations and specialized markets, is based on small towns and focuses on using private entrepreneurs' primitively accumulated capital instead of foreign or government funds to develop small industries. The core of this model is that its private nature obviously differs from the state-owned or collective nature of other economic development models.

7 The Eastern Zhejiang School of Utilitarianism is a school of Confucian thought but its understanding of 'righteousness' and 'profit' is vastly different from the thoughts of Confucius and Mencius. The school advocated enhancing righteousness with profit, not giving up profit for the sake of righteousness.

8 Neo-Confucianism first appeared in the Northern Song Dynasty (960–1126) and developed its final form in the Southern Song Dynasty (1127–1279). Its theoretical basis was still the Confucian thought of Confucius and Mencius but it also included some aspects of Buddhism and Taoism. Its main principle was to uphold heavenly principles and overcome human desires. The representatives of Neo-Confucianism were Sima Guang, Cheng Hao, Cheng Yi, Zhu Xi, etc. It should be said that Zhu Xi epitomized the thought of this school.

9 In the earlier period, Lingnan had embraced a broader scope involving Guangdong Province, Guangxi Autonomous Region, Hainan Province as well as Hong Kong and Macao, but in modern times, Lingnan mainly referred to Guangdong Province (Zhao 2003: 2).

10 From the day of its birth, Lingnan culture was most particular about being practical and utilitarian. This became even more prominent in recent modern times. Modern Lingnan thinkers He Qi and Hu Liyuan set forth the proposition that profit making is man's nature. They argued that a man who can benefit himself will certainly be able

to benefit others and that a man who cannot benefit himself is bound to bring trouble to the society (Zhao 2003: 195).

11 In terms of administrative jurisdiction, the Xiangjia Mountain area now belongs to Xikuo village, Kuoshan Township, Cangnan County in Zhejiang Province.

12 The village has been renamed from Duanjia to Fuxing since late 1996 due to the creation of the new institution of 'integrating village with company' (IVWC). This issue will be discussed in detail in Chapter 8.

13 Villager Group No. 9 of Fuxing village is the cradle of Fuxing Company. The farmland owned by this villager group has already been taken up by the company and, therefore, it has a certain particularity that needs special explanation.

14 The three heads of these households are Xiao Zuoming, Xiao Mucheng and Duan Jinxiang.

15 Family heads are Feng Tao, Hu Fengxiang, Li Liangbing, Liu Jin'an, Duan Xuelin, Li Sixiong, Duan Chuanxiang and Dai Zhongtao.

16 See also Wang Xiaoyi, Zhang Jun and Yao Mei, *Economic Growth and Societal Transition in Rural China: A Survey of Yantian Village, Dongguan City, Guangdong Province*, Shanxi: Jingji Chubanshe, 1996; and Zhang Xiaoshan and Hu Biliang (eds), *Small Town and Regional Integration*, Shanxi: Renmin Chubanshe, 2002.

5 Village trust and bidding ROSCAs

1 Rotating savings and credit associations (ROSCAs) is called *hehui* by Chinese people. As occurs in some other economies in the world, there are many different forms of ROSCA in different regions of China. ROSCAs in this chapter, based on the existing situation at the survey village, refer to *biaohui* – bidding ROSCA is determined through bidding the interest rates of the fund during a certain fixed time period.

2 The state banks' share of national total financial assets, total lending, total savings and the total employees in the financial sector were 67.8 per cent, 67.5 per cent, 65.4 per cent and 61.6 per cent respectively in 2003-end; the shares for joint-stock banks were 15.5 per cent, 15.7 per cent, 16.1 per cent and 5.7 per cent respectively; 16.7 per cent, 16.8 per cent, 18.5 per cent and 32.7 per cent for credit cooperatives (including urban and rural credit cooperative and urban commercial banks as well as rural commercial banks). (See *China Financial Year Book 2004*, China Financial Publishing House, 2004).

3 Non-bank financial institutions, post credit departments and foreign financial institutions in China have not been considered since they make up only a very limited share of the national total of the above mentioned indicators.

4 After the Republic of China, the government stopped issuing banknotes (Li 2000: 60).

5 As a matter of fact, 'underground private money houses' do exist in many areas. Due to government restrictions, these money houses cannot have open counter business. However, making use of their private connections, they have been a 'bridge' between depositors and loan seekers. We have found that these people are called money lenders or middlemen in our research area in Cangnan County, Zhejiang Province.

6 These organizations are more informal financing by nature.

7 By the end of 1995, the total number of RCFs had been 19,700 at the township and town level and 134,000 at the village level in 41.7 per cent and 18.3 per cent of China's townships and towns and villages in the same year respectively. They received a cumulative contribution of 72.3 billion yuan and granted cumulative loans of 82.8 billion yuan (Wei and Zhang 1998). In addition, the total amount of funds of these foundations was estimated at 150–200 billion yuan in 1997 (Jiang 1999).

8 *Rural Report* by The Agricultural Economy Department of the Central Agricultural Research Institute, Issue 11, Volume 2, 1934.

9   The head of the village Xiang Fanghuai told me that his family alone spent 6,000 yuan per month for the ROSCA. Every year, his family brings home nearly 100,000 yuan from various ROSCAs. Of course, we have to take into account that as the head of the village, he tries to help the less fortunate by taking part in their ROSCAs. Most families invest much less money in ROSCAs than he does.

10   The second method of interest rate calculation takes the time factor into consideration. Since the current value rate $= (1 + r)^n$ (where r indicates the interest rate, while n indicates the number of sequence of people gaining/paying the fund), then we get the average interest rate = total interest payment (income)/total funds received from the ROSCA (or the total funds paid to the ROSCA) in terms of current value/time (annually, quarterly or monthly).

11   The third method of calculation takes both the time factor as well as savings rate (when the 'feet' act more as depositors) and lending rate (when the 'feet' act more as lenders) of the formal credit market into consideration. Clearly, the head of the ROSCA is purely a lender, while the last 'foot' is purely a depositor, and the rest of the 'feet' play both roles in the ROSCA. Therefore, for those who play more role as depositors, they get the interest income = the funds they pay each time $\times \{[(1 + \text{savings rate})^{(n+1)} -1] / \text{interest rate} - 1\}$; for those who play more role as lenders, they pay the money = the funds they pay each time $\times \{[(1 + \text{lending rate})^{(n+1)} - 1] / \text{interest rate} \times (1 + \text{lending rate})^n]\}$. The results from such calculation, taking Xiang Sujiao's ROSCA as an example, show that the average annual deposit rate is somewhere between 8 per cent and 12 per cent, while the annual average lending rate is between 5.6 per cent and 15.2 per cent.

12   In order to keep clans from fighting each other with weapons, the local government in recent years has forcibly banned these boat races.

13   The nine scholars were Zhong Xingji, Xu Jingheng, Liu Anjie, Liu Anshang, Dai Shu, Zhao Xiao, Zhang Hui, Shen Gongxing and Jiang Yuanzhong.

6 *Guanxi* community and people's mobility

1   In addition to the author, the other three researchers are Li Hui, Liu Yongping and Zhao Hong.

2   There are also some exceptions for a male who might move to live with the woman's parents in some areas of rural China when the woman's parents have only one child. This was during the time before family planning policy was implemented or the male's social status is much lower than the woman's.

3   In some of the areas in 1994, for example, women were as many as 75 per cent of the 'floating population' in the Pearl River Delta (Sun 1996).

4   One of the customs in rural China before 1949 was 'not marrying people from the same village, neither from the same surname kinships'.

5   Lei Jiejing (1994) provides the detailed information about people's marriage distances in relation to different age groups in rural China in the mid-1980s.

6   Knight *et al.*'s research in this regard provides us a good example: the rural–urban migrants find a job relying on the Ministry of Labour and Social Securities organized official agencies spending 324 yuan on the average, but only 50 yuan if they find a job through the help of their relatives or friends (Knight *et al.* 1999).

7   However, Murphy (2002) thinks that the return orientation of the migrants is positive, not negative at all.

8   This might be due to the fact that the sample did not include the elderly or children. If these two population groups were included, the impact of age factors would have been more significant.

9   Basic information about Shanxi Yichen Industrial Co. Ltd. includes: (1) Domicile: Yuanma Road, Yuanping City; (2) Legal representative: Chen Jugao; (3) Registered capital: RMB 10.312 million; (4) Type of enterprise: Limited liability company; (5)

Business scope: manufacturing of general and chemical equipment, BR-class pressure vessels, D-class boiler and steel shuttering;(6) Registration no.: 1422021000010;(7) Establishment date: Dec. 30, 1998. Basic information about the Spark Boiler Plant of Shanxi Yichen Industrial Co. Ltd.: (1) Domicile: Yuanma Road, Yuanping City; (2)Responsible person: Zhao Youyou;(3) Business scope: Manufacturing of CWW 0.7-85/60AIII horizontal normal pressure boiler, drinking water boiler, oil tank, steel container and rivet welding parts;(4) Registration no.: 1422021600007; (5) Establishment date: March 5, 1997. Basic Information about Yuanping Jianda Machinery Engineering Co. Ltd. of Shanxi Province: (1) Legal representative: Chen Jugao; (2) Registered capital: RMB 9.77 million; (3) Enterprise type: Limited liability company; (4) Business scope: Mechanic excavation of earthwork, wholesale and retail of electric machinery and equipment, building materials and steel.

10 The following information is from the business licence of Chen Wenkai's enterprise: (1) Name: Yuanping Chuangda Machinery Co. Ltd.; (2) Domicile: Ping'an Avenue (Xizheng New District), Yuanping City; (3) Legal representative: Chen Yongsheng; (4) Registered capital: RMB 5.18 million; (5) Enterprise type: Limited liability company; (6) Business scope: Production and processing of construction-related steel form plates, steel form plates for bridges and tunnels, hoisting machinery, mining machinery, transportation machinery, and hardware; (7) Registered no.: 1422022000144; (8) Establishment date: Feb. 9, 2003.

11 Zhao's conclusion is that 'villages with high migration rate in year $t-1$ continue to have large migration rate in year t' (Zhao 2003).

12 One of the typical 'chain migration' stories was the famous case of how the New Territories in Hong Kong migrated to Britain during the period of 1957–1962. The result was that most of the families, large parts of clans and whole villages were gradually summoned to Britain based on a core of about 60 fellow villagers from San Tin already in Britain since the 1940s and 1950s. The mobility was very well organized mainly by five large clans – the Deng, Hou, Wen, Peng, and Liao. More interestingly, 'many of the overseas Chinese in Britain from the New Territories are still today organized in five "clansmen's associations" corresponding to the five clans' (Christiansen 2003: 50).

13 According to Kwong (1997: 9), only illegal immigrants from Fujian Province to the United States in the last 15 years before the end of the twentieth century was about 200,000 (re-quoted from Kyle and Liang 2001).

7 *Guanxi* community and TVE development in China

1 China did not introduce the National Accounting Method until the early 1990s. In order to make historical data comparable, the 'gross production' indicator is still retained while employing the new indicator of 'value-added'.

2 See also Wang *et al.* (1996) and Zhang and Hu (2002).

3 See also chapters in Hu and Hu (1996) and Hu (1998).

4 See also Li Jing (1996).

5 See also Wang and Zhu (1996).

6 For example, visiting a woman after her sterilization or abortion and presenting her with gifts are the new ritual forms after the implementation of family planning policy in China since the early 1980s (Yan 1996b).

7 According to Jin Yaoji (Ambrose King) (1989a), *renqing* or 'human feelings' are social in nature and requires empathy for others' emotional responses in accordance with one's own (Yan 1996a).

8 The political function of *guanxi* at the micro level has been well discussed by Yan (1996a).

9 See more relevant analysis in Chapter 8.

8 The institution of 'integrating village with company' (IVWC) and rural community development

1 'Integrating village with company', simply IVWC, is the English expression of *yichang daicun* in Chinese. It means that a company takes over a village under its administration and leadership, but the operation of both remains separate.

2 For convenience sake, 'Fuxing Science & Technology Shareholding Co. Ltd.' will hereafter be referred to as 'the Fuxing Company' or FSTSC.

3 In October 1985, the 'Fuxing Cooperative Iron & Wood Processing Factory' was renamed as 'Hanchuan Steel Wire Factory'.

4 After the Asian financial crisis, metal products from South Korea were sold to China in large quantity and at a low price, which greatly reduced the profit margin of the Fuxing Company in the following years and exerted great pressure on the long-term development of the Fuxing Company.

5 Wuhan Fuxing Huiyu Real Estate Development Co. Ltd., a subsidiary company controlled by the Fuxing Company (with 97.33 per cent shares), is dedicated to real-estate development and operation. It was incorporated in Wuhan in August 1999, with a registered capital of 100 million yuan. In a short period of four years, Wuhan Fuxing Huiyu Real Estate Development Co. Ltd. has invested nearly three billion yuan in the real estate market of Wuhan, and with its average annual profit and tax turnover exceeding 100 million yuan, it now ranks as one of the top companies in Wuhan's real estate market.

6 Wuhan Fuxing Bio-Pharmacy Co., Ltd., incorporated in Wuhan in October 2000, is a subsidiary solely owned by the Fuxing Company with 150 million yuan. In a period of only three years since its incorporation, the company has, through cooperation with universities, colleges and science and research institutes such as Huazhong University of Science and Technology, Wuhan University and Hubei Provincial Medical Industry Research Institute, developed many new high-tech products with their own independent intellectual property rights such as Arachidonic Acid, Fuxing Liver Protectors and can mass-produce biomedicine, biological series, healthcare series and nearly 100 daily medicines such as various high-capacity injections, low-capacity injections, tablets, granules, oral liquid, etc.

7 If the populations of Fuxing village, the Fuxing Company and other residents permanently living in the area are all taken into account, the current total population is about 30,000. It is estimated that the figure will reach about 50,000 in 2006.

8 Hanchuan County was changed to Hanchuan City (county-level city) on 8 November 1997 upon the approval of the Ministry of Civil Affairs. In terms of administration, it is under the jurisdiction and leadership of Xiaogan City (prefecture-level city), Hubei Province.

9 The full text of request for instruction submitted by Chenhu Town People's Government on 19 July 1996 to Hanchuan County People's Government regarding 'Application for "Fuxing Residents' Committee of Chenhu Town, Hanchuan County"' reads as follows:

> In recent years, Fuxing Area of our town has enjoyed over-speed economic development and a new type of Fuxing market town has taken shape. At present this area has a total population of 18,800, of whom there are 500 households of residents and a non-agricultural population of over 3,000. In order to strengthen administration of the market town and further promote the material as well as ethical progress in Fuxing area, in accordance with the relevant stipulations of City and Town Residents Organization Law, the town government hereby applies for establishment of "Fuxing Residents' Committee of Chenhu Town, Hanchuan County." The leadership of the Residents' Committee is proposed to consist of three members, to be elected by the general meeting of residents, and the salary

of the Committee members will be borne by Hanchuan Steel Wire Shareholding Co., Ltd. The office of the Residents' Committee is arranged at No. 15, 3rd Street, Fuxing Market Town.

The full text of 'Official Reply on Approving Setting up Fuxing Residents' Committee of Chenhu Town' made by Hanchuan County People's Government on 2 September 1996 reads:

> Chenhu Town People's Government: We have duly received your town's request for instruction on setting up Fuxing Residents' Committee. At present, Fuxing area has enjoyed rapid economic development and Fuxing Market Town has taken shape. In accordance with Place Name Administration Methods of Hubei Province and upon the examination and verification of the County Place Name Commission, the County Government hereby approves setting up Fuxing Residents' Committee, which shall be under the leadership of Chenhu Town Government.

10 The full text of '24 December 1996 Official Reply of the County Government Office on Approving Putting Duanjia Village of Chenhu Town under the Administration of Hanchuan Steel Wire Shareholding Co. Ltd. and Implementing the System of "integrating village with company"' reads

> Chenhu Town People's Government: we have duly received your town's 'Request for Instruction on Putting Duanjia Village of Chenhu Town under the Administration of Hanchuan Steel Wire Shareholding Co. Ltd. and Implementing the new institution of "integrating village with company"'. According to the principles of relevant documents of the higher authorities and in view of the actual conditions of local economic development, we hereby make the following replies upon the approval of the County Government, (1) We approve putting Duanjia Village of Chenhu Town, formerly under Fuxing Administrative Area, under the administration of Hanchuan Steel Wire Shareholding Co. Ltd. and implementing the new institution of 'integrating village with company'. (2) Duanjia Village is renamed as Fuxing Village. The original credits and debts shall be borne by the renamed Fuxing Village. (3) The renamed Fuxing Village shall assume the various assignments of the former Duanjia Village. The specific work assignments shall be sent down by Chenhu Town People's Government to Hanchuan Steel Wire Shareholding Co., Ltd., which shall be responsible to Chenhu Town People's Government. (4) The implementation of various tasks of 'integrating village with company' shall be organized by Chenhu Town Party Committee and Chenhu Town People's Government.

11 Actually, regarding the issue of renaming the village, Hanchuan County Bureau of Civil Affairs once presented different views on 12 November of that year: 'Regarding the issue of renaming the village, we suggest not changing the name, and the reasons are: (1) Article IV of *Ordinances of Place Name Administration* stipulates that "the villages in one township shall avoid identical names and the names shall avoid identical pronunciation." Chenhu Town already newly set up a "Fuxing Residents' Committee" in the area of Duanjia in September this year, and renaming Duanjia Village as Fuxing Village would constitute duplication of names in the same region and of the same administrative level. (2) Changing the name of the village is not of much significance and effect to rural economic development, so it is not quite necessary. (3) Place Name has certain historical significance and has been recorded in place name archive, administrative division, local chronicles, maps, historical data on place name, etc. and used consistently. It seems that changing the name would cause much inconvenience.' This is a proposal written by the Civil Affairs Bureau to

Magistrate Li. Apparently, this suggestion was not adopted by the county government leaders of the day.

12 The leaders of the company told us that this standard would be raised to a minimum of 50 yuan per square metre in 2004. The company planned to complete the villagers' house renovation project in the coming three years.

13 According to Directive No. 2 of the Fuxing Company in 2000 (issued on 18 March 2000), Tan Yeliang, the Secretary of the Village Party Branch is entitled to treatment as director of the company's branch factory, with a monthly salary of 1,560 yuan. The salary of other village cadres shall be paid out of the village's revenue. Their monthly salaries are as follows: Director of the Village Committee and Deputy Secretary of the Village Party Branch: 650 yuan; Deputy Director of the Village Committee: 600 yuan; Deputy Secretary of the Village Party Committee and the village treasurer: 600 yuan; the village broadcaster: 250 yuan; heads of Villager Groups Nos. 1, 2, 3, 4, 11 and 12: 120 yuan; heads of Villager Groups Nos. 5, 6, 7, 8, 9 and 10: 100 yuan.

14 Every 10 work points constituted one standard workload. At that time one standard workload in Fuxing village was equivalent to 0.1 yuan to one yuan. In an ordinary production team, each workload was equivalent to about 0.6 yuan. As the iron business in Fuxing village went well, compared with other areas in China, the value of work points in Fuxing village was relatively high.

15 The company altogether has six branch factories engaging in manufacturing these metal products. Branch Factory No. 1 manufactures steel wire, Branch Factory No. 2 manufactures steel wire rope, Branch Factory No. 3 manufactures steel curtain wire, Branch Factory No. 5 is a machine repair shop, Branch Factory No. 8 manufactures steel wire for tyres, and Branch Factory No. 9 manufactures PC steel strands.

16 Community mainly stresses the state of unity, harmony and stability within a specific group of people. The members in the group attach the greatest importance to their own sufficiency and their common sense of belonging. Generally speaking, a community does not pay much attention to the functions of the organization, nor does it attach much importance to the individual ability of its members (usually regards moral standing as more important than ability).

17 Generally speaking, a functional organization refers to one formed to materialize a certain external objective. To an enterprise, its most important external objective is to make maximum profit. The key to this objective of the enterprise as a functional organization is capacity building for fulfillment of the objective of maximizing profit. In particular, the capacity building of the entrepreneurs and employees of the enterprise is of great significance. Therefore, a functional organization regards such issues as the satisfaction, harmony and unity of its internal members only as the means to maximize profit, not as the objective itself (Sakaiya 1996).

18 Although the benefits that Tan Gongyan and his company have brought about to local development and villagers are still open to veiled censure of some villagers, many villagers indeed regard Tan Gongyan and his startup partners as the saviours that brought about prosperity. The fact that the name of the village was changed from the original 'Duanjia Village' to 'Fuxing Village' has actually expressed to a certain extent some villagers' gratitude towards Tan Gongyan. In the Chinese language, *fu* means happiness and *xing* means star and here refers to saviour. Fuxing literally means 'star of happiness' or 'saviour who brings happiness'. This indicates that many people in this area indeed regard Tan Gongyan as a saviour who can bring them happiness. Tan Gongyan has been very proud of this. In our judgment, compared with money, Tan Gongyan values more the local people's evaluation of him and the government's evaluation of him. He has indeed been recognized by local people and by the government at various levels. In January 1988, he won the title of 'the Provincial Peasant Entrepreneur' of Hubei Province; in February 1988, he won the title of 'Business Administration Star of Xiaogan Prefecture' of Hubei Province; in February 1990, he won the title of 'Special Class Model Worker of Hanchuan County' of Hubei

Province; in April 1991, he won the title of 'Model Worker of Hubei Province' and was awarded 'the National May 1st Labor Medal'; in 1993, he was elected as one of the deputies to the 8th National People's Congress; in 1994, he was appraised as 'National Township and Village Entrepreneur' by the Ministry of Agriculture; in 1995, he won the title of 'National Model Worker'; in 1998, he was re-elected the deputy to the 9th National People's Congress; and in 2003, he was elected again the deputy to the 10th National People's Congress.

19 Villagers with surname Tan have the third largest population in Fuxing village, accounting for 9.8 per cent of the total population of the village; villagers with the surname Duan have the largest population, accounting for 20 per cent of the village total; and the villagers with the surname Zhang have the second largest population in the village, accounting for 15 per cent of the village total.

20 In 1996, the Fuxing Company supported the village in running a disc spool factory to provide supplementary services for the production of steel wire. The company issued its planned production targets every month. It was up to the company to sell the products and settle the accounts in cash.

9 Conclusion: integration of tradition and modernity – towards understanding institutional arrangements in China's modernization

1 According to Blau (1975), social structure describes the pattern of recurrent and regularized interaction among two or more persons, hence implying the existence of norms for regulating behaviour (see also Landa 1997). From this point of view, social structure is referring to the similar meaning of social organization or social networks.

2 No special discussion in this book is dedicated to Wangjian village in Shaanxi Province, but detailed discussion has been dedicated to the development of Wangjian village in Hu (1996).

3 Max Weber's concept of hierarchical system mainly means that a legally based organization should be made available, an organization which must have clearly defined terms of reference and abide by certain hierarchical principles.

4 Mainly referring to eliminating as much as possible the impact of the holy factors such as religion and ethics from the social lives and basing people's behaviour on the orthodoxy and legitimate principles of secularized and formal-institutionalized legal provisions. However, according to Max Weber's analysis, some religious thoughts after the Reformation belong to the secular category (Weber 1958).

5 The modernization theory of Talcott Parsons, mainly based on the evolution theory, believes that modern society has only one fountainhead (occidental centrism) and that the development process of 'rationalization' which led to the 'modernity' of Western Europe has 'universal' significance. He also believed that this development process would become a main trend in the twenty-first century or in the longer run and that the final result would be what he called the completion of modern society (Parsons 1971; Jin 2002: 84). It is evident that the thought of Parsons is basically a mixture of Amercian centrism and universality.

6 We can have a deep understanding of this point from an incident related by Tu Wei-ming in one of his books: 'I participated in a seminar on "Is There Alternative to Western Modernism?" in Japan. When I exchanged views with American sociologist Daniel Bell on this, his answer was very straightforward: of course there are alternatives, but all tragic! He believed if the European modernization could not be steadily extended all over the world, the emergence of other so-called "modernities" in conflict with this would be disastrous for mankind, and those "modernities" mean fundamentalism, ultra-nationalism, irrationalism, oriental mysticism, etc.' (Tu 2001).

7 Industrialization will lead to increasingly similar social and cultural modalities.

8 According to Taylor's theory of alternative modernities, as different cultures of the various non-Western countries would exert an impact on the modernization process and its results, the results of modernization of non-Western countries must be the emergence of other similar modernities different from Western modernity, or what can be called the non-Western pattern of multiple modernities.

9 Eisenstadt believed that, although the modernity emerging in the Western world has had global consequences, such consequences are not the universal transplant of the Western modernity pattern but the emergence of modernity states of different characteristics in non-Western countries and regions. Therefore, Eisenstadt once clearly remarked that modernization and Westernization are not the same thing (Eisenstadt 2000).

10 Re-quoted from Jin Yaoji (Jin 2002: 87).

11 It was said that Chen Xujing was the first person in China who proposed 'wholesale Westernization', whereas Hu Shi only put forward the thought of sufficient modernization instead of 'wholesale Westernization'.

Bibliography

Adams, J.S. (1963) 'Toward an understanding of inequity', *Journal of Abnormal and Social Psychology*, 67: 422–36.

Agarwala, Ramgopal (2002) *The Rise of China: Threat or Opportunity?* New Delhi: Bookwell.

Akerlof, George (1970) 'The market for "lemons": quality uncertainty and the market mechanism', *Quarterly Journal of Economics*, 84: 488–500.

Alchian, A.A. (1984) 'Specificity, specialization, and coalitions', *Journal of Institutional and Theoretical Economics*, 140: 34–9.

Aldridge, Stephen (2001) *Social Mobility*, London: Performance and Innovation Unit.

An, Zuozhang (ed.) (1986) *Zhongguoshi Jianbian [A Short Course in Chinese History]*, Jinan: Shangdong Jiaoyu Chubanshe.

Anderson, Benedict (1991) *Imagined Communities: Reflections on the Origin and Spread of Nationalism*, London and New York: Verso.

Anderson, J.R. (1980) *Cognitive Psychology and its Implications*, San Francisco, CA: Freeman.

Aoki, Masahiko (2001) *Toward a Comparative Institutional Analysis*, Cambridge, MA: MIT Press.

Arrow, Kenneth J. (1962) *The Theory of Economic Progress*, New York: Shocken Books.

—— (1969) 'The organization of economic activity: issues pertinent to the choice of market versus nonmarket allocation', *The Analysis and Evaluation of Public Expenditure: The PPB System*, Vol. 1, US Joint Economic Committee, 91st Congress, 1st Session, Washington, DC: US Government Printing Office.

—— (1971) 'Political and economic evaluation of social effects and externalities', in M. Intrilligator (ed.) *Frontiers of Quantitative Economics*, Amsterdam: North-Holland.

—— (1974) *The Limits of Organization*, New York: W.W. Norton.

Ayres, C. E. (1961) *Toward a Reasonable Society*, Austin, TX: University of Texas Press.

Bailey, Adrian J. and Cooke, Thomas J. (1998) 'Family migration and employment: the importance of migration history and gender', *International Regional Science Review*, 21(2): 99–118.

Baker, Hugh (1968) *Sheung Shui: A Chinese Lineage Village*, Stanford, CA: Stanford University Press.

Barnard, C. (1938) *The Function of the Executive*, Cambridge, MA: Harvard University Press.

Baurmann, Michael (2002) *The Market of Virtue: Morality and Commitment in a Liberal Society*, The Hague: Kluwer Law International.

Bell, Daniel (1973) *The Coming of Post-Industrial Society*, New York: Basic Books.

—— (1976) *The Cultural Contradictions of Capitalism*, New York: Basic Books.

Benedict, R. (1946) *The Crysanthemum and the Sword: Patterns of Japanese Culture*, Boston, MA: Houghton-Mifflin.

Biggart, Nicole Woolsey (2001) 'Banking on each other: the situational logic of rotating savings and credit associations', *Advances in Qualitative Organization Research*, 3: 129–53.

Binswanger, H.P. and Ruttan, V.W. (1978) *Induced Innovation: Technology, Institutions, and Development*, Baltimore, MD: Johns Hopkins University Press.

Blau, P.M. (1955) *The Dynamics of Bureaucracy: A Study of Interpersonal Relations in Two Government Agencies*, Chicago, IL: Chicago University Press.

—— (1964) *Exchange and Power in Social Life*, New York: John Wiley & Sons.

—— (1975) *Approaches to the Study of Social Structure*, New York: The Free Press.

Boas, Franz ([1911] 1983) *The Mind of Primitive Man*, New York: Macmillan. Reprinted in 1983 by Greenwood Press.

Boon, James (1972) *From Symbolism to Structuralism: Lévi-Strauss in a Literary Tradition*, New York: Harper & Row.

Borjas, George J. (1987) 'Self-selection and the earnings of immigrants', *The American Economic Review*, 77(4): 531–53.

Bourdieu, Pierre (1984) *Distinction: A Social Critique of the Judgement of Taste*, London: Routledge.

—— (1986) 'The forms of capital', in John G. Richardson (ed.) *Handbook of Theory and Research for the Sociology of Education*, New York: Greenwood Press.

Bowles, S. (2001) *Economic Institutions and Behavior: An Evolutionary Approach to Microeconomic Theory*, Princeton, NJ: Princeton University Press.

Bradach, J.L. and Ecceles, R.G. (1989) 'Markets versus hierarchies: from ideal types to plural forms', in W.R. Scott (ed.) *Annual Review of Sociology*, 15: 97–118.

Braudel, Fernand (1981) *Civilization and Capitalism, 15th–18th Centuries, Vol. 1: The Structure of Everyday Life*, New York: Harper & Row.

Buchanan, James M. (1978) 'Markets, states, and the extent of morals', *The American Economic Review*, 68: 362–8.

Burke, Peter (1992) *History and Social Theory*, Cambridge: Polity Press.

Burt, Ronald S. (1980) 'Autonomy in a social topology', *American Journal of Sociology*, 85: 892–925.

—— (1992) *Structural Holes: The Social Structure of Competition*, Cambridge, MA: Harvard University Press.

—— (2000) 'The network structure of social capital', in Robert I. Sutton and Barry M. Staw (eds) *Research in Organizational Behavior*, Greenwich, CT: JAI Press.

Butterfield, Fox (1964) *Exchange and Power in Social Life*, New York: Wiley.

—— (1983) *China: Alive in Bitter Sea*, London: Coronet Books.

Byrd, W.A. and Lin, Q. (eds) (1990) *China's Rural Industry: Structure, Development, and Reform*, Oxford: Oxford University Press.

Cai, Fang (1996) 'An economic analysis for labor migration and mobility', *China Social Sciences Quarterly*, Spring: 120–35.

Callahan, W.A. (2002) *Diaspora, Cosmopolitanism and Nationalism: Overseas Chinese and Neo-Nationalism in China and Thailand*, Working Paper Series No. 35. Hong Kong: Southeast Asia Research Centre, City University of Hong Kong.

Casson, M. (1991) *The Economics of Business Culture: Game Theory, Transaction Costs and Economic Performance*, Oxford: Clarendon Press.

—— (1995) *The Organization of International Business: Studies in the Economics of Trust*, Aldershot: Edward Elgar.

—— and Godley, A. (eds) (2000) *Cultural Factors in Economic Growth*, Berlin: Springer.

Chamberlain, Neil W. (1962) 'The institutional economics of John R. Commons', in Joseph Dorfman, C.E. Ayers, Neil W. Chamberlain, Simon Kuznets and R.A. Gordon (eds) (1962) *Institutional Economics: Veblen, Commons, Mitchell Reconsidered*, Berkeley, CA: University of California Press.

Chan, Anita, Madsen, Richard and Unger, Jonathan (1984) *Chen Village: The Recent History of a Peasant Community in Mao's China*, Berkeley, CA: University of California Press.

Chan, Chi-chao (1987) 'A theoretical analysis and practical research on the face mentality', in Yang Kuo-shu (ed.) *The Psychology and Behavior of Chinese People*, Taipei: Laureate Publications Co.

Chan, Kam Wing, Ta Liu and Yunyan Yang (1999) '*Hukou* and non-*hukou* migrations in China: comparisons and contrasts', *International Journal of Population Geography*, 5: 425–48.

Chang, Pei-kang (1949) *Agriculture and Industrialization*, Cambridge, MA: Harvard University Press.

Chang, S.D. and Kwok, R.Y. (1990) 'The urbanization of rural China', in R.Y. Kwok, W. Parish and A.G.O. Yeh (eds) *Chinese Urban Reform: What Model Now?* New York: M. E. Sharpe.

Chen, Baoliang (1996) *Zhongguo de She yu Hui [Societies and Associations in China]*, Hangzhou: Zhejiang Renmin Chubanshe.

Chen, Jiyuan and He Mengbi (Carsten Herrmann-Pillath) (eds) (1996) *Dangdai Zhongguo de Cunzhuang Jingji yu Cunluo Wenhua [Village Economy and Culture in Contemporary China]*, Taiyuan: Shanxi Jingji Chubanshe.

Chen, Liang (1974) *Chen Liang Wenji [Collected Works of Chen Liang]*, Bejing: Zhonghua Shuju.

Chiao, Chien (1987) 'A discussion of relationships', in Yang Kuo-shu (ed.) *Zhongguoren de Xinli [Chinese Psychology]*, Taipei: Guiguan Chuban Gongsi.

Christiansen, Flemming (1990a) 'The de-rustication of the Chinese peasant? Peasant household reactions to the rural reforms in China since 1978, unpublished Ph.D dissertation, University of Leiden.

—— (1990b) 'The ambiguities of labour and market in periurban communities in China during the reform decade', in Jørgen Delman, Clemens S. Østergaard and Flemming Christiansen (eds) *Remaking Peasant China: Problems of Rural Development and Institutions at the Start of the 1990s*, Aarhus: Aarhus University Press.

—— (1993), 'The legacy of the mock dual economy: Chinese labour in transition, 1978–1992', *Economy and Society*, 22(4): 411–36.

—— (2003) *Chinatown, Europe: An Exploration of Overseas Chinese Identity in the 1990s*, London; New York: RoutledgeCurzon.

—— and Zhang Junzuo (1998) 'The village revisited', in Flemming Christiansen and Zhang Junzuo (eds) *Village Inc.: Chinese Rural Society in the 1990s*, London: Curzon Press.

Chu, Cathy Ruey-ling (1987) 'The social interaction of the Chinese: on the question of face', in Yang Kuo-shu (ed.) *Zhongguoren de Xinli [Chinese Psychology]*, Taipei: Guiguan Chuban Gongsi.

Coase, Ronald H. (1937) 'The nature of the firm', *Economica*, 4: 386–405; reprinted in O.E. Williamson and S.G. Winter (eds) (1991) *The Nature of the Firm*, Oxford: Oxford University Press.

—— (1960) 'The problem of social cost', *Journal of Law and Economics*, 3: 1–44.

—— (1988) *The Firm, the Market, and the Law*, Chicago, IL: University of Chicago Press.

Coate, Stephen and Ravallion, Martin (1993) 'Reciprocity without commitment: characterization and performance of informal insurance arrangements', *Journal of Development Economics*, 40(1): 1–24.

Cohen, Myron (1990) 'Lineage organization in North China', *The Journal of Asian Studies*, 49: 509–34.

Coleman, James S. (1988) 'Social capital and the creation of human capital', *Amerian Journal of Sociology*, 94 (supplement): 94–120.

—— (1990) *Foundations of Social Theory*, Cambridge, MA: Harvard University Press.

Commons, John R. (1932) 'The problem of correlating law, economics and ethics', *Wisconsin Law Review*, 8: 3–26.

—— ([1934] 1990) *Institutional Economics: Its Place in Political Economy*, New Brunswick, NJ: Transaction Publishers. Originally published in 1934 by the Macmillan Company.

—— (1950) *The Economics of Collective Action*, Madison, WI: University of Wisconsin Press.

Cook, Karen S., Emerson, Richard M., Gillmore, Mary R. and Yamagishi, Toshio (1983) 'The distribution of power in exchange networks: theory and experimental results', *American Journal of Sociology*, 89: 275–305.

CPC Central Committee (2002) 'Zhongguo Gongchandang Dangzhang' ['Constitution of the Communist Party of China'], in *Zhongguo Gongchandang di Shiliuci Quanguo Daibiao Dahui Wenjian Huibian [A Compilation of the Documents of the Sixteenth National Congress of the CPC]*, Beijing: Renmin Chubanshe.

Dasgupta, Biblab (1977) *Village Society and Labour Use*, Bombay, Calcutta, Madras: Oxford University Press.

Dasgupta, P. (1988) 'Trust as a commodity', in D. Gambetta (ed.) *Trust: Making and Breaking Cooperative Relations*, Oxford: Blackwell.

—— and Serageldin, I. (eds) (1999) *Social Capital: A Multifaceted Perspective*, Washington, DC: The World Bank.

DaVanzo, J. (1981) 'Microeconomic approaches to studying migration decisions', in G.F. De Jong and R.W. Gardner (eds) *Migration Decision Making: Multidisciplinary Approaches to Micro-Level Studies in Developed and Developing Countries*, New York: Pergamon.

David, Paul A. (1985) 'Clio and the economics of QWERTY', *American Economic Review*, 75(2): 332–7.

—— (1986) 'Understanding the economics of QWERTY: the necessity of history', in William N. Parker (ed.) *Economic History and the Modern Economist*, Oxford: Blackwell.

—— (1988) *The Future of Path-Dependent Equilibrium Economics: From the Economics of Technology to the Economics of Almost Everything?* Stanford, CA: Center for Economic Policy Research, Stanford University.

—— (1992) 'Path dependency and the predictability in dynamic system with local network externalities: a paradigm for historical economics', in C. Freeman and D. Foray (eds) *Technology and the Wealth of Nations*, London: Pinter.

Davin, Delia (1996) 'Migration and rural women in China: a look at the gendered impact of large-scale migration', *Journal of International Development*, 8(5): 655–65.

—— (1999), *International Migration in Contemporary China*, New York: St Martin's Press.

Deutsch, M. (1962) 'Cooperation and trust: some theoretical notes', in M.R. Jones (ed.) *Nebraska Symposium on Motivation*, Lincoln, NE: University of Nebraska Press.

Drobak, John N. and Nye, John V.C. (eds) (1977) *The Frontiers of the New Institutional Economics*, New York: Academic Press.

Du, Xuncheng (1993) *Chuantong Zhongguo Lunli yu Xiandai Zibenzhuyi [Traditional Chinese Ethic and Modern Capitalism]*, Shanghai: Shanghai Shehui Kexueyuan Chubanshe.

Duara, Prasenjit (1988) *Culture, Power and the State: Rural North China 1900–1942*, Stanford, CA: Stanford University Press.

Duncan, Jennifer and Li Ping (2001) *Women and Land Tenure in China: A Study of Women's Land Rights in Dongfang County, Hainan Province*, Seattle, WA: Rural Development Institute.

Durkheim, Emile (1933) *The Division of Labour in Society*, New York: Macmillan.

Ebanks, G.E. and Cheng, C. (1990) 'China: a unique urbanization model', *Asia-Pacific Population Journal*, 5(3): 29–50.

Eggertsson, Thrainn (1990) *Economic Behaviour and Institutions*, Cambridge: Cambridge University Press.

Eisenstadt, S.N. (1966) *Modernization: Protest and Change*, Englewood Cliffs, NJ: Prentice-Hall.

—— (2000) 'Multiple modernities', *Daedalus*, Special issue on *Multiple Modernities*, Winter: 1–3.

Elias, Norbert (1976) *Über den Prozess der Zivilisation: Soziogenetische und Psychogenetische Untersuchungen, Vol. 1: Wandlungen des Verhaltens in den weltlichen Oberschichten des Abendlandes Suhrkamp*. English edition edited by Eric Dunning, Johan Goudsblom and Stephen Mennell (2000) *The Civilising Process*, Oxford: Blackwell.

Elster, J. (1979) *Ulysses and the Sirens: Studies in Rationality and Irrationality*, Cambridge: Cambridge University Press.

—— (1989) *The Cement of Society: A Study of Social Order*, Cambridge: Cambridge University Press.

Epstein, Stephan R. (2000) 'Constitutions, liberty, and growth in pre-modern Europe', in M. Casson and A. Godley (eds) *Cultural Factors in Economic Growth*, Berlin: Springer.

Etzioni, Amitai (1988) *The Moral Dimension: Toward A New Economics*, New York: The Free Press.

Fairbank, John King (1958) *The United States and China*, Cambridge, MA: Harvard University Press.

Fei, Xiaotong (Fei, Hsiao-tung) (1939) *Peasant Life in China: A Field Study of Country Life in the Yangtze Valley*, New York: E.P. Dutton & Company.

—— (Fei, Hsiao-tung) (1947) *Xiangtu Zhongguo [Country China]*, Shanghai: Shanghai Guanchashe.

—— (1986) *Jiangcun Jingji [Peasant Life in China]*, Nanjing: Jiangsu Renmin Chubanshe.

Feng, Tianyu, He Xiaoming and Zhou Jiming (1991) *Zhonghua Wenhuashi [History of Chinese Culture]*, Shanghai: Shanghai Renmin Chubanshe.

Feyerabend, Paul Karl (1975) *Against Method: Outline of an Anarchistic Theory of Knowledge*, London: New Left Books.

Foa, E.B. and Foa, U.G. (1976) 'Resource theory of social exchange', in J.W. Thibaut, J.T. Spence and R.C. Carson (eds) *Contemporary Topics in Social Psychology*, Morriston, NJ: General Learning Press.

Ford Foundation (2001) *Labor mobility in China: an evaluation of a Ford Foundation program in Beijing 1997–2001*, Beijing: Ford Foundation, Beijing Office.

Freedman, Maurice (1958) *Lineage Organization in Southeastern China*, London: Athlone Press.

—— (1966) *Chinese Lineage and Society: Fukien and Kwangrung*, London: Athlone Press.

Freeman, Linton C. (1977) 'A set of measures of centrality based on betweenness', *Sociometry*, 40: 35–40.

Friedman, Edward, Pickowicz, Paul G. and Selden, Mark (1991) *Chinese Village, Socialist State*, New Haven, CT: Yale University Press.

Fukuyama, F. (1995) *Trust: The Social Virtues and the Creation of Prosperity*, New York: Free Press.

Fuller, L. (1954) 'American legal philosophy at mid century', *Journal of Legal Education*, 6(4): 457–85.

Fuxing Science & Technology Shareholding Co., Ltd. (ed.) (2003) *2002 Annual Report of Hubei Fuxing Science & Technology Shareholding Co., Ltd.* Author collected the material from his field survey to the company.

Gambetta, D. (1988) 'Can we trust trust?', in D. Gambetta (ed.) *Trust: Making and Breaking Cooperative Relations*, Oxford: Basil Blackwell.

Gao, Xiaoxian (forthcoming) 'Rural China entering the 21th century: marriage, family and women', unpublished paper, Shaanxi: Shaanxi Women's Federation.

Garnaut, Ross and Yiping Huang (eds) (2001) *Growth without Miracles: Readings on the Chinese Economy in the Era of Reform*, Oxford: Oxford University Press.

Geertz, Clifford ([1966] 1973) *The Interpretation of Cultures*, New York: Basic Books.

Giddens, Anthony (1984) *The Constitution of Society*, Berkeley, CA: University of California Press.

—— (1990) *The Consequences of Modernity*, Cambridge: Polity Press.

—— (1991) *Modernity and Self-Identity: Self and Society in the Late Modern Age*, Cambridge: Polity Press.

Ginsburg, Norton, Koppel, Bruce and McGee, T.G. (eds) (1991) *The Extended Metropolis, Settlement Transition in Asia*, Honolulu, HI: University of Hawaii Press.

Glaeser, Bernhard (ed.) (1987) *Learning from China?* London: Allen and Unwin.

Goffman, Erving (1955) 'On facework: an analysis of ritual elements in social interaction', *Psychiatry*, 81: 213–31.

Goodhart, Charles and Chenggang Xu (1996) 'The rise of China as an economic power', *National Institute Economic Review*, 155: 56.

Granovetter, Mark S. (1973) 'The strength of weak ties', *The American Journal of Sociology*, 78(6): 1360–80.

—— (1985) 'Economic action and social structure: the problem of embeddedness', *American Journal of Sociology*, 91: 481–510.

Greenwald, A.G. and Banaji, M.R. (1995) 'Implicit social cognitions: attitudes, self-esteem, and stereotypes', *Psychological Review*, 102: 4–27.

Greenwood, M. J. (1969) 'An analysis of the determinants of geographic labor mobility in the United States', *Review of Economics and Statistics*, 51: 189–94.

—— (1985) 'Human migration: theory, models, and empirical studies', *Journal of Regional Sciences*, 25(4): 521–44.

Greif, A. (1989) 'Reputation and coalitions in medieval trade: evidence on the Maghribi traders', *Journal of Economic History*, 49: 857–82.

—— (1990) *Culture Shift in Advanced Industrial Society*, Princeton, NJ: Princeton University Press.

—— (1993) 'Contract enforceability and economic institutions in early trade: the Maghribi traders' coalition', *American Economic Review*, 83: 525–48.

—— (1994) 'Cultural beliefs and the organization of society: a historical and theoretical reflection on collectivist and individualist societies', *Journal of Political Economy*, 102: 912–50.

Greif, A., Milgrom, P. and Wingast, B. (1994) 'Coordination, commitment and enforcement: the case of the merchant guild', *Journal of Political Economy*, 102: 745–76.

Gu, S. and Jian, X. (eds) (1994) *Dangdai Zhongguo de Liudong Renkou yu Chengshihua [Population Floating and Urbanization in Contemporary China]*, Wuhan: Wuhan Daxue Chubanshe.

Gulati, R. (1995) 'Does familiarity breed trust? The implications of repeated ties for contractual choice in alliances', *Academy of Management Journal*, 38: 85–112.

Guldin, G.E. (ed.) (1992) *Urbanizing China*, London: Greenwood Press.

Guojia Tongjiju (National Bureau of Statistics – NBS) (ed.) (1979) *Zhongguo Tongji Nianjian 1979 [China Statistical Yearbook 1979]*, Beijing: Zhongguo Tongji Chubanshe

—— (ed.) (1984) *Zhongguo Tongji Nianjian 1984 [China Statistics Yearbook 1984]*, Beijing: Zhongguo Tongji Chubanshe.

—— (ed.) (1985) *Zhongguo Tongji Nianjian 1985 [China Statistics Yearbook 1985]*, Beijing: Zhongguo Tongji Chubanshe.

—— (ed.) (1990) *Zhongguo Tongji Nianjian 1989 [China Statistical Yearbook 1989]*, Beijing: Zhongguo Tongji Chubanshe.

—— (ed.) (1995) *Zhongguo Tongji Nianjian 1994 [China Statistical Yearbook 1994]*, Beijing: Zhongguo Tongji Chubanshe.

—— (2000) *Zhongguo Tongji Nianjian 2000 [China Statistics Yearbook 2000]*, Beijing: Zhongguo Tongji Chubanshe.

—— (ed.) (2003) *Zhongguo Tongji Nianjian 2002 [China Statistical Yearbook 2002]*, Beijing: Zhongguo Tongji Chubanshe.

—— (2004) *Zhongguo Tongji Nianjian 2003 [China Statistical Yearbook 2003]*, Beijing: Zhongguo Tongji Chubanshe.

Guthrie, Douglas (1998) 'The declining significance of Guanxi in China's Economic transition', *The China Quarterly*, 154: 254–82.

Hamilton, Gary (ed.) (1991) *Business Networks and Economic Development in East and Southeast Asia*, Hong Kong: Center for Asian Studies, University of Hong Kong.

Hamilton, Gary G. and Biggart, Nicole Woolsey (1988) 'Market, culture and authority: a comparative analysis of management and organization in the Far East', *American Journal of Sociology*, 94 (Supplement): S52–S94.

Hare, Denise (1999) '"Push" versus "pull" factors in migration outflows and returns: determinants of migration status and spell duration among China's rural population', *Journal of Development Studies*, 35(3): 45–72.

Harrison, Lawrence E. (1985) *Underdevelopment is a State of Mind: The Latin American Case*, Lanham, MD: University Press of America and the Center for International Affairs, Harvard University.

—— (1998) *The Pan-American Dream: Do Latin America's Cultural Values Discourage True Partnership With the United States and Canada*, Boulder, CO: Westview Press.

—— and Huntington, Samuel P. (eds) (2000) *Culture Matters: How Values Shape Human Progress*, New York: Basic Books.

Hatada, Takashi (1972) *Chugoku Sonraku to Kyodotai Riron [Theory of 'Community' in Chinese Village]*, Tokyo: Iwanami.

Hatton, T.J. and Williamson, J.G. (1994) 'What drove the mass migration from Europe in the late nineteenth century?' *Population and Development Review*, 20(3): 533–59.

Hayami, Yujiro (2001) *Development Economics: From Poverty to the Wealth of Nations*. New York: Oxford University Press.

—— and Kawagoe, T. (1993) *The Agrarian Origins of Commerce and Industry: A Study of Peasant Marketing in Indonesia*, New York: St Martin's Press.

—— and Kikuchi, M. (1981) *Asian Village Economy at the Crossroads: An Economic Approach to Institutional Change*, Baltimore, MD: Johns Hopkins University Press.

Hayek, Friedrich A. (1945) 'The use of knowledge in society', *The American Economic Review*, 35: 519–30.

—— (1973) *Law, Legislation and Liberty, Volume 1: Roles and Order*, Chicago, IL: University of Chicago Press.

—— (1988) *The Fatal Conceit: The Errors of Socialism*, Chicago, IL: The University of Chicago Press.

He, Mengbi (Herrmann-Pillath, Carsten) (1993) 'Feizhengshi yueshu, wenhua he cong jihua dao shichang de guodu' ['Informal constraints, culture and Chinese transition from planning to market economy'], in Zhongguo Jingji Xuehui [Chinese Economists' Society] (eds) *Xiaolü, Gongping yu Shenhua Gaige Kaifang [Efficiency, Equity and Deepening Reforms and Opening-up]*, Beijing: Beijing Daxue Chubanshe.

—— (1996) *Wangluo, Wenhua yu Huaren Shehui Jingji Xingwei [Networks, Culture and the Chinese Socio-economic Behaviour]*, Taiyuan: Shanxi Jingji Chubanshe.

—— (2000a) 'Kexue yu wenhua zuowei zhuanxing guocheng zhong shehui de zhixu liliang' ['Science and culture as the factors of social order in the transition process'], in He Mengbi (Carsten Herrmann-Pillath) (ed.) *Deguo Zhixu Zhengce Lilun yu Shijian [Theory and Practice of Order Policies in Germany]*, Shanghai: Shanghai Renmin Chubanshe.

—— (2000b) 'Shichang jingji zhong shequ de zuoyong' ['The function of community in market economy), in He Mengbi (Carsten Herrmann-Pillath) (ed.) *Deguo Zhixu Zhengce Lilun yu Shijian [Theory and Practice of Order Policies in Germany]*, Shanghai: Shanghai Renmin Chubanshe.

He, Annai (Heufers, Rainer) and Hu Biliang (eds) (2000) *Nongcun Jinrong yu Fazhan [Rural Finance and Development]*, Beijing: Jingji Kexue Chubanshe.

Heath, A. and C. Payne (2000) 'Social mobility', in A. Halsey with J. Webb (eds) *Twentieth-Century British Social Trends*, Basingstoke: Macmillan Press.

Heider, F. (1958) *The Psychology of Interpersonal Relations*, New York: Wiley.

Heilbroner, Robert L. and Milberg, William (1972) *The Making of Economic Society*, Englewood Cliffs, NJ: Prentice-Hall.

Herder, F. (1958) *The Psychology of Interpersonal Relations*, New York: Wiley.

Herrmann-Pillath, Carsten (1992) 'Informal constraints, culture and incremental transition from plan to market', in Wagener, Hans-Jürgen (ed.) *On the Theory and Policy of Systemic Change*, Heidelberg: Physica-Verlag.

—— (1993) 'New knowledge as creation: notes when reading Nietzsche on evolution, power, and knowledge', *Journal of Social and Evolutionary System*, 16(1): 25–43.

—— (1994), 'Evolutonary rationality, "Homo Economy", and the foundations of social order', *Journal of Social and Evolutionary System*, 17(1): 41–69.

—— (2000a) 'Social capital and networks: a proposal for conceptual integration', Working Paper no. 63, Witten: University of Witten/Herdecke.

—— (2000b) 'Culture and observation in the study of economic system', Working Paper no. 52, Witten: University of Witten/Herdecke.

—— (2004) 'The true story of wine and cloth, or building blocks of an evolutionary political economy of international trade', paper presented at Sino-German Workshop on Evolutionary Economics, Beijing, March.

Hickey, Gerald C. (1964) *Village in Vietnam*, New Haven, CT: Yale University Press.

Hicks, John (1969) *A Theory of Economic History*, New York: Oxford University Press.

Hinton, William (1966) *Fanshen: A Documentary of Revolution in a Chinese Village*, New York: Vintage Books.

Ho, D.Y.F. (1975) 'On the concept of face', *American Journal of Sociology*, 81: 867–84.

Hodgson, Geoffrey M. (1988) *Economics and Institutions: A Manifesto for a Modern Institutional Economics*, Cambridge: Polity Press and Philadelphia, PA: University of Pennsylvania Press.

Homans, G.C. (1961) *Social Behavior: Its Elementary Forms*, New York: Harcourt Brace Jovanovich.

Hu, Biliang (1996) *Zhongguo Cunluo de Zhidu Bianqian yu Quanli Fenpei: Shaanxisheng Shangzhoushi Wangjiancun Diaocha [Institutional Change and Power Distribution in Rural China: Survey Report of Wangjian Village, Shangzhou City of Shaanxi Province]*, Taiyuan: Shanxi Jingji Chubanshe.

—— (1998) *Fazhan Lilun yu Zhongguo [Development Theory and China]*, Beijing: Renmin Chubanshe.

—— and Hu, Shunyan (1996) *Zhongguo Nongcun de Qiye Zuzhi yu Shequ Fazhan – Hubeisheng Hanchuanxian Duanjiacun Diaocha [Enterprise Organization and Community Development in Rural China: A Survey on Duanjia Village, Hanchuan County, Hubei Province]*, Taiyuan: Shanxi Jingji Chubanshe.

—— and Zheng, Hongliang (1996) *Xiangzhenqiye yu Zhongguo Xiangcun Fazhan [Township Enterprises and Rural Development in China]*, Taiyuan: Shanxi Jingji Chubanshe.

Hu, H.C. (1944) 'The Chinese concept of face', *American Anthropologist*, 46: 45–64.

Hu, Yunzhao (ed.) (2002) *Hubei Nianjian [Hubei Yearbook]*, Wuhan: Hubei Nianjian Chubanshe.

Huang, Philip C.C. (1985) *The Peasant Economy and Social Change in North China*, Stanford, CA: Stanford University Press.

—— (1990) *The Peasant Family and Rural Development in the Yangzi Delta, 1950–1988*, Stanford, CA: Stanford University Press.

—— (1998) 'Theory and the study of modern Chinese history: four traps and a question', *Modern China*, 24(2): 183–208.

Huang, Shu-min (1989) *The Spiral Road: Change in a Chinese Village Through the Eyes of a Communist Party Lerder*, Boulder, CO: Westview Press.

Huang, Xiyi (1998) 'Two-way changes: kinship in contemporary rural China', in Flemming Christiansen and Zhang Junzuo (eds) *Village Inc.: Chinese Rural Society in the 1990s*, London: Curzon Press.

Hume, David ([1739] 1965) 'A treatise of human nature', in T.H. Green and T.H. Grose (eds) *The Philosophical Works of David Hume*, Oxford: Clarendon Press.

Huntington, Samuel P. (1996) *The Clash of Civilizations and the Remaking of World Order*, New York: Simon & Schuster.

Huo, Hongwei (2002) 'Woguo beifang yige nongzhuang de hunyinquan yanjiu – dui shandongsheng jiyangxian jiangdianxiang jiazhaicun de gean yanjiu' ['Marriage distance in one of the northern villages in China: case study of Jiazhai village, Jiangdian township, Jiyang county of Shandong province'), *Shehui [Society Magazine]*, Issue 12: 36–40.

Hurwicz, L. (1993) 'Toward a framework for analyzing institutions and institutional change', in Samuel Bowles, Herbert Gintis and Bo Gustaffson (eds) *Markets and Democracy: Participation, Accountability, and Efficiency*, Cambridge: Cambridge University Press: 51–67.

Hwang, Kwang-kuo (1987) 'Face and favor: the Chinese power game', *American Journal of Sociology*, 92(4): 944–74.

Inglehart, Ronald (1977) *The Silent Revolution: Changing Values and Political Styles in Advanced Industrial Society*, Princeton, NJ: Princeton University Press.

—— (1997) *Modernizations and Postmodernization: Cultural, Economic, and Political Change in Forty-Three Societies*, Princeton, NJ: Princeton University Press.

—— (2000) 'Culture and democracy', in Lawrence E. Harrison and Samuel P. Huntington (eds) (2000) *Culture Matters: How Values Shape Human Progress*, New York: Basic Books, 80–97.

Jevons, William Stanley (1871) *Theory of Political Economy*, New York: Kelly and Millman.

Jiang, Wenheng (1999) 'Zhengdun nongcun hezuo jijinhui de jidian sikao' ['Reflections on rectifying rural cooperative foundations'], *Jingji Gaige yu Jingji Fazhan Zazhi [Economic Reform and Development Magazine]*, Issue 21.

Jiang, Zemin (2002) 'Quanmian jianshe xiaokang shehui, kaichuan zhongguo teshe shehui zhuyi shiye xinjumian' ['Build a well-off society in an all-round way and enter a new phase in building socialism with Chinese characteristics'], in *Zhongguo Gongchandang de Shiliuci Quanguo Daibiao Dahui Wenjian Huibian [A Compilation of the Documents of the Sixteenth National Congress of the CPC]*, Beijing: Renmin Chubanshe: 1–56.

Jin, Hehui and Yingyi Qian (1998) 'Public versus private ownership of firms: evidence from rural China', *Quarterly Journal of Economics*, August Issue: 773–808.

Jin, Yaoji (King, Ambrose) (1989a) 'Renji guanxi zhong renqing zhi fenxi' ['An analysis of *renqing* in interpersonal relations'], in Yang Guoshu (ed.) *Zhongguoren de Xinli [Chinese Psychology]*, Taipei: Guiguan Chuban Gongsi.

—— (1989b) 'Mian, chi yu zhongguoren xingwei zhi fenxi' ['An analysis of face, shame and the behavior of the Chinese'], in Yang Guoshu (ed.) *Zhongguoren de Xinli [Chinese Psychology]*, Taipei: Guiguan Chuban Gongsi.

—— (1991) 'Kuan-his and network building: a sociological interpretation', *Daedalus*, 120(2): 63–84.

—— (2002) *Jin Yaojin Zixuanji [Selected Works of Jin Yaoji]*, Shanghai: Shanghai Jiaoyu Chubanshe.

Johnson, Chalmers (1982) *MITI and the Japanese Miracle*, Stanford, CA: Stanford University Press.

Jones, E.E. (1964) *Ingratiation: A Social Psychological Analysis*, New York: Appleton.

Kandori, Michihiro (1992) 'Repeated games played by overlapping generations of players', *Review of Economic Studies*, 59(1): 81–92.

Kasper, W. and Streit, M.E. (1998) *Institutional Economics: Social Order and Public Policy*, Northampton, MA: Edward Elgar.

Katona, G. (1951) *Psychological Analysis of Economic Behavior*, New York: McGraw-Hill.

Kerr, Clark, Dunlop, John T., Harbison, Frederick H. and Myers, Charles A. (1960) *Industrialism and Industrial Man*, Cambridge, MA: Harvard University Press.

Kirkby, R.J.R. (1985) *Urbanization in China: Town and Country in a Developing Economy 1949–2000 AD*, New York: Columbia University Press.

Kluckhohn, C. (1962) *Culture and Behavior*, New York: Free Press.

Knight, F. (1921) *Risk, Uncertainty and Profit*, Boston, MA: Houghton Mifflin.

Knight, John, Lina Song and Huaibin Jia (1999) 'Chinese rural migrants in urban enterprises: three perspectives, *Journal of Development Studies*, 35(3): 73–104.

Koentjaraningrat, Raden Mas (ed.) (1967) *Villages in Indonesia*, Ithaca, NY and London: Cornell University Press.

Kong, Jingyuan (1990) 'Shougongye yu zhongguo jingji bianqian' ['Handicrafts and China's economic change'], in Peng Zeyi (ed.) *Zhongguo Shehui Jingji Bianqian [China's Social and Economic Change]*, Beijing: Zhongguo Caizheng Jingji Chubanshe.

Kroeber, A.L. and Kluckhohn, C. (1952) *Culture: A Critical Review of Concepts and Definitions*, New York: Random House.

Kuznets, S. (1955) 'Economic growth and income inequality', *American Economic Review*, 45(1): 1–28.

Kwong, Peter (1997) *Forbidden Workers: Illegal Chinese Immigrants and American Labor*, New York: The New Press.

Kyle, David and Liang, Zai (2001) 'Migration merchants: human smuggling from Ecuador and China', Working paper no. 43, Davis, CA: Center for Comparative Immigration Studies, University of California at Davis.

La Ferrara, Eliana (2003) 'Kin groups and reciprocity: a model of credit transactions in Ghana', *American Economic Review*, 93(5): 1730–51.

Landa, Janet Tai (1997) *Trust, Ethnicity, and Identity: Beyond the New Institutional Economics of Ethnic Trading Networks, Contract Law, and Gift-Exchange*, Ann Arbor, MI: University of Michigan Press.

Laquian, A.A. (1997) 'The effects of national urban strategy and regional development policy on patterns of urban growth in China', in G.W. Jones and P. Visaria (eds) *Urbanization in Large Developing Countries: China, Indonesia, Brazil, and India*, Oxford: Claredon Press.

Lee, Everett S. (1966) 'A theory of migration', *Demography*, 3: 47–57.

Lee, Yok-Shiu F. (1989) 'Small towns and China's urbanization level', *China Quarterly*, 120: 771–86.

Lei, Jiejing (ed.) (1994) *Gaige Yilai Nongcun Hunyin yu Jiating de Xinbianhua [New Changes of Marriage and Family Households since the Reform in Rural China]*, Beijing: Beijing Daxue Chubanshe.

Lewis, W. Arthur (1954)'Economic development with unlimited supplies of labour', *The Manchester School of Economic and Social Studies*, 22: 139–191.

Li, Daoxiang (2000) *Li: Renji Wenmin de Guifan [Rites: Standards for Interpersonal Civilization]*, Beijing: Hongqi Chubanshe.

Li, David (1996) 'A theory of ambiguous property rights in transition economies: the case of the Chinese non-state sector', *Journal of Comparative Economics*, 23(1): 1–19.

Li, Guoqing (2001) *Riben Shehui: Jiegoutezheng Jiqi Bianqian [Japanese Society: Structural Features and its Changes]*, Beijing: Gaodeng Jiaoyu Chubanshe.

Li, Jing (1996) *Zhongguo Cunzhuang de Shangye Chuantong yu Qiye Fazhan – Shanxisheng Yuanpingshi Tunwacun Diaocha [Commercial Tradition and Enterprise Development in Rural China – A Survey of Tunwa Village, Yuanping City, Shanxi Province]*, Taiyuan: Shanxi Jingji Chubanshe.

Li, Jinzheng (2000) *Jiedai Guanxi yu Xiangcun Bianqian [Lending Relationship and Rural Changes]*, Shijiazhuang: Hebei Daxue Chubanshe.

Li, Lizhi (2002) *Bianqian yu Chongjian: 1949–1956 Nian de Zhongguo Shehui [Change and Reconstruction: Chinese Society 1949–1956]*, Nanchang: Jiangxi Renmin Chubanshe.

Li, Yuanqing (2003) *Jinxue Chuji [A Preliminary Collection of Shanxi Studies]*, Taiyuan: Shanxi Renmin Chubanshe.

Liang, Shuming (1988) *Zhongguo Wenhua Yaoyi [Essentials of Chinese Culture]*, Beijing: Beijing Shifan Daxue Chubanshe.

—— (1992) *Liang Shuming Quanji [Collected Works of Liang Shuming]*, Jinan: Shandong Renmin Chubanshe.

Liang, Zhixiang (ed.) (1999) *Dangdai Shanxi Jianshi [A Brief History of Contemporary Shanxi]*, Beijing: Dangdai Zhongguo Chubanshe.

Ligon, Ethan, Thomas, Jonathan P. and Worrall, Tim (2002) 'Informal insurance arrangements with limited commitment: theory and evidence from village economies', *Review of Economic Studies*, 69(1): 209–44.

Lin, Nan (1990) 'Social resources and social mobility: a structure theory of "social attainment"', in Ronald L. Breiger (ed.) *Social Mobility and Social Structure*, New York: Cambridge University Press.

—— (1995) 'Local market socialism: local corporatism in action in rural China', *Theory and Society*, 24(3): 301–54.

Lin, Y.T. (1939) *My Country and My People*, London: William Heinemann.

Little, Daniel (1989) *Understanding Peasant China: Case Studies in the Philosophy of Social Science*, New Haven, CT and London: Yale University Press

Liu, Lianjun (2003) *Pingjia yu Fansi: Wanqing Wenzhou Weixin Zhishi Qunti [Evaluation and Revisit: Wenzhou's Intellectual Reformists in Later Qing Dynasty]*, Online. Available HTTP: <http://www.cuhk.edu.hk/ics/21c/supplem/essay/0305064g.htm> (accessed 4 August 2006).

Liu, Qiugen (1992) 'Zhongguo gudai gaolidai de qiyuan yu fazhan' ['On the origin and development of usury in ancient China'], *Hebei Xuekan [Hubei Journal]*, Issue 2: 37–44.

—— (1995) *Zhongguo Diandang Zhidushi [History of the Pawn Brokering System in China]*, Shanghai: Shanghai Guji Chubanshe.

Liu, Shiding (1999) 'Qianru yu guanxi hetong' ['Embeddedness and relational contract'], *Shehuixue Yanjiu [Sociology Research]*, Issue 4: 75–88.

Liu, Wenpu and Yang Xun (eds) (1996) *Zhongguo Guoqing Congshu: Cangnan Juan [China's National Conditions Series: Cangnan Volume]*, Beijing: Zhongguo Dabaike Quanshu Chubanshe.

Locke, J. ([1690] 1960) *Two Treatises of Government*, ed. P. Laslett, Cambridge: Cambridge University Press.

Long, Anzhi (Brahm, Laurence J.) (1997) *Zhongguo Diyi [China as No. 1]*, Beijing: Qiye Guanli Chubanshe.

Lovett, Steve, Simmons, Lee C. and Kai, Raja (1999) '*Guanxi* versus market: ethics and efficiency', *Journal of International Business Studies*, 30(2): 231–48.

Lu, Ruihua (ed.) (2002) *Guangdong Nianjian [Guangdong Yearbook]*, Guangzhou: Guangdong Nianjian Chubanshe.

Luhmann, N. (1979) *Trust and Power*, Chichester: John Wiley.

—— (1988) 'Familiarity, confidence, trust', in D. Gambetta (ed.) *Trust: Making and Breaking Cooperative Relations*, Oxford: Basil Blackwell.

Ma, Jiesan and Zhang, Yi (eds) (1989) *Zhongguo Xiangzhenqiye Nianjian 1978 – 1987 [China Township Enterprises Yearbooks 1978–1987]*, Beijing: Zhongguo Nongye Chubanshe.

Ma, Laurence J.C. and Xiang, Biao (1998) 'Native place, migration and the emergence of peasant enclaves in Beijing', *The China Quarterly*, 155: 546–81.

Ma, Xiaohong (1997) *Li yu Fa [Rites and Law]*, Beijing: Jingji Guanli Chubanshe.

Ma, Zhenduo, Xu Yuanhe and Zheng Jiadong (1999) *Rujia Wenming* (The Confucian Civilization), Beijing: Zhongguo Shehui Kexue Chubanshe.

Ma, Zhongdong and Liaw, Kao-Lee (1994) 'Education selectivity in the internal migrations of mainland China', *Journal of Population Studies*, 15: 135–59.

Ma, Zhongfu (2001) *Zhongguo Nongcun Hezuo Jinrong Fazhan Yanjiu [Research on the Development of Cooperative Financing in Rural China]*, Beijing: Zhongguo Jinrong Chubanshe.

McCloskey, Donald N. (1972) 'The enclosure of open fields: preface to a study of its impact on the efficiency of English agriculture in the eighteenth century', *Journal of Economic History*, 32(1): 15 – 35.

MacIntyre, Alasdair (1984) *Is Patriotism a Virtue?*, The Lindley Lecture, University of Kansas, reprinted in Richard J. Arneson (ed.) (1992) *Liberalism*, Vol. III: 246–63, Aldershot: Edward Elgar.

McKeown, Adam (2001) *Chinese Migrant Networks and Cultural Change: Peru, Chicago, Hawaii, 1900–1936*, Chicago. IL: University of Chicago Press.

Malinowski, Bronislaw ([1922] 1967), *Argonauts of the Western Pacific*, London: Routledge & Kegan Paul.

Malthus, Thomas Robert (1826) *An Essay on the Principle of Population*, 6th edn, London: John Murray.

Mann, Michael (1986) *The Source of Social Power*, Cambridge: Cambridge University Press.

Mao, Zedong (1969) 'Zhongguo geming he zhongguo gongchandang' ['Chinese revolution and the Chinese Communist Party'], in *Mao Zedong Xuanji [Selected Works of Mao Zedong]*, vol. II, Beijing: Renmin Chubanshe.

Marx, Karl (1973) *Grundrisse der Kritik der politischen Okonomie 1857–1858 (Ruhentwurf)* , trans. Martin Nicolaus as *Grundrisse, Foundations of the Critique of Political Economy*, Harmondsworth: Penguin.

Massey, Douglas S., Arango, Joaquin, Hugo, Graeme, Kouaouci, Ali, Pellegrino, Adela and Taylor, J. Edward (1993) 'Theories of international migration: a review and appraisal', *Population and Development Review*, 19(3): 431–66.

Mauss, Marcel ([1950] 1954) *The Gift: Forms and Functions of Exchange in Archaic Societies*, trans. Ian Cunnison, London: Cohen & West.

Mead, Margaret (1937) *Cooperation and Competition among Primitive Peoples*, New York and London: McGraw-Hill Book Company.

Meng, Xin (2000) *Labour Market Reform in China*, Cambridge: Cambridge University Press.

—— (2001) 'The informal sector and rural-urban migration: a Chinese case study', *Asian Economic Journal*, 15(1): 71–89.

Menger, C. ([1883] 1963) *Problems of Economics and Sociology*, Urbana, IL: University of Illinois Press.

Merton, Robert K. (1957) *Social Theory and Social Structure*, New York: Free Press.

Mill, J.S. ([1848] 1909) *Principles of Political Economy*, edited by W. Ashley, London: Longmans.

Montgomery, James F. (1991) 'Social networks and labor-market outcomes: toward an economic analysis', *American Economic Review*, 81: 1408–18.

Moore, Wilbert E. (1963) *Social Change*, Englewood Cliffs, NJ: Prentice-Hall.

Murphy, Rachel (2002) *How Migrant Labor is Changing Rural China*, New York: Cambridge University Press.

Murray, Charles A. (1977) *A Behavioral Study of Rural Modernization: Social and Economic Change in Thai Villages*, New York: Praeger Publishers.

Naughton, B. (1994) 'Chinese institutional innovation and privatization from below', *American Economic Review*, 84(2): 266–90.

Navril, F.J. (1977) 'The socioeconomic determinants of migration and the level of aggregation, *Southern Economic Journal*, 43: 1547–59.

Nee, Victor (1990) 'A theory of market transition: from redistributive to markets in state socialism', *American Sociological Review*, 54: 663–81.

—— (1992) 'Organizational dynamics of market transition: hybrid forms, property rights and mixed economy in China', *Administrative Science Quarterly*, 37 (1): 1–27.

—— and Su Sijin (1990) 'Institutional change and economic growth in China: the view from the villages', *The Journal of Asian Studies*, 49: 3–25.

Nelson, R. (1994) 'The co-evolution of technology, industrial structure, and supporting institutions', *Industrial and Corporate Change*, 3: 47–63.

Newbold, K. Bruce (2000) 'Return migration, entrepreneurship and local state corporation', *Journal of Contemporary China*, 9(24): 231–48.

—— (2001) 'Counting migrants and migrations: comparing lifetime and fixed-interval return and onward migration', *Economic Geography*, 77(1): 23–40.

Nongyebu Xiangzhenqiyeju [Bureau of Township and Village Enterprises of the Ministry of Agriculture] (2003a) *Zhongguo Xiangzhenqiye Tongji Ziliao 1978–2002* [*Statistics of Township Enterprises in China 1978–2002*], Beijing: Zhongguo Nongye Chubanshe.

—— (2003b) *Xiangzhenqiye Nianbao yu Juesuan Ziliao 2002* [*Statistical Annals and Financial Settlement Materials 2002*], Beijing: Zhongguo Nongye Chubanshe.

—— (ed.) (2004) *Xiangzhenqiye Nianbao yu Juesuan Ziliao 2003* (*Statistical Annals and Financial Settlement Materials 2003*), Beijing: Zhongguo Nongye Chubanshe.

Nooteboom, B. (1996) 'Trust, opportunism and governance: a process and control model', *Organization Studies*, 17: 985–1010.

—— (2000) 'Trust as a governance device', in M. Casson and A. Godley (eds) *Cultural Factors in Economic Growth*, Berlin: Springer.

—— (2002) *Trust: Forms, Foundations, Functions, Failures and Figures*, Cheltenham: Edward Elgar.

North, Douglass C. (1981) *Structure and Change in Economic History*, New York and London: W. W. Norton & Company.

—— (1990) *Institutions, Institutional Change and Economic Performance*, Cambridge: Cambridge University Press.

—— (1994) 'Economic performance through time', *American Economic Review*, 84: 359–68.

—— and Thomas, R.P. (1973) *The Rise of the Western World: A New Economic History*, Cambridge: Cambridge University Press.

Odgaard, Ole (1992a) 'Entrepreneurs and elite formation in rural China', *Australian Journal of Chinese Affairs*, 28: 89–108.

—— (1992b) *Private Enterprises in Rural China: Impact on Agriculture and Social Stratification*, Aldershot: Avebury.

Olson, M. (1982) *The Rise and Decline of Nations: Economic Growth, Stagflation and Social Rigidities*, New Haven, CT and London: Yale University Press.

Ostrom, Elinor (1990) *Governing the Commons: The Evolution of Institutions for Collective Action*, Cambridge: Cambridge University Press.

Pan, Jiawei and Tan Rongyao (eds) (2002) *Zhejiang Nianjian [Zhejiang Yearbook]*, Hangzhou: Zhejiang Nianjian Chubanshe.

Parish, William L. and Whyte, Martin K. (1978) *Village and Family in Contemporary China*, Chicago, IL: University of Chicago Press.

Parsons, Talcott (1940) 'The motivation of economic activities', *Canadian Journal of Economics and Political Science*, 6: 187–203; reprinted in N.J. Smelser (ed.) (1965), *Readings in Economic Sociology*, Englewood Cliffs, NJ: Prentice-Hall.

—— (1949) *The Structure of Social Action*, New York: The Free Press.

—— (1951) *The Social System*, Glencoe, IL: The Free Press.

—— (1968) *The Situation of Social Action*, New York: The Free Press.

—— (1971) *The System of Modern Societies*, Englewood Cliff, NJ: Prentice Hall.

Perotti, E. C., Sun, L. and Zou, L. (1999) 'State-owned versus township and village enterprises in China', *Comparative Economic Studies*, 41(2–3):151–79.

Platteau, Jean-Philippe (1994) 'Behind the market stage: where real societies exist', *The Journal of Development Studies*, 30: 533–77 (part I), 753–817 (part II).

Poffenberger, Mark and Zurbuchen, Mary S. (1980) 'The economics of village Bali: three perspectives', *Economic Development and Cultural Change*, November, 29(1): 91–133.

Polanyi, Karl (1944) *The Great Transformation: The Political and Economic Origins of Our Time*, Boston, MA: Beacon Press.

—— (1977) *The Livelihood of Man*, New York: Academic Press.

Polanyi, M. (1958) *Personal Knowledge*, New York: Harper and Row.

Popkin, Samuel L. (1979) *The Rational Peasant: The Political Economy of Rural Society in Vietnam*, Berkeley, CA: University of California Press.

Portes, Alejandro (1998) 'Social capital: its origins and applications in modern sociology', *Annual Review of Sociology*, 24: 1–24.

—— and Sensenbrenner, Julia (1993) 'Embeddedness and immigration: notes on the social determinants of economic action', *American Journal of Sociology*, 98(6): 1320–50.

Potter, S.H. and Potter, J.M. (1990) *China's Peasants: The Anthropology of a Revolution*, Cambridge: Cambridge University Press.

Powell, W.W. (1990) 'Neither market nor hierarchy: network forms of organization', in B.M. Staw and L.L. Cummings (eds) *Research in Organizational Behavior*, 12, Greenwich, CT: JAI Press.

Putnam, Robert (1993) *Making Democracy Work: Civic Traditions in Modern Italy*, Princeton, NJ: Princeton University Press.

—— (1995) 'Bowling alone: America's declining social capital', *Journal of Democracy*, 6(1): 65–78.

—— (2000) *Bowling Alone: The Collapse and Revival of American Community*, New York: Simon and Schuster.

Putterman, L. (1988) 'The firm as an association versus the firm as a commodity', *Economics and Philosophy*, 4: 243–66.

—— (1997) 'On the past and future of China's township and village-owned enterprises', *World Development*, 25(10): 1639–55.

Qian, Wenbao (1996) *Rural-Urban Migration and its Impact on Economic Development in China*, Aldershot: Avebury.

Qian, Xun (1999) *Tuichen Chuxin [Bringing Forth the New by Weeding Through the Old]*, Beijing: Qinghua Daxue Chubanshe.

Qian, Yingyi and Xu, Chenggang (1993) 'Why China's economic reforms differ: the M-form hierarchy and entry/expansion of the non-state sector', *Economics of Transition*, 1(2): 22–66.

Qin, Hui (2003) *Chuantong Shilun [Ten Articles on Tradition]*, Shanghai: Fudan Daxue Chubanshe.

Quine, W.V.O. (1960) *Word and Object*, Cambridge, MA: MIT Press.

Redding, S. Gordon (1993) *The Spirit of Chinese Capitalism*, Berlin: Walter de Gruyter & Co.

Redfield, Robert (1960) *Peasant Society and Culture*, Chicago, IL: University of Chicago Press.

Reyes, Belinda I. (1997) *Dynamics of Immigration: Return Migration to Western Mexico*, San Francisco, CA: Public Policy Institute of California.

Roberts, Kenneth, Rachel Connelly, Zhenming Xie, and Zhenzhen Zheng (2004) 'Patterns of temporary labor migration of rural women from Anhui and Sichuan', *The China Journal*, 52: 49–70.

Rostow, Walt Whitman (1960) *The Stages of Economic Growth: A Non-Communist Manifesto*, Cambridge: Cambridge University Press.

Rozelle, Scott, Li Guo, Shen Minggao, Giles, John and Tuan Yee Low (1997) 'Poverty, networks, institution, or education: testing among competing hypotheses on the determinants of migration in China', paper presented at the Annual Meeting of the Association for Asian Studies, Chicago, IL, 1997.

Rozman, Gilbert (ed.) (1981) *The Modernization of China*, New York: The Free Press.

Russell, B. (1922) *The Problem of China*, London: George Allen.

Sahlins, Marshall (1972) *On the Sociology of Primitive Exchange in Stone Age Economics*, New York: Aldine Atherton.

—— (2001) 'What is anthropological enlightenment: some lessons of the 20th century', manuscript of a lecture given at Peking University, June 1998; quoted from Naribilige (ed.) *Renleixue Lilun de Xingeju [New Developments of Anthropology]*, Beijing: Shehui Kexue Wenxian Chubanshe.

Sakaiya, Taichi (1996) *Soshiki no Seisui [The Rise and Fall of Organizations]*, Tokyo: PHP Kenkyujo.

Sako, M. (1992) *Prices, Quality, and Trust: Inter-firm Relations in Britain and Japan*, Cambridge: Cambridge University Press.

Schlicht, Ekkehart (1998) *On Customs in the Economy*, New York: Oxford University Press.

Schotter, A. (1981) *The Economic Theory of Social Institutions*, Cambridge: Cambridge University Press.

Schultz, Theodore W. (1964) *Transforming Traditional Agriculture*, New Haven, CT: Yale University Press.

—— (1968) 'Institutions and the rising economic value of man', *American Journal of Agricultural Economics*, 50(5): 1113–22.

Scott, James C. (1976) *The Moral Economy of the Peasant: Rebellion and Subsistence in Southeast Asia*, New Haven, CT and London: Yale University Press.

Shapiro, S. P. (1987) 'The social control of impersonal trust', *American Journal of Sociology*, 93: 623–58.

Shweder, Richard A. (1991) *Thinking through Cultures: Expeditions in Cultural Psychology*, Cambridge, MA: Harvard University Press.

Shi, Lin (2002) *Jingji Renleixue [Economic Anthropology]*, Beijing: Zhongyang Minzu Daxue Chubanshe.

Simmel, Georg ([1907] 1990) *The Philosophy of Money*, trans. Tom Bottomore and David Frisby (1990), London: Routledge.

—— ([1922] 1955) *Conflict and the Web of Group Affiliations*, New York: Free Press.

Simon, Herbert A. (1976) *Administrative Behavior: A Study of Decision-making Processes in Administrative Organization*, New York: Harper and Row.

Skinner, G. William (1964–65) 'Marketing and social structure in rural China', *Journal of Asian Studies*, 24(1) (November 1964): 3–44, 24(2) (February 1965): 195–228, 24(3) (May 1965): 363–99.

Skocpol, Theda (1979), *State and Social Revolutions: A Comparative Analysis of France, Russia, and China*, New York: Cambridge University Press.

Smith, Arthur Henderson (1894) *Chinese Characteristics*, New York: Fleming H. Revell.

—— (1899) *Village Life in China: A Study in Sociology*, New York: Fleming H. Revell.

Smyth, Russell (1997) 'The township and village enterprise sector as a special example of regionalism: some general lessons for socialist transformation', *Economic System*, 21(3): 235–64.

Solinger, D.J. (1995) 'The Chinese work unit and transition labor in the transition from socialism', *Modern China*, 21: 155–83.

—— (1999) *Contesting Citizenship in Urban China: Peasant Migrants, the State, and the Logic of the Market*, Berkeley, CA: University of California Press.

Spence, A. Michael (1974), *Market Signalling*, Cambridge, MA: Harvard University Press.

Sugden, R. (1986) *The Economics of Rights, Co-operation and Welfare*, Oxford: Basil Blackwell.

Sun, S. (1996) 'Market economy and female floating population', *Southern China Population*, 4: 41–4.

Tang, Yijie (2003) 'Zongxu' ['General Preface'] in Huang Jiande (ed.) *Ershi Shiji Xifang Zhexue Dongjin Shi Daolun [General Introduction on the Introduction of the Western Philosophy to the Orient in the 20th Century]*, Beijing: Zhongguo Shehui Kexue Chubanshe.

Taylor, Charles (1992) 'Inwardness and culture for modernity', in H. Honnath, T. McCarthy, C. Offe and A. Wallmer (eds) *Philosophical Interventions in the Unfinished Projects of Enlightenment*, Cambridge, MA: MIT Press.

—— (1999) 'Two theories of modernity', *Public Culture*, 11(1): 162.

Thibaut, J.W. and Kelley, H.H. (1959) *The Social Psychology of Groups*, New York: Wiley.

Thøgersen, Stig (2002) 'Village economy and culture in contemporary China', *Modern China*, 28(2): 254–75.

Thomlinson, J. (1999) *Globalization and Culture*, Cambridge: Polity Press.

Thompson, E.P. (1991) *Customs in Common*, London: Merlin Press.

Todaro, M.P. (1969) 'A model of labor migration and urban unemployment in less developed countries', *American Economic Review*, 59: 138–48.

—— (1976) *International Migration in Developing Countries*, Geneva: International Labor Organization.

Tönnies, F. (1955) *Community and Association*, London: Routledge and Kegan Paul.

Tsai, Kellee S. (2002) *Back-Alley Banking: Private Entrepreneurs in China*, Ithaca, NJ and London: Cornell University Press.

Tu, Wei-ming (2000) 'Multiple modernities: a preliminary inquiry into the implications of East Asian modernity', in Lawrence E. Harrison and Samuel P. Huntington (eds) *Culture Matters: How Values Shape Human Progress*, New York: Basic Books.

—— (2001) *Dongya Jiazhi yu Duoyuan Xiandaihua [The East Asia Value and Multiple Modernities]*, Beijing: Zhongguo Shehui Kexue Chubanshe.

Tylor, Edward B. ([1871] 1924) *Primitive Culture*, 2 vols, 7th edn, New York: Brentano's.

United States of America Department of Housing and Urban Development and Ministry of Urban and Rural Construction and Environmental Protection of The People's Republic of China (1987) *English-Chinese Glossary of Terms in Housing, Urban Planning, and Construction Management*, Washington, D.C. and Beijing: United States of America Department of Housing and Urban Development and Ministry of Urban and Rural Construction and Environmental Protection of The People's Republic of China.

Vaggi, Gianni (1987) *The economics of François Quesnay*, Basingstoke: Macmillan.

Veblen, Thorstein B. ([1899] 1934) *The Theory of the Leisure Class: An Economic Study of the Evolution of Institutions*, New York and London: Macmillan (1899); New York: Viking Press (1934).

—— (1901) 'Gustav Schmoller's economics', *Quarterly Journal of Economics*, 16(1): 69–93.

—— (1919) *The Place of Science in Modern Civilisation and Other Essays*, New York: Huebsch; reprinted in 1990 with a new introduction by W.J. Samuels, New Brunswick: Transaction Publishers.

Walder, Andrew (1983) 'Organized dependency and cultures of authority in Chinese industry', *Journal of Asian Studies*, 43(4): 51–76.

Wang, Dingding (1996) *Zai Jingjixue yu Zhexue Zhijian [Between Economics and Philosophy]*, Beijing: Zhongguo Shehui Kexue Chubanshe.

Wang, Hai (Heberer, Thomas) (2001) 'Dongya yu xifang: duikang haishi hezuo?: Lun shuangfangjian de wuhui yu qujie' ['East Asia and the West: Confrontation or cooperation? Misunderstanding and misinterpretation'], in Ma Rong and Zhou Xin (eds) *Ershiyi Shijie: Wenhua Zijue yu Kuawenhua Duihua [21st Century: Culture Consciousness and Inter-cultural Dialogue]*, Beijing: Beijing Daxue Chubanshe.

Wang, Jianhui and Liu Senmiao (1992) *Jingchu Wenhua [Jingchu Culture]*, Shenyang: Liaoning Jiaoyu Chubanshe.

Wang, Mingming (1996) 'Xiandai de zixing: tangdongcun tianye diaocha he lilun duihua' ['Self-awakening of modernity: field works and theoretical dialogue in Tangdong village'], in Pan Naigu and Ma Rong (eds) *Shequ Yanjiu yu Shehui Fazhan [Community Research and Social Development]*, Tianjin: Tianjin Renmin Chubanshe.

Wang, Wenfei W. (2004) 'Urban–rural return labor migration in China: a case study of Sichuan and Anhui Provinces', Department of Geography, UCLA. Online. Available HTTP: <http://www.iir.ucla.edu/research/grad_conf/2004/wang.pdf> (accessed 5 February 2007).

Wang, Xiaoyi and Zhu Chengbao (1996) *Zhongguo Nongcun de Siying Qiye yu Jiazu Jingji – Zhejiangsheng Cangnanxian Xiangdongcun Diaocha [Private Enterprises and Family Economy in Rural China – A Survey of Xiangdong Village, Cangnan County, Zhejiang Province]*, Taiyuan: Shanxi Jingji Chubanshe.

——, Zhang Jun and Yao Mei (1996) *Zhongguo Nongcun de Jingji Zengzhang yu Shehui Zhuanxing – Guangdongsheng Dongguanshi Yantiancun Diaocha [Economic Growth and Societal Transition in Rural China – A Survey of Yantian Village, Dongguan City, Guangdong Province]*, Taiyuan: Shanxi Jingji Chubanshe.

Wang, Zongpei (1935) *Zhongguo zhi Hehui [Rotating Savings and Credit Associations in China]*, Beijing: Zhongguo Hezuo Xueshe.

Wank, David (1995) 'Bureaucratic patronage and private business: changing networks of power in urban China', in Andrew G. Walder (ed.) *The Waning of the Communist State: Economic Origins of Political Decline in China and Hungary*, Berkeley, CA: University of California Press.

Ward, R.E. (1965) 'Japan: the continuity of modernization', in L.W. Pye and Sindey Verba (eds) *Political Culture and Political Development*, Princeton, NJ: Princeton University Press.

Weber, Max ([1904] 1949) *The Methodology of the Social Sciences*, New York: The Free Press.

—— (1947) *The Theory of Social and Economic Organization*, New York: Oxford University Press.

—— (1951) *The Religion of China: Confucianism and Taoism*, New York: The Free Press.

—— (1958) *The Protestant Ethic and the Spirit of Capitalism*, New York: Scribner's Press.

—— (1976) *The Agrarian Sociology of Ancient Civilizations*, London: NLB.

Webster's Third New International Dictionary of the English Language, Unabridged (1976), Springfield, MA: G. & C. Merriam Company.

Webster's New Twentieth Century Dictionary of the English Language, Unabridged (1979), New York: Prentice Hall Press.

Wei, Daonan and Zhang Xiaoshan (1998) *Zhongguo Nongcun Xinxing Hezuo Zuzhi Tanxi [An Analysis of the New Cooperative Organizations in Rural China]*, Beijing: Jingji Guanli Chubanshe.

Weitzman, Martin and Chenggang Xu (1994) 'Chinese township and village enterprises as vaguely defined cooperatives', *Journal of Comparative Economics*, 18: 121–45.

Wellman, B. and Berkowitz, S.D. (eds) (1988) *Social Structure: A Network Approach*, New York: Cambridge University Press.

White, Harrison C. (1981) 'Where do markets come from?' *American Journal of Sociology*, 87: 517–47.

Whyte, Martin K. (1992) 'Introduction: rural economic reform and Chinese family patterns', *The Chinese Quarterly*, 130: 317–22.

Williamson, O.E. (1975) *Markets and Hierarchies: Analysis and Antitrust Implications*, New York: Free Press.

—— (1979) 'Transaction cost economics: the governance of contractual relations', *Journal of Law and Economics*, 22: 233–61.

—— (1985) *The Economic Institutions of Capitalism*, New York: Free Press.

—— (1991) 'Comparative economic organization: the analysis of discrete structural alternatives', *Administrative Science Quarterly*, 36: 269–96.

—— (1993a) 'Calculativeness, trust and economic organization', *Journal of Law and Economics*, 36: 453–86.

—— (1993b) 'Transaction cost economics and organization theory', *Industrial and Corporate Change*, 2(2): 107–56.

—— (1996) *The Mechanism of Governance*, New York: Oxford University Press.

—— (1999) 'Strategy research: governance and competence Perspectives', *Strategic Management Journal*, 20: 1087–108.

Williamson, R.G. (1965) 'Regional inequality and the process of national development: a description of the patterns', *Economic Development and Cultural Change*, 13(4): 3–45

Wimmer, Andreas (1996) 'Kultur: zur Reformulierung eines sozialanthropologischen Grundbegriffs', *Kölner Zeitschrift für Soziologie und Sozialpsychologie*, 48(3): 401–25.

Wolff, Kurt (ed.) (1950) *The Sociology of Georg Simmel*, Glencoe, IL: Free Press.

World Bank (1997) *At China's Table: Food Security Options*, Washington, DC: The World Bank.

—— (1999) *Accelerating China's Rural Transformation*, Washington, DC: The World Bank.

—— (2000) *China: Overcoming Rural Poverty*, Washington, DC: The World Bank.

—— (2003) *World Development Report 2003*, Washington, DC: The World Bank.

Wu, Bannong (1932) 'Cong gongye youxian zhi chengdu guancha muqian zhongguo jingji zhi xingzhi' ['Study on the features of China's economy from industrial development'], *Qinghua Zhoukan – Shehui Kexue Zhuanhao [Qinghua Weekly – Special Issues on Social Sciences]*, November, Beijing: Qinghua Daxue.

Wu, Baoshan (1947) *Zhongguo Guomin Suode 1933 [China's National Income 1933]*, Shanghai: Zhonghua Shuju.

Xiao, Yunchun (ed.) (1997) *Cangnan Xianzhi [Annals of Cangnan County]*, Hangzhou: Zhejiang Renmin Chubanshe.

Xu, Haiqing (1999) 'Environmental policy and rural industrial development in China', *Human Ecology Review*, 6(2): 72–81.

Xu, Tangling (1996) *Zhongguo Nongcun Jinrong Shilue [Outline History of Rural Finance in China]*, Beijing: Zhongguo Jinrong Chubanshe.

Yan, Yunxiang (1996a) 'The culture of *guanxi* in a north China village', *The China Journal*, 35: 1–25.

—— (1996b) *The Flow of Gifts: Reciprocity and Social Networks in a Chinese Village*, Stanford, CA: Stanford University Press.

Yang, Lien-sheng (1957) 'The concept of "pao" as a basis for social relations in China', in John K. Fairbank (ed.) *Chinese Thought and Institutions*, Chicago, IL: University of Chicago Press.

Yang, Martin (1945) *A Chinese Village: Taitou, Shantung Province*, New York: Columbia University Press.

Yang, Mayfair (1989) 'The gift economy and state power in China', *Comparative Studies in Society and History*, 31: 25–54.

—— (1994) *Gifts, Favors and Banquets: The Art of Social Relationship in China*, Ithaca, NJ: Cornell University Press.

—— (2002) 'The resilience of *guanxi* and its new developments: a critique of some new *guanxi* scholarship', *The China Quarterly*, 170: 459–76.

Ye, Shi (1961) *Ye Shi Wenji [Collected Works of Ye Shi]*, Beijing: Zhonghua Shuju.

Yu, Chiqian and Huang Haiguang (eds) (1991) *Dangdai Zhongguo de Xiangzhen Qiye [Township Enterprises in Contemporary China]*, Beijing: Dangdai Zhongguo Chubanshe.

Yu, Lianjun (2002) 'Wenzhou moshi yu gongli bingju de wenhua chuantong' ['Wenzhou model and the cultural tradition of gaining righteousness and profits simultaneously'], *Zhongguo Jingji Kuaixun Zhoukan [China Economic News Weekly]*, 21 October: 25–6.

Yu, Wujin, Wang Xingfu, Yu Biping, Zhang Shuangli and Wu Xinwen (2002) *Xiandaixing Xianxiangxue [Phenomenology of Modernity]*, Shanghai: Shanghai Shehui Kexueyuan Chubanshe.

Zand, D.E. (1972) 'Trust and managerial problem solving', *Administrative Science Quarterly*, 17: 229–39.

Zhai, Xuewei (1994) *Mianzi Renqing yu Guanxi Wangluo [Face, Favor and* Guanxi *Networks]*, Zhengzhou: Henan Renmin Chubanshe.

Zhang, Guohui (1987) 'Qingdai qianqi de qianzhuang he piaohao' ['Private money houses and bill exchanges in the early Qing dynasty'], *Zhongguo Jingjishi Yanjiu [Research on China's Economic History]*, 4: 46–58.

Zhang, Lüping (1993), *Wenmin de Chongtu yu Ronghe: Riben Xiandaihua Yanjiu [Clash and Fusion: Study on Japan's Modernization]*, Beijing: Wenjin Chubanshe.

Zhang, Qizi (1999) 'Shehui wangluo yu jiceng jingji shenghuo' ['Social networks and grass-roots economic life'], *Shehuixue Yanjiu [Sociology Research]*, 3: 25–34.

Zhang, Xiaobo and Li Guo (2001) 'Does *guanxi* matter to nonfarm employment?' EPTD (Environment and Production Technology Division) discussion paper no. 74, Washingtong DC: International Food Policy Research Institute.

Zhang, Xiaoshan and Hu Biliang (eds) (2002) *Xiaochengzhen yu Quyu Yitihua [Small Town and Regional Integration]*, Taiyuan: Shanxi Renmin Chubanshe.

Zhang, Xiaoshan and Heufers, Rainer (eds) (2002) *Nongcun Jinrong Zhuanxing yu Chuangxin: Guanyu Hezuo Jijinhui de Sikao [Transition and Innovation of Rural Financing: Reflections over Rural Cooperative Foundations]*, Taiyuan: Shanxi Jingji Chubanshe.

Zhang, Zhengming (ed.) (1988) *Chu Wenhua Zhi [Annals of Chu Culture]*, Wuhan: Hubei Renmin Chubanshe.

Zhao, Chunchen (2003) *Lingnan Jindai Shishi yu Wenhua [Lingnan Modern Events and Culture]*, Beijing: Zhongguo Shehui Kexue Chubanshe.

Zhao, Shukai (2000) 'Organizational characteristics of rural labor mobility in China', in Loraine A. West and Yaohui Zhao (eds) *Rural Labor Flows in China*, Berkeley, CA: University of California Press.

Zhao, Yaohui (2003) 'The role of migrant networks in labor migration: the case of China', *Contemporary Economic Policy*, 21(4): 500–11.

Zhao, Zhong (2005) 'Migration, labor market flexibility, and wage determination in China: a review', *The Development Economies*, 43(2), June: 285–312.

Zhe, Xiaoye and Chen Yingying (1996) *Shequ de Shijian: 'Chaoji Cunzhuang' de Fazhan Licheng [The Practice of Community: The Development of the 'Super Villages']*, Beijing: Zhongguo Shehui Kexue Chubanshe.

Zhonggong Zhongyang Shujichu he Zhongyang Wenxian Yanjiushi [Research Center of the Secretariat of CPC Central Committee and the Party Literature Research Center of CPC Central Committee] (1987) *Jianchi Gaige, Kaifang yu Gaohuo –Shiyijie Sanzhong Quanhui Yilai de Zhongyao Wenxian Xuanbian [Adhering to Reform, Opening-up and Revitalization – Selected Important Literature Since the 3rd Plenary Session of the 11th CPC Central Committee]*, Beijing: Renmin Chubanshe.

Zhongguo Caijingbao [China Finance and Economics News] (2003) 'Xiaochengzhen yijing chengwei zhongguo nongcun laodongli zhuanyi de zhuqudao' ['Small towns have become an important channel for rural labor transfer in China'], October 30, section 3.

Zhongguo Shehui Kexueyuan, Yuyan Yanjiusuo [Institute of Linguistics of the Chinese Academy of Social Sciences–CASS] (ed.) (1987) *Xiandai Hanyu Cidian [Contemporary Chinese Dictionary]*, Beijing: Shangwu Yinshuguan.

Zhongyang Nongye Shiyansuo, Nongyejingjike [Agricultural Section of the Central Agricultural Experiment Institute] (1934) *Nongqing Baogao [Report on Rural and Agricultural Situations]*, vol. 2, issue 11.

Zhou, Changcheng (2003) *Jingji Shehuixue [Economic Sociology]*, Beijing: Zhongguo Renmin Daxue Chubanshe.

Zhou, Zhang Y., Dillon, John L. and Wan, Guang H. (1992) 'Development of township enterprise and alleviation of the employment problem in rural China', *Agricultural Economics*, 6(3): 201–15.

Zhu, Junming (1995) 'Multilevel analysis of rural outmigration in Guangdong, China', paper presented at the annual meetings of the Population Association of America meetings, San Francisco, April.

Zhu, Rongji (ed.) (1985) *Dangdai Zhongguo de Jingji Guanli [Economic Management in Contemporary China]*, Beijing: Zhongguo Shehui Kexue Chubanshe.

Zhuo, Yongliang (forthcoming) *Fanshu, Zhanzheng yu Qiyejia Jingshen: Yetan Wenzhou Moshi de Chengyin Jiqi Kunjing [Sweet Potato, War and Entrepreneur Spirit: How Wenzhou Model Constitutes and its Current Difficulties]*, Hangzhou: Zhejiang Reform and Development Institute.

Zucker, L.G. (1986) 'Production of trust: institutional sources of economic structure', in B.M. Staw and L.L. Cummings (eds) *Research in Organizational Behavior*, 8, Greenwich, CT: JAI Press.

Index

236; property rights 11, 12, 16, 17, 18, 19, 20, 21, 175, 278, 299; statute law 11; unified examination system 42
four olds (*sijiu*) 275
FSTSC 92, 193, 217, 218, 224, 228, 231, 236, 246, 283; diversification and rapid development of 221–2; preliminary expansion stage of 220; restructuring stage of 221; start-up stage of 220; traded on the Shenzhen Stock Exchange 233
Fukuyama, F. 22, 23, 24
functional organization 12, 245, 246, 247, 254, 255, 259
Fuxing village: area of 89; collective enterprises in 92–4; FSTSC in 92; households and population of 89; income difference in 96–7; iron industry in 90–1; location of 88; as a migrant village 89; private and individual business in 95
game theory 12, 125, 127
genealogy 90, 119, 251
genetic distance 33
Giddens, A. 22, 25, 264, 265, 280
Goffman, E. 61, 64, 65
governance: corporate 253, 269; indigenous 9; informal 175, 278; local 10, 68, 262; rural 28, 278; self-governance 28, 279; theories of 36, 38; village 262, *see also* IVWC; rural governance
Granovetter, M.S. 9, 23, 24, 25, 28, 29, 56, 124, 172, 265, 267
'Great Leap Forward' 3, 177
'Great Society' 23
Greif, A. 25, 29, 270
Gu, Yanwu 122
Guangdong Province: FDI in 78; Hong Kong and Macao compatriots from 77; land area of 77; location of 77; overseas Chinese from 77; population of 77; Taiwan compatriots from 77
guanxi and TVE development: in Fuxing village 193–202; regional differences of 214; in Tunwa village 203–6; in Xiangdong village 206–8; in Yantian village 189–93, *see also* Fuxing village; *guanxi* community; Tunwa village; TVEs; Xiangdong village; Yantian village
guanxi community: *3F theory* of 60; basic models and rules of the 60–5; blood relationships and 53, 56, 58, 59;

boundaries of 57–9; chain migration method and 173; Chinese network community (society) 59; Confucian rites and 62; definition of 56–7; differential mode of association in 58, 63; distant marriage and 139; dramaturgy theory and 64–5; Ego and 33; extended *guanxi* and 139, 173; extension of *guanxi* and 33, 57, 139, 211, 213; features of 210; five cardinal relationships of the 57, 58; forms of 173; geographical relationship and 55, 56, 58, 59; *guanxi* making and 58; Kula Ring exchange and 63, 64; 'little tradition' in 62, 121, 275, 283; model of favour and face of 60–3; occupational relationship and 59; reciprocity in 61–2, 211, 269; sanctions within the 211–12; shame in 48, 61–2, 211, 280, 281; social exchange and 63–4, 125–8; weak ties and strong ties in 172; 'Zhejiang village' in Beijing and 139, 173; *see also guanxi* and TVE development; *guanxi* networks and people's mobility
guanxi networks and people's mobility: 130–53, 164, 167, 172
guanxi: as a social institution 55, 211; definition of 55–6; and networks and social networks 55–6, *see also guanxi* networks and people's mobility
Guanzi: four cardinal virtues 48

Han, Fei 72
Hanchuan 88, 89, 92, 194, 195, 196, 216, 217, 218, 221, 224, 225, 226, 227, 246, 247, 249
Hangzhou 79, 81, 262
Harrison, L.E. 25, 272
Hayami, Y. 268, 270, 272, 280, 281, 463
Hayek, F.A. 14, 23, 27, 38, 260, 282
Henan Province 98, 162, 166, 169, 173, 198, 205
Herrmann-Pillath, C. 6, 7, 9, 11, 22, 23, 24, 25, 26, 188, 268, 281, 282
Heufers, R. 8, 102, 103
Hicks, J. 20
Hodgson, G.M. 9, 13, 20
Homans, G.C. 64
Hong Kong 77, 78, 97, 98, 99, 189, 190, 191, 192, 212, 214, 219, 242, 272, 283
Hu, Anguo 75
Hu, Biliang 8, 90, 92, 96, 102, 108, 109, 114, 138, 177, 209, 218, 221, 239, 240

of 278; as the root of cultural pattern 280; and ROSCAs 269; and society 269–71; and traditionalization 274; as 'the vehicle of culture' 260; versus development 280
transaction cost 9, 11, 12, 17, 18, 19, 22, 23, 28, 36, 38, 250, 253, 270
trust: basic 265; in China and in Sweden 23; collective 28, 261; enforceable 265; as general and universal phenomenon 23; importance of 22–3; or die 22; personal 23, 24; system 23, 24; trust advantage 30, *see also* village trust
Tu, Wei-ming 272, 280
Tunwa entrepreneurs 153, 158; age and educational status of 156; expansion of *guanxi* networks of 159, 164, 167, 172; family contract land status of 155; household registration status of 155, 162, 170; political environment and the mobility of 159, *see also guanxi* and people's mobility
Tunwa village: agriculture in 84–5; boiler plants in 86–7; cultivable area of 83; livestock breeding in 85; location of 83; as 'Mini-Beijing' 86; net per capita income of 88; population of 87; total revenue of 88, *see also* mobility
TVEs: and China's GDP 177; and China's national tax revenue 182; and Chinese industrial traditions 184–6; definition of 176–7; development (history) of 177; and employment 178; and farmers' per capita net income 179–80; *guanxi* and *guanxi* community and 188–208; *guanxi* as a special supporting factor for 208–11; manufacturing sector of 178–9; and small towns 181, *see also guanxi* and TVE development
Tylor, E.B. 25, 26

Veblen, T.B. 13, 14, 16, 20
vertical integration 38
village church 29, 122, 123
village community: concept of 49; Duara on cultural nexus 50–1; Japanese scholars on 49–50; moral economy 50; Philip Huang on 50; Skinner and local market community 51; Weber on 50; in Xiangdong 119–21
village economy and culture in contemporary China 7, 210
village study 7, 28, 210

village trust: and bidding ROSCAs in Xiangdong village 118; concept of 118; customs and social norms and 122–4; local culture and 121–2; social embeddedness and 124, *see also* trust
Volkswagen Foundation 6

Wang, Chong 77
Wang, Mingming 282, 283
Wang, Tong 72
Wang, Xiaoyi and Zhu, Chengbao 80, 120, 121, 124, 208
Wang, Yangming 72
Ward, R.E. 281
Weber, M. 22, 26, 50, 53, 188, 263, 264, 266, 267, 271, 278, 279
Wenzhou 62, 77, 78, 81, 103, 104, 121, 122, 128, 139, 215, 265; model 77, 121, 122
'Western-centralism' 6
Williamson, O.E. 36, 37, 38, 39, 140, 270
World Bank 1
Wuhan City 195, 209, 222, 223
Wuyue: culture 75; State of 79

Xiang Sujiao's ROSCA 110, 111, 113, 114
Xiang Xianliang's ROSCA 29, 31, 108, 113, 114
Xiang Zujian's ROSCA 29, 30, 113, 114
Xiang, Yu 76
Xiangdong village: agricultural resources of 80; arable land of 80; immigrants of 81–3; location of 78; population of 80; village industry in 80, 81; water and land transport of 79; Xiang family tree in 79
Xiaogan City 92
Xue, Xuan 72, 73

Yan, Yunxiang 208, 209, 210, 211
Yang, Lien-sheng 61
Yang, Martin 7
Yang, Mayfair 209, 210, 211
Yantian village: Deng lineage in 97, 98, 99; Deng lineage in Hong Kong from 99; large number of migrants in 98; location of 97; population of 97
Ye, Shi 62, 121, 122
Yongjia School 77, 122, *see also* Zhejiang Province
Yongkang School 77, 121, *see also* Zhejiang Province

Yuanping City 34, 35, 83, 86, 87, 130, 131,
    133, 149, 151, 154, 158, 160, 161, 162,
    163, 165, 166, 168, 170, 172, 173, 203
Zeng, Guofan 274
Zhai, Xuewei 61
Zhang, Xiaoshan 8, 103
Zhao, Yaohui 140, 151, 173
Zhejiang Province: facing out to the
    East China Sea 76; as the home

of the Eastern Zhejiang School of
    Utilitarianism 77; land area of 76;
    population of 76; Qiantang River in 76;
    Wenzhou model of 77; Yongjia School
    77; Yongkang School 77
Zhou, Dunyi 76
Zhu, Xi 62, 72, 77
Zhuangzi (or Zhuang Zhou) 75
Zuo Qiuming and *Zuo Zhuan* 75

For Product Safety Concerns and Information please contact our EU
representative GPSR@taylorandfrancis.com
Taylor & Francis Verlag GmbH, Kaufingerstraße 24, 80331 München, Germany